Interconnections

Addison-Wesley Professional Computing Series

Brian W. Kernighan, Consulting Editor

Ken Arnold / John Peyton, *A C User's Guide to ANSI C*

Tom Cargill, *C++ Programming Style*

David Curry, *UNIX System Security: A Guide for Users & Systems Administrators*

Scott Meyers, *Effective C++: 50 Specific Ways to Improve Your Programs and Designs*

Radia Perlman, *Interconnections: Bridges and Routers*

W. Richard Stevens, *Advanced Programming in the UNIX Environment*

Interconnections: Bridges and Routers

Radia Perlman

ADDISON-WESLEY PUBLISHING COMPANY, INC.

Reading, Massachusetts   Menlo Park, California   New York   Don Mills, Ontario
Wokingham, England   Amsterdam   Bonn   Paris   Milan   Madrid   Sydney   Singapore   Tokyo
Seoul   Taipei   Mexico City   San Juan

The publisher offers discounts on this book when ordered in quantity for special sales. For more information please contact:

Corporate & Professional Publishing Group
Addison-Wesley Publishing Company
One Jacob Way
Reading, Massachusetts 01867

Library of Congress Cataloging-in-Publication Data

Perlman, Radia.
    Interconnections : bridges and routers / Radia Perlman.
        p. cm. — (Addison-Wesley professional computing series)
    Includes index.
    ISBN 0-201-56332-0 (hardback)
    1. Computer network protocols. 2. Local area networks (Computer networks)
I. Title. II. Series.
TK5105.5P474 1992   91-37493
004.6'2—dc20   CIP

Cover design by Joyce C. Weston
Text design by Webster Design, Marblehead, MA
Set in 11 point Times by Gex, Inc.

ISBN 0-201-56332-0
Text printed on recycled and acid-free paper.
3 4 5 6 7 8 9 10 11- MU -96959493
Third printing February 1993

Contents

Preface

It is becoming apparent that people expect to interconnect just about every computer in the world, at least for the purpose of sending and receiving mail. Local area networks allow communication between a limited number of devices. Routers and bridges are required in order to build larger networks, and standards for such devices have only recently begun being proposed and adopted. Although routers of various types have been built for years, early routers experienced problems with performance or robustness, making their design unsuitable for really large networks.

Interconnections was written in response to the fact that there is considerable confusion regarding routers and bridges, with most of the terminology in the field being ill-defined and used in conflicting ways. Furthermore, both the terminology and the official specifications tend to be daunting, and information is spread among many different documents.

This book is intended for several types of readers. Novices should find it a nonthreatening introduction to the field. Implementers and others who really wish to understand the field deeply should benefit from the fact that *Interconnections* not only presents the algorithms and protocols in use but goes far beyond simply describing the technology: it explains the implications of design decisions, points out deficiencies, compares competing approaches, and weighs engineering trade-offs as well. Experts in the field will consider the book a convenient reference, but it is in no way intended to replace the specifications for the protocols themselves, for the details of individual protocols are subject to change.

Since many important router/bridge issues remain unresolved and would make an exciting topic for a course at the advanced undergraduate or graduate level, *Interconnections* should also be useful as a textbook. It contains numerous homework problems that are intended to further readers' intuitive understanding of the consequences of distributed algorithms. *Interconnections* can serve as a starting point for those interested in doing research in the field, too. It presents various suggestions for research, which, depending on the depth of the topic, could involve anything from a term paper to a Ph.D. thesis. And any of the suggested topics would be of interest in journals and conferences.

The first portion of *Interconnections* reviews the ISO reference model and the essential concepts behind LANs that affect bridges—namely, addressing, multicast ability, and the reasons for geographic, total traffic, and population limitations. The next portion of the book, which deals with bridging standards, describes the spanning tree algorithm, transparent bridging, and source routing bridging. This is followed by a discussion of routing standards, which covers routing algorithms in general and contrasts the TCP/IP style of routing with the ISO style of routing. The final portion of the book examines the directions in which both bridges and routers are evolving, such as brouters and multipro-tocol routers. A glossary is included as a reference for terminology and jargon.

And finally, I would like to call your attention to two categories of material that are set off from the regular text. First, *Interconnections* occasionally addresses issues that are very subtle and constitute something of a digression from the overall flow of the book. Novices should definitely skip these digressions, which are set off from the text by vertical rules. Second, the suggested research problems, mentioned earlier, are desig-nated by a heavy line in the left margin.

Throughout the book I have used the following symbols:

ⓇⓇ	L1 (level 1) router
Ⓡ	L2 (level 2) router
(SR-TB)	SR-TB bridge
(B7)	bridge

Acknowledgments

There are many people I'd like to thank. I've been fortunate to have had the opportunity to work with a lot of very perceptive and creative individuals, both within my group at Digital and in various standards committees. Tony Lauck has probably been the most inspirational and educational colleague, and I am particularly grateful to him for sug-gesting numerous interesting problems for me to work on, such as the requirement for a bridge spanning tree algorithm and a sabotage-proof network layer protocol.

Others to whom I'm grateful for contributing to designs and offering insight include Floyd Backes, Ross Callon, John Harper, Art Harvey, Bill Hawe, Charlie Kaufman, Paul Koning, Dave Oran, Mike Shand, Mike Speciner, and George Varghese. I greatly appre-ciate the efforts of the following individuals who reviewed the book, especially since they had to work with ugly, unformatted copy: Philip Almquist, Brian Kernighan, Phil Karn, Dave Piscitello, Kay Robbins, Mike Speciner, and especially Dan Pitt, who did a very thorough job and was particularly helpful. I was also impressed with Sue Cohan, my copy-editor. She not only improved the English but caught technical errors as well.

And finally, I'd like to thank my children, Dawn and Ray. Admittedly they did not contribute much to the content of this book, but they make life so much fun.

Chapter 1
Essential Networking Concepts

This chapter introduces some concepts that are essential to understanding the specific subfield of computer networking that includes bridges and routers. It covers the International Standard Organization's reference model, including layering and service models. It also discusses various dimensions along which network designs can differ, such as scope, scalability, robustness, and autoconfigurability. Chapter 1 also describes the typical techniques involved in providing reliable two-party communication because some of the techniques used by routers can interact with techniques used by other layers.

1.1   Layers

Understanding, designing, and building a computer network would be too difficult a task unless the problem were partitioned into smaller subtasks. This has traditionally been done by considering the problem as being divided into several layers. The idea behind layering is that each layer is responsible for providing some service to the layer above and does this by using the services of the layer below.

Each layer communicates with its *peer* layer in another node through the use of a *protocol*. This communication is accomplished through direct communication with the layer below. The communication between layer n and layer $n-1$ is known as an *interface*.

The OSI (Open Systems Interconnection) Reference Model defines seven layers. There is nothing magic about the number seven or the functionality in the layers, however. The reference model was designed before the protocols themselves, and then committees were set up to design each of the layers. Many of the layers were subsequently subdivided into further layers. The distinction between the layers is not always clear. Bridges and routers are a good example of a case in which people should rightfully be confused about which layers are which. But semantic arguments about layers are not very productive. Instead, the layering should be viewed as a useful framework for discussion, not as a bible.

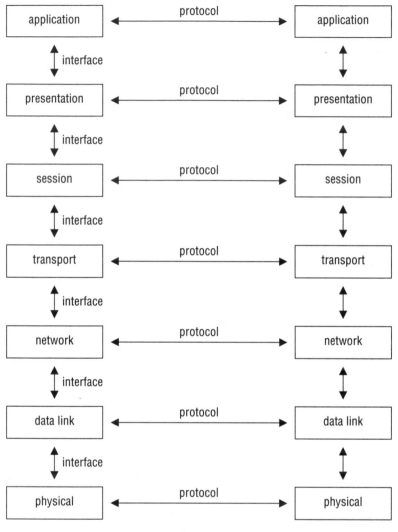

Figure 1.1

The layers defined by the ISO (International Standards Organization) are:

1. *Physical layer:* The responsibility of the physical layer is to transmit unstruc-
    tured bits of information across a link. It deals with such problems as size and
    shape of connectors, assignment of functions to pins, conversion of bits to elec-
    trical signals, and bit-level synchronization. It is usual for several different types
    of physical layers to exist within a network and even for multiple different types
    of physical layers to exist within a node, because each technology requires its
    own physical layer. For instance, a node with an attachment to FDDI (fiber dis-
    tributed data interface) and an attachment to a 56-KB synchronous line will
    have implemented two different physical layers.

2. *Data link layer:* The responsibility of the data link layer (sometimes called the link layer) is to transmit chunks of information across a link. It deals with such problems as checksumming to detect data corruption; orderly coordination of the use of shared media, as in a LAN (local area network); and addressing when multiple systems are reachable, as in a LAN. Again, it is common for different links to implement different data link layers and for a node to implement several data link layer protocols, one to support each of the different types of links to which the node is attached.

3. *Network layer:* The responsibility of the network layer is to enable any pair of systems in the network to communicate with each other. A "fully connected" network is one in which every pair of nodes has a direct link between them, but this kind of topology does not scale beyond a few nodes. Therefore, in the more typical case, the network layer must find a path through a series of connected nodes, and nodes along the path must forward packets in the appropriate direction. The network layer deals with such problems as route calculation, packet fragmentation and reassembly (when different links in the network have different maximum packet sizes), and congestion control.

4. *Transport layer:* The responsibility of the transport layer is to establish a reliable communication stream between a pair of systems. It deals with errors that can be introduced by the network layer, such as lost packets, duplicated packets, packet reordering, and fragmentation and reassembly (so that the user of the transport layer can deal with larger-size messages and so that less efficient network layer fragmentation and reassembly might be avoided).

5. *Session layer:* The responsibility of OSI's session layer is to offer services above the simple full-duplex reliable communication stream provided by transport, such as dialogue control (enforcing a particular pattern of communication between systems) and chaining (combining groups of packets so that either all or none in the group gets delivered).

6. *Presentation layer:* The responsibility of OSI's presentation layer is to provide a means by which OSI applications can agree on representations for data.

7. *Application layer:* Many OSI applications are currently, or are soon to become, standard, such as FTAM (file transfer, access, and management services) and VT (virtual terminal services). It is common for multiple applications to be running concurrently in a node.

In this book, the data link layer is relevant because bridges operate within the data link layer and because the service provided by the data link layer is relevant to routers, which operate at the network layer, thereby making the network layer obviously relevant as well. The transport layer is somewhat relevant because it is a user of the network layer and certain decisions that the network layer might make (such as whether to allow traffic to be split among several equivalent paths) affect the transport layer. The layers above transport are pretty much irrelevant to the study of bridges and routers.

Typically, the way layer n works is that it receives a chunk of data from layer $n+1$, along with additional information (such as the destination address) that might be required. Layer n must transmit the data to the layer n process in the destination node, which delivers it to the layer $n+1$ process in the destination node. Layer n often needs to include with the data certain information—for instance, the address of the destination—that will be interpreted by other layer n entities. In order to get the information to the destination node, layer n hands down a buffer to layer $n-1$, including the data received from layer $n+1$ and the control information added by layer n. Additionally layer n might pass other information in the layer $n/n-1$ interface along with the buffer.

Now for an example of how layering works. Assume that the physical layer allows a stream of bits to pass from one machine to another. The data link layer marks the bit stream, so that the beginning and end of a packet can be found, and adds a checksum to the packet, so that the receiving machine can detect whether noise on the line introduced errors.

There are various interesting techniques to ensure that the marker indicating that the packet is starting or ending does not appear inside the data. One technique is known as *bit stuffing*. In bit stuffing, the marker is a sequence of six 1's. To ensure that six consecutive 1's do not appear in the data portion of a packet, the hardware automatically adds an extra 0 after five consecutive 1's. The receiving hardware knows that if the next bit after five consecutive 1's is a 0, then the 0 should be removed and ignored. If the next bit after five consecutive 1's is a 1, then it is a signal for the beginning or end of a packet. Another technique involves using different physical signals for data bits (1's and 0's) than for markers.

The network layer allows communication across multiple hops by cooperating with the network layers in all the connected machines to compute routes.

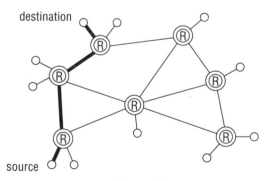

Figure 1.2

When the network layer receives a packet from the transport layer for transmission, the network layer adds a header, which includes information such as the destination address; chooses an appropriate link on which to dispatch the packet; and hands the packet plus the network layer header to the data link layer process responsible for the outgoing link.

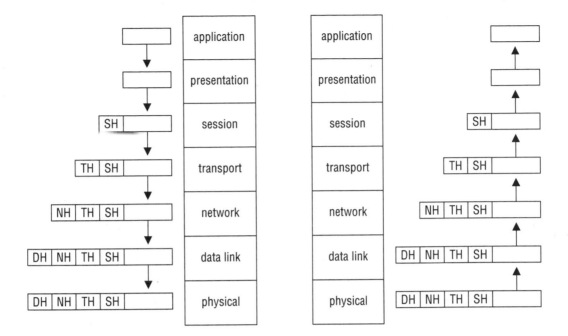

SH = session header
TH = transport header
NH = network header
DH = data link header

Figure 1.3

When the packet is received by an intermediate node, it is processed by the data link layer, the data link layer header is removed, and the packet is passed up to the network layer, where the packet looks exactly the way it did when the previous network layer handed the packet to the data link layer—i.e., it has everything transport sent down, plus the network layer header. The network layer process at the receiving node looks at the network layer header, makes a decision as to the direction in which the packet should go based on that header, modifies the header as necessary (for instance, incrementing a hop count), and gives the modified packet to the data link layer process responsible for the outgoing link (see Fig. 1.4).

In the preceding description, words like *packet* can be confusing. The ISO has invented terminology that makes everything precise. Each layer communicates with its peer layer through a *protocol data unit*, or *PDU*. To make it clear which layer is being discussed, a single-letter prefix is added to 'PDU.' The data link layer communicates with a peer data link layer by transmitting LPDUs. The network layer communicates with other network layers through NPDUs. The transport layer communicates with other transport layers through TPDUs.

When layer $n+1$ gives information to layer n for transmission, the information is known as an *SDU*, or *service data unit*. As with PDUs, a single-letter prefix is added to

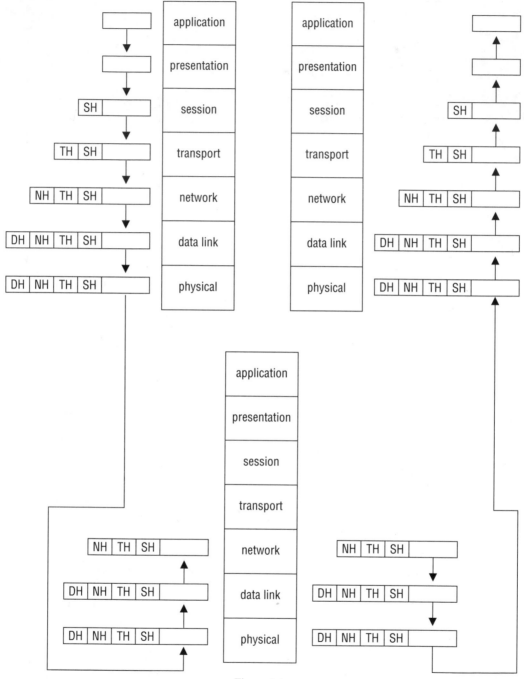

Figure 1.4

eliminate ambiguity. When the transport layer wishes to transmit a TPDU to another transport layer, it must do so by giving the network layer an NSDU. The network layer takes the NSDU, adds a header, and transmits it (through the data link layer) as an NPDU.

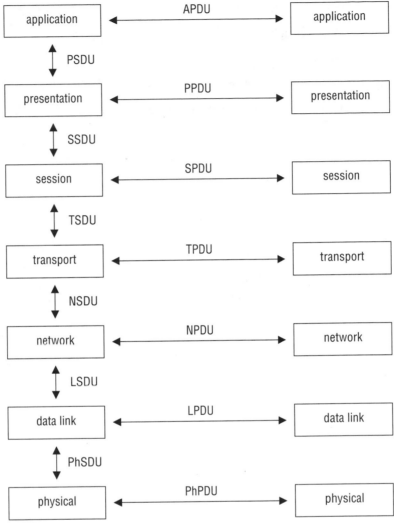

Figure 1.5

As a rule, the ISO terminology will not be used in this book, since it is wordy and hard to translate "in real time" until one has attended at least three standards meetings. However, the ISO terminology will occasionally be used, when it is necessary to be very precise.

1.2 Service Models

In general, the service provided by layer $n-1$ for layer n consists of transmitting data. Layer n provides layer $n-1$ with data (an SDU) plus some extra information, such as the address of the destination. Layer n must also be able to receive data from a peer layer n, which it does by having layer $n-1$ inform it that data is available.

Layer $n-1$ can provide two types of service:

1. Connectionless service

2. Connection-oriented service

A connectionless service offers layer n two functions:

1. It accepts packets for transmission from layer n.

2. It delivers packets to layer n.

With a connection-oriented service, a connection must be established before data can be transferred. Communication consists of three phases:

1. Connection setup

2. Data transfer

3. Connection release

Associated with each of these phases are two functions, one in which layer n initiates the function and another in which layer $n-1$ informs layer n that its peer has initiated the function.

The two functions for connection setup are:

1. Layer n requests that a connection be set up to some destination address.

2. Layer $n-1$ informs layer n that some layer n process in some other node is requesting a connection.

The same two data transfer functions that are available in connectionless service—namely, transmission and receipt of data—are also available in a connection-oriented service.

For connection release, the two functions are:

1. Layer n requests that a connection be released.

2. Layer $n-1$ informs layer n that the layer n process in the other node (or some other condition) requires release of the connection.

Various interfaces might provide other functions, but the preceding are the basic ones.

Another dimension along which services can vary is in their degree of reliability. A service that is purely *datagram* accepts data but makes no guarantees as to delivery. Data may be lost, duplicated, delivered out of order, or mangled. A reliable service will (at least claim to) guarantee that data will be delivered in the order transmitted, without corruption (mangling of the bits), duplication, or loss. Usually, connection-oriented service attempts to be reliable, whereas connectionless service is claimed only to be datagram.

Intuitively, it might seem strange to want anything but a reliable service. However, reliability is not free. It usually makes layer $n-1$ more costly and less efficient. Although there are sometimes good reasons for providing reliability at more than one layer, it certainly need not be provided at every layer.

The trade-offs between connection-oriented versus connectionless service and data-gram versus reliable service are discussed in later chapters. In the standards world, the advocates of connection-oriented, reliable service and the advocates of connectionless, datagram service can never convince each other, so both types of service tend to be offered at various layers. As will be seen in the discussion of LANs in Chapter 2, this is why two flavors of data link layer are offered for running over LANs. The service is known as *LLC*, for *logical link control*. LLC type 1 is a connectionless datagram service; LLC type 2 is a reliable, connection-oriented service.

In the network layer, CONS (connection-oriented network service) and CLNS (connectionless network service) have both been defined by the ISO.

Because there was no agreement about the kind of service provided by the network layer, five classes of transport exist in ISO, ranging from class 0, known as *TP0*, where the assumption is made that the network layer does just about everything, to class 4, known as *TP4*, where the assumption is made that the network layer is a datagram service.

1.3   Important Properties of a Network

It is possible for network designs to seem as if they offer equivalent functionality. However, there are subtle ways in which they might differ. When evaluating a network architecture, the following properties should be considered:

1. *Scope:* A network architecture should solve as general a problem as possible. It should be designed to support both a wide range of applications and a wide range of underlying technologies. It is possible for a network that is either designed with a specific application in mind or designed to be built upon a particular technology to perform better for that one case. However, it is unlikely that a totally different network can be designed and built for each specific case. Unless there is some reason why a general-purpose solution can't possibly meet the needs, it is better to design a network that can handle a large spectrum of applications and underlying technologies.

2. *Scalability:* The ideal network design would work well with very large networks and also be efficient with small networks. In the past, thousands of nodes might have been considered "large." Now, in standardizing any design, we should be thinking in terms of its operating well with millions or even billions of nodes. Ideally, efficiency would not be sacrificed if the same design were used on a very small network (say, 20 nodes), but this is unlikely. In such a case, a network designed for very few nodes could be more efficient. For instance, addresses could be smaller. But we are willing to compromise somewhat in order to get a complete answer, provided that the complete answer isn't grossly less efficient in the special case.

3. *Robustness:* Some aspects of robustness are obvious, and most network designs take this into account. For instance, the network should continue to operate even

if nodes or links fail. Most networks have routing algorithms that adapt to changing topology. However, robustness also has certain more subtle aspects.

Most networks will work properly in the theoretical world in which no undetected data corruption occurs, all nodes are properly executing all the algorithms, parameter settings are compatible across all nodes, and all nodes have sufficient processor power to execute all necessary algorithms in a timely fashion.

However, we do not live in a theoretical world. Undetected data corruption happens, due to undetected data errors in transmission, in a node's memory, or while data is being transferred internally across a bus. Defective implementations attach to the network. Hardware faults cause unpredictable behavior. Implementations run out of memory or CPU and behave unpredictably instead of immediately ceasing operation or doing something compatible with the continued effective functioning of the network.

So robustness in the sense of computing alternate routes is not sufficient. Other types of robustness that a network should have are:

a. *Firewalls:* With most networks, malfunctions can cause widespread disruption. Some networks, however, are designed with "firewalls." If a network is partitioned into pieces by firewalls, a disruption will spread only as far as a firewall and will therefore affect only a portion of the network.

   LAN broadcast storms, which have been an annoyance with the TCP/IP (transmission control protocol/internet protocol) network layer protocol, are a case in which firewalls can be used effectively. A broadcast storm is an event in which severe congestion is initiated; it is usually due to bugs in implementations, ambiguous protocol specifications, or misconfigurations. The broadcast storms with IP are capable of completely incapacitating a LAN. When two LANs are connected with a bridge, the bridge merges the LANs, and a broadcast storm on either LAN will incapacitate both LANs. If the LANs are connected instead with a router, the broadcast storm will be confined to the single LAN on which it started.

b. *Self-stabilization:* This concept means that after any sort of database corruption, due to such causes as malfunctioning hardware or undetected data errors, the network will return to normal operation without human intervention within a reasonable time, provided that the faulty hardware is disconnected from the network or repaired and no further data corruption occurs (for some time). Without this type of robustness, an error could cause the network to remain inoperative until every node in the network is simultaneously brought down and rebooted. As will be seen in Chapter 9, when routing algorithms are discussed, the routing protocol implemented in the ARPANET was not self-stabilizing.

   This type of robustness does not guarantee that a network will operate properly with a malfunctioning piece of equipment attached, but it does make the network easy to repair once the problem is diagnosed. All that is required is to remove the offending device. Many pieces of equipment get into "wedged states," and power-cycling them usually works as an instant repair. However, a network does not have an ON/OFF switch and cannot easily be power-cycled. The network's very robustness, in the sense of its being distributed so that it can remain operational even if some parts of it are down, means that all of it must be "killed" in order to eliminate any residues of a fault.

If a network is not self-stabilizing, a saboteur can inject a few bad packets and the network will remain down forever, or until complex and costly human intervention occurs. If the network is self-stabilizing, a saboteur must inject bad data continually in order to keep the network disrupted. Having to interact continually with the network in order to maintain disruption is far riskier than surreptitiously connecting at some off-hour, injecting a few packets, and quietly slipping away.

Again, if the network is self-stabilizing, repair is simple. Once the offending equipment is found, it must simply be removed in order to restore the network to operational status.

c. *Fault detection:* Although none of today's networks will operate properly in the face of actively malfunctioning nodes, it would be desirable for a network to have the ability to diagnose itself, so that a faulty piece of equipment could be identified. All networks have some ability to detect faults, but none has a perfect ability to do so, and networks vary greatly in the degree to which faults can be identified.

d. *Byzantine robustness:* The term *Byzantine failure* is taken from a famous problem in computer science known as the *Byzantine generals problem.* A Byzantine failure is one in which a node fails not by simply ceasing operation but instead by performing improperly. This can occur due to defective implementations, hardware faults, or active sabotage. A network with Byzantine robustness would be able to continue working properly even if some portion of the nodes had Byzantine failures. Although none of today's networks has this form of robustness, such networks are possible.

4. *Autoconfigurability:* Some network designs work well provided that very smart people do a lot of complex management and constantly tweak parameters. Such network designs are terrific for the ego and job security of the people who understand how to manage them. However, networks of that sort will not suffice in the future. They will become too large, portions of the network will be managed by different organizations, and people will be too dependent on networks to rely on a very few experts to keep them running.

Tomorrow's networks must "run themselves" as much as possible. Ideally, naive users should be able to buy a piece of equipment from the local discount department store, plug it into a network, and be operational. They should not have to configure complex parameters. They should not need to find the address guru to be given an address. (The address guru will be on vacation or will eventually

quit, and the envelope on which the address guru scrawled the address assign-
ments will be lost.) They should not have to find the manager of other nodes in
order to have information about their new node configured into databases.

5. *Tweakability:* Networks should come with reasonable defaults and should ideally
   be autoconfiguring. However, they should also come with parameters that adventurous network managers can play with so as to optimize performance for the
   specific conditions, since it is possible for significant performance gains to be
   achieved by tailoring timers and other parameters to fit a particular network.
   (Ideally, any setting of the parameters will result in reasonable, if not optimal,
   performance, so even overly adventurous network managers will not be able to
   inflict too much damage.)

6. *Determinism:* According to the property of determinism, identical conditions
   will yield identical results. For instance, in a deterministic network design,
   routes would always be identical given identical physical topologies. In contrast, in a network design that is not deterministic, routes might differ depending
   on the order in which nodes were brought up in the network.

   Not all people feel that determinism is an important property, but determinism advocates claim that by ensuring reproducible conditions, determinism
   makes network analysis much easier.

7. *Migration:* A particular network design will not last forever. It is therefore
   important to design network protocols such that new features can be added to
   nodes, one at a time, without disrupting current operations. It is also important
   to have a design that allows modifications like address changes to be done in a
   node-by-node fashion without disrupting network operations.

1.4   Reliable Data Transfer Protocols

Data link and transport protocols that provide reliable service all tend to have the same
general structure. This section introduces the basic ideas and brings up some of the
deeper issues involved—issues that are explored in more detail later in the book.

The problem to be solved is that there is a sequence of packets, which must be delivered to the recipient in the same sequence as was transmitted by the source. The protocol
has failed if any packets are lost or damaged, or any packet is duplicated, or packets are
received in a different order than transmitted. The basic solution is that a packet is transmitted, and the recipient acknowledges its receipt. The packet has a checksum so that the
recipient can detect (with high probability) whether the packet was damaged in transit.

In the overly simplified scheme, the transmitter sends a packet, waits for an acknowledgment (also known as an "ack"), and then transmits the next packet. Let us assume that
the data being transmitted is the message "1000 from acct A to acct B." Let us further
assume that only three characters fit into each message. If an acknowledgment does not

arrive, the transmitter must retransmit the data. Since the transmitter has no way of knowing for sure whether an acknowledgment will arrive, the only thing it can do is set a timer and assume that if the acknowledgment hasn't arrived within that time, the packet (or the acknowledgment) was probably lost.

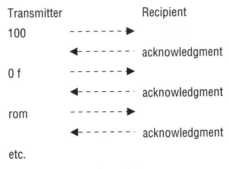

Figure 1.6

Establishing the value of the timer is tricky. If the recipient is a busy time-sharing system, its response time could be highly variable. When the system is heavily loaded, it might take so long to generate an ack that the transmitter will have given up and retransmitted. If the "link" over which the data is being transmitted is a computer network, some packets might take different paths, with the paths having different delays. Or the network might at times be congested (it takes longer to drive the same route at rush hour than at 3:00 A.M. in the U.S. highway network).

If the timer is too small, packets will be needlessly retransmitted, adding to congestion in the network or adding processing burden to the recipient that was already too overloaded to return an ack in time. If the timer is too large, then throughput will be delayed after packet loss, because the large timer will need to expire before further progress can be made on data transmission.

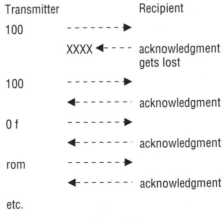

Figure 1.7

Perhaps a more serious problem than optimizing the timer, at this point, is that the preceding protocol does not work. If an acknowledgment is lost or delayed, the recipient will get two copies of a packet and will not know that they are duplicates.

The result of this is that the recipient will assume the message was "1001000 from acct A to acct B." The owner of account B might be delighted to receive over a million dollars instead of a thousand, but the owner of account A might object. Thus, the protocol must be modified somewhat.

The solution is to add message numbers, and corresponding numbers in the acknowledgments, so that an ack can be matched with the message being ack'ed.

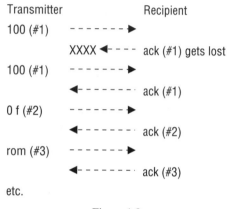

Figure 1.8

The recipient receives 100 (#1) twice but, since both packets are marked with (#1), knows that they are duplicates and only keeps one.

Often, data is being transferred simultaneously in both directions. In this case, the message numbers from right to left are totally independent of the message numbers from left to right. There is no ambiguity. An ack number on an ack transmitted from right to left pertains to the stream of numbered packets being transmitted from left to right. An ack number on an ack transmitted from left to right pertains to the stream of numbered packets being transmitted from right to left.

If the transmitter had to wait for an acknowledgment after sending each message, throughput would be needlessly low. Before the data transmitter can receive an ack, after it finishes transmitting a packet, the packet has to travel the route between the transmitter and receiver, the receiver has to process the packet and generate an acknowledgment, and the acknowledgment has to travel the route between the receiver and the transmitter. Since time is available after the transmitter finishes transmitting the packet and before the transmitter finishes processing the acknowledgment, it would be nice to utilize that time for transmitting more data.

Sending additional data before receiving an acknowledgment for earlier data is known as "pipelining." The number of messages the transmitter is allowed to have "outstanding" (i.e., without yet having received an ack) is known as the "window."

Another issue is the size of the message number. Ideally the number would be of unlimited size. The first packet of a conversation would be numbered 1, and the 12 billionth would be numbered 12000000000. This would make the protocol very simple. The transmitter could transmit all the packets as quickly as it could. The recipient would then ack all the ones it received, and the transmitter could fill in the holes (noting that acks were not received for, say, messages numbered 17, 112, and 3178).

However, protocols are usually designed to use as few bits as possible for information other than data. (If that were not the case, a government agency responsible for truth in labeling might demand that instead of being called "datagram," the service be

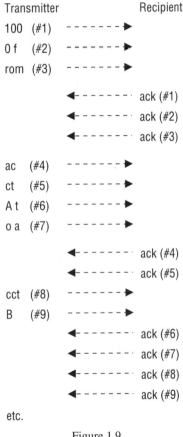

Figure 1.9

called "headergram.") Normally, a limited number of bits is set aside for the message number—for instance, in this example we'll use 3 bits although in real protocols a larger number would be desirable.

With a 3-bit message number, what happens after message 7 is transmitted? The answer is that the message number "wraps around." Messages are numbered 0, 1, 2, 3, 4, 5, 6, 7, 0, 1, 2, 3, 4 . . .

It is also usual for these types of protocols to be designed so that an ack need not be transmitted for every packet. Instead, each ack is cumulative in the sense that an ack of message 4 confirms that all messages up to 4 have been received properly.

The finite message number, together with pipelining and cumulative acks, can create problems unless implemented carefully. Some examples:

1. The transmitter transmits 0, 1, 2, 3, 4, 5, 6, 7, 0, 1, 2, 3. Assume that all messages from the first three to the last are lost, so the recipient gets 0, 1, 2, 3 and returns ack (#3). The transmitter and receiver will assume that all messages arrived properly.

2. The transmitter transmits the same sequence of messages, which are permuted into random order by a network that offers a datagram service. The recipient will have no way of knowing which message 2 comes first and which messages may be duplicates.

3. The transmitter transmits packets 0, 1, 2, 3, 4, 5, 6, 7. The recipient receives them all and returns ack (#7), which gets lost in transit. The transmitter retransmits all eight packets, which the recipient accepts as new data and returns another ack (#7).

The solution to these problems is to design timers and window sizes carefully. It is important that the message-numbering space be large enough so that the message number cannot wrap around during the worst-possible-case delay time. Thus, if it is conceivable that a network could delay a packet by 15 sec, it must not be possible for a transmitter, at maximum speed, to transmit enough messages so that a message number will wrap around within 15 sec. It is also important that if the recipient holds onto packets that arrive out of order (i.e., if the recipient receives 1 and then 3, it holds onto 3 hoping that 2 will eventually arrive), the window be no larger than half the message number. On the other hand, if the recipient is guaranteed to discard any message except the one with the next consecutive number, the window size can be as large as one less than the message number size.

Homework

1. Suppose that the session layer hands information down to the transport layer, which transmits that information (plus perhaps some control information) in a single packet. In ISO-ese, this would be stated as "a single SPDU results in a single TSDU, which results in a single TPDU."

   Suppose instead that the session layer gives the transport layer some information that is too large for the transport layer to send, and the transport layer instead transmits it as a set of packets, with enough control information so that the transport layer at the destination can reassemble the session layer's information. How would this be expressed in ISO-ese?

2. Now suppose that the transport layer is capable, for efficiency reasons, of taking lots of little pieces of information handed down by the session layer and putting

them all into one big "box" to be transmitted as a single packet, such that the transport layer at the destination can sort them back into individual pieces of information. Translate this situation into ISO-ese.

3. Now suppose that the network layer has a packet to send, but some intermediate router notices that the packet is too large to fit over the link on which it should be transmitted. The network layer at the intermediate node breaks the packet into smaller chunks, such that they can be reassembled at the destination network layer. Translate this situation into ISO-ese.

4. Assume a message number size of n. Give an example of a protocol failure in which the transmitter has a window size of n and the receiver discards packets received out of order. Prove that no problems will occur if the window size is $n-1$.

5. Now assume that the receiver does not discard packets received out of order. In other words, the receiver holds onto message number n, hoping that it will eventually receive message $n-1$, and when it does, it acknowledges them both. Give an example of a protocol failure in which the transmitter has a window size of $n/2+1$. Prove that no problems will occur if the window size is $n/2$.

6. Discuss the trade-offs of providing reliable versus datagram service at the data link layer. Assume that the transport layer will provide reliable connection-oriented service in either case.

   Points to consider:

   a. The probability of a packet's making it across a sequence of links (which depends on the error rates of the links)

   b. The total number of packet hops required to successfully get a packet to the destination node, as well as get an acknowledgment back to the source

   c. The desire to maximize throughput for the transport layer

   d. The need for the transport layer to estimate the round-trip delay in order to decide when to retransmit a packet that has not been acknowledged

Chapter 2
Data Link Layer Issues

The purpose of this chapter is to discuss data link layer issues that impact bridges and routers. One issue is the service provided by the data link layer. Should it be reliable or datagram-oriented? Another is how to have multiple network layer protocols coexist on a link. When a node receives a packet, how can it tell which protocol suite originated the packet? Although the chapter also discusses many aspects of LAN (local area network) technology, a fascinating topic, it is not meant to be a detailed reference on LANs. Rather, it is intended to explain those aspects of LANs in general, or of specific LAN technologies, that affect the bridging and network layer protocols.

2.1   Generic LANs

2.1.1   What Is a LAN?

"LAN" is not a well-defined concept. People use the term LAN when they refer to any of a number of technologies that have the properties usually associated with LANs—e.g.:

*   Multiple systems attached to a shared medium.

*   "High" total bandwidth (the total bandwidth is shared by all the stations).

*   "Low" delay.

*   "Low" error rate.

*   Broadcast capability, also known as multicast capability (the ability to transmit a single message and have it received by multiple recipients).

*   Limited geography (several kilometers).

*   Limited numbers of stations (hundreds).

- Peer relationship among attached stations (as opposed to a group of slaves with a master). In a peer relationship, all attached stations are equivalent. In a master/slave relationship, there is one special station, called the *master*, that polls the slaves, giving each one a turn to transmit.

- Being confined to private property and not subject to PTT (post, telegraph, and telephone) regulation.

Note that the meaning of terms like *low*, *high*, and *limited* is relative and changes with time. For the purposes of this book, it is not necessary to come up with a definition of a LAN that would distinguish it from a "MAN" ("metropolitan area network") or a "WAN" ("wide area network"). (This is fortunate because as LAN technology improves to expanded geographies, and WAN technology improves to increased bandwidth, the distinction between LANs and WANs becomes even less clear.)

Basically, a LAN (as well as a WAN) can be viewed as a "cloud" to which stations can be attached. If a station attaches to the cloud, it can transmit packets to, and receive packets from, every other station attached to the cloud.

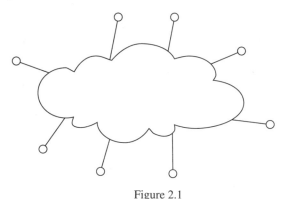

Figure 2.1

2.1.2 Taking Turns

In a shared medium, only one station can successfully transmit at a time. Some mechanism must therefore exist to allocate bandwidth among the stations so that:

- Each station gets a fair share of bandwidth

- Each station gains access to the medium within a reasonable amount of time

- The wastage of bandwidth due to arbitration mechanisms is minimized

The two most popular bandwidth-arbitration mechanisms used on LANs are token schemes and contention.

In a token scheme, each station is granted permission to transmit in some round-robin fashion. In the case of a *token ring*, a particular sequence of bits known as the *token* travels around the ring. A station is allowed to transmit when it sees the token.

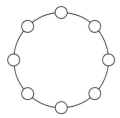

Figure 2.2   Token ring

In the case of a *token bus*, the token is a special packet that is sent from station to station, with each station being required to know the identity of the station to which it should transmit the token.

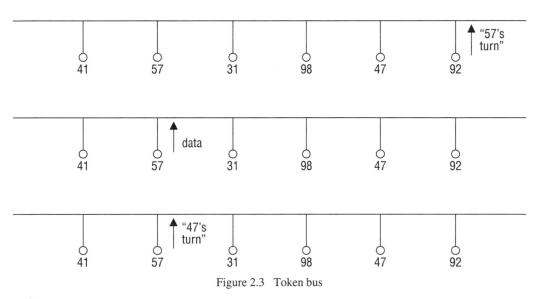

Figure 2.3   Token bus

In a contention scheme, stations transmit at will, and if two stations transmit simultaneously, there is a "collision," with neither station's transmission being successful. Mechanisms are built in to minimize the probability of collisions. Contention schemes are *probabilistically fair*, which means that theoretically, some station might never succeed in transmitting, because whenever it tries, some other station transmits at the same time. However, contention LANs are carefully designed to make this situation highly unlikely.

Relying on probability instead of a scheme that guarantees a desired outcome might seem worrisome, but it must be realized that we rely on probability every day. It is only probably true that enough oxygen atoms will remain in the room in which you are sitting to enable you to continue breathing. It is theoretically possible that through random motion, all oxygen atoms will leave the room and you will asphyxiate.

Even schemes that seem to provide guarantees are actually probabilistic. The token is merely a sequence of bits, which can become corrupted. In a token scheme, it is theoretically possible that one particular station will never succeed in transmitting because the token always gets lost before that station gains access. Or it is possible that every time some station succeeds in acquiring the token, its transmitted packet will get corrupted.

2.2   IEEE 802 LANs

The IEEE (Institute for Electrical and Electronic Engineers) has a committee with the descriptive title "802" whose purpose was to standardize LANs. Taking its job very seriously, the 802 committee standardized not one but several LANs.

LAN protocols really cover the bottom two layers of the ISO Reference Model (the physical and data link layers). The 802 committee chose to subdivide the data link layer into two sublayers:

1. *MAC*, which stands for *medium access control*, addresses issues specific to a particular type of LAN. For instance, it deals with channel management algorithms such as token passing (on 802.5 and 802.4), binary backoff after collision detection (802.3), priorities (802.5 and 802.4), error detection, and framing.

2. *LLC,* which stands for *logical link control*, defines the fields that allow multiple higher-layer protocols to share the use of the data link. Since some people felt that it was not enough for the data link layer to provide a simple datagram service, they pushed for additional functionality. The decision was to provide several different flavors of LLC. The following three have been standardized so far (but at least one more is in process):

    a. *LLC type 1* is simply a datagram protocol, meaning that a packet is delivered with "best-effort" service by the data link layer. There is no protocol at the data link layer to alert the source as to whether the packet was successfully received. Instead, error control of that sort is assumed to be carried out at a higher layer.

    b. *LLC type 2* is a connection-oriented protocol on top of the basic datagram. This means that in addition to the fields required by LLC type 1, there are fields to number messages, provide a piggybacked acknowledgment field, and provide for differentiating data packets from control packets such as acknowledgments and resynchronization messages. LLC type 2 is basically running the connection-oriented data link protocol HDLC (high-level data link control), which was designed for point-to-point links, on top of the LAN datagram-oriented protocol.

    c. *LLC type 3* is a semireliable protocol. It is less expensive to implement than LLC type 2, since it requires less state to be kept. It was developed primarily for use on a token bus by process control applications.

    This book describes LLC types 1 and 2 in detail, just to demystify what different types of LLC might provide, but the details of all the types of LLC are really not relevant to bridges and routers.

The various IEEE 802 committees relevant to this book are:

*   *802.1:* This committee deals with issues common across all 802 LANs, including addressing, management, and bridges.

*   *802.2:* This committee defines LLC. MAC and physical layer are defined for a specific type of LAN by the committee that defines that type of LAN.

*   *802.3:* This committee deals with the CSMA/CD (carrier sense multiple access with collision detection) LAN, which is derived from the Ethernet, invented by Xorox and developed by Digital, Intel, and Xerox.

*   *802.4:* This committee deals with the token bus LAN.

*   *802.5:* This committee deals with the 4-Mb and 16-Mb token ring LAN.

Although there are other 802 committees, dealing with such issues as metropolitan area networks and security, they are not particularly relevant to this book, which concentrates on bridges and routers.

Another type of LAN is FDDI (fiber distributed data interface), which is a 100-Mb token ring. It is not simply a faster version of 802.5 but rather is very different from 802.5. (Although the technical differences between them are fascinating, they are not really relevant to this book.) FDDI is not being standardized within 802 but is being standardized instead by ANSI.

2.3   Names, Addresses, Routes

Considerable confusion exists regarding the terms *name*, *address*, and *route*. Shoch[1] defines these terms as follows:

*   *Name:* What something is

*   *Address:* Where it is

*   *Route:* How to get there

Inevitably, the Schoch paper seems to be referenced whenever any mention is made of names, addresses, and/or routes. However, I have never found these definitions helpful, in the sense of enabling one to look at a string of bits and decide, based on the preceding taxonomy, whether the string should be classified as a name, an address, or a route.

An alternative method of defining the three concepts that I have found helpful is as follows. Suppose a particular string of bits refers to a particular station. We want to decide whether that string of bits should be considered a name, an address, or a route. In the following definitions, the *destination* is the station referred to by the string of bits, and the *source* is the station that is using the string of bits to refer to the destination.

1.   *Name:* A name is location-independent, with respect to both the source and the destination. If something is the name of a destination, it will remain

[1] "Internetwork Naming, Addressing, and Routing," *Compcon* (Fall 1978), 72–79.

unchanged even if the destination moves, and it is valid regardless of which source is attempting to reach the destination. An example of a name is a Social Security number, which remains unchanged even if the number's owner moves. Sometimes, fields that are names are referred to as *identifiers*, or *IDs*.

2. *Address:* An address is valid regardless of the location of the source station, but it may change if the destination moves. An example of an address is a postal address. The same destination postal address works regardless of the location from which a letter is mailed. However, if the destination moves, it is assigned a new address.

3. *Route:* A route is dependent on the location of both the source and the destination. In other words, if two different sources specify a route to a given destination, the routes are likely to differ. And if the destination moves, all routes to it are likely to change. An example of a route is, "To get to my house, go west 3 miles and take a right turn at the first light. It's the last house on the left."

Note that with the preceding descriptions, the entities known as "addresses" in 802 would really be classified as "names" rather than "addresses," since especially with globally assigned 48-bit "LAN addresses," the LAN address will not change if a station moves to a different LAN. There are probably several reasons why these fields are referred to as "addresses":

• Some people like to refer to something as a "name" if it is human-friendly—i.e., an ASCII string rather than a bunch of bits. Since 48-bit quantities are certainly unpleasant to type, remember, or look at, those who equate the word *name* with human compatibility prefer to refer to them as "addresses." I would prefer to refer to a human-hostile quantity that is location-independent as an "identifier," or "ID."

• From the viewpoint of a higher-layer process that may move from node to node, its "LAN address" really does become an address, because when the higher-layer process moves to a different node, its LAN address actually changes.

• If the 48-bit "LAN address" is stored in the interface to the LAN rather than in the node, then a node with multiple attachments to LANs has multiple LAN addresses. But then the 48-bit quantity is addressing not the node but one of the interfaces of the node, and I would therefore claim that the 48-bit quantity is an identifier of the interface.

Since everyone in the industry refers to the 48-bit elements as "addresses," I will do so in this book. It is important to realize, however, that most terms (*layer, address, route, node, network, LAN,* etc.) are at best vaguely defined in the industry and are used in conflicting ways by various communities. One should not take terminology too seriously.

2.4   LAN Addresses

Because every station on a LAN hears every packet transmission, it is necessary to include a **destination** field in each packet. And so that the destination can identify which station transmitted the packet, a **source** field is also included. To prevent software interrupts with every packet, LAN adapters filter out packets not addressed to the station.

The 802 committee needed to standardize addresses for its LANs. The first decision was to set the length of the address field. The committee apparently felt that if standardizing on one size was a good thing, standardizing on several sizes would be even better. The 802 committee gave the option of running a LAN (other than 802.6) with 48-bit addresses or 16-bit addresses. It gave the option of running 802.6 with 16-, 48-, or 60-bit addresses. Luckily, 16-bit addresses have not caught on and can safely be ignored. There is a good chance that 16-bit addresses will be removed from the standard.

The argument for 16-bit addresses is that this size is sufficient for any single LAN, provided that the manager of the LAN is capable of assigning addresses to the stations. Also, 802.4 used addresses to resolve an initial contention phase prior to building a logical ring and would come up or restart faster with 16-bit addresses.

The argument for 48-bit addresses is that they enable stations to be provided with a globally unique identifier at the time of manufacture. This allows networks to be truly *plug and play*, in the sense that a customer could buy an off-the-shelf system, plug it into the network, and have it operate, without having to first assign it an address.

The way globally unique addresses work is that a global authority is responsible for handing out blocks of addresses. Originally, Xerox was the global authority, though now the official global authority is IEEE. When a vendor wishes to manufacture equipment that will plug into a LAN, it first contacts the global authority to obtain a block of addresses. The current cost of a block of addresses is $1,000, for which the vendor is given 2^{24} addresses. In other words, the vendor is given 3 fixed-value octets, with the remaining 3 octets being for the vendor to allocate. The fixed value portion of the address is sometimes referred to in the industry as the *vendor code* or *OUI* (*organizationally unique identifier*), but that is really a misnomer (misoddresser?) because a vendor can purchase more than one block of addresses as well as donate addresses to other vendors.

The three fixed-value octets actually have additional structure. One bit represents **group/individual.** If that bit is 0, the address refers to a particular station; if that bit is 1, the address refers to some logical group of stations. Thus, the global authority does not really give 24 bits of fixed value, but rather 23 bits of fixed value, with the remaining bit being the group/individual bit. An entire address is 6 octets long. The 3 octets of constant leave an additional 3 octets (24 bits) that can be assigned by the vendor. Therefore, when a vendor purchases a block of addresses, it gets 2^{24} station addresses and 2^{24} group addresses.

The 802 committee was not sure everyone would want to go to the trouble (and expense) of obtaining a block of addresses from the global authority. Therefore, it designated another of the 48 bits to indicate whether the address was globally or locally assigned. If a vendor purchases a block of addresses from the global authority, the global/local bit will be set to 1. People are free to use any addresses with the global/local bit set to 0. However, if local addresses are used, it is up to the network manager to assign addresses and make sure there are no *address collisions* (which occur when two stations use the same address). Address collision becomes an important issue when two networks are merged.

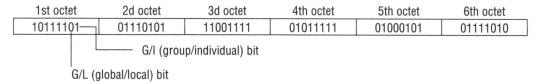

Figure 2.4

Group addresses are also sometimes referred to as *multicast addresses*. The most common use of multicast addresses is for discovering appropriate neighbors, which can be done by one of the following two methods:

1. *Solicitation:* Suppose the network contains one or more of a certain type of station—for instance, a naming server, a router, or a file server—that station A is likely to want to contact. Station A could be configured, by management, with the addresses of all those stations. However, it would be more desirable if station A did not need to know about specific servers a priori. Instead, it would know a single group address, ZSERVERS (where "Z" can be any type of service—for instance, those just suggested).

   When station A wishes to find a Z server, it transmits a packet with the destination address ZSERVERS. All the Z servers listen for, and respond to, packets directed to that address.

2. *Advertisement:* A different way to use group addresses is to define an address to be used for stations listening for a service. Instead of having service Z clients ask for help by transmitting to ZSERVERS, Z servers would periodically transmit packets to the address ZCLIENTS. A Z client would listen for packets addressed to ZCLIENTS until it heard such a packet. Then, based on the source address of the packet or on some other field explicitly contained in the data portion of the packet, the Z client would now know the address of a Z server.

   The human counterpart of this method is commercial advertising. The advertising industry would love to be able to transmit an advertisement that would be received only by people interested in hearing it, but the best advertisers can do is to advertise in magazines whose readership tends to match the type of person who might be interested in a particular product.

Why is it that a multicast address looks different from an individual address? Why can't just any address be used for a multicast, in that a particular address is designated to mean "all Z servers," and all Z servers are supposed to listen to that address in addition to their own?

The problem is that on a LAN, there are a lot of packets, and it would seriously degrade the performance of an attached station if the software had to process an interrupt every time a packet for any destination was transmitted on the wire. The hardware will receive every packet, and it is possible to request that it deliver every packet. This is known as listening *promiscuously*.

Although sometimes, as in the case of a bridge or a LAN-monitoring tool, it is appropriate for the hardware to deliver every packet, for most applications, promiscuity is not desirable. Instead, it should be possible for the hardware to look at enough of a packet to decide whether the software might conceivably be interested in the packet. If the packet is of interest, the hardware should pass it up to the software. If not, the hardware should just drop the packet (*filter* it).

Theoretically, it is not necessary to reserve a bit in the address to differentiate group and individual addresses. Ideally, the software would tell the chip all the different addresses that the software was interested in receiving, and the chip would pass packets up to the software if and only if the "destination address" field in the data link header matched one of the addresses requested by the software.

The problem with having the software request a certain number of addresses is that the chip designer would need to pick a maximum number of addresses that could be requested. If the designer picked too large a number, the chip would be too expensive. If the designer picked too small a number, the chip would be useless for a station that required more addresses than were provided for in the chip.

Many chips were designed with the following compromise:

- A bit in the address designates the address as individual or group.

- A station informs the chip of the single individual address it wants to receive.

- The chip partitions the set of group addresses into a number of groups (the technical term is *hash buckets*). If the station wishes to receive a particular group address, it must request the bucket into which that address hashes. Once a bucket is selected, the chip will send up all packets whose destination addresses hash into that bucket.

The theory is that a station will only be interested in a single individual address (its own) and some number of group addresses. The chip could have been designed to allow the software to specify exactly which multicast addresses to pass up, but again, the problem was picking the right maximum number. So instead of exactly specifying group addresses, the chip has several hash buckets into which to sort group addresses, and the software specifies any subset of the hash buckets for the chip to pass up. This chip design means that a station cannot avoid software interrupts for group addresses in which it is not interested, since the chip will pass up all group addresses that hash into a requested bucket.

An alternative chip design provides:

- Some fixed number of exact addresses (either group or individual) that the station can request to receive.

- Some number of hash buckets for addresses, with the provision that the station can request any subset of the hash buckets.

With this design, if a station does not need to receive more than the number of addresses allowed for in the chip, it can get perfect filtering (it will not get software interrupts for addresses in which it is not interested). If the station does need to receive more than the specified number of addresses, it can fall back on the hashing scheme and hope that a foreign address with a lot of traffic does not happen to hash into a bucket containing an address that the station needs to receive.

One particular group address has been named the *broadcast address*. It consists of all 1's. It is intended to mean "all stations," and theoretically, all stations should receive any packet transmitted to the broadcast address. In the case of a protocol that must be implemented by every station on the LAN, it makes sense to use the broadcast address. However, it does not make sense for other protocols to use the broadcast address, since they really do not mean "all stations"; instead, they mean "all stations that have implemented this particular protocol." Unfortunately, some protocols implemented by only a subset of stations do use the broadcast address.

2.5   Multiplexing Field

It is possible for multiple higher-layer protocols to be implemented in the same station. When a packet arrives addressed to that station, there must be some way to determine which protocol should receive the packet. Likewise, many different protocols (unfortunately) send packets to the broadcast address. When a station receives a packet, it must determine how to interpret the bits of the packet (i.e., find out which protocol constructed the packet).

For example, it might be possible to examine the packet and determine that it could not possibly be a legal TCP/IP packet and thus must be an OSI packet. However, since most protocols were designed without worrying about disambiguating packets valid in one protocol from packets valid in other protocols, there really is no way to determine from the data alone which recipient is intended.

We have the same problem in human language, which is fundamentally nothing more than a set of sounds. If you walk up to someone on the street and ask, "Can you please tell me how to get to the nearest subway stop?" the individual you've asked may be unable to speak English and may instead speak Martian. Worse yet, there is the danger that the sequence of sounds you uttered means something very rude in Martian—in which case, the creature, instead of directing you to a subway stop, may melt you with its ray gun.

To solve this problem, there should be a universally defined method by which, before delivering your message, you first identify the language in which you are about to speak. Although there is no such method for human speech, a method has been defined for LANs. Included in the LAN header is a field that specifies the protocol being used. In the original Ethernet design, there was a 2-octet-long field known as the *protocol type*. The field was globally administered by Xerox, and anyone who wanted to define a protocol would negotiate with Xerox to obtain a number for the protocol.

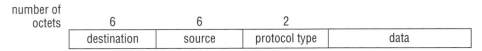

Figure 2.5   Protocol type multiplexing

When the 802 committee standardized LANs, it decided that a more flexible scheme would be to have separate fields for the source and destination. These fields were known as service access points (SAPs). Included in the 802 header are SSAP (source service access point) and DSAP (destination service access point). This gives the flexibility of assigning numbers to protocols differently in each machine.

Figure 2.6   SAP multiplexing

The SAP fields are 8 bits long. However, as with the LAN addresses, two of those bits are reserved. One of the reserved bits is for "global/local," which, as with the similar bit in the LAN address field, indicates whether the 802 committee has assigned the number, to guarantee its uniqueness, or whether the owner of the network or system manages the number.

The other reserved bit is for "group/individual." This gives the capability of sending a packet that would be received by multiple higher-layer protocols within a system. The reason for reserving a bit in the LAN address had to do with convenience in making chips. This reasoning is not applicable in the case of the SAP, since filtering based on SAP is not done in the hardware. Another reason why the group/individual address makes sense in the LAN address but does not make as much sense in the SAP is that it seems likely that many different stations on the same LAN would implement the same protocol and would thus want to receive the same message. It seems less likely that a common protocol would be implemented by multiple upper-layer processes within the same station. However, with an entire 8 bits to play with, why not reserve 1 for the purpose, even though the justification for its need is slight? (Hint: The preceding statement is sarcastic, with a touch of bitterness. In fact, 8 bits are not nearly sufficient to make the scheme usable. Only due to the invention of the SNAP SAP kludge, which is described later in this section, was it possible for protocols other than ISO or IEEE protocols to use the 802-defined LLC.)

The SAP consisting of all 1's is reserved to mean "all SAPs," like the broadcast address. The SAP consisting of all 0's is reserved to mean the data link layer itself, not a user of the data link layer. (Actually, to be nitpicky, the 802 committee shouldn't have assigned meaning to the SAP consisting of all 0's, because that SAP has G/L set to 0 and, as such, should really be locally defined.)

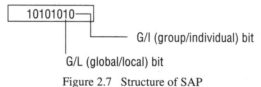

Figure 2.7   Structure of SAP

With only 6 bits of globally assigned individual SAP numbers, the 802 committee cannot grant numbers to every organization that might want to design a protocol. Rather than assign numbers on a first-come, first-served basis until they are all gone, the 802 committee has strict rules for the sorts of organizations and protocols that can be granted a SAP number. In order to be eligible, a protocol must have been designed by a standards body approved by the 802 committee.

For those protocols privileged to receive a global SAP value, the SAP fields are used like a single protocol type field, since the SSAP and DSAP will both be equal (they will equal the global SAP value assigned to that protocol).

Other protocols (those without globally assigned SAP values) could use locally assigned SAP numbers, and the manager of a system could ensure that each protocol had a unique number within that system. However, this approach makes conversation startup difficult, because it is hard to send a protocol message to another machine when the SAP numbering within the foreign machine is unknown.

A plan to make the SAP system usable was proposed within 802. It consisted of requesting a single globally assigned SAP. When the DSAP was set to that value, it would indicate that the header was expanded to include a "protocol type" field. The protocol type field could then be large enough so that a global authority could assure that every protocol was granted a globally assigned number.

Originally, the plan was that the protocol type field be 2 octets, on the theory that it was 2 octets in the original Ethernet, and Xerox must have known what it was doing. But then someone noticed that the 802 header was an odd number of octets. If the protocol type field were an odd number of octets, it would make the entire header an even number of octets, which would enhance performance on machines that like fields to be word-aligned.

Then someone noticed that if the protocol type field were longer than 3 octets, administration of the field could be done "for free" by linking the administration of the protocol type field with the administration of the addresses. In other words, when a vendor bought a block of addresses, it received 3 octets of constant (including the group/individual bit), with the remaining 3 octets assignable by the vendor. The vendor could use those same 3 octets of constant as the higher-order portion of protocol types, which the vendor could then assign. So for instance, if the protocol type field were 4 octets long, then when a vendor purchased a block of addresses, it also received a block of 2^8 protocol types.

The agreed-upon size of the protocol type field was 5 octets, not only because 5 is larger than 3 but also because 5 is odd and is the smallest odd number bigger than 3.

The globally assigned SAP value that indicates the presence of the protocol type field is known as the *SNAP (subnetwork access protocol)* SAP. It is equal to 10101010 (binary), which equals aa hex. When the SNAP SAP is used, both DSAP and SSAP are set to aa hex. The protocols that have a globally assigned SAP set DSAP and SSAP to the same value—namely, the value of the globally assigned SAP. And the protocols that do not have a globally assigned SAP also set DSAP and SSAP to the same value—in this case, the SNAP SAP, aa hex.

To summarize, the structure of an address is:

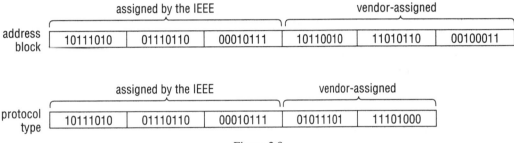

Figure 2.8

When an organization purchases a block of addresses, it receives a 3-octet quantity such as XYZ, and its addresses have the form XYZ***. The organization can assign stations addresses having the form XYZ***. It can assign multicast addresses having the form X'YZ***, where X' is X with the G/I bit set. It can assign protocol types having the form XYZ**.

Note that this description applies only to the assignment of addresses, not to the use of addresses. Suppose organization A buys a block of addresses XYZ*** and assigns XYZAB to a protocol it has designed. Now suppose organization B buys a block of addresses YYY and implements organization A's protocol within a machine it has manufactured. Organization B assigns its machine the address YYY***, but organization A's protocol will still be numbered XYZAB within Y's machine.

2.6 Bit Order

A serious problem with addresses is how they should be represented and transmitted. Different machines store bits and bytes in different ways. The 802.1 committee has defined a canonical format for writing addresses—namely, 6 octets separated by hyphens. Each octet is represented by two hex digits. For instance, an address might be written as a2-41-42-59-31-51.

With 802.3 and 802.4, the least significant bit is transmitted first, and with 802.5 (and FDDI), the most significant bit is transmitted first. This would not be an issue (adapters on receiver and transmitter for a particular LAN would presumably be symmetric, and the order of transmission would be irrelevant) except for the fact that the group bit in addresses was defined not as "the most significant bit" or "the least significant bit," but rather as "the first bit on the wire." Thus, an address that was a group address on 802.3 would not necessarily look like a group address when transmitted on 802.5, since a different bit would be transmitted first.

The canonical format for addresses assumes least-significant-bit-first order. Therefore, the address a2-41-42-59-31-51 is not a group address, since the least significant bit of the first octet (a2, which equals 10100010 binary) is 0.

When addresses are stored for transmission onto 802.5 or FDDI, which transmit the most significant bit first, they must be stored in a different format.

The address a2-41-42-59-31-51, as stored for transmission least significant bit first:

10100010	01000001	01000010	01011001	00110001	01010001

Figure 2.9

The address a2-41-42-59-31-51, as stored for transmission most significant bit first:

01000101	10000010	01000010	10011010	10001100	10001010

Figure 2.10

Therefore, bits in the address fields must be shuffled when forwarding between 802.5 (and FDDI) and any of the other LANs. This is a problem for bridges.

An even more difficult problem is the inclusion of LAN addresses in higher-layer protocol messages (such as management messages or ARP messages, which are described in Chapter 8). If the implementers of the higher-layer protocol do not convert the LAN address into a canonical format before placing it into a protocol message, then the destination cannot interpret the field that contains the LAN address without determining the type of LAN from which the protocol message originated—information that is not generally available to upper-layer protocols, since it should be irrelevant.

The failure of the 802 committee to agree upon a bit ordering for all the LANs has caused immense amounts of confusion and interoperability problems. For instance, at least one protocol was implemented so that it broke if the address in the data link header was not identical to the address as represented in the higher-layer header. If bridges did the appropriate bit shuffling when forwarding between 802.3 and 802.5, then the protocol would break. The solution that the bridge vendors were forced to adopt was to specifically check for the protocol type of this particular protocol and not shuffle the address bits in the data link header on packets with that protocol type. As a result, bridged packets from that protocol will have different addresses than they should. There are two major problems that this can cause: (1) the station address—when the bits are in the flipped order—might appear on the LAN to be a multicast address, which may in turn confuse source routing bridges into misparsing the packet and cause transparent bridges to refuse to forward the packet; or (2) the station address with the flipped order might turn into an address used by another station.

2.7 LLC

LLC (which stands for *logical link control*) is described in the specs as if it were a sub-layer separate from the MAC sublayer. If people had agreed upon a datagram model for LANs, the 802 committee might not have felt the need to subdivide the LAN data link layer into MAC and LLC.

As stated earlier in this chapter, three types of LLC are currently defined. Type 1 is datagram, type 2 is connection-oriented, and type 3 is semireliable.

The sublayering defined by the 802 committee has only the data link layer fields **DSAP**, **SSAP**, and **CTL** within LLC. The source and destination addresses are actually considered part of the MAC sublayer, which technically means that each individual LAN committee (802.3, 802.5, etc.) can define addresses as it chooses. It is lucky that addresses across different LANs are pretty much the same. Unfortunately, they are not identical, because of bit-ordering issues and problems in 802.5 with arbitrary multicast addresses, to be described later in this chapter. In fact, with 802.5, the addresses started out being different—they were originally hierarchical, with a portion of the 6 bytes indicating the ring number on which a station resided and the remainder of the address indicating the station number with respect to that ring. That has been changed to be 6 bytes of station address, as on the other LANs.

The **CTL** ("control") field in LLC type 1 (datagrams) is always 1 byte long and is always equal to one of three values:

1. *UI*, which stands for "unnumbered information." (This just means it's a datagram.)

2. *XID*, which stands for "exchange identification." There are two types of XID, "response" and "command." **Command** informs the recipient of the identity of the transmitter of the XID command message, and which LLC types the transmitter supports. **Response** is the required reply to an XID command message. It contains the same information as the XID command—i.e., it includes the identity of the transmitter of the XID response message and which LLC types the transmitter supports.

3. *TEST*. As with XID, there are two types of TEST message, "command" and "response." TEST is used to check whether a packet can be sent to the recipient and returned. Included in the command is any arbitrary data. The data in the TEST response is copied from the data in the TEST command.

Command and response packets in XID and TEST are distinguished based on a bit in the SSAP field! The 802.2 committee decided that there was no reason anyone would want to transmit a packet from a group SAP, so the bit in the SSAP designated to indicate group or individual actually indicates command or response.

In LLC type 2, the CTL field is either 1 or 2 bytes long, depending on what type of packet it is. The packet types for which the CTL field is 2 bytes contain at least one sequence number. These packets are:

1. *I* (stands for "information") is a data packet. In this case, the CTL field is 2 bytes long and includes 7 bits of sequence number for the data packets being transmitted from source S to destination D, plus 7 bits of sequence number for the acknowledgments for packets being received from D by S.

2. *RR* ("receive ready") is an acknowledgment. It contains a sequence number and indicates that all packets with sequence numbers lower than that have been received. It also indicates that the receiver is prepared to receive more data.

3. *RNR* ("receive not ready") is an acknowledgment for previously transmitted packets (with numbers lower than the number in the receive sequence number field in the RNR), just like the RR. However, it also indicates that the receiver is temporarily busy and that further packets should not be transmitted until the receiver indicates it can accept new packets, by transmitting an RR.

4. *REJ* ("reject") indicates that the receiver is requesting retransmission of packets starting with the number in the receive sequence number field.

The other LLC type 2 packet types, which use a 1-byte CTL field, are:

1. *SABME* ("set asynchronous balanced mode extended"—aren't you sorry you asked?) requests that a connection be started. The bizarre name for the command is historical.

2. *DISC* ("disconnect") requests that a connection be ended.

3. *DM* ("disconnected mode") is transmitted in response to a DISC, indicating that the recipient of the DISC has indeed received the DISC.

4. *FRMR* ("frame reject") indicates receipt of an invalid packet —for example, one containing an out-of-order sequence number.

5. *UA* ("unnumbered acknowledgment") acknowledges a DISC or SABME message.

2.8   Issues in 802.3

The 802.3 LAN access is based on contention. The technology is known as *CSMA/CD*, which stands for "carrier sense multiple access with collision detection." *Carrier sense* means that a station wishing to transmit first listens, and if another station is transmitting, the first station does not transmit but rather waits until the medium is idle. *Multiple access* merely means that many stations share the same medium. *Collision detect* means that stations monitor the medium even while they are transmitting, so that they can detect the occurrence of a collision—i.e., another station transmitting while they are transmitting.

A collision can occur if the medium is idle and two stations attempt to initiate transmission simultaneously. However, the transmission initiations need not be absolutely simultaneous, since once one station starts transmitting, it takes time for its signal to be detected, especially if the second transmitter is far away. The shorter the wire, the lower the probability of collisions.

The original CSMA/CD LAN was designed at Xerox and was called the Ethernet. It was designed to guarantee that the transmitting station could tell whether its transmis-

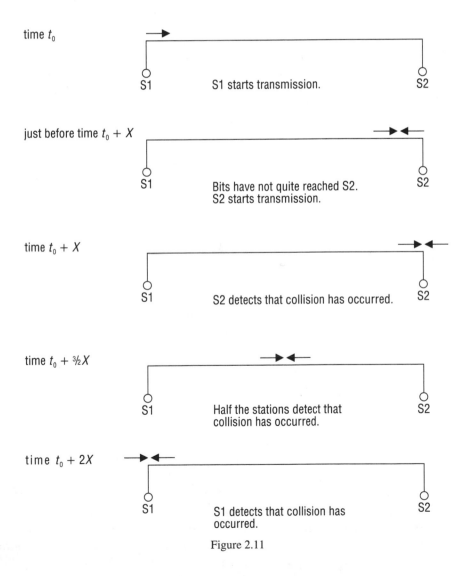

Figure 2.11

sion had failed due to a collision. In order to meet the conditions of this guarantee, the length of the wire had to be limited and a minimum size had to be established for packet lengths. The worst case is when a station at one end of the wire initiates transmission. If a station at the other end initiates transmission just before the bits from the first station arrive, the first station will not detect that its packet has collided until twice the length of time it takes for a signal to go from one end of the wire to the other.

This time is known as a *slot time*. Given that the maximum length of the wire is set at 2.5 km, given the speed of electricity on the wire, and given the transmission speed of 10 Mb/sec, it might take as long as 512 bit times to detect a collision. Thus, each packet must be at least 512 bits long, because if a station finishes transmitting a packet and does not discover during that time that a collision occurred, it will assume its transmission was successful. Some protocols might want to issue packets shorter than that, but those packets must be padded to minimum length.

One problem specific to the 802.3 LAN is that the committee did not merely standardize the Ethernet. Instead, it made some modifications. Although 802.3-compliant hardware is compatible with Ethernet hardware, in that both types of stations can coexist on the same cable, header formats do differ slightly.

In particular, the Ethernet and 802.3 header are as follows:

Ethernet

8	6	6	2	46–1,500	4
preamble	destination	source	protocol	data	FCS

802.3

8	6	6	2	1	1	1	43–1,497	4
preamble	destination	source	length	DSAP	SSAP	CTL	data	FCS

Figure 2.12

It was desirable to build stations that could receive packets in either format (Ethernet or 802.3). Luckily, these formats can be distinguished, because of the 2-byte field that is **length** in 802.3 and **protocol type** in Ethernet. The maximum legal packet length in 802.3 is 1500 bytes. Xerox just made sure that none of the assigned protocol types used with the Ethernet format was smaller than 1,500. In fact, some protocol types assigned before the 802.3 standard had values smaller than 1,500, and these had to be reassigned as a result. Thus, if a station receives a packet, and the field in question has a value smaller than 1,500, the packet is assumed to be in 802.3 format; otherwise, it is assumed to be in Ethernet format.

Another difference between the two formats is the use of **protocol type** in Ethernet and two **SAP** fields in 802.3. Currently, the way the SAP fields are used in 802.3 is that (except for XID and TEST) either an 802-approved protocol is used—in which case, DSAP = SSAP, and they equal the globally assigned SAP value—or DSAP = SSAP, and they equal the globally assigned SNAP SAP value, and following the CTL field is a 5-byte **protocol type** field.

2.9   Issues in 802.5

> Yes, but I'd rather go by bus. There is nothing nicer in the
> world than a bus.
>
> —Charles, Prince of Wales, when asked whether he was
>   excited about sailing to Tobruk on the royal yacht,
>   news summaries of May 21, 1954. [2]

A token ring has the interesting property that each packet travels through every station. The source removes the packet from the wire. Thus, it is possible for the destination to mark the packet, to indicate to the source that the packet was successfully received (at least, by the hardware—congestion at the destination could force the packet to be dropped even though the hardware successfully received it).

In 802.5, there are 2 bits at the end of a packet, used as an acknowledgment by the destination. One is the "A" bit, which means that the address was recognized. That, in turn, means that the destination is on the LAN. The "C" bit indicates that the packet was copied into the destination's buffer. If the "A" bit is on and not the "C" bit, this indicates that the destination was (presumably, only temporarily) congested, so that although the destination knew the packet was supposed to be copied, it could not copy the packet. Theoretically, if the source transmits a packet, it can examine the state of the A and C bits and surmise the following:

1. If the A bit is clear, the destination does not exist or is down, so there is no point in attempting to retransmit the packet.

2. If both the A and C bits are set, the destination has successfully received the packet, so no retransmission is necessary.

3. If the A bit is set and the C bit is clear, the hardware was temporarily congested at the destination, so an immediate retransmission will probably succeed.

4. The case of the A bit's being clear and the C bit's being set was not originally assumed to be useful, and some implementations might have been built to handle this case as an error.

Although these bits seem like a nice idea, it is very difficult for bridges to do anything meaningful with them. A number of options for what bridges could do were discussed, including the following:

1. Always clear both bits.

2. Don't modify the bits at all.

3. Set A and C if the bridge decides to forward the packet.

4. Clear A and set C if the bridge decides to forward the packet.

[2] James B. Simpson, *Contemporary Quotations* (New York: Thomas Y. Crowell Company, 1964), 1970.

The last option—i.e., that bridges should clear the A bit and set the C bit—was the one selected.

> Note that the A and C bits have other uses. These bits help stations determine the order in which they physically appear in the ring. The way this works is that a station emits a packet with the ALL-STATIONS destination address. The next station in the ring will note that the A bit has not been set and that it therefore is the next station. It sets the A bit, and downstream stations do not conclude they are the next station. Each station, in turn, emits a special packet to identify itself to the neighbor immediately downstream. But these other uses of the A and C bits, although interesting, are not relevant to bridges and routers.

Another issue in 802.5 is that the chips being used (at least as of the writing of this book) do not support true multicast addresses. Instead, they support "functional addresses," of which there are only 31, because there are 17 bits of constant, followed by 31 bits, and an 802.5-style multicast address has only a single bit on. The fact that the 802.5 chips do not support receipt of true multicast addresses means that a protocol that has been specified to use a particular multicast address must instead attempt to get one of the 31 functional addresses assigned to it, and a bridge between 802.5 and some other LAN must know the mapping between the multicast address that a protocol uses on a LAN other than 802.5 and the functional address assigned to that protocol for use on 802.5. If more than 31 multicast addresses are used, there must be a mechanism for multiplexing several multicast addresses onto a single functional address, because the number of functional addresses (31) is not quite as large as the number of multicast addresses (2^{47}, which is greater than 100 trillion).

Even if new 802.5 chips are developed that support true multicast addresses, backward compatibility with existing devices will continue to make bridging 802.5 to other LANs more complicated as a result of the need to convert between multicast addresses and functional addresses.

2.10   Packet Bursts

Many stations are designed so that they cannot over a long period of time process packets at the rate of the LAN. The assumption is that if the total bandwidth of the LAN were, say, 10 Mb, a single station does not need to process packets that quickly because the amount of traffic destined for a particular station will be far less than 10 Mb.

Unfortunately, it is possible for a burst of packets to arrive, exceeding the station's ability to receive. Although some buffering is usually available, it can quickly be exceeded, depending on the number of buffers and the speed with which the station can actually process the packets. If this situation occurs, the station will correctly receive and process the first few packets in the burst, and later ones will get lost.

It is important to understand this typical behavior, because naive protocols might never work under these circumstances. Suppose that there were a query response protocol by which a station requested data from another station. If all the data were not received, the station would repeat the identical request. Suppose that the data required transmission of ten packets, the transmitter transmitted them all immediately, and the requester could only buffer two of the packets. Then every time the requester received the response, the first two packets would be accepted by the hardware and the remaining packets would be lost.

2.11 Reasons for Bridges

Each of the technologies discussed in the preceding sections has certain limitations:

1. *Limited number of stations:* In token rings, each station that is attached causes increased delay around the ring, even if it is not transmitting.

2. *Limited size:* In 802.3, the cable must be sufficiently short that when a station at one end of the cable transmits a packet of the legally minimum size, the transmitter will detect a collision.

3. *Limited amount of traffic:* In all LANs, the available bandwidth must be shared by all stations. The more stations that there are, and the more stations that are attempting to transmit, the smaller the share of bandwidth for each station.

For these reasons, a single LAN is often insufficient to meet the requirements of an organization. If stations have been designed with the assumption that packets will need to get forwarded by routers in order to reach destinations in other locations, the stations will have implemented a network layer protocol that cooperates with routers. However, if stations have been designed with the assumption that their entire world is a single LAN, they will not have a network layer and thus cannot use a router. Because many stations were designed without a network layer protocol, it was deemed desirable to provide some sort of box that would allow LANs to be "glued" together such that packets could be forwarded from one LAN to another without any cooperation by the stations. These boxes, known as "bridges," are discussed in Chapter 3.

2.12 Point-to-Point Links

Two of the issues relevant for LANs are also relevant for point-to-point links:

1. *Service:* Traditionally, data link layer protocols designed for point-to-point links provided reliable service. Hop-by-hop reliable service is vital if the error rate on each link is high. Otherwise, the probability of successfully transmitting a packet across many hops becomes very small, meaning that an unreasonably

large number of retransmissions from the source would be required. Examples of data link protocols providing reliable service are HDLC [3] and DDCMP.[4]

With improved technology, datagram service at the data link layer not only becomes acceptable but improves performance. "PPP" (which stands for point-to-point protocol[5]) is an emerging standard developed by the TCP/IP community for a datagram data link layer protocol for point-to-point links. It is basically a simplified HDLC. PPP as compared with HDLC is very similar to LLC type 1 as compared with LLC type 2.

Basically, the HDLC format is:

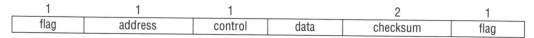

Figure 2.13

Flag is a special bit pattern that indicates the start and end of a packet. **Address** is necessary when more than two stations share the link. On a LAN, two addresses are necessary, one to identify the source and one to identify the destination. However, HDLC was designed not for LANs but for multiaccess links with a master and several tributaries. Tributaries on that sort of link do not send packets to each other. Rather, packets are either transmitted by the master to a tributary or transmitted by a tributary to the master. In the former case, the address specifies which tributary is supposed to receive the packet; in the latter case, the address specifies the source. **Control** specifies the sorts of things that LLC type 2 specifies. The meaning of **data** and **checksum** is obvious.

2. *Multiplexing:* Just as on a LAN, if multiple upper-layer protocols are being multiplexed over the same link, unless all the protocols have been designed in such an extraordinarily fortuitous way as to make all packets unambiguous (incapable of being mistaken for a packet from a different protocol), there has to be some field to disambiguate the packets. On a LAN, there is the protocol type field. Traditional data link layer protocols do not have a protocol type field. PPP has provided that functionality by adding a 16-bit **protocol** field.

The PPP format is:

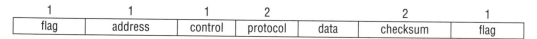

Figure 2.14

[3] **International Organization for Standardization, ISO Standard 3309-1979. "Data Communication— High-level Data Link Control Procedures—Frame Structure," 1979.**

[4] **DNA Digital Data Communications Message Protocol (DDCMP) Functional Specification, Version 4.1.0, Order No. AA-K175A-TK.**

[5] **D. Perkins, "Point-to-Point Protocol for the Transmission of Multiprotocol Datagrams over Point-to-Point Links." RFC 1171.**

Address is set to the constant 11111111. **Control** is a single byte, set to the value 3, which would be considered "unnumbered information" by HDLC. **Protocol** is a 2-byte field, and the assigned values are listed in the "assigned numbers" RFC (currently, RFC 1010, but that will change when a new one is issued as more numbers are assigned).

Homework

1. Is the address 53-21-ab-41-99-bb a group address? Has it been globally or locally assigned? Show bit-by-bit how it would be stored for transmission on 802.3. Show bit-by-bit how it would be stored for transmission on 802.5.

2. There are two methods for running a meeting. In the first, a moderator presides, and people raise their hands when they have something to say, then wait until the moderator calls on them and gives them permission to speak. The second method is contention. Anyone who has attended a meeting where the protocol is contention knows that certain people talk a lot in such meetings and certain others never manage to get a word in edgewise. Assuming that 802.3 is fair (every station does get a chance to transmit if it has data), in what respects does 802.3 differ from a meeting of human beings?

3. Given that there is a "protocol type" field (or SAP fields), there is theoretically no need for group addresses. Instead, all protocols that wanted to send a multicast packet could send packets to the broadcast address and differentiate their packets from packets originating with other protocols based on the protocol type field.

   What is gained by using a group address specific to a particular protocol instead of using the broadcast address and specifying the protocol based on the protocol type field?

4. Assuming that every protocol uses a separate group address when transmitting multicast packets, why is it necessary to include a protocol type field in the packet header?

5. Assume that a particular station has limited buffering and loses all but the first few packets of a rapid packet burst addressed to it. What provisions should be made by a request/response protocol involving many packets in the response, so that the requester will (with a reasonable probability) receive all the data?

6. Now suppose that the query/response is not something aimed at a particular destination but is something like an XID directed at the broadcast address, to which many destinations are expected to respond and the requester should receive all the replies. If we assume a high probability that some replies will get lost and that the requester will need to try several times, what provisions can be made in the protocol to ensure that the requester will eventually receive all the replies (i.e., so that the same ones don't always get lost)?

Chapter 3
Transparent Bridges

Transparent bridges were originally developed by Digital Equipment Corporation and were adopted by the 802.1 committee. For clarity, I will "build" a transparent bridge by adding features.

The Digital bridges and the standardized 802.1 bridges have all the following features:

- The promiscuous listen and the store and forward capabilities of the "no-frills" bridge, as described in section 3.1.

- The station learning cache of the "learning" bridge, as described in section 3.2.

- The spanning tree algorithm of the "complete" bridge, as described in section 3.3.

Note: The intermediate forms of bridge ("no frills" and "learning") are not standard bridges. In order to conform to 802.1d, a bridge must implement both learning and the spanning tree. Some early bridge implementations were built without these features, but they are presented here primarily because it is easier to understand bridges if each feature is described separately.

3.1 The "No-Frills" Bridge

The most basic form of transparent bridge is one that attaches to two or more LANs (each attachment to a LAN is known as a *port*), listening promiscuously to every packet transmitted and storing each received packet until it can be transmitted on the LANs other than the one on which it was received. This will be called the "no-frills" bridge.

The transparent bridge was developed to allow stations that were designed to operate on only a single LAN to work in a multi-LAN environment. The stations expect to transmit a packet, exactly as they would in a single-LAN environment, and have the packet delivered. The bridge must therefore transmit the packet exactly as received. If the bridge modified the packet in any way—for instance, by overwriting the source address portion of the header with its own address—then protocols in the stations might no longer work properly. The bridge does change the delay characteristics, which might affect protocols with tight timers that expect a single-LAN environment. However, most protocols either don't have such tight timers or can be adjusted.

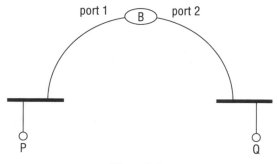

Figure 3.1

With just this basic idea, a no-frills bridge extends the capabilities of a LAN. For instance, in the case of 802.3, it allows the length restriction necessitated by the 802.3 hardware to be exceeded. If the box connecting the two LANs were a repeater instead of a bridge, the repeater would forward each bit as it was received, and a station's transmission on one side of the repeater could collide with a station's transmission on the other side of the repeater.

However, with a no-frills bridge, the packet is not transmitted by the bridge while it is being received. Instead, the entire packet is first received by the bridge and then stored, waiting for the LAN on the other side to become idle. It is therefore possible for two stations on opposite sides of the bridge to be transmitting simultaneously without a collision.

Another example of how a no-frills bridge can extend the limits of a LAN is the ability to increase the number of stations in 802.5. In 802.5, the total number of stations that can be in the ring is limited, due to the fact that clock jitter accumulates at each station and phase lock loop will be lost with too many stations. A bridge solves this problem because it implements a completely independent instance of the ring MAC protocol on each ring to which it attaches. Each ring has an independent token and a separate active monitor (the station on which all the stations synchronize their clocks).

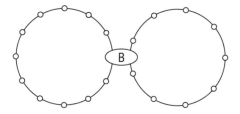

Figure 3.2

However, the no-frills bridge does not overcome the LAN total bandwidth limit. If the LANs connected by the no-frills bridge each have a capacity of 10 Mb/sec (as in 802.3, 802.4, and 802.5), the total bandwidth that can safely be utilized will still be 10 Mb. This is because the no-frills bridge attempts to ensure that every packet transmitted on any LAN eventually winds up appearing on every LAN. Since each packet will appear on each LAN, the combined transmissions of all stations on all LANs cannot exceed 10 Mb.

Nit alert: The statement that "the combined transmissions of all stations on all LANs cannot exceed 10 Mb" is not exactly true, for two reasons:

1. A temporary traffic peak could occur such that more than 10 Mb of traffic were transmitted within a short interval, and as long as the buffer capacity of the bridge were capable of storing the excess packets, none of the packets would get lost.

2. If the buffering capacity of the no-frills bridge were exceeded and the bridge needed to drop packets, the bridge might be lucky enough to drop packets that didn't need to be forwarded because the source and destination were on the same LAN. Therefore, the throughput could theoretically exceed 10 Mb.

   However, in practice, since the no-frills bridge cannot distinguish between packets that can safely be dropped and those that must be forwarded, if total bandwidth exceeds 10 Mb, then packets will be dropped before reaching their destination.

The next enhancement to the bridge solves the problem of allowing the bridge to intelligently choose which packets to drop and also allows the aggregate bandwidth to exceed 10 Mb.

3.2 The "Learning" Bridge

Suppose a bridge were to "know" which stations were on which LANs. Here are some strategies that could be used (but are not):

1. The network manager could manually enter the addresses of all stations on each LAN into a database kept at the bridge. (Some vendors actually made bridges like this before 802.1 standardized the transparent learning bridge.)

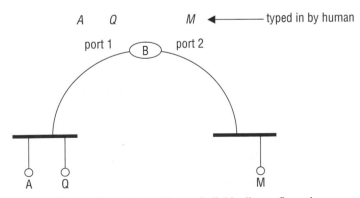

Figure 3.3 Station addresses individually configured

2. The network manager could place stations so that each LAN had only stations whose addresses were within a certain range. For instance:

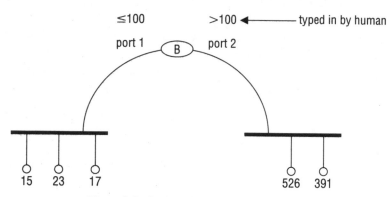

Figure 3.4   Station address ranges configured

3. The network manager could assign station addresses so that a portion of the address specified the LAN to which the station was attached. So for instance, an address could be partitioned into two parts, one being the "LAN number" and the other indicating the station on the LAN.

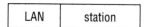

Figure 3.5   LAN number part of station address

In this case, an address could be written as a two-part quantity, with the LAN number separated from the station number. For instance, an address might read "5.21," which would mean station 21 on LAN 5.

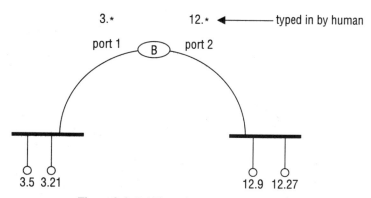

Figure 3.6   LAN number part of station address

All the preceding strategies involve difficult management. It would obviously be preferable if stations could use a globally assigned 48-bit ID stored in a ROM by the manufacturer and be plugged into the topology in any location, and the bridge could just "figure out" where the stations were.

This does turn out to be possible, based on the assumption that a station puts its address in the "source address" field in the packet header when it transmits a packet. (Note: Why do I call this an "assumption"? Wouldn't it violate "all sorts of standards" if a station put anything other than its own address into the source address field? Well, consider the fact that bridges do not put their address into the source address field when they forward packets! Luckily, it's a good assumption in general that the source address in the packet header identifies the transmitter of the packet.)

The strategy used by the bridge is as follows:

1. The bridge listens promiscuously, receiving every packet transmitted.

2. For each packet received, the bridge stores the address in the packet's source address field in a cache (which I'll refer to as the "station cache"), together with the port upon which the packet was received.

3. For each packet received, the bridge looks through its station cache for the address listed in the packet's **destination address** field.

    a. If the address is not found in the station cache, the bridge forwards the packet onto all interfaces except the one from which it was received.

    b. If the address is found in the station cache, the bridge only forwards the packet onto the interface specified in the table. If the specified interface is the one from which the packet was received, the packet is dropped (*filtered*).

4. The bridge ages each entry in the station cache and deletes it after a period of time (a parameter known as *aging time*) in which no traffic is received with that address as the source address. (Actually, the 802 spec spells the parameter "ageing," because the editor of 802.1d is British and the country seems to have a surplus of vowels.)

Assume the following topology. B initially knows nothing about any of the stations.

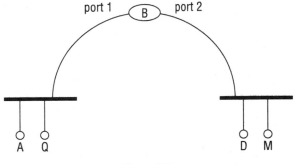

Figure 3.7

Now assume that station A transmits a packet with destination address D. The packet looks like this:

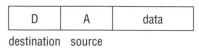

D	A	data

destination source

Figure 3.8

The bridge concludes, by looking at the packet's source address and noting that the packet was received on port 1, that A resides on port 1. The bridge does not know where D resides, so it forwards the packet.

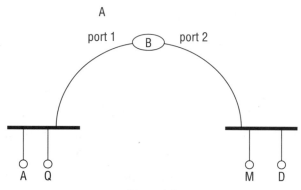

Figure 3.9

Now assume that D transmits a packet for A.

A	D	data

destination source

Figure 3.10

The bridge concludes, by looking at the packet's source address and noting that the packet was received on port 2, that D resides on port 2. The bridge has learned A's address, and since it is on port 1, the bridge knows that it must forward the packet onto port 1 in order for A to receive the packet.

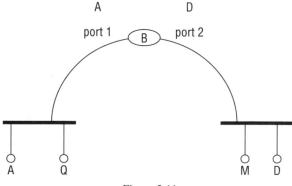

Figure 3.11

Now assume that Q transmits a packet for A.

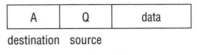

destination source

Figure 3.12

The bridge concludes, by looking at the packet's source address and noting that the packet was received on port 1, that Q resides on port 1. The bridge has learned A's address, and since it is on port 1, the bridge knows that it does not need to forward the packet, since A also resides on port 1.

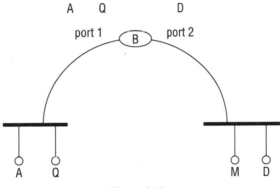

Figure 3.13

The learning bridge concept is actually quite powerful and works for many topologies. For instance, a bridge can have more than two ports.

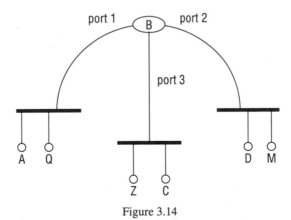

Figure 3.14

Initially, B just knows that it has three ports. Assume that A transmits a packet with destination D. B will note that A resides on port 1. Since B does not know where D resides, B must forward the packet onto both ports 3 and 2.

After this initial packet, the state of B's learning is as follows:

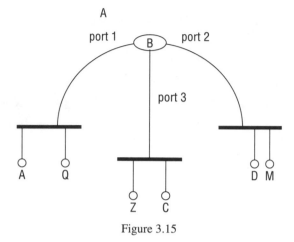

Figure 3.15

Now assume that D transmits a packet with destination A. B will note that D resides on port 2, and since B knows that A resides on port 1, B will forward the packet, but only onto port 1.

Now assume that Q transmits a packet with destination A. B will note that Q resides on port 1, and since A also resides on port 1, B will not need to forward the packet (see Fig. 3.16).

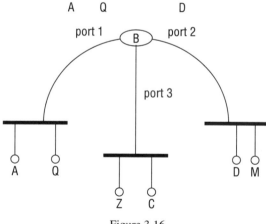

Figure 3.16

Now assume that Z transmits a packet with destination C. B will note that Z resides on port 3, but since B does not know where C resides, it must forward the packet onto both ports 1 and 2.

Now that I've shown that the bridge concept works for any number of ports, let us examine multiple bridges. For instance, consider the topology in Fig. 3.17:

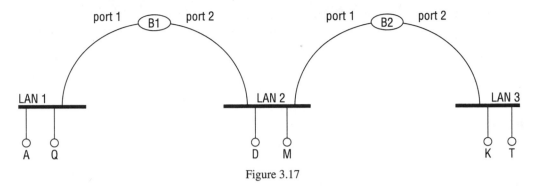

Figure 3.17

Bridge B1 cannot distinguish stations on LAN 2 and LAN 3. As far as B1 can tell, it is connected to two LANs, the one on its port 1 and the one on its port 2. B2 connects LAN 2 and LAN 3 transparently, so B2's existence is hidden from B1, just as B2's existence is invisible to the stations.

Once all the stations have transmitted something, the state of the caches in the two bridges will be as follows:

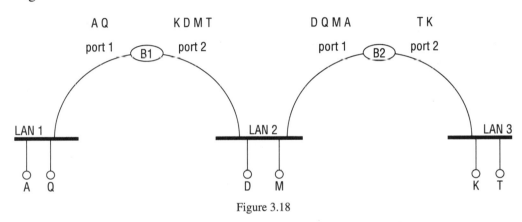

Figure 3.18

Thus, the topology in Fig. 3.18 looks to B1 like Fig. 3.19:

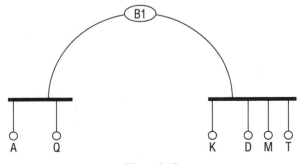

Figure 3.19

Whereas the topology in Fig. 3.18 looks to B2 like Fig. 3.20:

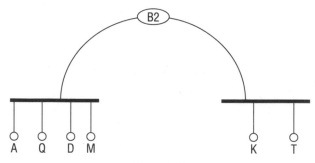

Figure 3.20

The learning bridge concept actually works for any *tree* (loop-free) topology.

Does the concept extend to all topologies? Consider the following system:

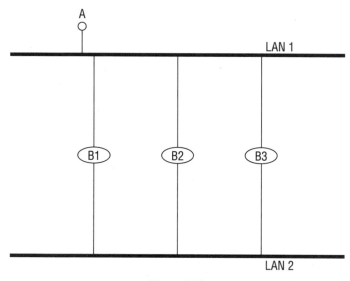

Figure 3.21

What happens when station A transmits a packet? The destination to which A sends is irrelevant. Assume that it is a destination that has not yet transmitted anything, so the bridges do not have the destination in their station caches.

The first guess as to the behavior of this system is usually that three copies of the packet are transmitted to LAN 2. If that were indeed the way the system behaves, things wouldn't be so bad. However, the behavior is much worse than that. Infinitely worse, to be precise.

Initially, each of the three bridges:

1. Receives the packet

2. Notes that A resides on LAN 1

3. Queues the packet for forwarding onto LAN 2

Then, by the laws of LANs, one of the bridges (let's say bridge 3) will be the first to succeed in transmitting the packet onto LAN 2. Since bridge 3 is transparent to bridges 1 and 2, the packet will appear, on LAN 2, exactly as if station A had transmitted the packet onto LAN 2. Thus bridges 1 and 2 will:

1. Receive the packet

2. Note in their tables that A now resides on LAN 2

3. Queue the packet for forwarding onto LAN 1

Next suppose that bridge 1 succeeds in transmitting its first received packet onto LAN 2. Bridges 2 and 3 will also receive the packet. Bridge 2 will merely note that A is still on LAN 2, and bridge 3 will note that A has moved onto LAN 2; both will then queue the packet for transmission onto LAN 1.

Now suppose that bridge 1 succeeds in transmitting onto LAN 1. Bridges 2 and 3 will note that A has moved to LAN 1 and will queue the "new" packet for forwarding onto LAN 2.

Thus, not only do the packets loop, but they proliferate. Every successful packet transmission results in two packets in the system. For those familiar with routers, it is worth noting that although packet looping does occur with routers, it is not nearly so bad. With routers, each packet transmitted is directed to a specific router, and each router only transmits a packet onto a single interface. Therefore with routers, a packet might be transmitted an infinite number of times, but it will not spawn additional copies at each hop. At any point in time, only a single copy of the packet will exist. And finally with routers, there is generally a "hop count" in the packet so that a looping packet will eventually be dropped. With bridges, since bridges are supposed to be transparent, a packet looks the same on its 25-thousandth transmission as it did on its first transmission.

Now that it is clear how badly learning bridges will perform in a topology with loops, we have several options. We can:

1. Decide that bridges were a stupid idea after all.

2. Document the fact that the topology must be kept loop-free. Then if someone accidentally plugs the topology together with a loop somewhere, we can smirk and tell the offender to read the documentation more carefully next time.

3. Design bridges to detect the existence of loops in the topology and complain, so that at least the customer doesn't have to learn about the problem from field service.

4. Design into the bridges an algorithm that prunes the topology into a loop-free subset (a spanning tree).

Option 1 is clearly not correct, since in loop-free topologies, bridges are quite useful. Options 2 and 3 are undesirable because allowing loops in a topology is extremely useful. Without loops, the topology has no redundancy. If anything breaks, connectivity is

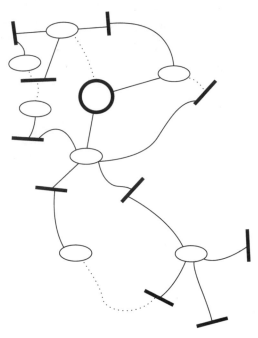

Figure 3.22   Topology pruned to spanning tree by bridges

lost. Loops should not be viewed as misconfiguration, but as good design strategy. An additional drawback of option 2 is that it represents a poor customer relations strategy. Option 4 is clearly desirable, if such an algorithm can be devised. Luckily, such an algorithm exists and is quite simple.

3.3   Spanning Tree Algorithm

Algorhyme

**I think that I shall never see
A graph more lovely than a tree.**

**A tree whose crucial property
Is loop-free connectivity.**

**A tree that must be sure to span
So packets can reach every LAN.**

**First, the root must be selected.
By ID, it is elected.**

**Least cost paths from root are traced.
In the tree, these paths are placed.**

**A mesh is made by folks like me,
Then bridges find a spanning tree.**

— Radia Perlman

The purpose of the spanning tree is to have bridges dynamically discover a subset of the topology that is loop-free (a tree) and yet has just enough connectivity so that where physically possible, there is a path between every pair of LANs (the tree is *spanning*).

The basic idea behind the spanning tree algorithm is that bridges transmit special messages to each other that allow them to calculate a spanning tree. These special messages have been given the catchy name *configuration bridge protocol data units*—or *configuration BPDUs*, for short—by 802.1. I was torn between using ISO terminology and something friendlier. In this chapter, "configuration BPDU" will be called a "configuration message," as a compromise between familiarizing you with ISO terminology and making the chapter readable.

The configuration message contains enough information so that bridges can:

1. Elect a single bridge, among all the bridges on all the LANs, to be the "root" bridge.

2. Calculate the distance of the shortest path from themselves to the root bridge.

3. For each LAN, elect a "designated bridge" from among the bridges residing on that LAN. The elected bridge is the one closest to the root bridge. The designated bridge will forward packets from that LAN toward the root bridge.

4. Choose a port (known as the "root port") that gives the best path from themselves to the root bridge.

5. Select ports to be included in the spanning tree. The ports selected will be the root port plus any ports on which "self" has been elected designated bridge.

Data traffic is forwarded to and from ports selected for inclusion in the spanning tree. Data traffic is discarded upon receipt and never forwarded onto ports that are not selected for inclusion in the spanning tree.

3.3.1 Configuration Messages

A configuration message is transmitted by a bridge onto a port. It is received by all the other bridges residing on the LAN attached to the port. It is not forwarded off that LAN.

A configuration message has an ordinary LAN data link layer header.

destination	source	DSAP	SSAP	configuration message

Figure 3.23   Configuration message transmitted with data link header

The data link layer destination address is a special multicast address assigned to "all bridges." (A functional address is assigned for this purpose in 802.5, because of the inability of the 802.5 implementations to handle true multicast addresses.) The data link layer source address is the address on that port of the bridge transmitting the configuration message. (The bridge architecture requires a bridge to have a distinct data link layer address on each port.) The SAP value is 01000010, which is a wonderful value because there is no way to get the bit ordering incorrect.

Although a bridge has a separate address on each port, it also has a single ID that it uses as its ID in the data portion of a configuration message. This bridgewide ID can be the LAN address on one of the ports, or it can be another address, just as long as it is a unique 48-bit address.

Contained in the data portion of a configuration message (among other stuff to be described later) are the following:

- **Root ID:** ID of the bridge assumed to be the root

- **Transmitting bridge ID:** ID of the bridge transmitting this configuration message

- **Cost:** Cost of the least cost path to the root from the transmitting bridge (at least, the best path of which the transmitting bridge is currently aware)

A bridge initially assumes itself to be the root and transmits configuration messages on each of its ports with its ID as root and transmitting bridge and 0 as cost.

A bridge continuously receives configuration messages on each of its ports and saves the "best" configuration message from each port ("best" is described in the next paragraph). The "best" configuration message is determined by comparing not only the configuration messages received from a particular port but also the configuration message that the bridge would transmit on that port.

Given two configuration messages, C1 and C2:

1. C1 is "better than" C2 if the root ID listed in C1 is numerically lower than the root ID listed in C2.

2. If the root IDs are equal, then C1 is "better than" C2 if the cost listed in C1 is numerically lower than the cost listed in C2.

3. If the root IDs and costs are equal, then C1 is "better than" C2 if the transmitting bridge ID listed in C1 is numerically lower than the transmitting bridge ID listed in C2.

4. There's an additional field in the configuration message known as **port identifier.** The transmitting bridge has some internal numbering of its own ports, and when it transmits a configuration message onto port *n*, it places "*n*" in the port identifier field. If the root IDs, costs, and transmitting bridge IDs are equal, then the port identifier serves as a tiebreaker. This field is primarily useful for detecting the case in which two ports of a bridge attach to the same LAN. This can be caused by connecting two different LANs with a repeater or simply by attaching two bridge ports onto the same physical LAN. For simplicity, the port identifier field will be ignored in the following examples.

	C1			C2		
	root ID	cost	transmitter	root ID	cost	transmitter
a.	29	15	35	31	12	32
b.	35	80	39	35	80	40
c.	35	15	80	35	18	38

Figure 3.24

In all three cases (a, b, and c), the configuration message C1 is "better than" the configuration message C2. In case a, the root ID is lower in C1. In case b, the transmitting bridge ID is smaller, and the root ID and cost are the same. In case c, the root is the same, but the cost is better in C1.

Note that with the preceding rules, configuration messages can be ordered by the multiprecision number consisting of root ID as the most significant portion concatenated with cost as the next most significant portion and designated bridge ID as the least significant portion.

If a bridge receives a "better" configuration message on a LAN than the configuration message it would transmit, it no longer transmits configuration messages. Therefore, when the algorithm stabilizes, only one bridge on each LAN (the "designated bridge" for that LAN) transmits configuration messages on that LAN.

3.3.2   Calculation of Root ID and Cost to Root

Based on received configuration messages from all interfaces, each bridge B independently decides the identity of the root bridge. This will be the minimum of B's own ID and the root IDs reported in any configuration message received by B on any of its ports.

Let us assume that B has an ID of 18. Suppose that the "best" configuration message B receives on each of its ports is as follows:

	Root	Cost	Transmitter
port 1	12	93	51
port 2	12	85	47
port 3	81	0	81
port 4	15	31	27

In this case, the "best" root heard about by B is 12. If B's ID had been smaller than 12, then B would be the root.

Bridge B also determines its own distance to the root bridge. If B is the root bridge, then B's distance to the root is defined to be 0. Otherwise (if B is not the root), B will calculate its cost to the root to be 1 higher than the smallest reported cost in any of the received configuration messages (assuming for now that the "cost" of a path is the number of "hops"—i.e., the number of times a packet needs to be transmitted to be delivered from one end of a path to another). If B is not the root, B selects one of the ports from which it received the smallest reported cost to the root to be its preferred path to the root (its root port).

In the preceding example, B will assume that 12 is the root and will further assume that its own distance to the root is 86, since it received a cost of 85 on port 2. B will assume that port 2 is its root port.

Once B determines the identity of the root and its own distance to the root, B knows what its own configuration message would contain and can compare that with the best received configuration message on each port to determine whether B should be the designated bridge on that port. In this case, B's configuration message would be 12.86.18. B's configuration message is better than the ones it has received on ports 1, 3, and 4, so B will assume (until it hears a better configuration message on one of those ports) that it is the designated bridge on ports 1, 3, and 4 and will transmit the configuration message 12.86.18 on those ports.

3.3.3 Selecting Spanning Tree Ports

Once B calculates the root, its own cost to the root, and the designated bridge for each of its ports, B decides which ports are in the spanning tree and which are not. The following ports are selected for inclusion in the spanning tree:

1. The port chosen by B as its preferred path to the root (B's root port). In the example we're working with, it would be port 2.

2. All ports for which B is the designated bridge. In the example we're working with, these would be ports 1, 3, and 4.

The ports selected by B for inclusion in the spanning tree are placed in the "forwarding" state, meaning that B will forward data packets to and from those ports. All other ports are placed in the "blocking" state, meaning that B will not forward data packets to or from those ports.

3.3.4 An Example

In Fig. 3.25, the bridge with ID 92 has five ports. On port 1, the best configuration message it has received is 81.0.81, where 81 is the root ID, 0 is the cost to the root, and 81 is the ID of the bridge transmitting the configuration message, which, in this case, obviously

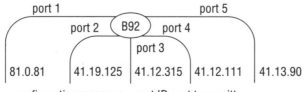

configuration message = root ID.cost.transmitter

Figure 3.25 Configuration messages received

assumes at the moment that it is the root. On port 2, the bridge has received 41.19.125; on port 3, 41.12.315; on port 4, 41.12.111; on port 5, 41.13.90.

Bridge 92 will assume that the best known root is 41, and that the best cost to the root from bridge 92 is 12 + 1, or 13, via either port 3 or port 4. Bridge 92 must select one of these ports to be its root port. Since it uses the ID of the neighboring designated bridge as a tiebreaker, it will select port 4, because the neighboring designated bridge's ID there is 111, which is numerically lower than 315.

The configuration message that bridge 92 can transmit—i.e., 41.13.92—is a better configuration message than the ones received on ports 1 and 2. Therefore, bridge 92 will assume that it is the designated bridge on ports 1 and 2 and will discard the configuration messages it had previously received on those ports. Bridge 92's configuration message (still 41.13.92) is not better than the one received on port 5—namely, 41.13.90—because of the designated bridge ID tiebreaker.

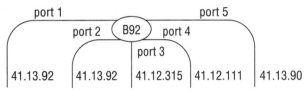

configuration message = root ID.cost.transmitter

Figure 3.26   Bridge overwrites message on ports 1 and 2

The result of this calculation is that bridge 92 will select port 4 (because 4 is its root port) and ports 1 and 2 (because bridge 92 is the designated bridge on those LANs) for inclusion in the spanning tree. Bridge 92 will classify ports 5 and 3 as in the blocking state—i.e., bridge 92 will continue to run the spanning tree algorithm on those ports but will not receive data messages from those ports, learn the location of station addresses from them, or forward traffic onto them.

Note that if the example is changed so that the bridge's own ID is 15, then it will decide that the root ID is 15, the cost to the root is 0 (since it is the root), and it will be the designated bridge on all its ports, transmitting the configuration message 15.0.15.

3.4   Spanning Tree Algorithm Refinements

3.4.1   Failures

The algorithm presented in the preceding section describes how a network initially starts or how it adapts to new bridges' or links' coming up. However, it does not adapt to failures of bridges or links.

The stored configuration message for each each port contains a **message age** field, which is incremented after each unit of time. If the message age reaches a certain threshold (known as "max age"), the configuration message is discarded, and the bridge recalculates as if it had never received a configuration message from that port.

In the normal course of events, the root bridge periodically transmits configuration messages (every hello time). When the root bridge generates a configuration message, the message age field is set to 0. When bridges receive the root's configuration message, this causes them to transmit a configuration message on each of the ports for which they are designated, with a message age field of 0. Likewise, when the bridges downstream from any designated bridge receive a configuration message with message age 0, they transmit their own configuration message, on the ports for which they are designated, with message age 0.

If the root fails, or if any component on the path between a bridge and the root fails, the bridge will stop receiving "fresh" (i.e., message age = 0) configuration messages on the root port, and it will gradually increase the message age on the configuration message stored for that port until it reaches max age—at which point, the bridge will discard that configuration message and recalculate the root, root path cost, and root port. For instance:

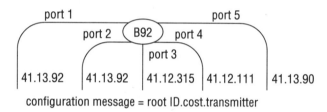

configuration message = root ID.cost.transmitter

Figure 3.27

Assume that the configuration message on port 4 times out. If the configuration message on port 3 has not timed out, then bridge 92 will simply switch its root port from port 4 to port 3. Bridge 92's configuration message on ports 1 and 2 will not change.

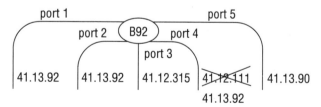

configuration message = root ID.cost.transmitter

Figure 3.28

Now assume that the configuration message on port 3 times out as well. In that case, bridge 92 will choose port 5 as its root port. Switching to port 5 causes bridge 92 to change its configuration message to 41.14.92.

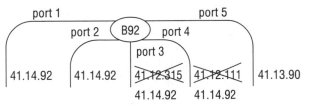

Figure 3.29

If the configuration messages on all three ports—3, 4, and 5—time out, then bridge 92 will assume itself to be the root and will transmit 92.0.92 on all five ports until it receives fresh configuration messages from any of its ports regarding a better root.

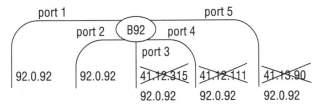

Figure 3.30

The following events cause spanning tree calculation:

1. *Receipt of a configuration message on port X:* In this case, the bridge compares the received configuration message with the stored configuration message from port X. If the received configuration message is "better" or has a smaller age, the stored configuration message is overwritten, and the bridge recalculates the root, root path cost, and root port.

2. *Timer Tick:* In this case, the bridge increments the message age field in the stored configuration message for each port. If this causes the message age field in any stored configuration message to reach max age, the bridge discards that stored configuration message and recalculates the root, root path cost, and root port.

If the only time the designated bridge issued a configuration message were upon receipt of a configuration message from the direction of the root, there would be no reason to include the age field in the configuration message, since upon transmission, it would always be 0. However there is another situation in which a designated bridge will issue a configuration message, even if one has not been received recently from the root port.

Suppose that B is the designated bridge on a particular port. Suppose, too, that B has not recently received a configuration message from the direction of the root, so that the stored configuration message from the direction of the root now has age X (B has been aging the message while holding it in memory). If another bridge, B2, were to come up, it would issue its own configuration message, since it will not have heard B's configuration message on that LAN. It would be dangerous for B to ignore this situation until B hears a new configuration message from the root, since it will cause the new bridge to be very unsynchronized with respect to the rest of the network. If the new bridge does not hear B's configuration message, the new bridge will assume that it should become designated on that port, causing extra connectivity— i.e., a loop. If B retransmitted its configuration message without the age field (or with age field 0), then it would slow down discovery of any failure of the root in that subtree, since B's retransmission of the configuration message will look like assurance that the root (and the path to the root) was still functioning at the time B retransmitted its configuration message.

B must issue its configuration message, but with age field X. The result will be the same as if the new bridge had heard B's configuration message when B transmitted it originally (X seconds ago).

3.4.2   Avoiding Temporary Loops

After a topological change (a new bridge or link coming up, or a bridge or link failing), it will take some time for news of the event to spread throughout the topology. Until news of the changed topology has reached all bridges, the bridges will be operating on inconsistent data—a situation that has two possible outcomes (both of which may occur simultaneously in various portions of the network):

1. There may be temporary loss of connectivity if a bridge port that was off in the old topology hasn't yet found out that it needs to be on in the new topology.

2. There may be temporary loops in the topology if a bridge port that was on in the old topology hasn't yet found out that it needs to be off in the new topology.

Although it was stated earlier, it is worth repeating that loops with bridges are far more frightening than loops with routers for two reasons:

1. There is no hop count in the data link header, so with bridges, packets will loop indefinitely until the topology stabilizes.

2. Packets can proliferate with bridges, since a bridge might forward the packet onto several LANs, and several bridges might pick up the packet when it is transmitted onto a LAN. In contrast, routers forward the packet in only one direction and specify the router to which the packet is being forwarded. Therefore, a loop with routers will not cause packet proliferation.

Temporary partitions in a bridged topology are better than temporary loops. (Just about anything is better in a bridged topology than a temporary loop.) The probability of temporary loops is minimized by requiring that a bridge wait some amount of time before allowing a bridge port that was in the blocking state to transition to the forwarding state. Hopefully, the amount of time is sufficient for news of the new topology to spread, so that all bridge ports that should be off in the new topology have already heard the news and turned themselves off before any additional ports start forwarding data packets.

This timer should be at least twice the maximum transit time across the network, for the following reason. Suppose that bridge B1 is the root of the "old topology." Suppose also that B1 issues one configuration message, which transits the network essentially instantaneously (no congestion). Then suppose that its next configuration message is maximally delayed, by X sec. B1 then crashes. Bridges close to B1 will time out B1 and start to compute a "new topology" X sec before bridges maximally far from B1.

Now suppose that the root in the new topology is B2, which is maximally far from B1. And suppose that the first configuration message transmitted by B2 travels maximally slowly—i.e., it takes X sec to reach the portion of the network that is near the ill-fated B1. Then bridges near B2 will find out about the new topology X sec before bridges that are close to B1.

In the worst case, news of the new topology will take twice time X to reach all bridges. Therefore, the algorithm does not allow a bridge that has a port in the blocking state and that hears spanning tree information advising the bridge that the port should be in the forwarding state to immediately transit the port into the forwarding state. Instead, the bridge temporarily puts the port into a different state in which it still does not forward packets. If no information is received while the bridge is in this temporary state that would cause it to revert the port into the blocking state before a timer expires, the bridge transits the port into the forwarding state.

The 802.1 standard actually calls for two intermediate states. This is designed to minimize learning of incorrect station locations while the topology has not yet stabilized. The committee deemed it desirable not to allow a bridge to start forwarding until it has built up its learned cache, to minimize unnecessarily forwarded frames. During the initial portion of the intermediate state, the bridge does not learn station addresses; and then during the latter part, the bridge still does not forward packets over that port, but it does start learning station locations on that port. In other words, the intermediate state is actually subdivided into two substates: "listening" and "learning."

> Note: In the original spanning tree algorithm, I had only a single intermediate state, known as "preforwarding." The committee asked whether bridges should learn station addresses in the preforwarding state. I said I didn't think it mattered. The committee decided to break preforwarding into the two aforementioned states. I believe that having two states is unnecessary and that bridges would work fine regardless of whether or not they learn station addresses in preforwarding. Breaking this period into two states makes the algorithm more complicated to understand but does no harm. It would be an interesting project to study the trade-offs between the three strategies:
>
> 1. One intermediate state in which station learning is done.

2. One intermediate state in which station learning is not done.

3. Two intermediate states, as in the spec, in which learning is not done in the first half of the time, and is done in the second half.

3.4.3 Station Cache Timeout Values

Bridges learn and cache the location of stations. Since a station might move, it is important for a bridge to "forget" station locations unless it is frequently reassured that the learned information is correct. This is done by timing out entries that have not been recently verified.

Choosing a suitable timeout period is difficult. If an entry is incorrect for any reason, traffic may not be delivered to the station whose location is incorrectly cached. If an entry has been deleted, traffic for the deleted station will leak into other portions of the bridged network unnecessarily. If the timeout is too long, traffic will be lost for an unreasonably long time. If the timeout is too short, performance in the network will degrade because traffic will be forwarded unnecessarily.

If the only reason for the learned station locations' becoming incorrect is that a station might be moved, then a timer on the order of minutes is reasonable, since:

1. It would probably take someone 15 min or so to unplug a station, physically move it to a new location, and then plug it in.

2. Even if a station were moved more quickly than that, it is understandable that things might take a few minutes to start working again.

3. There are strategies that the moved station can employ to cause things to start working more quickly. For instance, the moved station can transmit a packet to a multicast address. Packets transmitted to multicast addresses are forwarded throughout the spanning tree (unless it's a multicast address that the bridges have been explicitly configured not to forward). Once all the bridges see a packet from source S, they will correct their entry for S. Since station S's multicast packet might get lost and not reach all parts of the extended LAN, S can either transmit a few multicast packets when it first comes up or live with the fact that 95% of the time, things will work immediately when it moves, and occasionally, it might take a few minutes. If indeed, it takes at least 15 min to physically move a station, no special mechanisms are necessary.

However, a reconfiguration of the spanning tree can cause many station locations to change. It is unreasonable to have many stations become unreachable for up to 15 min after a topology change. None of the aforementioned arguments holds for topological reconfiguration because:

1. The spanning tree takes considerably less than 15 min to reconfigure (if it didn't, bridges would be more useful as boat anchors than as LAN interconnection devices).

2. A station user would not understand why things mysteriously stop working every so often, since a spanning tree reconfiguration happens without any action on the part of the user.

3. A station cannot correct its entry with a special mechanism such as transmitting a multicast packet, because a spanning tree reconfiguration occurs without the station's being aware of it.

Therefore, a station cache timeout of 15 min is too long. What about a station cache timeout on the order of 15 sec? I feel that performance would not differ significantly with a station cache timeout on the order of 15 sec as opposed to 15 min. My reasoning is that if a station has not transmitted anything for 15 sec, then it is probably not in the process of receiving a high bandwidth of traffic. After a gap of 15 sec, it would probably not degrade network performance significantly if the first few packets destined for that station were sent unnecessarily to other portions of the network.

It would be interesting for someone to study the effect of shorter cache timeout values on network performance. If someone could positively identify the smallest cache timeout value before network performance degraded significantly, and if that timeout were on the order of a few seconds, then bridges could just use that timeout value.

Unfortunately, the question of timeout value cannot be answered definitively, since it depends on the types of applications and the topology. It might be definitively shown that a cache timeout of, say, 3 sec works fine in a particular network with a particular set of applications, but there might be other applications for which such a timeout would be unsuitable.

Since a suitable cache timeout value could not be definitively established, it was decided that the cache timeout value should be network-management-settable, and further, assuming that a cache timeout value longer than the spanning tree reconfiguration time would often be desirable, it was felt that there should be two cache timeout values:

1. A long value, to be used in the usual case

2. A shorter value, to be used following a reconfiguration of the spanning tree algorithm

Can bridges detect that the spanning tree has reconfigured? In some cases, some bridges can. However, in the general case, the spanning tree can reconfigure without all the bridges' being aware of it, and many station entries can become incorrect in a bridge's station cache, even when that bridge cannot detect that the spanning tree algorithm has reconfigured.

Therefore, the spanning tree algorithm had to be enhanced with some method for reliably advising all the bridges that the spanning tree has reconfigured. The enhancement should keep the "spirit" of the original spanning tree algorithm, in that the required bandwidth should not grow with the size of the network. For instance, having each bridge that noticed a topology change send a multicast message would cause the overhead to grow as the total number of bridges grew. The basic idea behind the enhancement is that when a bridge B notices that the topology has changed, B must inform the root bridge of the change. However, instead of having B inform the root bridge directly, B notifies the bridge on B's root port. That bridge, in turn, informs its parent, and so on, until finally the root has been informed that the topology has changed.

When the root has been informed of the change, it sets a flag in its configuration message, known as the "topology change flag," indicating that the topology has changed. Bridges set the topology change flag in the configuration messages they transmit on the LANs for which they are the designated bridge as long as the flag is set in the configuration message from the root port.

The following steps occur:

1. A bridge notices that the spanning tree algorithm has caused it to transition a port into or out of the blocking state.

2. It periodically transmits a topology change notification message on its root port, with the same period as the hello timer. It continues to do this until the parent bridge acks, by setting a bit in its configuration message. The data link destination address of a topology change notification is the same multicast address as is used for configuration messages.

3. A bridge that receives a topology change notification on a port for which it is the designated bridge does two things:

   a. It performs step 2 (i.e., informs its parent bridge through topology change notifications).

   b. It sets the "topology change acknowledgement flag" in the next configuration message it transmits on the LAN from which the topology change notification was received.

4. The root bridge sets the topology change notification flag in its configuration messages for a period equal to the sum of the forward delay time parameter and the max age parameter if the root bridge either:

   a. Notices a topology change because one of its ports has changed state

   b. Receives a topology change notification message

5. A bridge that is receiving configuration messages with the topology change flag set (or the root bridge that is setting the topology change flag in its configuration messages) uses the short station cache timer until it starts receiving configuration messages without the topology change flag set.

Note that the long cache value is a network management parameter and that the short cache value is equal to the forward delay timer, which is also a network management parameter.

3.4.4 Networkwide Parameters

There are several parameters upon which all bridges need to agree in order for the spanning tree algorithm to work properly. These parameters are network-management-settable.

This might seem unworkable. What happens if the parameters are set incompatibly at different bridges? What happens if all bridges are set compatibly but someone then decides to change the networkwide value to a value that is incompatible with the first value? Will the network cease operating properly once a few bridges have been told to use an incompatible parameter value? And might the network become so nonfunctional that network management commands intended to fix the problem could not get through?

Luckily, there is a nifty solution. The root bridge includes in its configuration messages the values of the parameters upon which all bridges must agree. If network management commands a bridge to set one of the parameters, that bridge notes the network-management-configured value in nonvolatile storage. If the bridge becomes the root, it uses its own values and puts them into its configuration messages. A bridge that is the designated bridge on some port copies the values it received in the configuration message from the root port into the configuration messages it transmits. Also, all bridges use the current root's values (as discovered through receipt of configuration messages from the root port) for the parameters.

The parameters dictated by the root in this way are:

1. *Max age:* The time at which a configuration message is discarded

2. *Hello time:* The time interval between issuing configuration messages

3. *Forward delay:* The amount of time in the "learning" and "listening" states—i.e., half the amount of time that must elapse between the time when it is decided that a port should become part of the spanning tree and the time when data traffic is allowed to be forwarded to and from that port

3.4.5 Port ID

A configuration message also contains the "port ID." This field has two purposes:

1. (Admittedly, a not very exciting purpose.) It allows the computed spanning tree to be "deterministic," in the sense that there's always a unique decision a bridge would make. In the case of picking the root port, it is possible for a bridge to be faced with two ports, both of which have the same designated bridge, reporting the same root and the same cost to the root. This can occur totally naturally, as in:

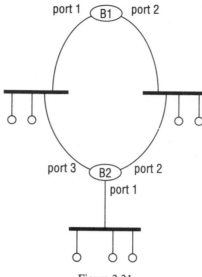

Figure 3.31

Assuming that B1 is the root, which port should B2 choose as its root port? It can be either the one on its top left or the one on its top right.

Each bridge has an internal representation of the number of each of its ports. The designated bridge puts its internal value of the port number into its configuration message.

On B2's port 3, B2 will receive the configuration message that B1 is the root, the cost to B1 is 0, the designated bridge is B1, and the port is 1. On B2's port 2, B2 will get a similar configuration message, but with the port being 2. Since "1" is less than "2," B2 selects its own port 3 as the root port instead of its own port 2.

2. (A more exciting purpose.) It allows loops formed through means other than bridges to be dealt with properly.

Suppose that a bridge has more than one port connected to what appears to the bridge to be a single LAN. This can happen for several reasons:

a. Someone could hook two ports of a bridge onto the same LAN.

b. Someone could hook two ports of a bridge onto two LAN segments connected with a repeater.

c. Someone could hook two ports of a bridge onto different LAN segments but connect them with a "simple bridge"—i.e., one that does not run the spanning tree algorithm.

Let us assume that some bridge B5 thinks that the root is B1 and that B5 is 12 from the root. Assume that B5 thinks it should be the designated bridge on its ports 3, 5, and 6. Further assume that ports 3 and 5 form a loop. B5 will transmit (B1, 12, B5, port 3) on port 3, (B1, 12, B5, port 5) on port 5, and (B1, 12, B5, port 6) on port 6. However, since ports 3 and 5 are directly connected, B5 will hear its own configuration message from

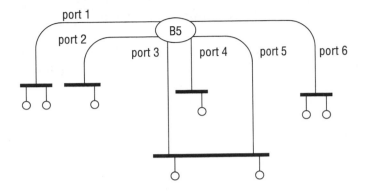

Port Number	Received	Transmitted
1	B1, 11, B7, 2	
2	B1, 12, B2, 1	
3	B1, 12, B5, 5	B1, 12, B5, 3
4	B1, 11, B17, 5	
5	B1, 12, B5, 3	B1, 12, B5, 5
6	B1, 12, B4, 3	

Figure 3.32

port 3 on port 5 and vice versa. When B5 hears its configuration message from port 3 on port 5, it will resign as the designated bridge on port 5 because "another bridge" is transmitting a "better configuration message" on that port—i.e., giving the same information as B5 would on that port but with a lower port number.

3.4.6 Performance Issues

The spanning tree algorithm has two properties that make performance critical:

1. Lack of receipt of messages causes bridges to add connectivity. For instance, if a bridge does not receive any configuration messages on some port, it will take over as the designated bridge on that port.

2. Extra connectivity (i.e., loops) is potentially disastrous.

It is important to design the system so that if the network becomes congested, the spanning tree algorithm will run properly. Otherwise, the network's becoming temporarily congested might prompt the spanning tree algorithm to incorrectly turn extra bridge ports on, causing loops and dramatically increasing the amount of congestion to such a point that the algorithm never recovers.

A bridge must be engineered to have sufficient CPU power. If the bridge's CPU becomes a bottleneck, then the bridge will start throwing away packets before it even looks at them. In this situation, there is no way for the bridge to avoid throwing away configuration messages, since it can't distinguish a configuration message from a data message without looking at it.

Another requirement is that a bridge must be able to transmit a configuration message no matter how congested the LAN is. All LANs enforce fairness, allowing each station at least a minimal amount of bandwidth. Therefore, no matter how congested the LAN, the bridge will be able to transmit a packet eventually. Since it is so critical that configuration messages get sent in a timely fashion, a bridge should be engineered so that a configuration message can be put at the front of a queue.

The 802.1 standard does not require adequate performance. It is possible for a bridge to be underpowered and still fully conform to the standard. Extended LANs with underpowered bridges do not perform well and can become totally unstable in the face of congestion.

It is not necessary for a bridge to completely process every configuration message it receives in "real time" in order for the algorithm to work correctly. It might be possible for a bridge to have just enough processing power to receive every message on the LAN, worst case, and decide whether it is a data message or a configuration message but not have enough CPU to run the spanning tree algorithm until there is some idle time on the LAN. This is OK, provided that the bridge keeps the "best" configuration message it has seen since it had sufficient CPU to actually process a configuration message. This can be done by simply looking at the multiprecision number consisting of the root ID as the most significant part, the cost to the root as the next most significant, and the transmitter's ID as the least significant.

I feel that the bridge spec should have outlawed underpowered bridges. In practice, underpowered bridges are a problem. A temporary congestion situation causes lost configuration messages, which, in turn, causes loops. Then the congestion resulting from looping and proliferating data packets makes the situation worse.

Loops caused by congestion can occur if links have the property of being able to lose messages without the transmitter's being aware of it. In such a case, the designated bridge on a link transmits configuration messages, but the link itself, due to congestion, loses them before they reach the other bridges. The 802 LANs do not behave this way, but there are technologies that have this problem. For such links, bridges are just not an appropriate solution.

3.4.7 One-Way Connectivity

It is possible for hardware to fail in such a way that connectivity between two bridges on a LAN can be one-way, in the sense that bridge A can hear bridge B, but bridge B cannot hear bridge A. This can be caused by bridge B's receiver being dead or weak, or bridge A's transmitter being dead or weak, or some other component like a repeater transmitting or receiving badly.

One-way connectivity between bridges is bad because a loop can be created. For instance, assume that B1 cannot hear B2. If the cause is that B1's receiver is dead, B1 will not hear data packets on the LAN either. However, B1 might forward packets onto the LAN, creating a loop.

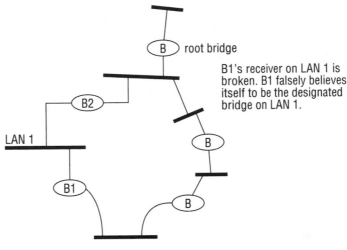

Figure 3.33

If the cause is that B2's receiver is dead, B2 will not be forwarding packets from the LAN; however, B2 will be forwarding packets onto the LAN, creating a loop.

The bridge standard does not say what to do in this case. One possibility is for any bridge that detects one-way connectivity on a LAN to stop forwarding packets to and from that LAN until the condition is no longer detected.

3.4.8 Settable Parameters

1. *Bridge priority:* A 2-octet value that allows the network manager to influence the choice of root bridge and the designated bridge. It is appended as the most significant portion of a bridge ID. A lower numerical value for bridge priority makes the bridge more likely to become the root.

2. *Port priority:* A 1-octet value that allows the network manager to influence the choice of port when a bridge has two ports connected in a loop.

    In my opinion, I can't imagine why anyone would care enough to have this parameter, but it doesn't do any harm.

3. *Hello time:* The time that elapses between generation of configuration messages by a bridge that assumes itself to be the root. The recommended time is 2 sec. Shortening the time will make the protocol more robust, in case the probability of loss of configuration messages is high. Lengthening the time lowers the overhead of the algorithm (because the interval between transmission of configuration messages will be larger).

4. *Max age:* The message age value at which a stored configuration message is judged "too old" and discarded.

If the selected max age value is too small, then occasionally, the spanning tree will reconfigure unnecessarily, possibly causing temporary loss of connectivity in the network. If the selected value is too large, the network will take longer than necessary to adjust to a new spanning tree after a topological event such as the restarting or crashing of a bridge or link.

A conservative value is to assume a delay variance of 2 sec per hop. The value recommended in 802.1d is 20 sec.

5. *Forward delay:* A parameter that temporarily prevents a bridge from starting to forward data packets to and from a link until news of a topology change has spread to all parts of a bridged network. This should give all links that need to be turned off in the new topology time to do so before new links are turned on.

Actually, forward delay only needs to be half the time necessary for news of the new topology to have reached all parts of the network, because it is invoked twice. When a bridge decides that a port should be switched from the blocking state to the forwarding state, it initially places the port in the listening state. In the listening state, the bridge continues running the spanning tree algorithm and transmitting configuration messages on the port, but discards data packets received on that port and does not transmit data packets to that port. The bridge keeps the port in the listening state for forward delay and then moves the port into the learning state, which is like the listening state except that data packets are received on that port for the purpose of learning some of the stations located on that port. After forward delay, if the bridge still hasn't heard any information that would make it transition the port back to the blocking state, the bridge transitions the port to the forwarding state.

Setting the forward delay value too small would result in temporary loops as the spanning tree algorithm converges. Since loops in bridged networks are bad, it is good to be conservative in setting this parameter. Setting the forward delay value too large, on the other hand, results in longer partitions after the spanning tree reconfigures. This can be sufficiently annoying to tempt people to be brave and set the value smaller.

The value recommended in 802.1d is 15 sec, which means that a bridge will delay forwarding packets to or from a port that was in the blocking state in the previous topology and should be in the forwarding state in the new topology for 30 sec after that bridge discovers that the port should be included in the new spanning tree.

Note that forward delay also serves as the value of the short cache timer, the one used following topology changes.

6. *Long cache timer:* A network-management-settable value. The default recommended in the 802.1 spec is 5 min.

7. *Path cost:* The cost to be added to the root path cost field in a configuration message received on this port in order to determine the cost of the path to the root through this port. This value is individually settable on each port.

Setting this value to be large on a particular port makes the LAN reached through that port more likely to be a leaf or at least low in the spanning tree. The closer a LAN is to being a leaf in the tree, the less through traffic it will be asked to carry. A LAN would be a candidate for having a large path cost if it has a lower bandwidth or if someone wants to minimize unnecessary traffic on it.

(Note: I would have called this parameter "link cost" or "port cost," so as not to confuse anyone into thinking that its value refers to an entire path.)

3.5   Bridge Message Formats

# of octets	Configuration message
2	protocol identifier
1	version
1	message type
1	TCA | reserved | TC flags
8	root ID
4	cost of path to root
8	bridge ID
2	port ID
2	message age
2	max age
2	hello time
2	forward delay

Figure 3.34

1. **Protocol identifier:** The constant 0.

2. **Version:** The constant 0.

3. **Message type:** The constant 0.

4. **Flags:**

   a. **TC**, the least significant bit, is the topology change notification flag. If set in the configuration message received on the root port, it indicates that the receiving bridge should use forward delay (a short cache timer) for aging out station cache entries rather than aging timer (the normal, longer timer for station cache entries).

   b. **TCA**, the most significant bit, is the topology change notification acknowledgment. If set in the configuration message received on the root port, it indicates that bridges receiving this configuration message no longer need to inform the parent bridge that a topology change has occurred. The parent bridge will take responsibility for advising the root of the topology change.

c. The remaining bits in the flags octet are unused.

5. **Root ID:** Each bridge is configured with a 2-octet "priority," which is added to the 6-octet ID. The priority portion is the numerically most significant portion. The 8-octet "root ID" consists of the priority followed by the ID of the bridge that is the root.

6. **Cost of path to root:** 4 octets, taken as an unsigned binary number, which is the total cost from the bridge that transmitted the configuration message to the bridge listed in the root ID.

7. **Bridge ID:** 2 octets of configured priority followed by the 6-octet ID of the bridge transmitting the configuration message.

8. **Port ID:** The first, and most significant, octet is a configurable priority. The second octet is a number assigned by the bridge to the port upon which the configuration message was transmitted. The bridge must assign a (locally) unique number to each of its ports. (In my opinion, having a priority configured for a port is an unnecessary but harmless frill.)

9. **Message age:** Estimated time, in 1/256ths of a second, since the root originally transmitted its configuration message, upon which the information in this configuration message is based.

10. **Max age:** Time, in 1/256ths of a second, at which the configuration message should be deleted.

11. **Hello time:** Time, in 1/256ths of a second, between generation of configuration messages by the root bridge.

12. **Forward delay:** Length of time, in 1/256ths of a second, that bridges should stay in each of the intermediate states before transiting a port from blocking to forwarding.

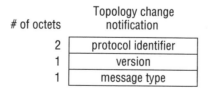

	Topology change notification
# of octets	
2	protocol identifier
1	version
1	message type

Figure 3.35

1. **Protocol identifier:** The constant 0

2. **Version:** The constant 0

3. **Message type:** The constant 128 (decimal)

3.6   Other Bridge Issues

The remainder of this chapter covers more advanced issues with standard transparent bridges, including implications of station behavior on bridge operations, implications of bridged environments on stations, and configuration of bridge filtering. Section 3.7 discusses nonstandard extensions to transparent bridges that allow the use of routes other than spanning tree paths.

3.6.1   Multiply Connected Stations

The consequence of having an incorrect entry in a bridge's station cache is that traffic may not get delivered to the station. One particularly ironic example of how bridge caches can become incorrect is a station with multiple connections into an extended LAN. The problem does not occur if the station uses different data link addresses on each attachment, but some endnode implementations use the same address on multiple links.

Assume the following topology, where station S is attached to two different LANs, LAN 1 and LAN 7:

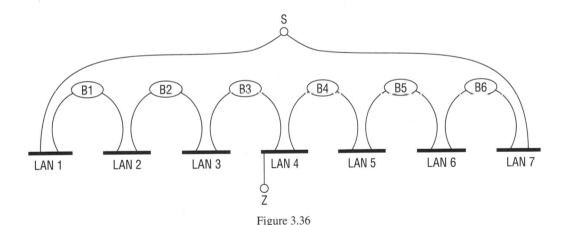

Figure 3.36

Suppose that S issues two packets at about the same time. Packet 1 is issued on LAN 1, and packet 2 is issued on LAN 7. Packet 1 travels toward the right, convincing each bridge that S resides on the left. Meanwhile, packet 2 travels toward the left, convincing each bridge that S resides on the right.

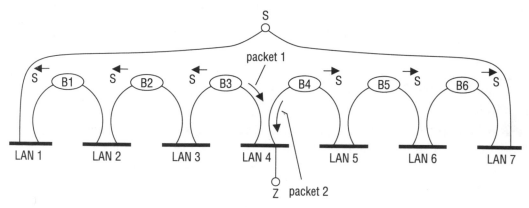

Figure 3.37

Assume that the two packets "cross" on LAN 4 (B4 has packet 2 queued for transmission onto LAN 4 while B3 has packet 1 queued for transmission on LAN 4). When B3 succeeds in transmitting the packet, it will cause B4 to change S's location from residing on the right to residing on the left, and B4 will forward the packet on, convincing B5 and B6 that S resides on the left. When B4 succeeds in transmitting the packet, B3 will become convinced that S resides on its right, and B3 will forward the packet on. Now the picture looks like this:

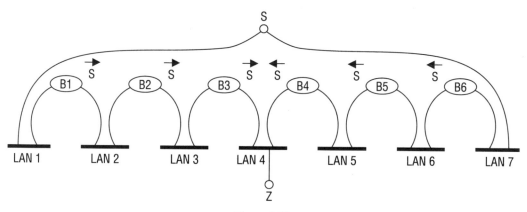

Figure 3.38

Now assume that Z, residing on LAN 4, transmits a packet for S. Since B3 thinks that S resides on its right, B3 will not forward the packet. Since B4 thinks that S resides on its left, B4 will not forward the packet either. Presumably, S is multiply attached into the extended LAN for increased availability, but indeed, the multiple points of attachment make it possible for the bridges to become confused as to S's whereabouts and refuse to forward packets for S.

3.6.2 Configuration of Filtering

A bridge that discards a packet rather than forwarding it is said to *filter* the packet. The standard transparent bridge automatically learns station addresses and performs *filtering*, in the sense that it does not always forward every packet throughout the spanning tree. Once all bridges have learned the location of a particular station, traffic destined for that station should travel along the shortest path in the spanning tree from the source to that station and not "leak" to other parts of the spanning tree.

Filtering is useful for another reason. For instance, it is sometimes desirable to keep certain kinds of traffic confined to portions of the topology. A case in point would be some type of protocol such as a time synchronization protocol that would not work with delays imposed by multiple hops and should therefore be kept confined to a single LAN. Or there might be terminal servers and hosts managed by different organizations in different portions of the spanning tree. It might be desirable to keep the terminal server protocol messages from leaking between the portions of the network.

The 802.1 standard specifies that network management have the ability to set certain addresses as being permanently in the filtering database of a bridge, with instructions as to which ports the bridge should allow the packets to traverse. Ordinarily, this would be used for multicast addresses.

The mechanism specified in the standard is that a particular address is entered into the filtering database with an input port number, together with flags indicating the output ports upon which a packet from the specified input port should be forwarded. Usually, the addresses that are manually entered into the filtering database are multicast addresses, but station addresses can also be configured.

First, a simple example. Suppose that one wanted a particular protocol to flow between ports 2, 4, and 5 and not flow on ports 1, 3, 6, and 7.

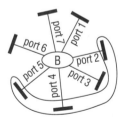

Figure 3.39

This would require three management commands that look approximately like the following. The user interface is not standardized at this time, and again, this tutorial is only helpful for understanding the commands; it is not a replacement for the applicable standard, which should be the reference for the current details. Assume that the multicast address used by the protocol in question is FOO.

1. *Create filter address FOO:* Input port 2; outbound 1—no, 2—no, 3—no, 4—yes, 5—yes, 6—no, 7—no.

2. *Create filter address FOO:* Input port 4; outbound 1—no, 2—yes, 3—no, 4—no, 5—yes, 6—no, 7—no.

3. *Create filter address FOO:* Input port 5; outbound 1—no, 2—yes, 3—no, 4—yes, 5—no, 6—no, 7—no.

Now suppose that there are two domains for FOO running the same protocol, and traffic for these two domains should not comingle. For instance, assume in the preceding example that besides having FOO flow between ports 2, 4, and 5, it should also flow separately between 1 and 7.

Figure 3.40

Then, in addition to the commands indicated earlier, the following commands below must be given:

1. *Create filter address FOO:* Input port 1; outbound 1—no, 2—no, 3—no, 4—no, 5—no, 6—no, 7—yes.

2. *Create filter address FOO:* Input port 7; outbound 1—yes, 2—no, 3—no, 4—no, 5—no, 6—no, 7—no.

Many products offer vendor-specific additional filtering—for instance:

• Filtering based on SAP value rather than specific address

• Filtering based on source address

Note that setting up filtering can be very tricky and counterintuitive, since the boundaries that one could imagine with a particular physical topology might no longer work once the spanning tree defines the logical topology. For instance:

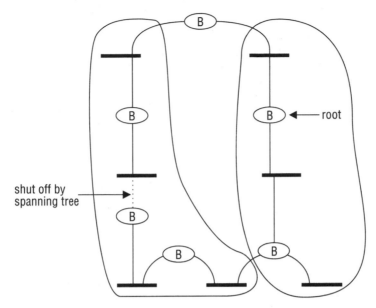

Figure 3.41   Confining protocols to regions of an extended LAN

3.6.3   **Not Quite Transparent**

Now that I've described the basic idea behind the transparent bridge, I'll discuss why it really should be called something like the "translucent bridge."

One obvious way in which adding bridges alters the environment for the stations is that the following performance changes occur:

1. *The probability of packet loss increases.*

    Even if every bridge were engineered to have sufficient CPU to read every packet and determine the ports to which to queue it, links can become congested, and thus, packets may need to be dropped. Queues cannot become arbitrarily large because bridges do not have infinite buffering, and even if they did, as queue lengths increased indefinitely, so would delays.

2. *The delay increases.*

    At each hop, the bridge must wait until it acquires the channel. Also, a congested link along the path can cause a packet to be queued behind several others.

3. *The packet lifetime increases.*

    For the same reasons that delay increases, so, too, can packet lifetime increase when bridges are introduced. This has implications for higher-layer protocols, in that counters set just large enough to avoid wrapping around during lifetimes on a LAN might wrap around during lifetimes across several bridged hops.

4. *The error rate increases.*

There are two places where data corruption can occur. One is while data is being transmitted. The CRC included in the data link layer protocol detects transmission errors. Another place where data corruption can occur is in memory or while a packet is being transmitted across the bus inside a system. If bridges were to strip off the CRC upon packet reception (after checking it for correctness) and then regenerate a CRC upon transmission on the next hop, then errors introduced while the packet was inside the bridge would not be detected. For this reason, it is desirable for the bridge to keep the CRC that was received with the packet and use the same CRC upon transmission. Then, data corruption errors occurring inside the bridge will be detected.

However, bridges cannot always preserve the original CRC. In the case of 802 LANs, no two LANs have the same packet format, and 802.5 even has a different bit order. Thus, the CRC can only be preserved if a bridge is forwarding between two LANs of the same type.

The standard doesn't *require* bridges to preserve the CRC when possible, so even if the extended LAN consists entirely of like LANs, some bridge implementations will not preserve the CRC. In the case of heterogeneous LANs in an extended LAN, bridges cannot preserve the CRC, and thus, the rate of undetected data corruption may increase by orders of magnitude when bridges are introduced.

5. *Packet misordering becomes possible.*

Although bridges go to great lengths to minimize the probability of out-of-order packets, packets can get misordered if spanning tree reconfigurations occur.

6. *The probability of duplicate packets increases.*

Again, bridges go to great lengths to minimize the probability of duplicate packets, but it is still possible for packets to get duplicated in a bridged extended LAN. For instance, if a repeater were to come up, joining two LANs that were previously separated within the spanning tree, there would be a temporary loop, and packets on that loop would be duplicated, perhaps a dramatic number of times.

Besides the quantitative performance-type changes that are introduced by bridges, certain qualitative functional differences result as well:

1. *Stations cannot use the LAN maximum packet size.*

Suppose that different types of LANs having different maximum packet sizes are interconnected with bridges. Then, a station emitting a maximum-size packet on its LAN will have a 100% probability of that packet's being lost if the packet needs to be forwarded by a bridge over a LAN with a smaller maximum packet size.

Stations can be configured to use smaller packet sizes, and one solution to the problem of differing LAN packet sizes is to configure all stations in the extended LAN to use the packet size of the LAN that has the smallest maximum packet size. This isn't a totally satisfactory solution, though, because, in many cases, the source and destination might be on the same LAN and could converse with no problem using a large packet size. Mandating a smaller-than-necessary packet size degrades throughput. Another strategy involves having the transport layer in the stations attempt to discover a larger packet size, but that is not guaranteed for the lifetime of a transport connection because spanning tree reconfigurations can reroute the conversation. Yet another strategy is left as an exercise for you, in homework problem 12.

Chapter 4 discusses source routing, which solves the problem of determining the maximum packet size for a conversation. It is interesting that source routing solves the packet-size problem, since even network layer protocols do not provide very satisfactory solutions. With network layer protocols, packets can be fragmented and reassembled at the destination, but this severely degrades performance. With transparent bridges, not only can bridges not fragment a packet, but they can't even issue an error report to a source that is using an overly large packet size explaining why the packet needed to be dropped, because no such protocol messages are defined for the data link layer.

2. *LAN-specific information in the data link layer may be lost.*

Some LANs have LAN-specific information fields, such as priority. If a packet is transmitted from a LAN with a priority field onto a LAN without such a field, and then onto another LAN with a priority field, there is no way to reconstruct the original priority, since it cannot be carried in the intermediate LAN.

3. *Unexpected packet format conversion may occur.*

There is a convention (RFC 1042) for an 802 format equivalent to the Ethernet format. This is done by using the SNAP SAP as both the DSAP and SSAP, and using 3 octets of 0 for the OUI, followed by the 2-octet Ethernet protocol type to form the 5-octet protocol type field.

Ethernet

6	6	2	
D	S	P	data
destination	source	protocol type	

Translated into 802.3

6	6	2	1	1	1	3	2	
D	S	length	aa	aa	3	0	P	data
destination	source		DSAP	SSAP	CTL	protocol type		

Figure 3.42

Once a packet is translated into 802 format, it can be forwarded onto other LAN types with minimal translation (for instance, adding a priority field, deleting the length field). If the packet is eventually transmitted back onto an Ethernet and the first 3 octets of protocol type are 0, there is no way for the final bridge to know whether the packet was originally transmitted in Ethernet format or 802 format.

In order to keep compatibility with old stations that only understand Ethernet format, a bridge will translate a frame in which SNAP SAP is used and the top 3 octets of the protocol type are 0 into Ethernet format. For this reason, newer stations, if they use the SNAP SAP and 5-octet protocol type with OUI = 0 on 802.3, must be able to accept a packet in Ethernet format and treat it exactly as they would treat the translated version. This rule is documented in RFC 1122. Unfortunately, the RFCs really only apply to IP implementations. There are protocols that use the SNAP SAP encoding with OUI = 0 and get confused if the packet is received in a format different from the one in which it was transmitted.

In particular, bridge vendors became aware of one protocol that assumed the version number of their own protocol based on whether the packet was received in Ethernet or 802.3 format. To protect the guilty, I will refer to this as "protocol X." It was essential for the correct operation of protocol X that if the transmitter emitted a packet with an Ethernet header, it ultimately be received in Ethernet format. Likewise, if the transmitter emitted the packet in 802.3 format, the packet ultimately had to be received in 802.3 format.

The bridge vendors got together and agreed to solve this problem by having bridges specifically check the protocol type for the value assigned to "X." If the packet was in Ethernet format, with protocol type = X, then instead of using the 5-octet protocol type field in 802 format normally used for translation—i.e., 3 octets of 0 followed by X—they'd instead use a different value (which happens to be 00-00-f8). When forwarding onto an 802.3 LAN, a bridge checks the protocol type and translates into Ethernet format if:

1. DSAP = SNAP SAP, the first 3 octets of protocol type = 00-00-00 and the last 2 octets of protocol type are anything other than X.

2. DSAP = SNAP SAP, and the first 3 octets of protocol type = 00-00-f8.

Bridges also make certain assumptions about station behavior, which, if violated, can have consequences ranging from annoying to severe:

1. *They assume that a given data link source address can appear in only one location in the extended LAN.*

    Some implementations of stations with multiple links use the same data link layer address on all ports. This confuses bridge caches. As a result, packets might not be delivered at all to a station that presumably had multiple attachments for greater availability.

2. *They assume that a station receiving a lot of traffic will also be transmitting.*
     If a destination never transmits, packets destined for that station cannot be localized within the extended LAN but rather must be transmitted to all the LANs throughout the spanning tree.

3.7   Extensions to Transparent Bridges

3.7.1   Remote Bridges

When people wish to connect two geographically distant LANs, they cannot attach a single box to both LANs. Instead, they attach a bridge to each LAN and connect the bridges with a point-to-point link. Bridges connected by point-to-point links are sometimes called "remote bridges." They are also sometimes referred to as "half bridges," because the combination of the two bridges plus the point-to-point link can be thought of as a single bridge.

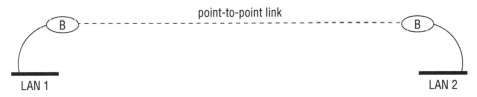

Figure 3.43

The spanning tree algorithm works just fine with point-to-point links. The two bridges on each side of the point-to-point link just regard the link as a LAN.
     One issue to consider is that the spanning tree algorithm makes sure that packets reach every LAN. One of the two bridges will be the designated bridge on the point-to-point link. That bridge will definitely consider the point-to-point link to be in the spanning tree and will forward data packets onto that link. The other bridge either will or will not consider the point-to-point link to be its root port. If the second bridge considers the link to be its root port, then it will also forward data packets to and from the link, and the point-to-point link will be useful in the spanning tree. If the second bridge does not compute the link to be its root port, then that bridge will not forward data packets to the point-to-point link and will ignore packets transmitted to that link.
     On some point-to-point links, tariffs are traffic-sensitive. In such a case, it makes sense for the second bridge to alert the first bridge that it will be ignoring its data packets. The standard does not specify a means to do this. Instead, it assumes that remote bridges will be bought in pairs, from the same vendor. The standard (at least as of the writing of this book) did not deem it necessary to standardize the protocol between remote bridges.

Another issue with remote bridges is the representation of the packet as it travels over the point-to-point link. Usually, the point-to-point link has some sort of header information that must be added to a packet. Bridges typically take the entire packet (including the LAN header) and treat it as the data portion of a packet on the point-to-point link. In this way, it is possible to preserve the CRC.

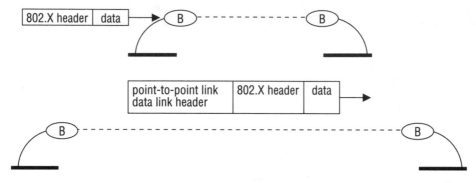

Figure 3.44

This same technique can be used if the point-to-point link is not a direct wire but rather is a "WAN cloud" to which both bridges connect. Since most WANs do not provide multicast capability, a collection of bridges attached to a WAN cloud needs to be pre-configured with the network layer addresses of all the other bridges. Each bridge communicates with all the other bridges.

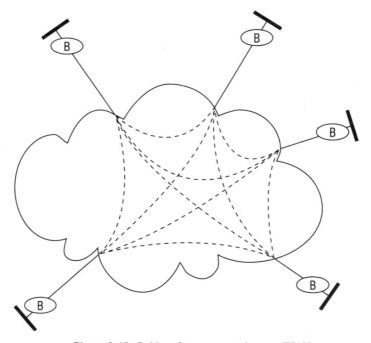

Figure 3.45   Bridges Interconnected over a WAN

Yet another issue with remote bridges is the need to pass the type of packet along with the packet. For instance:

Figure 3.46

If B1 merely packages a packet, as received from one of the LANs, and transmits it to B2, then B2 does not know whether the packet originated on 802.3 and can therefore be transmitted verbatim onto the 802.3 LAN attached to B2, or whether the packet originated on a different type of LAN and the header therefore requires modification. There are several solutions:

1. B1 and B2 could have a proprietary mechanism for passing along the type of LAN on which the packet originated.

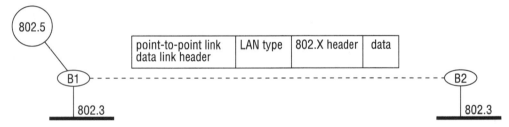

Figure 3.47

2. B1 and B2 could agree on a particular "canonical format" for packets and convert the packet into that canonical format before transmitting it on the point-to-point link. If the canonical format is not equal to one of the LAN types, then all packets will need to be reformatted both before and after transmission on the point-to-point link. The problem with reformatting packets is that there is no way to preserve the CRC end-to-end.

3. B1 and B2 could agree on a particular type of LAN—for instance, 802.3—and then convert non-802.3 packets to that format before transmitting them on the point-to-point link. This enables 802.3 packets to be passed along unmodified. But a packet that originated on an 802.5 and needs to be transmitted back onto an 802.5 would have been needlessly reformatted, and the CRC will have been lost. Also, information specific to a particular type of LAN (like priority) will get lost if the preferred format does not have the necessary field.

The 802 committee is considering doing the work necessary to standardize remote bridges.

3.7.2   Using Extra Links

Warning: The entire rest of this chapter (until the homework problems) is technically detailed and should be skipped unless you are really interested in bridge load sharing.

3.7.2.1   Vitalink's Proprietary DLS Protocol

John Hart, from Vitalink, invented a protocol known as "DLS," which allows point-to-point links not selected for inclusion in the spanning tree to be used, in certain cases, for bridge forwarding (see Figure 3.48).

This proprietary protocol, which has never been documented, is rather complex. It requires all of the following to be true before a point-to-point link can be used:

1. The bridges B1 and B2 that are endpoints of the point-to-point link both implement DLS.

2. The bridge B3 that is the root of the spanning tree has implemented DLS.

3. B3 is on the spanning tree path between B1 and B2.

4. The path cost (as computed by the spanning tree algorithm) from B1 to the root plus the cost from B2 to the root is less than the configured cost of the point-to-point link.

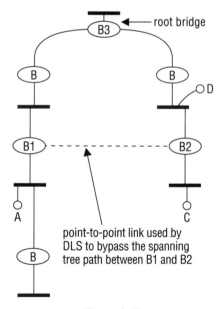

Figure 3.48

The way DLS works is that one of the bridges—say, B2—notices that the point-to-point link has not been selected by the spanning tree algorithm. (As stated earlier, at least one of the bridges will think the point-to-point link is in the spanning tree.) B2 sends a special message to B1 over the point-to-point link informing it that B2 would like to perform DLS on the point-to-point link. This also informs B1 that the point-to-point link has not been selected for the spanning tree algorithm, so B1 can cease sending spanning tree data packets over the point-to-point link. B2 also sends B1, over the spanning tree, a special packet whose purpose is to discover whether B3 is indeed on the path between B1 and B2. If B3 has implemented DLS, it will mark the special packet as having visited the root before forwarding it on toward B2 through the spanning tree. When B2 receives the special packet, reassuring it that the root is between B1 and B2, then it can decide whether the spanning tree path between B1 and B2 has a greater computed cost than the configured cost of the point-to-point link between B1 and B2. B2 knows B1's cost to the root because B1, which is the designated bridge on the point-to-point link, transmits configuration messages on the point-to-point link that include B1's cost to the root. If B2 decides to use the link, then the two bridges have to carefully use the link only to bypass the spanning tree path between B1 and B2.

B2 looks at its station learning cache for stations located in the subtree below B2—i.e., on B2's ports in the spanning tree other than the root port. For instance, C is such a station. B2 sends a special message to B1 over the point-to-point link informing B1 that traffic for destination C can traverse the point-to-point link. If B1 receives data traffic destined for C from a port in the spanning tree other than the root port, B1 can forward the packet over the point-to-point link rather than forwarding it through the spanning tree.

Likewise, B1 informs B2 of stations for which B2 can send traffic over the point-to-point link (for instance, A).

When B1 receives a data packet from a port in the spanning tree other than the root port, B1 checks the set of destinations for which B2 has requested traffic over the point-to-point link. If the destination address in the packet is one that B2 has requested, B1 forwards the traffic over the point-to-point link rather than through the spanning tree.

Bridges are supposed to try really hard not to misorder packets. Therefore, B1 cannot suddenly switch from forwarding traffic for C over the spanning tree to forwarding it over the point-to-point link. DLS provides a special protocol for B1 to determine when it is safe to transmit a packet over the point-to-point link, by ascertaining that any packets previously transmitted over the spanning tree have already been delivered or lost. B1 sends a special packet to B2 through the spanning tree. When B2 receives the special packet, it forwards the packet back to B1 over the point-to-point link. Upon receiving that packet, B1 knows that it is now safe to transmit data for the set of stations for which B2 had requested traffic.

3.7.2.2   A Simplified and More General Algorithm

DLS, as described, has certain strange topological restrictions. Given two identical spanning trees, a point-to-point link might be eligible for DLS in one topology and not in another, depending on which bridge is the root bridge.

I'd suggest a slight generalization and simplification of DLS. In the proposed generalization, the restriction that the root bridge must implement DLS is removed, and the root bridge can be an ordinary bridge. I'll call this algorithm "GDLS," for "generalized DLS." GDLS has not been implemented anywhere.

Assume a point-to-point link between two bridges, B1 and B2. Suppose, as before, that B2 notices that the link is not in the spanning tree. The topology can now be thought of as having four separate pieces:

1.   The spanning tree path between B1 and B2.

2.   The point-to-point link between B1 and B2.

3.   The subtree consisting of all branches of the spanning tree from B1 that do not lead to B2. Call this subtree S1.

4.   The subtree consisting of all branches of the spanning tree from B2 that do not lead to B1. Call this subtree S2.

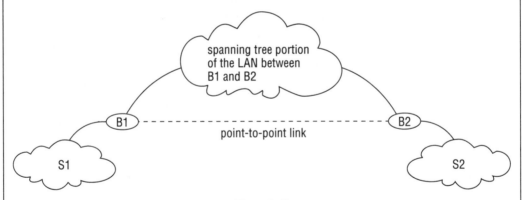

Figure 3.49

It does not matter where the root bridge is. B1 can forward traffic from S1 destined for S2 over the point-to-point link. B1 must first determine which of its ports in the spanning tree lead toward B2, and B2 must determine which of its ports in the spanning tree lead toward B1. Each of the bridges can do this by sending a special packet through the spanning tree to the other bridge.

For instance, B2 might inform B1, via a special packet over the point-to-point link, that B2 would like to use the point-to-point link for load sharing. B2 also launches a special packet on each spanning tree port, with source address equal to B2's data link address on that port and destination address equal to some predefined multicast address. (This is necessary because B1 has a different data link address on each port.) B1 will know, based on the data field in the packet, that the packet is for B1.

When B1 receives B2's special packet from the spanning tree, B1 knows B2's data link address on the port in the spanning tree in the direction of B1. B1 can then send B2 a message on that port, so that B2 will know B1's data link address on the spanning tree path between B2 and B1 as well as which port leads to B1.

DLS uses the configured cost of the point-to-point link and the spanning-tree-computed cost of the path between the two bridges to determine whether the point-to-point link should be used. Once a point-to-point link is determined to be useful, all possible traffic is diverted onto that link. There is no method for determining whether the point-to-point link has become overly congested.

Unlike DLS, GDLS does not have a mechanism for determining whether the root is on the spanning tree path between B1 and B2, nor does it wish to make use of the point-to-point link contingent on that fact. Likewise, GDLS does not compute the cost of the path between B1 and B2. How, then, can GDLS determine whether it is reasonable to use the point-to-point link to bypass the spanning tree path between B1 and B2?

GDLS accomplishes this by comparing the speed of the B1–B2 link with the speed of the spanning tree path connecting B1 and B2. Each of the bridges periodically launches two special packets, each containing the same sequence number (or timestamp). One is launched on the point-to-point link, the other on the spanning tree path. When B2 receives a packet with sequence number X on one of the paths to B1, it starts a timer and waits for the corresponding packet (also with sequence number X) from the other connection to B1. If B2 receives sequence number X first on the point-to-point link, then the point-to-point link can be used for more destinations, and B2 can inform B1 of more destinations for which B1 can use the point-to-point link. If B2 receives sequence number X first on the spanning tree path, then it means that the point-to-point link is slower than the spanning tree path (perhaps because the link is overutilized) and B2 can stop requesting new destinations for the link or perhaps even unrequest some previously requested destinations. In this way, B1 and B2 can work to really equalize the load. In DLS, it is an all-or-nothing proposition. Once the link is determined, to be better, based on cost, as many destinations as table space allows will be requested.

3.7.2.3 Extended DLS

Both DLS and GDLS only work if a bridge has at least three ports—one port for the point-to-point link, one for the spanning tree path to the other bridge, and one for destinations in the spanning tree besides the port toward the other bridge.

John Hart invented an enhancement to DLS (which I'll call "EDLS," for "extended DLS") that uses a cross-link like the following, but only for traffic between the adjacent LANs (LAN 1 and LAN 2 in the accompanying diagram).

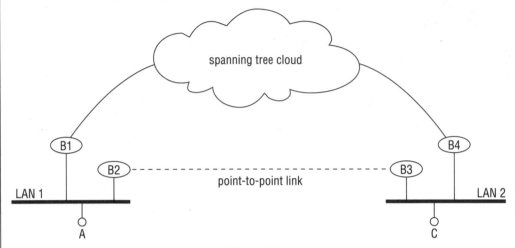

Figure 3.50

Notice that B2 and B3 have only two ports, and the basic DLS (or GDLS) scheme would not allow use of the cross-link.

The way DLS handles this situation is that B2 tells B1 (the designated bridge on the LAN) about the desire to use a cross-link off the LAN to B3. Likewise, B3 tells B4 that it would like to use a cross-link to B2. EDLS now needs to determine which stations reside on LAN 1 and which stations reside on LAN 2.

B1 sends a special packet to B3 saying "Let's do a cross-link and send traffic for destinations D1, D2, D3, etc., on that link." In the packet, B1 includes destinations it thinks reside on LAN 1. The special packet gets forwarded through B2, which inspects the list of stations and deletes any that B2 has in its cache as residing on a port other than LAN 1.

Assume that A is in the list of stations B1 requests from B3. B3 must inform B4 not to forward traffic from LAN 2 destined to A. When B3 forwards a packet—say, from C to A—through the DLS link, it is essential that B1 not get confused into thinking that C resides on LAN 1. Thus, B2 must somehow inform B1 not to learn from source addresses of packets destined for A.

I have seen only a very sketchy description of EDLS. I do not know exactly how it works, nor even whether it works.

3.7.2.4 Tunnels

Suppose that the topology consists of several LANs, connected with bridges that attach to some sort of WAN cloud.

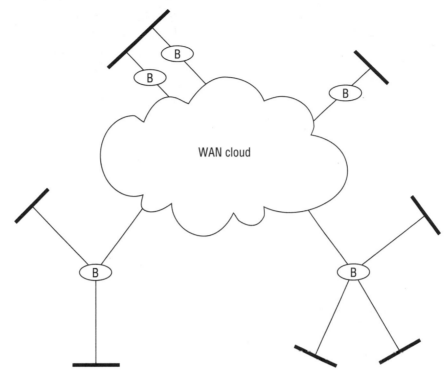

Figure 3.51

Each of the LANs can actually be an extended bridged LAN. Suppose that some protocol (like LAT) that cannot be routed (due to its not having a network layer) is operating in the LANs. Suppose, too, that the boxes are supposed to "glue" the LANs together so that LAT traffic can move from one LAN to another, through the WAN cloud, as if the boxes were bridges. This can be accomplished by configuring the boxes to know about each other. One constraint is that only a single box may forward traffic to or from a LAN. Otherwise, loops can occur. So the boxes on a LAN must use some sort of protocol to elect a single box for forwarding traffic to or from the LAN.

In order to forward traffic onto the WAN cloud, a box must put the network layer header used by the WAN cloud onto the packet and direct the packet to one of the other special boxes. If the box wishes to transmit the packet to all the other boxes, then it needs to send a copy to each of them. I will call the WAN path between two boxes—say, B1 and B2—a "tunnel." B1 has five tunnels in this illustration—one to B2, one to B3, and so forth. Each of the boxes in the illustration has a tunnel to each of the other boxes (see Fig. 3.52).

B1 can consider each of the tunnels to be a special "port" and can do learning on packets received from the tunnels. For instance, if B2 sends B1 a packet over the B2–B1 tunnel, B1 removes the network layer header to discover the original data link header transmitted by the source. If the source

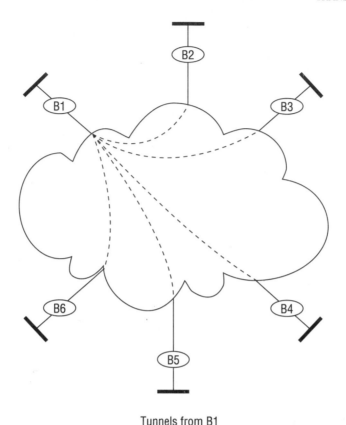

Tunnels from B1

Figure 3.52

address in the data link header is A, then B1 knows that future traffic for data link address A need not be sent over all tunnels but rather can be sent solely on the tunnel to B2.

Tunnels have some attractive properties. They can be used to bridge traffic across portions of the network connected with routers. In this way, the spanning tree need not become infinitely large. Very large spanning trees are dangerous because they take a long time to settle down, and they reconfigure too frequently because the larger the number of components participating in the spanning tree, the more likely it is that one of them will be coming up or going down at any particular time. Tunnels do not increase the size of the spanning tree.

Another attractive property of tunnels is that they make filtering much more sensible. People really want to configure which LANs should be "glued together" for a particular protocol. With bridges, filtering is done on a hop-by-hop basis. If the spanning tree reconfigures, the bridge filtering may no longer make sense. Boundaries that are right for a particular protocol in one topology may be wrong in a different topology. Also, it may be the case that a particular protocol's traffic should be bridged from one LAN to another

LAN that is not adjacent and that the intervening LANs should merely be used for route-through. This can be accomplished with tunnels, but not with bridges.

Still another attractive property of tunnels is that they permit traffic to take an optimal route from source LAN to destination LAN. Once a network layer header is added to the packet, the packet can be routed.

The only disadvantage of tunnels is that manual configuration is required to let the boxes know about each other and know which protocol types they should tunnel. Furthermore, the manual configuration can be fairly complex.

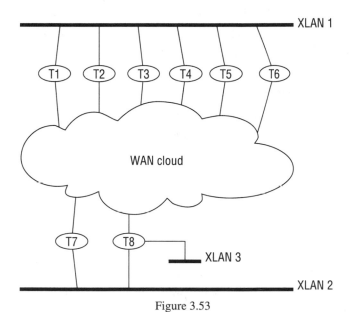

Figure 3.53

In the preceding illustration, only one of the tunnelers on XLAN 1 can forward traffic to and from XLAN 1. Likewise, only one of the tunnelers on XLAN 2 can forward traffic to and from XLAN 2. Presumably, there are six tunnelers on XLAN 1 because five of them are backups in case of the failure of several tunnelers. Therefore, all of them have to be configured with a tunnel to XLAN 2 in case they get elected the official tunneler.

When configuring a tunnel between XLAN 1 and XLAN 2, the network manager must specify the network layer address of the other end of the tunnel. In case a tunneler has several ports attached to extended LANs (as in the case of T8), the network manager has to specify not only the network layer addresses of the tunnel endpoints but the port numbers as well.

To configure a tunnel between XLAN 1 and XLAN 2, the network manager must configure into each of the six tunnelers on XLAN 1 a tunnel to the appropriate port on both T7 and T8. Likewise, T7 and T8 each have to be configured with a tunnel to each of the six tunnelers (with the appropriate port numbers as well) on XLAN 1. This may seem really awful, but it is unlikely that there would be more than two tunnelers on any particular extended LAN.

If a tunneler gets elected to be the official tunneler of the extended LAN, it attempts to form all the configured tunnels. A tunnel might succeed, or it may fail due to:

1. Failure to reach the other endpoint

2. Receipt of a refusal from the other endpoint, because the other endpoint either has not been configured to accept a tunnel from that node or is not a primary tunneler

I am not aware of any implementation of tunnels but do think the idea would be useful for protocols such as LAT that cannot be routed.

3.7.2.5 My Opinion

Bridges already make me nervous. They are solving what should be a network layer problem with the constraint that the packet header does not contain any fields helpful to multihop operation, nor do the endnodes cooperate in the protocol (as they would with routers).

Although bridges work reasonably well in simple topologies, extending the bridge protocol with complex algorithms like DLS, GDLS, and especially EDLS makes it even more likely that problems will occur, such as loops (which are a disaster with bridges), misordered packets, and packet loss due to confused station caches. If operating within the spanning tree is too much of a restriction, then the correct solution is to use a proper network layer protocol. Also, as more vendors invent proprietary enhancements, there is no guarantee that all these enhancements will interwork.

Homework

1. What problems occur if a bridge's cache is incorrect about the direction in which some station resides?

2. Suppose that the number of stations exceeds the capacity of a bridge's station cache. Will this cause problems? Should the bridge overwrite existing entries with new entries before the old entries have timed out, or should the new entries be ignored?

3. Despite careful configuration of timers, temporary loops can occur with bridges. For instance, a repeater can come up, connecting two LANs that had not previously been connected. What design decisions in bridge implementation can assure that the network will recover?

4. Why does using a smaller packet size degrade throughput on a long file transfer?

5. Suppose that someone built an "introduction" service to allow nodes to find other nodes' data link layer addresses. An "introduction server" has a well-known data link address—say, "INTRO"—and it knows the data link addresses of all other nodes, but other nodes do not a priori know the data link addresses of other nodes. The protocol is as follows:

    A node keeps a cache of data link layer addresses of nodes with which it is currently corresponding. This cache is learned based on the data link layer source address of received packets.

    When a node does not know another node's data link layer address, it sends the packet to data link layer destination INTRO. When the introduction server receives a packet, it finds the destination node's higher-layer address in the appropriate header of the packet, looks up that node's data link layer address, substitutes that node's data link layer address as the destination data link layer address in the packet, and forwards the packet on. The destination node will learn the source's data link layer address from the source address in the data link header of the received packet. Once the destination replies, the source will learn the destination node's data link layer address as well. Although this protocol works fine on a LAN, will it still operate properly on an extended LAN with transparent bridges (see Fig. 3.54)?

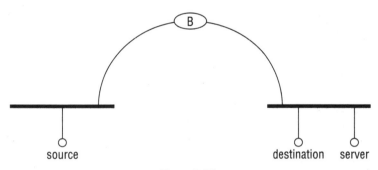

Figure 3.54

6. Consider the following alternative to the topology change notification protocol and the variable station timeout: When a bridge notices a topology change, it multicasts a special "flush cache" packet to all the other bridges. A bridge that receives a flush cache packet deletes its entire station cache.

    How does this compare with the topology change notification protocol? Will all incorrect entries be deleted? Will the network's performance be any different if the station cache is completely deleted in one step rather than having the station cache slowly cleansed of incorrect entries by setting the cache timer smaller?

7. Demonstrate a topology in which the spanning tree can reconfigure without some particular bridge's being aware that the topology has changed (assuming the topology change notification protocol was not implemented). Demonstrate how portions of that bridge's station learning cache can become invalid as a result of that reconfiguration.

8. Assume that a bridge has seven ports and that there are three protocols, using multicast addresses MULT1, MULT2, and MULT3, respectively. Suppose you want to allow MULT1 to travel freely between all ports; you want MULT2 to travel between ports 1, 2, and 3 and also between 5 and 7; and you want MULT3 not to travel between any of the ports. What network management commands would you give to the bridge to set up the filtering?

9. Where would filtering based on source address be useful? For example, a bridge might be configured with a set of source addresses and refuse to forward a packet unless the source was in the configured set. Also, a bridge might be configured with a set of disallowed source addresses—in which case, it would refuse to forward a packet whose source address was in the disallowed set.

10. Imagine a protocol in which clients and servers find each other based on multicast advertisements or solicitations. Suppose that for that protocol, there are specific regions of the extended LAN, and the person responsible for the extended LAN only wants clients and servers from the same region talking to each other. Assuming nonmalicious nodes, suppose that the manager configures bridges outside each of the regions to drop the multicast addresses used by the protocol. Further, assume that the bridges do not filter based on protocol type. Will filtering based solely on the multicast addresses keep the separate regions segregated with respect to that protocol?

11. Discuss methods (both hardware and software) for organizing the station learning cache in order to speed up the forwarding of packets. Adding entries to the cache based on newly learned source addresses should also be reasonably efficient but is not as critical as lookups of addresses already in the cache, since those must be done at LAN speeds, whereas adding entries can be done in background.

12. Assume for simplicity that there are only two types of LANs in the topology, FDDI and 802.3. FDDI allows 4,500-octet packets; 802.3 has a maximum packet size of 1,500 octets.

    FDDI has a priority field, which is not present in 802.3. The bridge spec states that when a bridge transmits a packet from 802.3 to FDDI, the bridge should transmit it at priority = 0. It is recommended that FDDI stations not originate traffic with priority 0. Use this information to devise a simple scheme that two stations can use to discover whether they can communicate with 4,500-octet packets or 1,500-octet packets.

13. As stated in section 3.4.2, the original spanning tree algorithm had only a single intermediate state between blocking and forwarding, and did not indicate whether a bridge should do learning of station addresses on a port in the intermediate state. The 802 bridge spec subdivides the intermediate state into two states. In the first, learning is not done; in the second, learning is done. Compare the following three strategies:

    a. A single intermediate state, in which learning is done

b. A single intermediate state, in which learning is not done

c. As in the spec, two intermediate states

Consider the implications of each strategy, such as unnecessarily forwarded frames and incorrect cache entries.

14. Compare the functionality of n-port bridges with two-port bridges. Can every configuration built with n-port bridges be built with two-port bridges? Suppose a topology consists of n LANs interconnected with a single n-port bridge; in that topology, a packet always requires just a single hop to get from any LAN to any other LAN. Can the same be accomplished with two-port bridges? If a customer wanted n LANs interconnected, and only two-port bridges were available, what configuration of LANs and two-port bridges would you suggest?

Chapter 4
Source Routing Bridges

"Source routing" was at one time a proposal before the IEEE 802.1 committee, competing against transparent bridging as the standard for connecting LANs in the data link layer. When the 802.1 committee decided to adopt transparent bridging, the source routing proponents brought the concept of source routing to the 802.5 committee to standardize as a method of interconnecting 802.5 LANs.

For some time, transparent bridges and source routing bridges evolved independently. Then there arose the need to design some means of interconnecting extended LANs attached via source routing bridges with extended LANs attached via transparent bridges. This type of bridge was known as the "SR-TB" bridge, or "source routing to transparent bridging" bridge. This approach proved quite complex, especially when people attempted to have networks in which both types of bridges attached to the same LAN.

It was subsequently decided that all standard bridges must support transparent bridging and that source routing would be an optional additional feature in a bridge. A bridge that does source routing in addition to transparent bridging is known as an "SRT" ("source routing transparent") bridge.

As of the writing of this book, the source routing standard is still changing. Thus, the details presented here may not match the standard at the time you read this book. However, as stated in the Preface, the purpose of this book is *not* to replace reading the standards. The purpose is to make the concepts understandable, so that subsequently reading the actual standards can be a rewarding and enjoyable experience.

I believe it will be easier for you to understand source routing if I start by explaining the pure SR bridge. Then I will provide a brief overview of the issues involved in designing an SR-TB bridge. The complexity and topology restrictions involved in the SR-TB bridge account for the development of SRT bridges, which I will then explain, after which, I will discuss end-system operation with source routing.

4.1   Pure Source Routing

The basic idea behind source routing bridges is that a packet header contains a route and that route is inserted by the source end station.

99

In order for the source end station to know a route to the destination end station, it must "discover" a route by transmitting a special kind of packet that replicates itself as it reaches route choices, sending a copy over each possible path. Each copy collects a diary of its travels, so that when the copies reach the destination station, a route can be selected.

When a station discovers a route to another station, it caches the route so that it can be used for subsequent packets to the same destination.

4.1.1   The Routing Header

Ordinarily, the data link layer header of a packet on a LAN looks roughly like this:

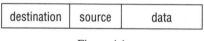

Figure 4.1

There are other fields—for instance, the SAP and/or protocol type field, the checksum, and LAN-specific fields such as length or priority—but these fields are not relevant here.

A source routing packet requires additional fields in the header. There must be a method for distinguishing packets that have the additional fields from those that don't, since it could be unfortunate if a user's data were interpreted as source routing header information.

Distinguishing between packets whose headers include routing information and those whose headers do not was accomplished by taking advantage of an "otherwise useless bit" in the preceding packet format. (Those of you unfamiliar with source routing should stop reading for a while at this point, examine the aforementioned packet format [i.e., the one with only three fields—destination, source, and data], and figure out where that magic bit might be.)

The magic bit is the multicast bit in the source address field. The reasoning was that nobody should be transmitting a packet *from* a multicast address. (Luckily, before the source routing bridge proposal, no applications did utilize that bit.) If that bit in the source address is 0, the assumption is that the packet is ordinary, whereas if that bit is set, then the assumption is that the information following the regular data link layer header should be interpreted as a source routing header.

Thus, a packet without a source routing header looks like this:

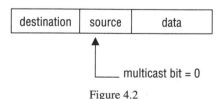

Figure 4.2

A packet with a source routing header looks like this:

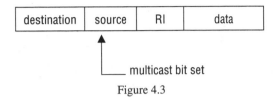

Figure 4.3

The **RI** ("routing information") field contains the additional source routing information. It consists of the following fields:

- **Type** (3 bits): One of the following:

  a. Specifically routed. (The route appears in the header.)

  b. All paths explorer. (The route gets collected as packet copies traverse the network.)

  c. Spanning tree explorer. (The route gets collected as packet copies traverse the network, just as with the all paths explorer, but the packet only travels along branches in the spanning tree.)

- **Length** (5 bits): Specifies the number of bytes in the RI field.

- **Direction** (1 bit): Specifies whether the route should be traversed from right to left or vice versa.

- **Largest frame** (3 bits): A value representing one of a few popular packet sizes (516, 1500, 2052, 4472, 8144, 11407, 17800, 65535).

- **Route**: A sequence of 2-byte-long fields, called "route designators," each of which consists of 12 bits of LAN number followed by 4 bits of bridge number.

Route Designator

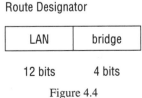

12 bits   4 bits

Figure 4.4

Within an extended LAN, each LAN must be assigned a unique LAN number.

Suppose that a route were designated as a sequence of LAN numbers and you have the following topology:

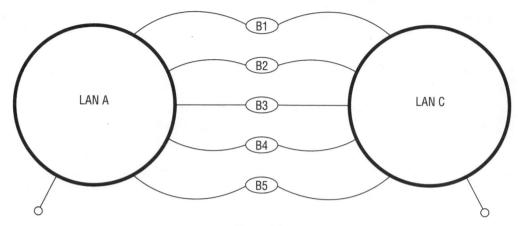

Figure 4.5

If a packet were routed with the route "LAN A, LAN C," then five copies would arrive, since each of the five bridges between LAN A and LAN C would assume that it should forward the packet. If there are multiple hops with parallel bridges, the number of copies grows exponentially with the number of hops.

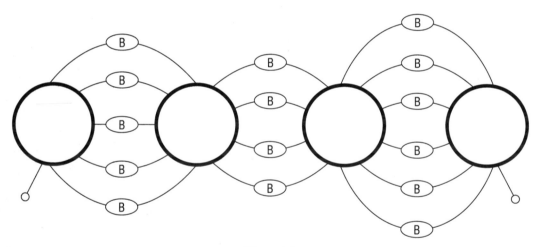

Figure 4.6

To solve this problem, each bridge is further assigned a 4-bit number to distinguish it from other bridges that connect the same pair of LANs. Each bridge must be configured with the LAN numbers for each port, plus a bridge number, the assignment of which must follow the rule that no two bridges interconnecting the same two LANs are allowed to have the same bridge number.

Note: The standard calls for a single bridge number per bridge instead of a separate number with respect to each pair of LANs that the bridge connects. If bridges have many ports, and each bridge has only a single bridge number instead of one for each of its pairs of ports, then there may be topologies in which there is no way to assign bridge numbers. The "right" thing is for a bridge to have a separate number for each pair of LANs. But that can be a management nightmare, especially for a bridge with hundreds of ports. (See homework problem 7.)

A route is really an alternating sequence of LAN and bridge numbers, always starting and ending with a LAN number. The fact that a LAN number and a bridge number are packaged together into a single route designator is merely an artifact of storing the information into octets. It is simpler to think of a route as (LAN, bridge, LAN, bridge, LAN, bridge, LAN). The final route designator's 4 bits indicating "bridge" are irrelevant (ought to be 0 probably, but the standard just has the bridges ignore that field, so a route would work no matter what the value of the final 4 bits).

There are several reasons for having parallel bridges (two or more bridges interconnecting the same pair of LANs):

1. *Robustness:* If one bridge fails, another is available.

2. *Underpowered bridges:* If a single bridge cannot support full-bandwidth forwarding, it is possible that different conversations will choose different bridges, so that the load might be shared between the bridges.

3. *Low-bandwidth links.*

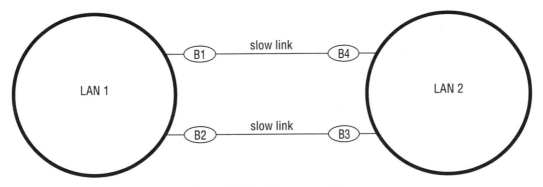

Figure 4.7 Parallel remote bridges

In the accompanying illustration, B1 is attached to B4 with a slow point-to-point link, and B2 is attached to B3 in a like fashion. In order to bridge LAN 1 to LAN 2, traffic must traverse at least one of the slow links. If all traffic went via the link between B1 and B4, then the amount of traffic would be limited to the capacity of the B1–B4 link. However, if some of the traffic were diverted to the B2–B3 link, then the bandwidth between LAN 1 and LAN 2 would be increased.

Note: If transparent bridges were used in Fig. 4.7, the spanning tree would select one of the links (B1–B4 or B2–B3) as being in the spanning tree, and all traffic would flow on that single link, making load sharing impossible.

However, it is possible to use multiple parallel low-speed links with transparent bridges by employing an alternate topology, which uses parallel links instead of parallel bridges.

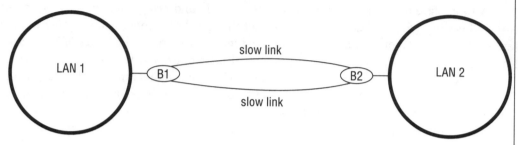

Figure 4.8   Parallel links

In Fig. 4.8, B1 and B2 use the parallel links as a logical single higher-bandwidth link. They must employ some sort of bridge-to-bridge protocol to reorder packets.

Parallel bridging (Fig. 4.7) has an advantage over the parallel links link-sharing method (Fig. 4.8) in that parallel bridging will allow operation (with degraded service due to decreased bandwidth) in the event of bridge failures. However, the parallel links configuration has two advantages over parallel bridge configuration:

1. The bridges control how much traffic goes over each link, so they can equalize the loads on the multiple links. With parallel bridges, it can only be hoped that end stations happen to choose paths in such a way as to distribute the load well.

2. Packets from a single large-bandwidth conversation can go over different links within the group of parallel links and be reassembled into the proper order afterward. With parallel bridges, if all of the traffic is due to a single large-bandwidth conversation, there is no way to utilize multiple paths.

4.1.2   Bridge Algorithms

From the viewpoint of a bridge, there are four types of packets to be handled:

1. Packets without an RI field, to be known as *transparent packets*

2. Specifically routed packets

3. All paths explorer packets

4. Spanning tree explorer packets

This section discusses how a bridge handles each of these types of packet.

4.1.2.1 Transparent Packets

A pure source routing bridge explicitly ignores packets without an RI field. To avoid confusion in case both source routing and transparent bridges attach to the same LAN, the transparent bridge standard requires that a transparent bridge ignore packets with the RI field. So transparent packets will be handled by the transparent bridges, and packets with the RI field will be handled by the source routing bridges.

4.1.2.2 Specifically Routed Packets

Assume that bridge B receives a specifically routed packet on a port P1 attached to a LAN that B knows as "X." B checks the direction bit in the header and scans the route in the appropriate direction searching for LAN X. B forwards the packet onto port P2 if all of the following are true:

1. X appears in the route. Now assume that the bridge number following X is some number, B_n, and the LAN number following X is some number, Y.

2. The LAN number that B associates with port P2 is Y.

3. B's bridge number with respect to the pair of ports (P1, P2) is B_n. (Or the single bridge number that B uses for any pair of ports is B_n.)

4. Y does not appear anywhere else in the route.

4.1.2.3 All Paths Explorer Packets

Assume that bridge B receives an all paths explorer packet on a port P1 attached to a LAN that B knows as "X."

An end system initially transmits the packet without any hops in the route. B must first check to see whether or not the packet has accumulated a route. If the RI field just contains the packet type and flags, but no actual hops yet, B does the following for every port P2 other than port P1:

1. Adds "X, B_n, Y," where Y is the LAN number with which B has been configured for P2 and B_n is B's bridge number with respect to P1 and P2 (or simply B's bridge number if there's a bridgewide bridge number rather than a specific bridge number for each pair of ports).

2. Adjusts the value of the largest frame field to be the minimum of the value the end system placed in that field, the value configured into B as the largest frame possible on P1, and the value configured into B as the largest frame possible on P2.

3. Recalculates the CRC (cyclic redundancy check) on the packet, since the packet has been modified.

4. Transmits the packet onto P2.

If the all paths explorer packet has been through other bridges (the **length** field is between 6 and 28 bytes, inclusive), B does the following for every port P2 except the port (P1) from which it received the all paths explorer packet. B forwards it onto port P2 (for which B has LAN number Y configured) if the following is true:

1. The final hop in the collected route is X. (If it isn't, B drops the packet and logs an error.)

2. Y does not appear anywhere in the route collected so far.

Before forwarding the packet onto port P2, B:

1. Adjusts the length of the RI field by adding 2 to the length field in the RI header.

2. Adds its bridge number to the bottom 4 bits of the route designator field that contains LAN number X.

3. Adds Y as the next LAN number.

4. Adjusts the largest frame field if the value configured into B as the largest frame possible on P2 is smaller than the value presently indicated in the largest frame field.

5. Recalculates the CRC, since the packet has been modified.

If the route in the received all paths explorer packet is full, the packet is discarded.

4.1.2.4   Spanning Tree Explorer Packets

The spanning tree explorer packet has the same function as an ordinary transparent packet. It travels along the spanning tree. One obvious use of spanning tree explorer frames was in the transmission of multicast packets. Multicast packets could not be specifically routed, because they needed to reach multiple destinations. It was undesirable for them to be sent via all paths explorer, since multiple copies of each multicast packet would be delivered to each LAN.

Other than in multicast situations, the standard was never clear about when this type of packet would be used. There were many possible scenarios for how an end system discovered a route. In one scenario, the conversation initiator sent the first packet of a conversation via spanning tree explorer and the destination replied with an all paths explorer, so that it was the source rather than the destination that chose the route.

To support this type of packet, source routing bridges run the spanning tree algorithm, discussed in Chapter 3.

A bridge handles a spanning tree explorer packet almost the same way as it handles an all paths explorer. The only differences are:

1. The bridge does not check whether the output LAN already appears in the collected route.

2. The bridge only accepts a spanning tree explorer packet if it arrives on a port in the spanning tree and only forwards it to other ports in the spanning tree.

4.2   SR-TB Bridges

Assume that extended LANs are neatly partitioned into portions connected solely via transparent bridges and portions connected solely via source routing bridges. There then arises the need to interconnect these portions, using a type of bridge known as an SR-TB bridge.

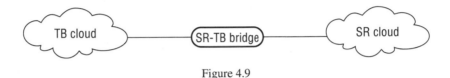

Figure 4.9

Although this type of bridge was never standardized, implementations would have had to do something similar to what is described in this section. Basically, such a device would have to make decisions about which packets should be forwarded, and remove or add a source routing header as appropriate.

4.2.1   Packets from a TB Port

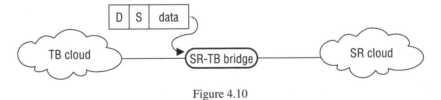

Figure 4.10

When a packet arrives from the transparent side, an SR-TB bridge must make a decision as to whether or not it should be forwarded. If the destination is an address that the TB portion of the SR-TB bridge has learned is on the port on which the packet was received, the SR-TB bridge will not forward the packet.

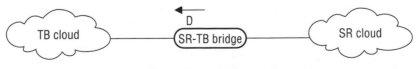

Figure 4.11

If a route to the destination address has been cached on the SR side of the bridge, the bridge will forward the packet, using the cached route, as a specifically routed packet.

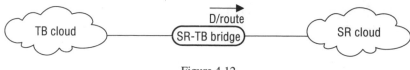

Figure 4.12

If no cache entry exists for the destination, the SR-TB bridge must forward the packet. It has several choices:

1. Forward the packet as an all paths explorer packet.

2. Forward the packet as a spanning tree explorer packet.

3. Cache the packet, go through a route discovery procedure, and forward the packet if/when a route is discovered to the destination.

4. Drop the packet (hope that the users will attribute the loss to congested LANs), go through some sort of route discovery procedure, and assume that the source will retransmit the packet if it was important. With luck, by the time the packet is retransmitted, a route to the destination may have been found.

The choice depends on how routes are being discovered, which has not been standardized. Two possible ways that the SR-TB bridge can learn a route to station S are:

1. Record the route from received specifically routed packets from S.

2. Choose routes based on received all paths explorer packets launched by S.

Once a route is stored, there is the problem of maintaining it. The SR-TB bridge does not necessarily know whether the packets it forwards along a route to station S actually reach that station. There can be no notification by the higher layer that a route is no longer working. Thus, there are only two possibilities for removing cache entries:

1. Remove the route to S if no traffic from S, with a route identical to the stored route, is received within a specified amount of time.

2. Remove the route to S periodically, regardless of received traffic.

Neither of these schemes is particularly satisfactory. If routes are deleted quickly, then the overhead increases greatly because of the need to rediscover routes frequently. Also, the more frequently routes change, the greater the probability of out-of-order packets. If the timers are very slow, then a nonfunctional route will persist for a long time.

4.2.2   Packets from an SR Port

To deal with packets from the SR side, each portion of the network interconnected with transparent bridges will be assigned a LAN number.

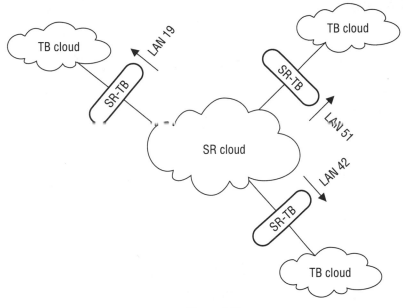

Figure 4.13

The SR-TB bridge can receive three types of packets:

1. Specifically routed

2. Spanning tree explorer

3. All paths explorer

The first two cases are fairly straightforward. If the SR-TB bridge receives a specifically routed packet whose LAN number indicates that it should be forwarded onto the TB side, the SR-TB bridge forwards the packet, first removing the source routing header. If the SR-TB bridge receives a spanning tree explorer packet, it removes the source routing header when forwarding to ports into the TB portions of the network.

The third case is more difficult. If the SR-TB bridge receives an all paths explorer packet, and the launcher of the packet is expecting replies from the packet's target, the SR-TB bridge must respond on behalf of the target station. If the SR-TB bridge has learned that the target exists on the TB port, it can respond by adding the LAN number of the TB port and replying with a specifically routed packet along the reverse path. If the SR-TB bridge has not learned the location of the target station, it could forward the all paths explorer packet, minus the source routing header, into the TB portion of the network and hope that the target station will transmit something in response. This would allow the SR-TB bridge to acquire a cache entry for the target, thereby enabling it to respond to a subsequent all paths explorer packet if one should arrive shortly.

The protocols for an SR-TB bridge are inherently confusing because the protocols for discovering routes have not been standardized. It is certainly in no way obvious that all strategies interwork.

4.2.3 Loops

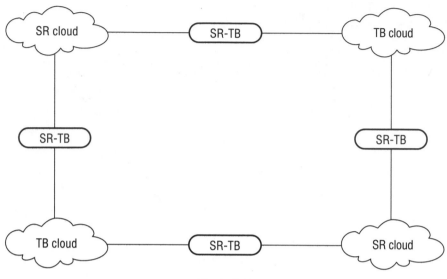

Figure 4.14

As Fig. 4.14 indicates, it is possible for SR-TB bridges to create a loop. It is essential that one of the following strategies be employed to prevent this:

1. The entire extended LAN (SR bridges, SR-TB bridges, and TB bridges) can participate in one instance of the spanning tree. If that is done, there is the danger that the spanning tree would configure itself by breaking up a cloud, and stations within the cloud would have to communicate via SR-TB bridges and clouds of different types, which would certainly degrade performance within the cloud.

2. The SR-TB bridges can run a separate instance of the spanning tree just among themselves. In this case, some SR-TB bridge will break the loop. The clouds will remain intact.

4.3   SRT Bridges

The strategy of having independent sections of the network tied together with source routing bridges and independent sections of the network tied together with transparent bridges, and then having those two types of sections interconnected with SR-TB bridges, proved unsatisfactory. SR-TB bridges have unsolvable problems (they function as "black holes" when their route caches have bad routes; their route find strategy must be compatible with all possible source routing end-system implementations). And the restriction that no LAN can contain both types of bridges proved unworkable when both the transparent bridge community and the source routing community wanted to bridge to FDDI. The dramatic resolution was that the source routing proponents came to the standards body with the SRT proposal, which outlawed pure source routing bridges. Source routing would be removed from the 802.5 standard and would instead be an optional "enhancement" to transparent bridges.

That means there are only two standard types of bridges:

1. Transparent bridges

2. SRT bridges, which are transparent bridges that are also capable of doing source routing

Once one understands transparent bridges and pure source routing bridges, SRT bridges are easy to understand. The SRT bridge handles packets with an RI field in the header exactly as a pure source routing bridge would, and it handles packets without an RI field exactly as a transparent bridge would.

Customers can build networks with an arbitrary mix of the two standard types of bridges (TB and SRT). If an end system wants, for whatever reason, to employ source routing, it attempts to find a route to the destination using that approach. If that fails, it can always communicate with the destination through the spanning tree using transparent packets.

There is one serious problem with an arbitrary mix of SRT and TB bridges. A station that goes to the trouble of attempting to find a route via source routing presumably does so to get a better route to the destination than the spanning tree path that it would otherwise use with transparent packets. If only some of the bridges are SRT bridges, then the source routes that can be found must go through whatever SRT bridges happen to be available. Given that constraint, it is possible for the best source routing path to be vastly inferior to the spanning tree path.

4.4   End-System Algorithms

The source routing standard has always left end-system operation "open," in the sense that there are many methods an end system could use to establish and maintain routes. The rationale for not specifying a single strategy is that all the suggested strategies have their pluses and minuses. No one strategy is better than all others according to all measures.

In my opinion, although flexibility might sometimes be a good thing, in this case it would be better if the standard chose a single algorithm. Otherwise, each individual end-system implementer is forced to consider various strategies, and it is not obvious that independently chosen strategies will interwork. It is important for two source routing end systems designed by different organizations to have compatible route find strategies.

If there is at least one strategy that works sufficiently well in all cases, then it ought to be standardized. It doesn't matter whether some other strategy might be marginally better in certain circumstances. If no strategy works adequately for all end systems, this should cast suspicion on the viability of source routing as a bridging mechanism.

This section discusses and compares the suggested strategies. It does not definitively answer the question, "How should my end system operate?" because the standards bodies have not specified end-system operation. Rather, this section raises the issues that should be considered when designing an end system capable of utilizing source routing.

The basic idea is that an end system keeps a cache of routes for destinations with which it is currently having conversations. If no route for a particular destination is in the cache, then the end system can employ some protocol to find a route or set of routes. If a route in the cache no longer works, and the end system discovers this, the end system can either attempt to find another route or use one of the alternate routes it has stored for that destination.

It is important that any strategy allow an end station that is capable of source routing to communicate with an end station that only uses transparent packets. It is also important to realize that even though these two end stations are capable of communicating via source routing, if the only paths between them involve at least one transparent-only bridge, the two stations must in that case communicate with transparent packets.

4.4.1   When to Find a Route

When should an end system try to find a route to another end system? One possibility is for the end system to attempt to find a route when it needs to transmit a packet to a destination for which it has no cache entry. Assuming that only some of the bridges and end systems have implemented source routing (but that it is mandatory for all end systems and bridges to have implemented transparent bridging), there will be some destinations that can only be reached via transparent bridging. Thus, it is important that any strategy:

1. Not declare a destination unreachable if source routing fails to find a route to the destination

2. Not continually (for instance, on every packet transmitted to the destination) attempt to find a source route to a destination for which no route is cached.

A natural time to attempt to find a route to a destination is when the end system wishes to transmit a packet to that destination, the cache contains no route to that destination, and the end system has not attempted to find a route to that destination very recently. Care must be taken to note the failure of recent attempts to find a route to that destination, so that the presence of stations only reachable via transparent bridging doesn't cause the source to continually search for routes.

If the communication process in the end system is connection-oriented, it might be natural to attempt to find a route every time a conversation is initiated. However, it might also be desirable to keep a cache of routes found on previous conversations rather than attempt to find a new route to a destination for which a route is still remembered.

If a connection is no longer working, it might be desirable to attempt to find a new route before declaring the connection down, since it is possible that the destination itself remains reachable but the previous route to that destination is no longer working.

Now suppose that a route had been found to destination D, but a much better route becomes available. Should an end system periodically attempt to find better routes, or should it only attempt to find a route if the currently cached route stops working?

Suppose that an end system S is having a conversation with destination D and then subsequently discovers a source route (or a new source route) to D. In this case, packets from S to D can be delivered out of order, since the ones transmitted on the previous source route (or transmitted transparently and therefore routed on the spanning tree) are traveling on a different route than the ones transmitted on the new source route. Depending on what applications are running, out-of-order packets might be a problem.

Suppose that a route is no longer working and the end system is using LLC type 1 (connectionless). There are three possible methods for making sure that the defunct route is removed from the cache:

1. Assuming that a connection-oriented transport layer is running in the end system, provide an interface between the transport layer and the process P that maintains the route cache to alert P to delete the cache entry when a connection breaks or fails to come up.

2. Delete a route cache entry for destination D if no traffic from D has been received on that route for some time.

3. Delete a route cache entry for destination D after a specified amount of time has elapsed since the cache entry was originally made, regardless of use.

The first possibility is reasonable, provided that:

- A connection-oriented transport layer is running.

- An interface exists between the transport layer and the process maintaining the route cache.

This strategy will not find a better route if one exists, nor will it work if the traffic flow is one-way, since the source would never know whether or not its packets were reaching the destination. Another instance in which the strategy would not work is if the route cache is being maintained in a different node than the actual source. This was the case, for instance, with the SR-TB bridge. That device needed to keep routes on behalf of all the end systems in the transparent extended LAN, and since there was no protocol from the end stations to the device to alert the device that a route was not working, the device would not know whether packets were failing to reach a particular destination.

The second strategy (deleting a cache entry if it is not periodically validated by receipt of traffic) must be used with care, since the route from S to D may not be the same as the route from D to S. A route to D must not be assumed to be working based on receipt of traffic from D if the traffic to and from D uses a different route. However, it would slow the end system down if it had to check the route received against the route in the cache every time a data packet was received. Also, this strategy will not find a better route. Rather, once the end system finds a route that works, no matter how suboptimal it might be, the end system will continue using that route.

The third strategy (deleting a cache entry periodically, regardless of use) must also be employed with some care, since it will cause the end system to find new routes in the middle of conversations, leading to the possibility of misordered packets. It is also difficult to select a reasonable timer value. If the value is short, then the network will have a lot of overhead due to frequent route discoveries. If the value is long, then a nonworking cache entry will cause traffic to a destination to "black hole" for an intolerably long time. Note that with the second strategy, a fairly short timer can be used, since as long as packets for a conversation on a working route arrive faster than the cache value, the cache entry will not be deleted and will persist for the duration of the conversation.

4.4.2   How to Find a Route

It would be desirable if the protocol for finding routes could distinguish between the following scenarios, which require differing strategies as to the advisability of retrying, using the source route, or communicating transparently:

1.   The destination might be down completely.

2.   The destination might be up, but reachable only via transparent bridging.

3.   The destination might be reachable by source routing, and the source routing paths by which the destination can be reached are much better than the spanning tree path.

4.   The destination might be reachable by source routing, but the source routing paths by which the destination can be reached are much worse than the spanning tree path.

Note that when source routing was an alternative to transparent bridging rather than an optional feature, a reasonable strategy was for an end system to first attempt to establish communication transparently (which would work if both stations were on the same LAN) and attempt to find a source route only if that failed. Once transparent bridging became mandatory, this same strategy would continue to work, but it would never attempt to find a source route (unless the destination was down or completely unreachable), because a destination that was reachable would always be reachable transparently.

4.4.2.1   Route Find Strategy 1

The source sends an all paths explorer packet to the destination. The destination receives multiple copies of the explorer packet and returns all these copies to the source as specifically routed packets, routed via the collected route (with the direction bit flipped). The destination does not store a route, nor does it modify its own route cache if it already has a route to the source. This strategy allows the source to choose the route.

source   destination

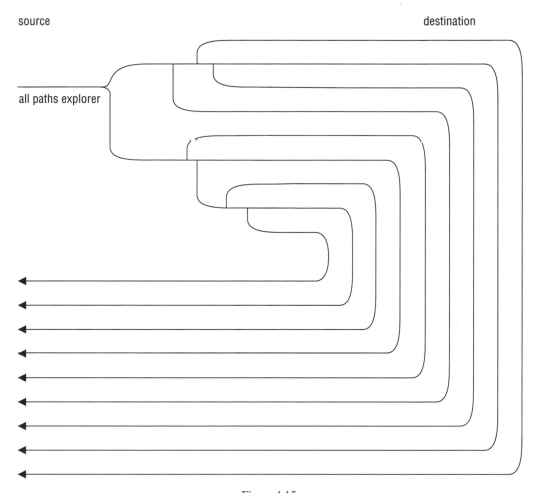

Figure 4.15

This scheme has its disadvantages, though. If a single all paths explorer packet generates X packets, this strategy generates $2X$ packets, since every copy of the all paths explorer that reaches the destination results in a packet from the destination to the source. Also, if the source is a client and the destination is a server with multiple clients, the many interrupts at the server for each client can be a performance problem.

There are several reasons why this scheme might fail to find a route: the destination might be down or reachable only via transparent packets, or the all paths explorer packet(s) and/or replies might have gotten lost in a congested network. The source must choose whether to try again with another all paths explorer, try to reach the destination with a transparent packet, or give up.

4.4.2.2 Route Find Strategy 2

Strategy 2 is the same as strategy 1, except that the source also sends a special "need route" packet, transparently, to the destination. The destination replies to the need route packet with another special packet, a "need route response."

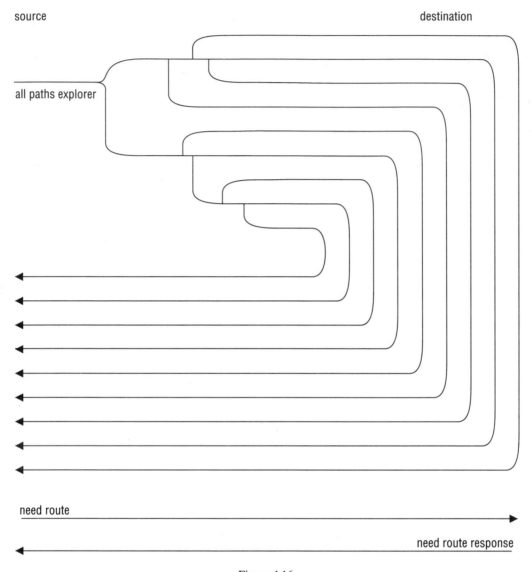

source   destination

all paths explorer

need route

need route response

Figure 4.16

The advantage of this scheme over scheme 1 is that it enables the source to quickly find out whether the destination is actually up.

The paper submitted as a contribution to 802.1 that made this recommendation suggested using a special packet but left it up to end-system implementers to independently invent compatible need route packets. This is a clear example of a case in which the standard must specify the exact details of end-station operation in order to enable end stations from different vendors to interoperate. Allowing each implementation the flexibility to define its own special packets just does not work.

4.4.2.3   Route Find Strategy 3

The source S sends a special need route packet, transparently, to the destination D. D responds with an all paths explorer packet. S chooses a route.

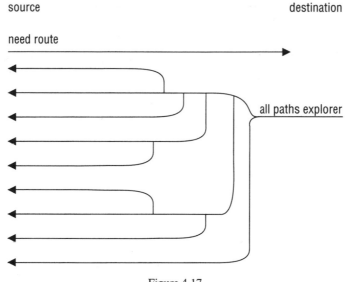

Figure 4.17

An advantage of this strategy over the first strategy is that it generates only half as much traffic. Like strategy 1, it allows the source to choose the route.

A disadvantage of this scheme is that it fails to find a route if the need route packet is launched during a time when the spanning tree is reconfiguring. It also fails to distinguish between a destination's being down and a destination's being reachable, but only via transparent packets. The need route packet must be one that the destination understands, regardless of whether the destination supports source routing.

4.4.2.4   Route Find Strategy 4

The fourth strategy is the same as strategy 3, but the destination should reply to a received need route packet with two packets:

1.   An all paths explorer packet

2.   A transparent need route reply

This strategy allows the source to discover the case in which the destination is reachable, but not via source routing.

This strategy requires that the destination transmit two packets as a result of receiving a single packet, which, in turn, requires that both source and destination implement compatible need route reply packets.

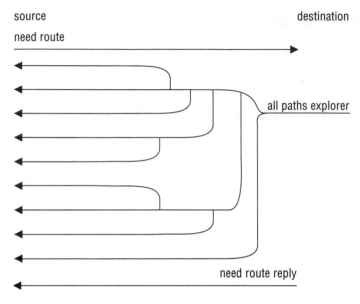

Figure 4.18

4.4.2.5 Route Find Strategy 5

The source transmits an all paths explorer packet. The destination chooses a route and replies with a single specifically routed packet, using that chosen route. The source stores the route from the received specifically routed packet.

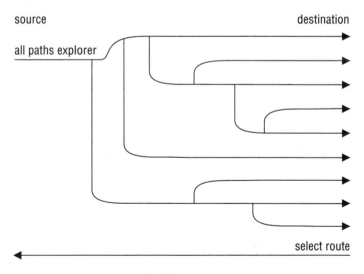

Figure 4.19

This scheme requires stations to store routes based on received specifically routed packets. It also burdens the destination with the task of selecting a route. It generates half as much traffic as strategy 1, though.

4.4.2.6 Route Find Strategy 6

Strategy 6 is the simplest one possible (and is incidentally what I would recommend). Always use transparent bridging. Do not maintain a route cache. This strategy offers the advantages of being simple, always working, and creating no overhead in the network due to route discovery. Its disadvantage is that if there exists a more optimal source route to a particular destination, the source will not attempt to find it. However, I believe it is impossible for a station to determine whether the route discovered through source routing is better or worse than the route used by the spanning tree. Another disadvantage of using simply transparent bridging is that the end station is not informed of the maximum packet size that can be used on the route to the destination, as it is with source routing. A third disadvantage is that data traffic cannot be spread over multiple paths, but all traffic instead traverses the spanning tree. However, I believe that these areas in which source routing offers advantages over transparent bridging do not warrant its increased complexity for the end stations or the bandwidth overhead required for discovering routes.

4.4.3 Route Discovery by the Destination

The various strategies presented in the preceding subsection do not specify how the destination finds a route. In some of the schemes, the destination sees the possible routes and could select and store one. But if it chooses a different path to reach the source than the source chose to get to the destination, then neither end system can be reassured, based on receiving packets from the other end system, that its cached route is correct.

Alternatively, the destination could wait until it has traffic to send to the source—at which point, it would reverse roles and obtain a route as the source. This scheme also results in asymmetric routes, and it generates a lot of traffic because both the source and the destination eventually issue all paths explorer packets.

Another possibility is for the destination to learn a route from received specifically routed packets. The advantage of this approach is that routes will be symmetric. A disadvantage is that the route discovery process must examine all incoming data packets. If the route cache already contains a route to end system S and a packet is received from S with a route that differs from the one in the route cache, the destination can either overwrite the cache entry or keep it.

4.4.4 Route Selection

Suppose that an end station receives multiple copies of an all paths explorer packet. What criteria should the station use to select a route? Again, the standard leaves it up to the end-station implementer. Some possibilities are:

1. Select the first packet received, on the theory that it traveled on the fastest path.

2. Select the one that indicates a path with the maximum packet size.

3. Select the one with the fewest hops.

4. Select some combination of the above (e.g., select the packet that arrived first, from among the ones with at least a certain packet size; or select the one that has the fewest hops, from among the ones that arrived within a certain amount of time).

5. Select the most recently received route. (Note: I've heard of an implementation that employed this strategy. Hint: It is a bad idea. Why?)

4.5 Source Routing Versus Transparent Bridging

Suppose that you were on a standards body evaluating the technical merits of source routing versus transparent bridging or that you were making a decision as to which scheme to adopt in your own network. What sorts of criteria could be used?

4.5.1 Bandwidth Overhead

The number of paths in a network is exponential. Theoretically, an all paths explorer packet will generate a copy of itself for each path through the network. Thus, theoretically, the number of copies of one all paths explorer packet that will be generated is exponential. Exponential grows very fast, especially with rich connectivity.

Basically, every time there is a choice (if many bridges are on a LAN or a bridge has many ports), the number of packets is multiplied by the number of choices. The maximum route length is 14 route designators, but there are actually 26 choice points in a path. (Each route designator contains both a LAN number and a bridge number, which is why there are about twice as many choice points as route designators. The reason there are not 28 choice points in a route is that the first item is the source's LAN, which is fixed. The last item is the bridge portion of the final route designator, which is blank.) When an all paths explorer packet is transmitted on a LAN, all the bridges on that LAN take a copy. Each bridge then generates a copy of its copy for each additional port to which the bridge attaches.

The number of packets spawned as a result of a single endnode's attempting to start a conversation with a single other endnode is on the order of the average number of bridges on each LAN to the 13th power multiplied by the average number of ports (more than two) on each bridge raised to the 13th power. Even if the destination can be reached with a route of length 2, once an all paths explorer packet is launched, there is no way to stop it until it has spawned all its copies.

In my opinion, this exponential overhead, invoked every time any endnode wishes to communicate with any other endnode, is a fatal flaw of source routing. In small topologies that are pretty much just a tree, with bridges that have only two ports, the exponential factor might not be too serious. But some people have raised the idea of building bridges with hundreds of ports. If there were two such bridges in a network, the proliferation of all paths explorer packets would be very serious.

> It would be an interesting exercise to determine the actual behavior of source routing in a richly connected topology. The potential number of packets is sufficiently astronomical that the vast majority will get lost. If the first few packets got through and the remainder got lost, the performance would not be particularly bad, since in general, the first few will find better routes than later copies. However, when the network capacity is exceeded and most copies of an all paths explorer packet are being lost, data traffic and initial copies of all paths explorer packets for other station pairs will also be lost in the congestion.

Source routing bridges also use extra bandwidth because the headers must be larger, but that's hardly worth mentioning given the exponential proliferation of explorer packets.

Transparent bridges do not make optimal use of bandwidth either (they waste bandwidth by using only a subset of the topology, by not using optimal routes, and by forwarding packets needlessly before cache entries are established), but their bandwidth waste is not nearly as spectacular as with source routing.

4.5.2   Configuration Ease

Transparent bridges are truly "plug and play." Although there are plenty of parameters a network manager can use to fine-tune performance in a specific situation, there is no need to modify any parameters unless desired.

In contrast, source routing requires that every LAN be assigned a number and that every bridge be configured both with the LAN number for each of its ports and with a 4-bit bridge number for each pair of LANs it connects (although establishing restrictions on the topologies might enable a bridge to have only a single 4-bit number that would be unique for each pair of LANs it connects). Misconfiguration can cause problems such as loops or severe duplication of data packets.

4.5.3   Universality

Source routing requires support in the endnodes. Thus, any endnodes built without source routing designed in would be unable to have their packets routed through a source routing bridge. Such stations would still be able to communicate with other stations on their local LAN but could not communicate with any stations on remote LANs.

On the other hand, transparent bridges are not completely transparent, especially when used to connect different types of LANs. The packet size problem can be solved if the network manager configures all the endnodes to use the smallest maximum packet size allowed by any of the LANs. Alternatively, some sort of clever procedure in the end stations can be used to determine the best packet size. One such procedure employs the priority field on FDDI to signal that somewhere along the path between the source and the destination, the packet is bridged through an 802.3 LAN. Although admittedly, such a procedure is an inelegant hack, it works, is useful, and is deployed in some FDDI stations to enable them to use large packet sizes when possible.

The source routing protocol does a fair job of solving the packet size problem, since when a route is discovered, the maximum packet size on the path is discovered as well. It is not necessarily easy to make use of the information about the maximum packet size on a route. This requires that the low-layer source routing process be able to share this information with the transport layer process, which makes decisions about packet sizes. If a source route changes in the middle of a transport connection, many end station implementations would not be able to change the packet size.

4.5.4   Cost/Performance of Bridges

It was originally asserted that source routing bridges would be cheaper/simpler/higher-performance than transparent bridges. Even if this were true, the number of endnodes in a network is vastly larger than the number of bridges, so an increase in a bridge's cost in order to ensure its adequate performance would likely be negligible compared to the cost of the network as a whole. Since source routing requires more complicated endnodes, it might increase the cost of the endnodes. When the additional endnode cost is multiplied by the number of endnodes, the resulting figure would probably far outweigh any increase in the cost of the bridge.

However, implementations of transparent bridges proved that transparent bridges with adequate performance could be built at a reasonable cost. People have stopped arguing that transparent bridges would be more expensive or slower.

Homework

1. Suppose that source routing were not allowed to use the multicast bit in the source address to flag that the LAN header contains the routing information field. What other encoding could have been used in order to signal that the header contains the extra field? The encoding must be such that packets emitted by stations that have not implemented source routing will not accidentally get parsed as if they contained the RI field.

2. Assuming that the maximum packet lifetime is X seconds in an extended LAN, what strategy can an end system use to ensure that packets to a destination will not arrive out of order, even if in the middle of a conversation, the source changes source routes or switches from using transparent packets to using a source route?

3. How can it be possible for a destination to be reachable by source routing but for the source routing path to be much worse than the spanning tree path?

4. Why is it a bad strategy for an end station that receives an all paths explorer packet giving a route from D to routinely overwrite the existing cache entry for D with the newly received route?

5. Is it a good or bad idea for SRT bridges to learn the location of the source address, and forward based on the learned location of the destination address, in each of the following cases?

   a. Spanning tree explorer packets

   b. Specifically routed packets

   c. All paths explorer packets

6. How many copies of a spanning tree explorer packet (approximately) would arrive on a typical LAN in a topology in which every LAN had k bridges attached and every bridge had j ports? How many copies would arrive on the LAN from which the source station launched the packet?
   Now answer the preceding questions for an all paths explorer packet.
   Now assume that $k = 4$ and $j = 3$. What is the actual number of packets?

7. The contention is (as of the April 2, 1990, draft of source routing) that each bridge requires only a single "parallel bridge number." Assuming a topology in which

   a. between any pair of LANs, there are never more than 15 bridges, and

   b. no bridge has more than one port onto the same LAN,

   is it always possible to assign each bridge a single 4-bit parallel bridge number, such that no two bridges between the same pair of LANs are ever assigned the same parallel bridge number? Prove that a single parallel bridge number per bridge will suffice, even if the bridge connects to multiple LANs; or show a topology in which (even though there are never more than 15 bridges between any two LANs) it is impossible to assign a single number per bridge without having multiple bridges between the same pair of LANs assigned identical numbers.

   What happens if a bridge is allowed to have multiple ports on a LAN?

   Assuming that the answer to the preceding questions is that it's not possible in all topologies to get by with a single bridge number, suppose that your job were to document which topologies will work with a single bridge number and also explain how to assign bridge numbers. What would you do?

8. What problems can arise if two LANs are given the same LAN number?

9. What problems can arise if two bridges between the same pair of LANs are given the same bridge number?

10. What problems can arise if bridges don't agree about the LAN number? (i.e., some bridges on a particular LAN think its LAN number is X, whereas others think it is Y.)

11. Since bridges check whether the output LAN already appears in the collected route before forwarding an all paths explorer, is it necessary for bridges to also check for duplicate LAN numbers when forwarding specifically routed packets?

12. Write code in your favorite language to handle forwarding of a specifically routed packet (make sure to take into account the direction bit and checking for the output LAN's appearing multiple times). Compare the processing required to route a specifically routed packet with that required to route a transparent packet (taking into account the need to efficiently scan a station learning cache of 8,000 or so station addresses).

13. What happens if an end system launches a specifically routed packet with extra hops following the destination LAN and/or extra hops preceding the source LAN?

14. What procedure can a bridge B follow to determine whether there is another bridge between the same pair of LANs as B whose bridge number is identical to B's? If B has n ports, how many times would B need to carry out this procedure?

15. In a network in which only some of the bridges support the source routing option (but all of the bridges support transparent bridging), compare the following two end-system strategies:

    a. The end system sends every packet transparently.

    b. The end system sends every packet using spanning tree explorer packets.

    Consider such factors as destination reachability and bridge forwarding speed.

16. Suppose that a network is interconnected with some SRT bridges and some TB bridges. Suppose, too, that stations A and B are both capable of using source routing and that they have successfully found a source route connecting them. As pointed out earlier in the chapter, it is possible for the source route to be much worse than the spanning tree path. Is there any way the stations can compare the spanning tree path with the source route they found? (Hint: Is the use of spanning tree explorer packets guaranteed to tell them the spanning tree path?)

17. Design several plausible end-system strategies for operation in a network with a mix of TB and SRT bridges and a mix of transparent and source-routing-capable end stations. Can you design two plausible end-station schemes such that an end station using one scheme will fail to establish communication with an end station using a different scheme?

18. In the following topology, there are two extended LANs interconnected with pure source routing bridges and an extended LAN interconnected with transparent bridges. An SR-TB bridge connects the SR clouds to the TB cloud.

Figure 4.20

Can the LAN numbers assigned to the LANs in the SR cloud on the left overlap with the LAN numbers assigned to the LANs in the SR cloud on the right?

Chapter 5
Network Layer Service Interface

5.1   What Is the Network Layer?

A network is made up of a bunch of packet switches connected through various types of technology such as point-to-point links or LANs (see Fig. 5.1). I'll call a packet switch a *router*, although other names are in use, including:

1. Intermediate system, or IS (used by the ISO).

2. Interface message processor, or IMP (used by ARPANET).

3. Gateway (used by the IP community).

The purpose of a network is to enable users who attach their equipment to the network to transmit data to and receive data from other users' equipment. This is similar to the telephone network, which allows you to attach your phone to the network in order to communicate with other users who have attached their phones to the network. I'll call the equipment attached to the network an *endnode*, which is commonly used terminology, although, again, other names are in use, including:

1. Host (used by the IP community)

2. Data terminal equipment, or DTE (used by the X.25 standard)

3. End system, or ES (used by the ISO)

Thus, as far as an endnode is concerned, the network is one big "cloud" to which it attaches, thereby enabling itself to communicate with other endnodes that are also attached to the cloud (see Fig. 5.2).

Additionally, the term *node* is often used to mean both endnodes and routers.

5.1.1   Network Service Types

There are two models for how a network should look to the endnodes. One model is known as *connectionless* (sometimes called *datagram*). In this model, an endnode

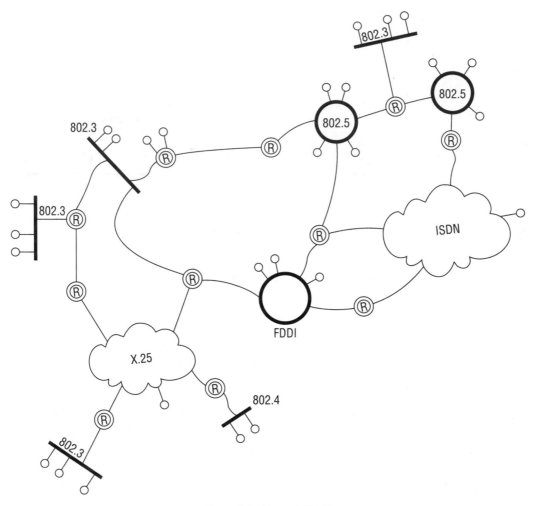

Figure 5.1   General WAN

transmits a piece of data to the network, together with the address to which the data should be delivered. The network does its best to deliver the data, but with some probability of the data's getting lost, duplicated, or damaged (the data might become altered). Also, each item of data (usually referred to as a "packet") is independently routed, and the network does not guarantee that the packets will be kept in order, meaning that if packet 1 is given to the network, followed by packet 2, packet 2 might be delivered before packet 1.

The connectionless model is similar to the postal system, in which each letter is deposited into the system with a complete address; there is a high probability of the postal service's delivering the letter to the destination, although there is some probability of the letter's being lost or damaged; and a letter posted on Monday might get delivered after a letter posted on Tuesday, even if both were posted from the same location and addressed to the same destination.

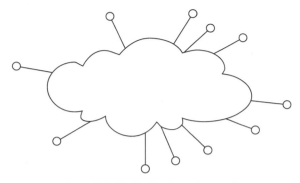

Figure 5.2   Endnode view of network

The other model is known as *connection-oriented* (sometimes called *virtual circuit*). In this model, an endnode first informs the network that it wishes to start a conversation with some other endnode. The network then notifies the destination that a conversation is requested, and the destination accepts or refuses. This is similar to using the telephone system. The caller informs the telephone system of the wish to start a conversation by dialing the telephone number of the destination. After the destination's telephone number has been dialed, the telephone system establishes a path, reserves whatever resources are necessary, contacts the destination (by ringing its phone), and after the call is accepted, the conversation can take place. I use the term *call* to mean the virtual circuit set up by the network and the term *conversation* to mean the information flowing on the call, but the distinction is not important because there is a one-to-one correspondence between conversations and calls.

Often, a connection-oriented service has the following characteristics:

1. The network guarantees that all packets will be delivered in order, without loss or duplication. If anything occurs to prevent the network from keeping those guarantees, it disconnects the call.

2. A single path is established for the call, and all data follows that path. If anything along the path causes the path to cease working, the network disconnects the call.

3. The network guarantees a certain minimal amount of bandwidth when it connects a call, and this bandwidth is reserved for the duration of the call. If the endnodes participating in the call do not utilize those resources (they send less data than the bandwidth reserved for them), the resources are wasted.

4. If a network becomes overly utilized, future call requests are refused (like a fast busy signal in the U.S. phone system).

The ISO never agreed on a service model. Thus, the ISO network layer designers broke into two independent camps. The connection-oriented camp adopted CCITT's (Comité Consultatif Internationale de Telegraphiqué et Telephoniqué) connection-oriented X.25 protocol. The connectionless camp designed CLNP ("connectionless network protocol" ISO 8473). The IP community has always been in the connectionless camp.

The distinction between a connection-oriented network and a connectionless network is not always clear. Some examples of service models that fall somewhere between the two types include:

1. A network in which a call-setup procedure is required before a conversation takes place and all packets are routed on the route established during the call setup, but there is no guarantee as to bandwidth or packet loss.

    The purpose of designing a network this way is to enable the call setup to assign a small number to the call, which, in turn, enables routers to make the forwarding decision by performing a simple table lookup rather than by having to parse a general network layer header and deal with a large network layer address. The network would still offer datagram service, in the sense of allowing packet loss and providing no bandwidth or latency guarantees.

2. A network in which a call-setup procedure is required before a conversation takes place, but only for the purpose of synchronizing an end-to-end connection between the first router and the final router. Packets are routed independently, but lost and reordered packets are recovered by handshaking between the first and final routers (using a protocol similar to a transport layer protocol), so that the packets as delivered to the destination endnode are in order, and no packets are lost. No bandwidth guarantees are provided.

    The purpose of designing a network this way is to support a connection-oriented interface. Not providing the uniform service normally associated with such an interface allows network resources to be shared.

3. A network in which an explicit call-setup protocol is not required, but routers initiate a call-setup protocol on behalf of the endnodes when a new source-destination pair is encountered.

    The purpose of this type of network design is to support a connectionless interface to the endnodes while allowing small numbers to be assigned to conversations, so that intermediate routers can make quick forwarding decisions.

Is one type of service better than the other? Connection-oriented proponents argue that:

1. The network is being used primarily for file transfer and remote terminal protocols. Both of these applications require that packets remain in order and cannot tolerate lost packets. Providing this service is complicated, and it is better to off-load this complexity into the network and out of the endnodes.

2. Connection-oriented service enables faster routers to be built. During call-setup time, the complicated route calculation and address lookup can take place, and calls can be assigned small identifiers. Routers can then do a simple table lookup based on the small identifier when forwarding data packets.

3. If a network accepts a call, it is duty-bound to provide reasonable bandwidth. It is better to lock out new calls than to degrade the quality of service on current calls.

4. It is easier for the transport layer to deal with uniform service from the network. For instance, if the network routes each packet independently (as is usually done in a connectionless network), it is difficult for the transport layer to calculate the round-trip delay to the destination (which is necessary in order to decide when a packet needs to be retransmitted because an ack has not yet been received from the destination).

   Another example is packet size. It is desirable to send the largest packet possible, but different link types allow different maximum packet sizes. The maximum-size packet that can be transmitted on a route is equal to the smallest maximum packet size allowed on any of the links along the route. In a connectionless network, packets might get routed along routes with different packet sizes. In (most) connection-oriented networks, a single path is used for all packets, and the endnodes can be informed of the maximum packet size along the path.

5. Interfacing to a connection-oriented network layer is easier than interfacing to a connectionless network layer because a connection-oriented network layer eliminates the need for a complicated transport layer.

Connectionless proponents argue that:

1. Most connection-oriented networks are built in such a way that if anything along a call's route fails, the network hangs up the call automatically, since it can no longer determine which packets have reached the destination and which have not, and it may be unable to recover packets "in the pipe" at the time of the failure. For this reason, a full-service transport layer is required even though the network layer claims reliable delivery. Therefore, rather than doing the endnode a favor, the connection-oriented network is only duplicating effort.

2. Interfacing to a connectionless network layer is simpler than interfacing to a connection-oriented network layer, even when the need for a fully general transport layer is taken into account. But especially if the first argument is correct (that a full-service transport layer is required anyway), then it is clear that the network layer code in an endnode is vastly simpler when the endnode is attached to a connectionless network layer.

3. Many applications—in particular, those now in the design stage—do not require sequential delivery of packets. For those applications, lost packets can be tolerated. One example is packet voice, where a modest percentage of lost packets can be tolerated, but delayed packets are useless and might as well be dropped. A connection-oriented network will sometimes delay otherwise deliverable packets because it will refuse to deliver a packet until an earlier lost packet has been recovered.

   Another example of an application that does not require sequenced delivery of packets is an alternative design for file transfer. Currently still in the experimental stage, this style of file transfer protocol seems promising and more appropriate for high-bandwidth technology. Each packet contains enough information so that the data can immediately be put into the proper place on disk when received by the destination. After a file transfer is completed, the application can determine which blocks are missing and specifically request them. The order in which packets are received is irrelevant.

4. Network traffic is inherently bursty, so it is wasteful to reserve resources. If an application tends to send data, then remain quiet for some time, then send more data, the bandwidth reserved for that endnode will be wasted when the endnode is not transmitting.

   File transfer is usually assumed not to be bursty. However, if the transmitter is a busy time-sharing system, the file transfer traffic can be quite bursty. Also, if bandwidth is really large, most file transfers would appear as bursts of short duration.

   Terminal traffic is universally regarded as being very bursty.

   Assuming that most traffic is bursty, it is better to budget resources optimistically and allow network resources to be shared. If too many users request resources simultaneously, data will be dropped. However, this is not fatal because any application requiring loss-free service will be using a transport layer protocol that will retransmit lost data.

5. It is better to allow all users onto the network and have service degrade equally for everyone rather than allow some lucky users onto the network and completely lock out others.

6. For many applications, particularly client-server request-response applications, maintaining state at the server (or at the router that services the server) regarding all current conversations would be difficult, since the server might have hundreds or thousands of clients.

In terms of today's technology—where "connection-oriented" means X.25 (see the next section)—I am in the connectionless camp. However, to build much higher-speed networks, it will probably become necessary for route-caching techniques to be used, such that some hybrid of connectionless and connection-oriented service would be optimal. Most likely, routes would be set up before a conversation takes place (which is similar to connection-oriented service), but the data transfer phase of the conversation, although restricted to that route, would be datagram in the sense that the network would not attempt to retransmit lost packets or to put packets back in order if they were misordered (although misordering would be very unlikely if a single path were used and the links themselves were sequential).

   Note that a connectionless network layer is similar to a LAN (with LLC type 1). Source and destination addresses are added to the data, which is then transmitted onto the network, and the network delivers the data to the destination with best-effort service.

5.2   X.25: An Example of Connection-Oriented Service

X.25, which was designed by CCITT, was adopted (except for very minor modifications) by the ISO as its connection-oriented network layer, with the name "ISO 8208."

X.25 does not specify how to build a connection-oriented service. Instead, it specifies the interface between an endnode (known in X.25 as a "DTE") and a router (known in X.25 as a "DCE").

In this section, I discuss what the interface looks like to the endnode. In section 9.9, I discuss implementation issues involved in building routers that support X.25 service.

The X.25 standard comes in three levels:

1. *Physical level:* This specifies the physical layer, including the size and shape of the connector, what voltage levels appear on each pin, what the signaling on the pins means, etc. It is not really relevant to network layer issues.

2. *Link level:* This specifies a data link layer protocol, including how to delimit the start and end of packets, number packets, acknowledge them, enforce flow control, etc. The link level, like the physical layer, is not extremely relevant to network layer issues.

3. *Packet level:* This really is the network layer interface, which is described in the balance of this section.

5.2.1   The Basic Idea

The service as seen by the DTE involves the ability to carry on multiple simultaneous "calls" over a single link to a DCE. Each call must first be established, then data can flow in both directions between the endpoints of the call, after which the call must be cleared.

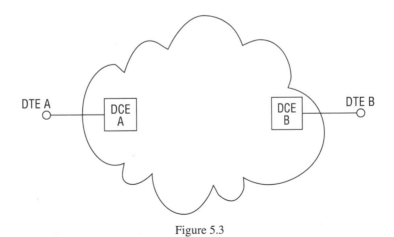

Figure 5.3

From DTE A's viewpoint, there are three ways to establish a call:

1. DTE A can initiate the call by informing DCE A of its desire to place the call (informing DCE A of the destination's *DTE address*—for instance, "DTE B"). This is similar to dialing a telephone, where the telephone number corresponds to the destination's DTE address. A call of this sort is known as an *SVC* (*switched virtual circuit*).

2. DCE A can notify DTE A that some other DTE—for instance, DTE B—has asked to place a call to DTE A (similar to having your telephone ring). This form of call is also an SVC. From DTE A's viewpoint, this is known as an *incoming call*.

3. The call can be permanently up. This is known in X.25 as a PVC (permanent virtual circuit). PVCs are set up administratively. Data flows on a PVC in the same way as on the first two types of calls, but call setup and call clearing are not done, or at least are not visible to the DTEs.

Each call is assigned a *virtual circuit number* upon setup. This number is only of significance between the DTE and the DCE to which it is attached. The DTE that is the other endpoint of the call will typically associate a different virtual circuit number with that call. Each data packet carries the virtual circuit number in the packet header rather than the source and destination DTE addresses. This is desirable, because the virtual circuit number is generally shorter than a DTE address, and it is easier for the routers to make a high-speed forwarding decision based on a shorter field.

X.25 provides *multiplexing*, which means that multiple calls can be taking place simultaneously over the same connection to the DCE. Thus, for instance, there might be several processes within the source DTE, each of which might be carrying on multiple conversations with different destinations. Each call will have its own virtual circuit number. When the DCE gives the DTE a data packet, it contains a virtual circuit number so that the DCE can identify the call to which the packet applies. Likewise, when the DTE gives the DCE a data packet, the virtual circuit number in the header informs the DCE of the call to which the packet applies.

Again, X.25 only specifies what happens between a DTE and its local DCE. In order for a network to provide X.25 service, there must be protocols and algorithms between the DCEs so that paths can be established, data can be transmitted, etc. However, these protocols are not standardized. They are proprietary to an individual X.25 network.

5.2.2   Virtual Circuit Numbers

Virtual circuit numbers are actually 12 bits long. In specifications of X.25, however, packet formats are written out byte-by-byte. This makes it pictorially awkward to represent a 12-bit field. So the virtual circuit number is actually written as though it consisted of two fields, which, concatenated together, form the virtual circuit number. One field, which the standard calls the "logical channel group number," is 4 bits long; the other, which the standard calls the "logical channel number," is 8 bits long. For brevity, I'll refer to the concatenation of the two fields as the *call number*.

By convention, call number 0 is reserved for control packets (for instance, restart packets and diagnostic packets) that refer to all virtual circuits. Then, a block of call numbers is reserved for PVCs. Next, a block is reserved for incoming calls (calls for which the DCE must assign a call number and notify the attached DTE that a remote

DTE is "ringing its phone"). Next, a block is reserved for either outgoing or incoming calls. Next, a block is reserved for outgoing calls—i.e., calls initiated by the DTE and for which the DTE must assign a call number. This convention avoids a *call collision*, which occurs when the DTE decides to initiate a call and chooses call number X, and almost simultaneously, the DCE receives notification of an incoming call for the DTE and chooses call number X to alert the DTE to the incoming call. The fact that the call numbers reserved for outgoing calls are different from the call numbers reserved for incoming calls prevents call collisions.

5.2.3 Call Setup

Assume that DTE A wishes to converse with DTE B. DTE A chooses a call number— say, X—which is not in use for any of DTE A's currently ongoing calls. DTE A issues a *call request* packet to DCE A. The format of a call request packet is:

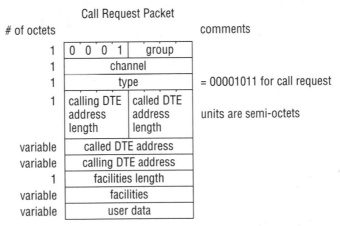

Figure 5.4

DTE A writes its own address into the **calling DTE address field**, DTE B's address into the **called DTE address field**, and X into the call number field (actually, it puts 4 bits of the call number into **group** and the remaining 8 bits into **channel**).

By some mechanism not specified in the standard, DCE A informs DCE B that DTE A wishes to talk to DTE B. DCE B chooses a call number—say, Y—that is not in use for any of DTE B's currently ongoing calls and issues an *incoming call* packet to DTE B. The incoming call packet has the same format as the call request packet. The call number will (almost always) be different, because the call number in the incoming call packet will have been selected by DCE B. (Only by coincidence would DCE B choose the same call number as DTE A had chosen, and this would never happen if all DCEs used the same convention as to which portion of the numbers the DTEs were allowed to assign [outgoing calls] and which portion of the numbers the DCEs were allowed to assign [incoming calls].) Other fields might differ as well. For instance, the packet size in the facilities might be different because the packet size between the source DTE and the source DCE might differ from the packet size between the destination DCE and the destination DTE.

If DTE B accepts the call, it sends a *call accepted* packet to DCE B. The call number on the call accepted packet transmitted by DTE B will be the same as the call number received from DCE B in the incoming call packet.

When DCE B receives the call accepted packet, it somehow (in a manner not specified by the standard) informs DCE A, which notifies DTE A with a *call connected* packet, which is identical to the call accepted packet, but with X (the call number that was chosen by DTE A) rather than Y (the call number that was assigned by DCE B and that DTE B associates with the call).

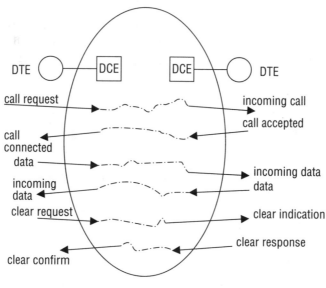

Figure 5.5

5.2.4   Data Transfer

Once the call has been established, data exchange is *full-duplex*, which means that data can flow simultaneously in both directions.

Data packets have two formats. One format has 3-bit sequence numbers; the other has 7-bit sequence numbers. With some providers, the choice of 7-bit or 3-bit sequence number is made at the time of subscription. With others, the choice is made on a per-call basis. It is not possible to switch between 3- and 7-bit sequence numbers in the middle of a call.

The standard allows the DTEs to use the **Q** bit for any purpose. A data packet transmitted with the Q bit set will be delivered to the destination DTE with the Q bit set, and it is up to the application running in the DTEs to interpret the meaning of the Q bit. (For those who are curious, "Q" stands for "qualified.")

The **M** bit defines whether "more data follows." It is used to transmit a packet larger than the maximum packet size allowable on the DTE/DCE link. When a DTE wishes to transmit a packet larger than the maximum size allowable on the link to its DCE, the

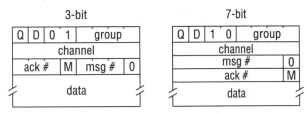

Figure 5.6

DTE breaks the packet into maximum-allowable-size pieces and sets the M bit on each piece except the last.

By the time the data reaches the destination DTE, it may be fragmented still more if the destination DTE/DCE interface has an even smaller maximum packet size. The destination DTE receives data packet after data packet, finally receiving one with the M bit clear. It then treats the entire collection of data as if it were a single large packet transmitted from the source DTE.

The **D** bit determines whether an acknowledgment means that the packet was received by the destination DTE or just by the DCE (and it is network-specific whether an acknowledgment when the D bit is 0 indicates that the packet was received by the source DCE or by the destination DCE).

When a DTE wishes to transmit data on a particular call, it sends a data packet, marked with the call number and with a sequence number, which increments for each packet on that call. If a DTE is transmitting data for several calls simultaneously, the sequence numbers for packets on different calls are unrelated.

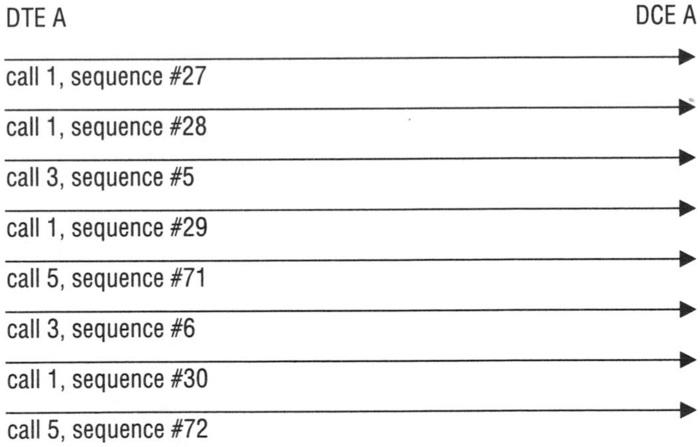

DTE A   DCE A

call 1, sequence #27

call 1, sequence #28

call 3, sequence #5

call 1, sequence #29

call 5, sequence #71

call 3, sequence #6

call 1, sequence #30

call 5, sequence #72

Figure 5.7

On a particular call, it is possible for a single data packet to have one sequence number when it is transmitted by the source DTE and a different sequence number when it is received by the destination DTE.

First, assume that the application's data size can be carried within the packet size allowed by the DCE/DTE link at both the source and the destination. In this case, each packet transmitted by the source DTE will be delivered as a single packet to the destination DTE.

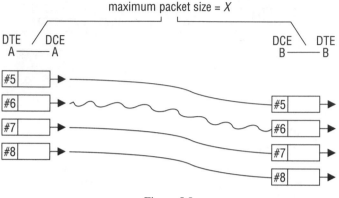

Figure 5.8

Now assume that the application's data size is bigger than the packet size at the destination DCE/DTE link. In this case, each packet transmitted by the source will result in several packets delivered to the destination, with every packet except the final one in each group having the M bit set. When the destination DTE receives a packet with the M bit clear, it transmits the data it has received on that call (since the last packet with a clear M bit) to the application as a complete packet.

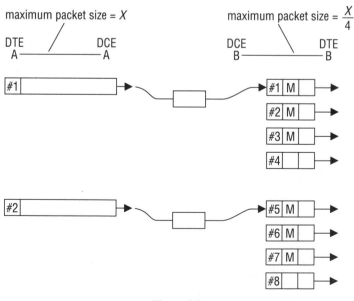

Figure 5.9

If the maximum packet size used by the source DCE/DTE link is smaller than the packet size used by the application, something similar happens, except it is the source DTE that transmits a sequence of packets to the source DCE, with all but the final one having the M bit set.

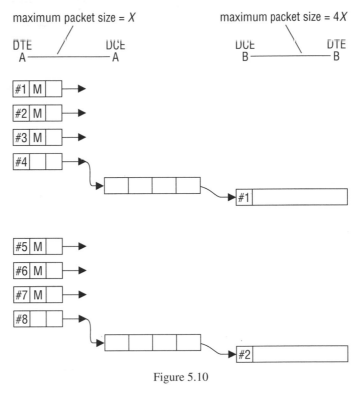

Figure 5.10

In general, if the maximum packet size at the source and destination DCE/DTE links differs, a data packet will have a different sequence number when transmitted by the source DTE than when received by the destination DTE.

An interesting problem arises because the standard does not allow the M bit to be set if the packet is not full (except if the D bit is set—see homework problem 3). Thus, if the DCE/DTE link allows a certain packet size—say, 1,024 bytes—a packet must contain 1,024 bytes if the M bit is set.

This creates a curious complication when the source DCE/DTE link has a smaller maximum packet size than the destination DCE/DTE link. When the source DTE transmits a sequence of packets, each with the M bit set, the destination DCE cannot transmit the data to the destination DTE until it has enough data for a maximum-size packet. Thus, for instance, if the maximum packet size on the source DCE/DTE link is one-eighth the maximum packet size on the destination DCE/DTE link, and the packet size used by the application is at least as large as the size on the destination DCE/DTE link, the destination DCE must hold onto eight packets with the M bit set in order to accumulate enough data to transmit a maximum-size packet with the M bit set to the destination DTE.

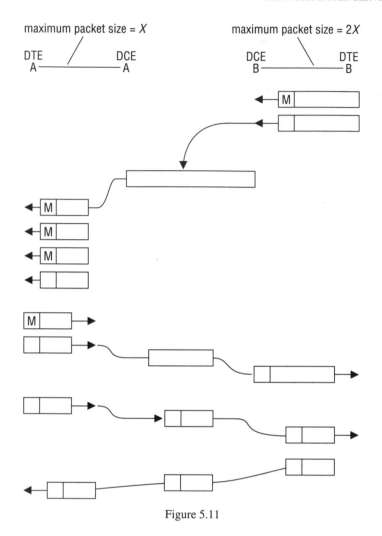

Figure 5.11

5.2.5   Flow Control

In addition to a message sequence number **(msg #)**, each data packet contains an **ack #**, whose purpose is to acknowledge received data. Assume a call between DTE A and DTE B. When DTE A transmits a packet to DTE B, it might have sequence number k when received by DCE A. When DTE A receives from DCE A a packet that originated from DTE B, it will have a totally unrelated sequence number—say, j. If DTE A has just received sequence number j from DCE A on that call, and DTE A is about to transmit data with sequence number k on the same call, it will set the **msg #** field in the data packet to k and the **ack #** field to j.

The protocol is symmetric. When DCE A is transmitting data to DTE A, it also transmits a msg # and ack # in each data packet.

The ack # field serves two purposes:

1. It acknowledges that the data packet with the indicated sequence number (as well as all previous ones) was received correctly.

2. It indicates that the receiver is ready to receive data packets beyond the indicated sequence number.

If the receiver does not have data to transmit and simply needs to acknowledge received data, it transmits a *receive ready* packet, which contains the sequence number of the packet being acknowledged.

Suppose that the DTE cannot receive more data on that call. Suppose, too, that the window for the call is w—i.e., the transmitter is permitted to transmit w packets beyond the last one acknowledged. Assume that an application is transmitting data to a user's terminal and the user has typed "pause," gotten distracted, and gone to lunch. If the DTE has acknowledged sequence number j, either in the ack # of a data packet or in the acknowledgment sequence number included in a *receive ready* message, then the DCE will transmit up to sequence number $j + w$ and then not send any more data on that call until the user returns from lunch and types "resume."

There is another mechanism for flow control in X.25 besides just refusing to acknowledge further packets. A node (DTE or DCE) can transmit a *receive not ready* packet, which includes the sequence number, j, of the most recently received data packet. This indicates that packet j was received correctly but that the DTE cannot receive additional data packets. Later, the node can transmit a *receive ready* packet, with sequence number j. If the node transmits data after the *receive not ready*, it will have j in the ack # field, which in this case, is not the same as a receive ready with j in the msg # field. It does not give the transmitter permission to transmit beyond sequence number j. After a receive not ready has been sent, the only way to give permission to transmit more data is to send a *receive ready*.

The receive not ready mechanism really does not make a lot of sense. Suppose that the receiver sends a receive not ready with sequence number j but then gets sequence number $j + 1$, since the transmitter transmitted sequence number $j + 1$ before the receive not ready arrived. If the transmitter assumes that the receiver has discarded $j + 1$ and therefore retransmits $j + 1$ after it gets a receive ready, then the receiver might notice that it has gotten a duplicate of sequence number $j + 1$, which would cause it to reset the call (hang up).

The only way this mechanism can work properly is if the receiver realizes that an acknowledgment of j requires that it be willing to receive w packets beyond j, even though it sends a receive not ready. But if the receiver realizes this, and implements the procedure accordingly, then a receive not ready is really a no-op, since merely not acknowledging sequence numbers beyond j would have the same effect as sending a receive not ready with sequence number j.

5.2.6   Facilities

Some facilities are contracted and therefore set up manually at the DCE (not part of the X.25 protocol as seen by the DTE). Examples of these are:

1. Fixing the window size at some value or letting it be negotiated on a per-call basis.

2. Fixing the packet size at some value or letting it be negotiated on a per-call basis.

3. Allowing throughput to be negotiated on a per-call basis (with values between 75 bps and 64 Kbps).

4. Establishing a *closed user group*—a set of DTEs such that only members of the set can communicate with each other over the X.25 network. A DTE can be a member of multiple closed user groups—in which case, the DCE can determine whether an incoming or outgoing call should be allowed, based on the specification of the identity of the closed user group in the call request packet and the DCE's configured information regarding the closed user groups to which the DTE belongs.

     The numbering of a closed user group is local to a particular DTE/DCE interface. In other words, if DTE A and DTE B are in a closed user group, DTE A might refer to the closed user group as *n* and DTE B might refer to it as *m*.

5. Allowing no incoming calls.

6. Allowing only incoming calls.

7. Establishing the lowest outgoing virtual circuit number, which defines the boundary between virtual circuit numbers that can be chosen by the DTE and virtual circuit numbers that can be chosen by the DCE.

The following list provides examples of other facilities that are selected on a per-call basis. Note that in the first three cases, the facilities can be selected on a per-call basis only if the ability to do so has been contracted.

1. Window size for this call

2. Maximum packet size

3. Throughput

4. Closed user group, which specifies the closed user group to which the call applies

5. Reverse charging

5.2.7   Call Release

The standard method for releasing a connection is for one of the DTEs involved in a call to request that the call be cleared by transmitting a *clear request* to its DCE. That DCE will inform the network that the call is being cleared, and the other DCE will inform the other DTE that the call is being cleared. When the noninitiating DTE acknowledges that it knows the call has been cleared, its DCE informs the network, which informs the initiating DTE's DCE, which, in turn, informs the DTE that originally requested that the call be cleared.

When the network detects a problem with a call, it might do one of the following:

1. The DCE might issue a *clear request*, which causes the call to be disconnected, with no guarantee regarding unacknowledged packets—they may or may not have been delivered to the destination.

2. The DCE might issue a *reset*, which also offers no guarantee regarding the fate of unacknowledged packets. It restarts the sequence numbers for the call at 0 but keeps the call up.

3. The network might recover transparently. (This is unfortunately not common.)

The sorts of problems that could trigger one of the preceding responses include the following:

1. A DCE or link along a call's route goes down. (X.25 networks can be designed so that a call could be rerouted when a route fails, but many are not.)

2. The DTE transmits a packet for a call with an unexpected sequence number, indicating that the DCE and DTE are no longer coordinated with each other regarding that call.

It is also possible for a DCE to inform a DTE that all the DTE's current calls have been torn down. This is usually the result of a restart by the DCE, since it has lost state with respect to any calls that might have been in progress.

5.2.8 Interrupts

X.25 offers the ability for a DTE to transmit a single packet (with 1 to 32 bytes of data) on a call, which the network will deliver to the destination DTE as quickly as possible—i.e., without having to wait for all previously transmitted data to be delivered to the destination. There is no flow control on *interrupt* packets, so even if the destination has transmitted a receive not ready, the interrupt packet will be delivered. An *interrupt confirmation* packet is used to acknowledge an interrupt packet. A DTE can transmit a second interrupt packet only after the DCE informs the DTE (via an interrupt confirmation packet) that the destination DTE has acknowledged the previous interrupt packet.

5.3   A Datagram Network Layer Service Interface

The connectionless network layer standards seem complicated in comparison with X.25. That is because they deal with issues that X.25 does not address. For example:

1. The algorithms and protocols involved in building routers (for instance, routing algorithms)

2. The protocols involved in having the network automatically (i.e., without humans' modifying tables) assimilate a new subscriber

3. The algorithms and protocols involved in attaching to the network on a LAN rather than a point-to-point link

These issues are dealt with in Chapters 8 and 9. In this section, I consider only the portions of a connectionless network layer service that address the same issues as X.25. Since the portions of the protocol involved in the interface to a connectionless network service over a point-to-point link are sufficiently similar in different protocols, the present discussion is not specific to any one protocol. Details regarding specific protocols are presented in Chapter 7.

5.3.1   Data Transfer

The most important service provided by the connectionless network is data transfer. An endnode (the equivalent of a DTE) attaches to a router (the equivalent of a DCE) via a point-to-point link.

Just as the X.25 standard has three levels, an attachment to a router in a connectionless network has to have three layers of protocol. There must be a physical layer (analogous to X.25's physical level), a data link layer (analogous to X.25's link level), and a network layer (analogous to X.25's packet level). Usually, the connectionless network service does not specify the physical layer or the data link layer, because routers often offer a choice of technologies. The endnode must implement some physical and data link layers provided by the router, and then it can connect to that router.

The connectionless network layer visible to an endnode on a point-to-point link is usually very simple. It consists mostly of a definition of a packet format. The header contains source and destination addresses, and usually a hop count to detect and destroy vagrant packets that are lost and wandering aimlessly. The hop count is unfortunately called "time to live" in both the ISO and TCP/IP protocols. The theory is that the endnode might have some traffic (like packet voice) that should be dropped if delayed beyond its time to live, and the network would have the capacity to measure elapsed time with sufficient accuracy. In practice, time to live fields do not have the granularity, nor can delays be measured with sufficient accuracy, for time to live to be any more useful than a simple hop count, and it is common for implementations to treat the field as a hop count.

Other items sometimes found in the data packet format are:

1. Information enabling the destination endnode to reassemble packets that the network had to fragment. The reassembly mechanism in X.25 is very simple: All fragments except the final one have the M bit set. But this mechanism would not work with a network layer in which fragments can be duplicated, arrive out of order, or get lost. Thus, the source includes a packet identifier in

the original unfragmented packet, so that fragments of the same packet can be identified as belonging together, and each fragment is marked with an offset. Fragmentation and reassembly are discussed in greater detail in section 5.3.3.

2. Service class information, which would advise the network of any special requirements pertaining to this packet. An example might be priority or a request for a route that does not incur per-packet charges. This is analogous to X.25's "facilities" field, which, in X.25, is only carried in the call request packet.

5.3.2   Network Feedback

In addition to receiving and transmitting data packets, an endnode might receive certain types of advisory information from the network, the two most common instances of which are:

1. Error reports, indicating that a packet could not be delivered for some reason. Usually, the error report gives a hint as to the reason. For instance, the destination might have been unreachable, or the packet might have been illegally formatted or too big.

2. Congestion information, indicating that the network is becoming overly utilized and that the endnode should reduce its use of the network by setting its transport layer window smaller.

5.3.3   Fragmentation and Reassembly

As stated in section 5.3.1, the X.25 mechanism of marking each fragment except the last with a flag indicating that more data follows does not work in a datagram network, in which fragments can be lost, duplicated, or arrive out of order. Neither would a mechanism in which a router marked each fragment with a "fragment number," since a router could fragment a packet into fragments 1, 2, 3, and 4, and then some hops later, fragment 2 could encounter a link that required fragment 2 to be fragmented further.

The common solution is for the network layer data packet format to contain an "offset" field. For example, if a packet whose size is 8,000 octets encounters a link that can only handle 4,000 octets, the router might fragment the packet into two pieces, each 4,000 octets long. (Each fragment must also carry header information, so the router must take into account the size of the header when it calculates what size fragment it will produce.) The first fragment will have the offset field set to 0. The second fragment will have the offset field set to 4,000. If the second fragment encounters a link on which it needs to be further fragmented—say, into 1,000-octet chunks—then the second fragment will become four fragments, with the offset fields set to 4,000, 5,000, 6,000, and 7,000, respectively.

It is essential for the destination to know when a packet has been completely reassembled. One issue is for it to be able to determine the total length of the packet before fragmentation. ISO's CLNP (connectionless network protocol) protocol provides a "total length" field. IP provides a "more fragments" flag, which is set on all but the final fragment.

Once the destination knows that it has received the final fragment, it still does not know that the packet has been successfully reassembled, because some of the packet's intermediate fragments may have gotten lost. Nor can it simply count the number of octets received, because some of the received fragments may be duplicates. Even if exact duplicates were discarded, a simple count of the octets received might not work because different copies of duplicated fragments may have taken different paths and been fragmented in different, overlapping places.

One possible solution is to allocate a bitmask, 1 bit per octet in the reassembly buffer. As data arrives, it is copied into the reassembly buffer, and the relevant bits in the bitmask are marked off. This solution requires the bitmask to be ⅛ as big as the reassembly buffer. However, both the IP and CLNP standards require reassembly on 8-octet chunks, so the bitmask can be ¹⁄₆₄ as big as the reassembly buffer.

Another possible solution is to keep pointers right in the reassembly buffer itself, in locations that have not yet been filled in with data. Initially, a reassembly buffer of some size is allocated—say, 8,000 octets. (In CLNP, each fragment's header gives the prefragmentation size of the packet, so the size of the required reassembly buffer is known.) Associated with the reassembly buffer is a pointer that points to the first location within the reassembly buffer that has not yet been filled in with data. Initially, the pointer will point to the beginning of the buffer. At the location where the pointer points is written a pointer to the next such location in the buffer and the size of the current "hole." As fragments arrive, the pointers and lengths are modified accordingly. When the initial pointer points to the end of the buffer, the packet has been completely reassembled.

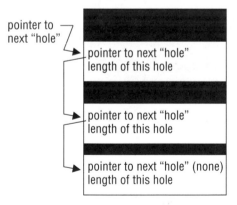

Figure 5.12

Another issue is for the destination to be able to determine when to discard partly reassembled packets. If a fragment has been lost in transit, the partly reassembled packet can never be successfully reassembled. Memory must be freed up for future packets. If all buffers are used for partly reassembled packets and a fragment arrives for a packet other than one of the packets currently being reassembled, various strategies can be employed. The destination can discard the most recently received fragment, the least recently received fragment, or a fragment chosen at random.

Network layer reassembly is CPU-intensive, especially because it usually involves extra copies at the destination. High-bandwidth applications would really be better served if the source transport layer chose a packet size such that packets would not need to be fragmented inside the network. Research is being done on strategies to enable the source to choose an appropriate packet size. Ideally, the source will want the largest possible packet size that won't require fragmentation, because throughput is degraded both if the packet size is smaller than necessary and if the packet size is so large that network layer fragmentation is required.

With connectionless networks, maximum packet size is a very difficult issue. Even if the appropriate size is found for a given path, the network may reroute packets in the middle of a conversation or do path splitting.

Homework

1. The link layer of X.25 includes flow control, in which the DTE can inform the DCE that it cannot receive any more packets. What is the difference in functionality between flow control performed at the link layer and flow control performed in X.25's network layer?

2. How would you design an X.25 net such that both endpoints of a call knew the call by the same number? Compare this approach to having a virtual circuit number with only local significance. Is either scheme better?

3. The X.25 standard allows an exception to the rule that a packet must be maximum-size in order to have the M bit set—the exception being when the D bit is set. What problems could arise if this exception were not made?

4. If the source DTE/DCE link allows a maximum packet size one-quarter the size allowed by the destination DTE/DCE link, and the source DTE has transmitted a packet to the source DCE with sequence number N, what can be said about the sequence number on that data when it is delivered by the destination DCE to the destination DTE?

5. Discuss the relative merits of the three proposals for discarding partly reassembled packets (discard the oldest fragment, discard the newest fragment, discard a fragment chosen at random).

6. Many connectionless network layer data packet formats include a flag that indicates "don't fragment." If the source sets the flag, the network is not allowed to fragment the packet en route. If the packet requires fragmentation but the flag is set, the packet must be discarded, and often, an error message is sent back to the source by the router R that cannot forward the packet. In such a network,

suppose that the error message sent back to the source merely says, "the packet was too big." What strategy could be used to find the real maximum packet size? Suppose that the error message actually indicates the maximum packet size that router R could have forwarded. Is the size indicated in the error message really the maximum packet size that the source could send on that route?

Chapter 6
Network Layer Addresses

This chapter describes the structure of ISO and IP network layer addresses. One of the major differences is that the ISO address is variable-length, up to 20 octets, whereas the IP address is always 4 octets. Another major difference is that in ISO, a node (router or endnode) usually has a single network layer address. In contrast, in IP, an address indicates an attachment to a link. An IP node with multiple links will have a different IP address for each link. The IP case is analogous to a house built on a corner, with an entrance onto two streets—say, Router Road and Bridge Boulevard. The house might then have two addresses, one for each street—say, 110 Router Road as well as 31 Bridge Boulevard.

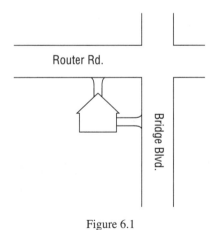

Figure 6.1

6.1 Hierarchical Addresses

When there are too many destinations for a network to keep track of, routing is designed to be "hierarchical," in the sense that the network is partitioned into pieces. Then one portion of the address indicates the "piece" of the network in which the destination resides, and another portion of the address distinguishes destinations within that piece.

149

The post office uses hierarchical addresses. A portion of the address indicates the country in which the destination is located. The first step in routing is to get the letter to the correct country. Once the letter has reached the correct country (say, the United States), the portion of the address that indicates the state in which the destination is located becomes relevant. Then routing delivers the letter to the correct state, ignoring the remainder of the address. Only when the letter has reached the correct state does the "city" portion of the address become relevant, and then the street and number, and finally the name.

Network layer addresses in ISO and IP are also hierarchical. A large network is broken into chunks, which I will call *level 1 subnetworks*. Within a level 1 subnetwork, routers keep track of all the individual links and nodes. The routers routing within a level 1 subnetwork are known as *level 1 routers*.

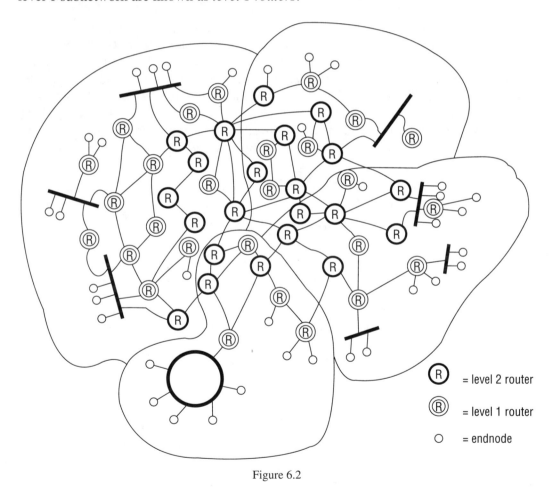

Figure 6.2

Level 2 routing concerns itself with where all the level 1 subnetworks are, but not with details internal to the level 1 subnetworks. If the size of the level 1 subnetworks is kept manageable, the job of level 1 routing is tractable. If there are not too many level 1 subnetworks, then the job of level 2 routing is tractable. If there are too many level 1 subnetworks, then the network can be partitioned into *level 2 subnetworks*, with *level 3 routers* routing to the proper level 2 subnetworks.

In a network with three levels of hierarchy, an address would look like this:

level 2 subnetwork	level 1 subnetwork	endnode

Figure 6.3

An address would have three components and look something like 27.91.12, where "27" would indicate the level 2 subnetwork, "91" would indicate the level 1 subnetwork, and "12" would indicate the endnode within level 1 subnetwork 27.91.

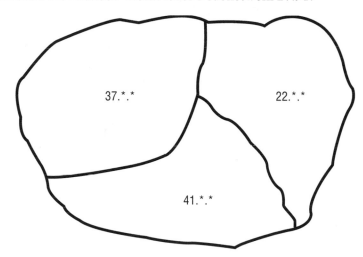

Figure 6.4   Level 2 subnetworks

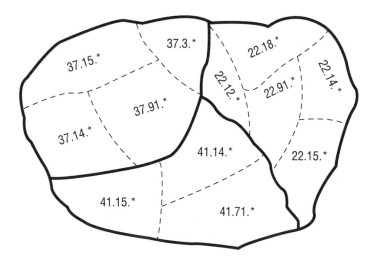

Figure 6.5   Level 1 subnetworks

Network layer addresses in both protocol suites are hierarchical. In contrast, for the purpose of routing, IEEE 802 addresses are not hierarchical. Although IEEE 802 addresses seem hierarchical, since the top three octets are named the "OUI," these addresses are in fact hierarchical only for ease of address assignment. No assumption can be made about the location of a LAN node based on its OUI. Any sort of routing based on IEEE 802 addresses (such as bridge station learning) must treat each address as an individual 48-bit quantity. If the 802 address were geographically hierarchical, then bridges would be able to do something like assume that all stations with an address whose first octet was equal to "X" would be located in the same place.

6.2 IP Network Layer Addresses

In IP, network layer addresses are 4 octets long. A portion of the address indicates a link number, and a portion indicates the system on the link, which in IP terminology is referred to as the *host*. (Note: There is really no IP terminology exactly corresponding to the *link*, except perhaps the word *subnet*, which does not exactly correspond because what I refer to as the *link number* is often referred to in IP as containing two fields: *net* and *subnet*. This should become clearer in a few paragraphs).

An IP address looks like this:

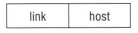

Figure 6.6

Which bits in the address belong in the "link" field and which bits belong in the "host" field is not fixed, but rather can differ for each link in the network. It is important for a node to know, for each link to which it is attached, which bits correspond to the link portion of its address on that link and which bits correspond to the host portion.

For each link in an IP network, the human planning the network decides the value of the link number and which bits in the address will correspond to the link number. A link (such as a LAN) has a link number and a mask indicating which bits correspond to the link number. An example is:

mask

| 11111111 | 11111111 | 11000000 | 00000000 |

link number

| 11101000 | 01010101 | 01000000 | 00000000 |

Figure 6.7

In this case, the leftmost 18 bits of all addresses of nodes on that link will equal 111010000101010101, and the rightmost 14 bits will be used to distinguish attachments to the link.

IP allows the mask to have noncontiguous 1's. That means the bits that indicate the link number need not be all together but can be sprinkled throughout the address. I believe this not only is incredibly confusing, and liable to create ambiguous addresses (addresses that could reside on more than one link, because the masks are different), but also results in inefficient routing, since this makes it computationally expensive for a router to identify the destination link toward which to route.

Each node on a link must know the mask for the link as well as its own IP address. An IEEE 802 address can be installed in ROM in a node and always be applicable no matter where the node is plugged into a network. IP addresses cannot work that way, since a node must acquire an IP address that matches the link's address (for the portion of the address that has 1's in the mask) and is different from the IP addresses of any other nodes on that link. Typically, IP nodes either are configured with their IP address and mask, or use the BOOTP protocol (RFC 951)[1] or, less commonly, the RARP protocol (RFC 903)[2] to acquire the information. They must start with some information—generally, their LAN address (which can be stored in ROM at the node) and the address of a BOOTP server. Assuming that the BOOTP server has been configured to know that node's IP address on that link as well as the link's mask, the BOOTP server will inform the endnode of its IP address and mask.

Originally, in IP, the boundary between the link number and host number was less flexible. Also, the link was known as the *network*. The boundary was after either the first, second, or third octet. If the leftmost bit in an address was 0, the boundary was after the first octet; the address was known as a *class A* address and had the following form:

Class A Address

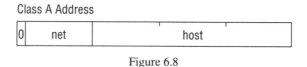

Figure 6.8

If the leftmost 2 bits in an address were 10, the boundary was after the second octet; the address was known as a *class B* address and had the following form:

Class B Address

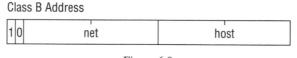

Figure 6.9

If the leftmost 3 bits in an address were 110, the boundary was after the third octet; the address was known as a *class C* address and had the following form:

Class C Address

Figure 6.10

[1] B. Croft and J. Gilmore, "Bootstrap Protocol," RFC 951 (Network Information Center, SRI International, Menlo Park, Calif., September 1985).
[2] R. Finlayson, T. Mann, J. Mogul, and Marvin Theimer, "A Reverse Address Resolution Protocol," RFC 903 (Network Information Center, SRI International, Menlo Park, Calif., June 1984).

The idea of making the boundary between net and host more flexible was known as *subnetting*. The original assumption was that a mask for a class A address would always have 1's for the highest octet (and an arbitrary mixture of 1's and 0's for the remaining octets), a mask for a class B address would always have 1's for the two highest octets, and a mask for a class C address would always have 1's for the three highest octets.

The portion of the class A address which had 1's in the bottom 3 octets of its mask, was known as the *subnet*. Likewise for a class B address—the 1 bits in the bottom 2 octets of the address mask correspond to the subnet. And likewise for a class C address, in which the 1 bits in the bottom octet correspond to the subnet. Usually, IP addresses are referred to as having three fields—the *net* number, the *subnet* number, and the *host* number. For instance, in a class B address, the top 2 octets would be the net portion, any bits in the bottom 2 octets corresponding to 1's in the mask would be the subnet portion, and the remainder of the bottom 2 octets would be the host portion.

However, it turns out to be potentially useful to allow masks with 0's in what used to be known as the net portion of the address (to get more levels of hierarchy), and addressing conventions that made a distinction between net and subnet were not found useful. If all protocols provided a mask when reporting a reachable destination, knowing about class A, B, and C addresses would become unnecessary. Most (but unfortunately not all) new IP routing protocols do include a mask. Old ones (RIP, EGP) did not. When a protocol does not include a mask when reporting a reachable destination, the portion of the address corresponding to the link number must be calculated implicitly based on whether the address is class A (in which case, the "link number" is the first octet), class B (the first two octets), or class C (the first three octets).

The link number in IP really indicates the level 1 subnetwork in which an endnode resides. Level 1 routing in IP is mostly trivial, supplied by the LAN or by bridges. Some "links" in IP are actually entire mesh topology networks (like the ARPANET or a bridged LAN)—in which case, level 1 routing would be the routing within that mesh topology network (like ARPANET routing or bridging protocols).

Additional levels of hierarchy can be attained in IP by clumping links together into level 2 subnetworks, assigning all the links in the level 2 subnetwork some portion of

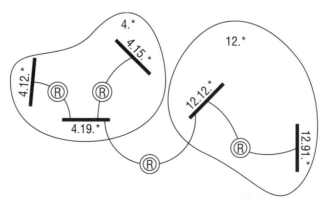

Figure 6.11   Hierarchical IP network

the address in common, and denoting that portion of the address as the level 2 subnetwork number. Outside the level 2 subnetwork, the level 2 subnetwork would be represented as a single link with a short mask (fewer 1's than the masks of the individual links within the level 2 subnetwork).

Note: IP terminology does not tend to recognize that level 1 routing merely involves forwarding onto a single IP link. The newer IP routing protocols that support hierarchy allow the network to be broken into chunks called "areas." Each area contains several links and, as such, already has two levels of hierarchy, but the IP routing protocols call routing within an area "level 1 routing" and routing between areas "level 2 routing."

IP addresses have the conventions that all "1's" in a field means "all," and all "0's" means "this." The uses for these conventions are as follows:

1. <link = 0><host = 0>

    This is employed when a host boots knowing only its data link address and uses RARP or BOOTP to find out its IP address.

2. <0><host>

    This would theoretically be employed by a host using RARP or BOOTP to determine the net and/or subnet portions of its address. This is not very useful, because there is no rational reason why a host would know its host number relative to a link but would not know the link number.

3. <−1>

    This destination address indicates that the packet should be transmitted as a data link broadcast packet on the attached link. Using all 1's in the source address of an IP packet is illegal and quite a nuisance. (Just because it's illegal doesn't mean it isn't done, however, especially by implementations with bugs.)

4. <net = X><−1>

    This indicates that the packet should be transmitted as a broadcast packet to all of net X. If net X is actually partitioned into multiple subnet numbers, this address implies that the packet should be transmitted as a broadcast packet on all those subnets, but none of the routing protocols supports this functionality.

    Again, transmitting a packet with a network layer source address of this form is illegal and quite a nuisance.

5. <net = X><subnet = Y><−1>

    This indicates that the packet should be transmitted to the link known as <X> <Y>, and when it arrives, it should be transmitted on that link as a broadcast packet.

    Again, an address of this form is legal only as a destination address.

An additional addressing convention is <127><X>, which is to be used as an internal host loopback address, regardless of the value of X. This form of address is illegal except when used internally (sort of like committing adultery in one's mind).

A host's IP address cannot have 0 or –1 in any of the fields <net>, <subnet>, or <host>.

The standard method of writing an IP address is as the decimal value of each of the four octets, separated by periods. For example, the IP address 15.29.13.4 would equal:

00001111	00011101	00001101	00000100

Figure 6.12

One additional convention for IP addresses has been established to support "IP multicasting." (This is discussed in the "WAN Multicast" section of Chapter 9. An IP multicast address is distinguished by its top 4 bits' being "1110" and is known as a *class D* address. In case IP ever invents some other form of address, its top 4 bits will be equal to "1111" (but not all the bits in the first octet will be 1's, or else this form would conflict with one of the broadcast conventions defined earlier in this section). This form of address, which is currently known as a *class E* address, is not yet defined for any purposes.

6.3   ISO Network Layer Addresses

ISO network layer addresses could be explained in highly complex detail. Luckily, most of the details are unimportant for understanding the network layer, and I will therefore refrain from discussing them.

ISO network layer addresses are variable-length, with a maximum of 20 octets. Because they are variable-length, any packets that contain an address must contain an additional octet specifying the address's length.

An ISO address can be thought of as follows:

area	ID	SEL

Figure 6.13

The **area** portion defines the level 1 subnetwork in which a node resides. If the area portion of a packet's destination address matches the address of the area in which the packet exists, then the packet should be routed via level 1 routing, based on the contents of the **ID** field in the destination address.

Originally, the **ID** field was 6 octets, which is a convenient number because it is the same length as an 802 address. A 6-octet ID field enables an endnode to automatically figure out its network layer address based on a globally assigned 802 address as the ID portion. The remainder of the address can then be obtained by copying the portions of the address other than ID from a router's address.

Endnodes built to attach to an 802 LAN automatically have a globally assigned 802 address. (I suppose some vendors might build equipment not preconfigured with a unique address ROM for the 802 attachment, but anyone buying such a beast deserves all the joys of figuring out how to configure addresses.) Endnodes not built to attach to an 802 LAN can also be preconfigured with a globally assigned 802 address, since 802 addresses are not that difficult to obtain. Vendors can (and in my opinion, should) obtain a block of 802 addresses for their systems and configure each system at the time of manufacture with a ROM containing a unique 802 address; then even endnodes that are not attached to an 802 LAN can have a globally unique ID.

Some members of the ISO committee objected to actually standardizing the size of the ID field. Some members felt that 6 octets were far too many; others felt that 6 octets were not enough. The committee compromised by allowing each routing domain (a portion of a network under the same administrative control) to use whatever size ID field it wanted (from 0 to 8 octets). Theoretically, routers could be configured with an ID size to use (but in practice, many products are likely to support only the 6-octet size). Since routing would be incredibly confused if routers within a routing domain disagreed on the size of the ID field, a field was added to various routing control packets indicating the size of the ID field as understood by the router generating the packet. This enables misconfiguration to be detected. Since the configurable ID length was added late in the standards process, the **ID length** field, which appears in the appropriate routing control packets, is encoded such that the value 0 means that the ID is 6 octets. Values between 1 and 8 correspond to ID lengths from 1 to 8 octets (which means that an ID length of 6 can be encoded as either 0 or 6). The value "255" indicates that the ID length is 0.

(Note: In my opinion, failing to establish a single ID size will have economic and/or performance implications for ISO routers. To do efficient data packet forwarding, level 1 routers must have specialized data structures and algorithms, and perhaps even specialized hardware assistance for address lookups, in order to deal with whatever ID size is implemented. It is unlikely that a vendor will be able to implement a high-performance router that can be configured at the last minute with the proper ID size for the routing domain.)

The purpose of the **SEL** octet is to differentiate among multiple network layer users. It is like the DSAP and SSAP octets in 802.1.

The area field actually has more structure and can yield many levels of routing hierarchy. The next level of complexity involves dividing the field into two parts:

Figure 6.14

The globally defined portion is variable-length (of course—it's a standard!). The locally defined portion is also variable, but the global addresses are assigned in such a way that there is always room for at least another 2 octets of area. Someone in charge of a routing domain can get a single globally defined number for the entire routing domain, and if the routing domain is so large that it needs to be hierarchical, the locally defined portion of the area field can be used to identify the level 1 subnetworks within the routing domain. The locally defined field can even be assigned hierarchically—for instance, by having the upper octet signify the level 2 subnetwork and the lower octet signify the level 1 subnetwork within the level 2 subnetwork.

ISO calls the globally defined portion an *IDP*, which stands for "initial domain part" (this, of course, makes everything clear). ISO does not administer all of the IDP values directly but rather assigns various authorities to define their own addresses. The first octet of the IDP is known as the *AFI*, which stands for "authority and format identifier." The remainder of the IDP is known as the *IDI*, or "initial domain identifier." The portion of the address that is not globally defined is known as the *DSP*, or "domain-specific part." (Yes, there will be a quiz.)

area		ID	SEL
globally assigned		locally assigned	
IDP		DSP	
AFI	IDI	DSP	

Figure 6.15

The globally defined portion of the address is hierarchical for the purpose of address assignment. However, in practice, a great deal of geographic information can be inferred from the IDP. This gives even more levels of routing hierarchy, which will allow ISO networks to scale, in practice, to arbitrary sizes.

The simplest way to think of a hierarchical address with many levels of hierarchy is to regard the address as being divided into fields such as:

level n subnet	level $n-1$ subnet	. . .	level 1 subnet	ID

Figure 6.16

It is not necessary to standardize the size of these fields in order for routing to work (which is indeed lucky given how enthusiastic the standards organizations seem to be about standardizing the size of fields). For instance, in one level n subnetwork, the level $n-1$ subnetwork numbers could be 4 octets long, whereas in another, they could be 2 octets long. Provided that level n routing gets the packet to the correct level n subnetwork, the level $n-1$ routers within that level n subnetwork will know which portion of the address to use for routing purposes.

Even within a level n subnetwork, it is not necessary for all the level $n-1$ subnetworks to have the same address length. Just as with IP class A, B, and C addresses, it is possible to have different address lengths within a subnetwork.

This would all be terribly confusing if one tried to understand exactly how many levels of hierarchy there were in an ISO address and where the boundaries were. Luckily, one need not think about that. Level 1 routing routes based on the ID field, which can be found by looking at the final 7 octets (where the number 7 is variable, thanks to committee politics) of an address (and ignoring the last octet, which is the SEL field). It is possible to find the end of an address because an ISO address is always preceded by an octet indicating "address length."

Level 1 routers know their own area address and compare a destination address against it. If the area portion of the destination address matches the area's address, the level 1 router routes based on the ID field. Otherwise, the level 1 router routes the packet to a level 2 router.

Level 2 routing routes based on "address prefixes." An analogy might be the best way to explain why this routing approach is useful. Assume that the postal service establishes the rule that envelopes must be addressed using a text string, with no spaces, starting from the country downward. Addresses might look like this:

USAMACAMBRIDGEMASSAVE77ROOM202JANEDOE

USAMABOSTONELFRD12APT3JOESHMOE

USAMABOSTONELFRD10JOESMITH

There is no fixed allocation of how many characters in the text string denote the level 1 subnetwork, how many denote the level 2 subnetwork, and so forth, and yet the postal system would be able to route properly. For instance, starting from the left, there is no problem figuring out the destination country, provided that no country name is an initial substring of another country name (for instance, a country called "USABIGSTICK" would be confused with the country "USA," state "BIGSTICK"). There is no problem with having variable-length country names, such as the three-letter name "USA" or the six-letter name "BRAZIL." Once the country is recognized, the remainder of the address is also parsed. The next level of hierarchy is read (and again, there will be no problem as long as no subnetwork name at that level is an initial substring of another subnetwork name at that level), and so forth.

ISO routing works pretty much like that (although addresses are not text strings). Assuming that ISO routing worked on text strings, the routers on the boundary of the United States would indicate that they can reach the address prefix "USA." Within the United States, routers on the boundary of a state, such as Massachusetts, would indicate that they can reach the address prefix "USAMA." A router on the boundary of the United States might wish to indicate that although it can reach all addresses in the United States, it will be more expensive to reach California than Massachusetts. Therefore, it might advertise reachability to "USA" at some cost—say, 80—and reachability to "USACA" at 75 and reachability to "USAMA" at 40. Once the router receives a packet with a destination address starting "USAMA," the packet is injected into Massachusetts, where the routers will be advertising longer address prefixes, so that the packet can be routed to the proper city within Massachusetts.

True ISO addresses work the same way. They just look uglier than text strings. Someone skilled in ISO network layer addresses could examine the first several bits and say, "That's a telephone number in the United States." He or she could then examine a few more bits and say, "That telephone number is in area code 617." A few more bits and the person could say, "The telephone number is (617) 555-1234."

Given the length and flexible hierarchy in ISO addresses, they can be used to achieve truly enormous networks.

6.3.1 NSAPs and NETs

ISO purists have probably been cringing during the preceding discussion of network layer addresses, since ISO does not actually call anything a "network layer address." There are actually two concepts. One is known as a *network service access point* (*NSAP*), and the other is known as a *network entity title* (*NET*). I have never found the distinction interesting, useful, or completely comprehensible. However, the two terms are employed in the ISO documents, so I will explain them.

In ISO terminology, the network layer provides a service, and a user of the network layer "attaches" to the network layer with an NSAP. A particular node will have many NSAPs if there are multiple users of the network layer in that node.

The network layer itself is not allowed to have an NSAP, since for layering purists, the network layer cannot be a user of the network layer. Instead, it has an NET.

A network entity title is not intended to appear as the source or destination address in a network layer header. However, NETs do appear in certain protocol messages, in certain option fields in data packets, and even as source or destination addresses in network layer headers in certain cases, such as when encapsulation is used.

In the IP data packet format, there is a "protocol" field in addition to a "destination address" and "source address" field. The protocol field serves a purpose similar to the SEL field in an ISO address. ISO would consider an IP address as an NET, and the combination of IP address and protocol field as functionally similar to an NSAP.

The IP form of address is similar to the original Ethernet data link header, in that there is a single protocol field, globally administered. The ISO form of address is similar to the 802.2 format, in that there is a separate SEL field tacked onto the destination address and one tacked onto the source address. Although at the data link layer, the 802.2 format was unworkable without the SNAP encoding, having separate, locally administered SEL values in the source and destination network layer addresses is not a problem, because those values merely become part of the network layer address. When an application needs to talk to another application, it looks up the name in a naming service, which returns an entire NSAP, including the SEL value.

The ISO specs were vague about what an NET would look like. Some implementers interpreted an NET as being an NSAP without the "selector" octet, which made sense because the selector octet really specifies the client of the network layer. Others interpreted an NET as being an NSAP whose selector octet had a special value (0) that by convention, means the network layer itself.

It didn't really matter, as long as all implementers agreed. Unfortunately, initial implementations did not agree and therefore did not interwork properly. Paulina Knibbe, from Cisco Systems, Inc., noticed the discrepancies among implementations and sent the following delightful electronic mail message to the relevant people. (An "ISH" is an intermediate system hello message, which is explained in Chapter 8.)

> **Well, folks we've got trouble right here in River City. . .**
> **Over the last month, I have spoken with many of you about**
> **whether or not the NET in an ISH should include a selector.**
> **The answers vary. (Mostly "Huh?") :-)**
>
> > **— E-mail sent by Paulina Knibbe, who originally noticed**
> > **the problem of the multiple interpretations of NET by**
> > **various implementation groups**

The decision was that an NET should take the same form as an NSAP and that the selector value of 0 would be reserved to mean the network layer itself. As a result of this decision, we can stop worrying about network entity titles versus network service access points and instead regard both of them as simply network layer addresses. (Thank you, Paulina Knibbe!)

6.3.2 Autoconfiguration

Autoconfiguration was touched on briefly earlier in the chapter, but it is so wonderful that it is worth mentioning again. An ISO address enables the user to buy an off-the-shelf endnode that has been endowed by its creator with a globally unique 6-byte ID in ROM. The endnode can then be hooked into any ISO network that uses a 6-byte ID field and employs the IS-IS (10589) and ES-IS (9542) protocols. Through the ES-IS protocol, it will discover the network layer address of an adjacent router. The endnode can then copy the area field from the router's network layer and use that for the area portion of its own address. The SEL field is locally administered among the network layer users in the node.

Autoconfiguration is, in my opinion, essential if a network is to scale to truly large size.

IP addresses are too small for autoconfiguration. In order to attach to an IP network, you must find the human who manages the host addresses on the link to which you will attach and ask for an IP address for your node. Once an IP address is assigned, it must be manually configured into the appropriate databases (either at the endnode or at a BOOTP server). This, of course, must be done correctly, since misconfiguration is difficult to detect, especially by users who just want to avail themselves of the services of the network—not glory in the network layer protocols.

6.3.3   Embedded DTE Addresses

Another feature of ISO addresses is the ability to embed a DTE address in the area address. For instance, a common type of network is the following, in which pieces of the network are interconnected via a big common-carrier network, like the phone company or an X.25 network. I'll call each piece a "network fragment" because the word *subnet*, which I'd rather use, has too many other meanings.

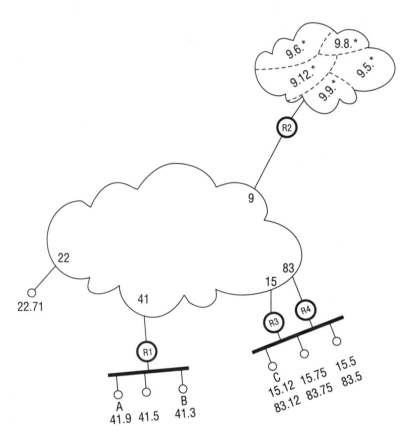

Figure 6.17   Using embedded DTE addresses

Assume that the area address of each of the network fragments shown in the illustration contains the DTE address of the point of attachment of the fragment to the X.25 network. This approach completely eliminates the need for a potentially expensive routing protocol operating on the X.25 network in order to keep the fragments aware of each other.

Assume that endnode A wants to talk to endnode B. The area address portion of A will match the area address portion of B. The level 1 routers within that fragment will route the packet correctly. Now assume that A transmits a packet with destination address "C." The level 1 routers within A's fragment recognize that the destination does not reside in that fragment and thus route the packet toward a level 2 router—in this case, R1, which attaches directly to the X.25 network. R1 will have no previous knowledge of C's area address, other than having been configured to know that any packet whose address prefix indicates that the address is on that X.25 network can be routed over the link by extracting the DTE address from the area address. R1 thus knows (based on its having matched the configured address prefix) that the packet should be forwarded over the X.25 network. R1 then extracts the DTE address from C's area address and places a call to that DTE address, whereupon the packet magically gets delivered to a router that knows how to reach C.

A network fragment can be composed of multiple level 1 subnetworks and still have the DTE address of its attachment embedded in the area address of each of the level 1 subnetworks. This is possible because the DTE address is embedded in the "globally defined" portion of the area address, and the area address can be expanded by at least another 2 octets.

Assume that the fragment containing D is sufficiently large that it must be broken into multiple level 1 subnetworks. Assume, too, that the IDP corresponding to R2's DTE address is X. Then the area address of each of the level 1 subnetworks will have the form X.y ("X" concatenated with a locally assigned field to distinguish the level 1 subnetworks within that network fragment). Note that the fragment containing C is reachable via either R3 (DTE address 15) or R4 (DTE address 84). In this case it is convenient to allow that fragment to have two area addresses.

Again, this sort of magic no-overhead routing cannot be accomplished with IP because the addresses are too small for a DTE address to be embedded.

Homework

1. With IP addressing, find two different (value, mask) pairs and an IP address that would match either link. Make sure that each mask has at least one "1" where the other mask has a "0."

2. Suppose that a router had a list of destination links, as a table of (value, mask) pairs, with instructions for each entry about how to route a packet, given a destination address matching that entry. Assuming noncontiguous subnet masks, is there, in the general case, any algorithm (including any way of organizing the table), other than trying each (value, mask) pair in turn, that will indicate which entry matches the destination address? (I think the answer is no. It would be of great interest if someone were to devise an efficient algorithm.)

3. Assuming that noncontiguous masks in IP are disallowed, IP routing becomes similar to ISO level 2 routing—the (value, mask) pairs become address prefixes and can be expressed as a (mask length, value) pair.

   How many bits need to be allocated to the "mask length"? Is an encoding of (mask length, value) more efficient than an encoding of (mask, value)?

4. Some people have attempted to get noncontiguous IP subnet masks banned, but there are those who defend noncontiguous subnet masks as being useful. Can you think of anything that can be done with noncontiguous subnet masks that cannot be done without them?

5. Assume a problem that requires finding, from a table of entries, the entry that is the longest matching initial substring of a given quantity. Devise an algorithm to do this efficiently.

6. Suppose you are told that you must implement a high-performance ISO level 1 router and that the customer must be able to set a management parameter indicating which size ID field is to be used. What kind of strategies could be employed? Keep in mind that high-performance forwarding usually requires specialized hardware. What kinds of economic trade-offs can be made? For instance, the router might theoretically support all address sizes but be higher-performance on some. Also keep in mind that your product should be competitive both economically and in terms of performance.

7. The rule in IP is that none of the three fields (net, subnet, host) in an IP address is allowed to be all 1's or all 0's. Why does this rule exclude a single-bit host or subnet field?

Chapter 7
Connectionless Data Exchange

In this chapter, I describe connectionless-style network layer protocols in detail, concentrating on two such protocols. One is the connectionless network layer protocol defined by ISO, which I will refer to in this chapter as simply "CLNP." The other is the network layer protocol defined by the Internet community, which I will refer to as "IP." The Internet protocol suite is sometimes called the "TCP/IP" protocol suite, but that name is misleading, since TCP and IP are only two of the layers in the Internet protocol suite. (TCP, or "transmission control protocol," is the transport layer protocol. IP is the network layer protocol.)

Connectionless network layer protocols tend to be described in several separate documents. Although having to read multiple documents is somewhat confusing, a single document that described everything would be daunting in its size and complexity, even more daunting than the individual pieces are today.

The more or less separable pieces consist of:

1. *Basic connectionless service:* This part of the network layer is the connectionless analog to the X.25 specification. It consists of the format for data packets and certain error messages or other notifications that the network can send to an endnode. The generic version is discussed in Chapter 5. Here, I discuss the specifics of the ISO and Internet protocols.

   In ISO, this part of the protocol is defined in ISO 8473, entitled "Protocol for Providing the Connectionless-mode Network Service." I'll refer to the ISO protocol by its common nickname "CLNP," for "connectionless network protocol." In the Internet protocol suite the equivalent protocol is defined in RFC 791, known as "The Internet Protocol," or "IP."

   The titles of these standards imply that the packet format is the entire network layer protocol, and perhaps this is a fair claim, since it is analogous to the functionality in the X.25 standard, which also only standardizes the interface between a network and a host attached to the network with a point-to-point link.

   In ISO, error reports to the source about problems with packet delivery are included in the 8473 document. In IP, error reports are discussed in a different document—ICMP (for "Internet Control Message Protocol," RFC 792).

2. *Neighbor greeting:* This aspect of the protocol enables neighbors to discover each other. It allows endnodes to know which routers are available on their LAN and to find out that it is possible to communicate directly with other endnodes on the same LAN. It allows routers to find their endnode neighbors, both so that the routers can tell all the other routers how to reach those endnodes and so that the neighbor routers will know the data link layer destination addresses needed to deliver packets the final hop to destination endnodes.

    In ISO, this is defined in ISO 9542 and is known by the catchy name of "End system to Intermediate system routeing exchange protocol for use in conjunction with the Protocol for providing the connectionless-mode network service." Somehow, nobody seems able to say or remember this title. Instead, this protocol tends to be called either "9542" or "ES-IS," with *ES* meaning "end system" and *IS* meaning "intermediate system." Note that *routeing* is not a typo; rather, it was spelled that way at the insistence of the British delegation to ISO. I won't wantonly waste *e*'s when writing *routing*, except when quoting the title of an ISO document. Also note that the capitalization in the title is copied exactly from the ISO document, and I make no claim about understanding the capitalization rules.

    In the Internet protocol suite, parts of the neighbor-greeting protocol are defined in ICMP and parts are defined in RFC 826 (known as "ARP," or "Address Resolution Protocol").

    A neighbor-greeting protocol is not present in X.25 because X.25 makes the assumption that an endnode will be directly attached, via a point-to-point link, to a router, and the endnode's network layer address either contains the attached router's address or the endnode's address is manually configured into the attached router.

3. *Routing:* This aspect of the network layer concerns the protocol and algorithms that routers should use so they can cooperate to calculate paths through a mesh topology.

    In ISO, this is defined in DP 10589, known (by very few people) as "Intermediate system to Intermediate system Intra-Domain routing information exchange protocol for use in Conjunction with the Protocol for providing the Connectionless-mode Network Service." More commonly, it is referred to as "IS-IS" (for "intermediate system to intermediate system").

    In the Internet protocol suite, there has never been a single standard for routing. The assumption was that all routers in a "routing domain" would be a single implementation or would belong to a group of implementations that have been cooperatively developed so as to speak the same protocol. The most widespread example of a routing algorithm for IP is RIP ("Routing Information Protocol," RFC 1058). Its popularity is due to the fact that it was distributed free.

    The Internet community would like a single standard routing protocol. The two main contenders are OSPF (documented in RFC 1131) and Integrated

IS-IS, which is actually ISO's DP 10589 enhanced to carry IP address reachability information in addition to ISO network layer reachability information.

Just when you think you're starting to understand the proliferation of routing protocols, I must tell you that the picture is actually a bit more confusing than what I've just described. Both ISO and IP have recognized the need for separate pieces of network, with each piece defined roughly as being managed by a single organization and running a single routing protocol. ISO calls these pieces *routing domains*; IP calls them *autonomous systems.*

The ISO jargon for the routing protocol running within a routing domain is *intra-domain routing protocol.* The IP jargon for the routing protocol running within an autonomous system is *interior gateway protocol*, or *IGP.*

In order to interconnect routing domains, routing must be done with either static tables or a routing protocol. The ISO jargon for a routing protocol to interconnect routing domains is *interdomain routing protocol.* The Internet jargon for a routing protocol to interconnect autonomous systems is *exterior gateway protocol*, or *EGP.* The only existing proposal for an ISO interdomain routing protocol is IDRP, for "InterDomain Routing Protocol" (which is not far enough along in the ISO standards process for the authors to realize they need to add an *e* to the title). IP has had an EGP of sorts, known as EGP. It is widely conceded to be technologically unsatisfactory (an issue that is examined in Chapter 10), and a replacement has long been sought. The most promising contender is BGP ("border gateway protocol"), documented in RFC 1105, upon which the ISO IDRP proposal is based.

The X.25 standard does not specify anything equivalent to a routing protocol. It is assumed that one organization will build a network that provides X.25 service and that there will be some proprietary algorithm for route calculation. Thus, connection-oriented networks have the same problems to solve, but the connection-oriented standards don't discuss this aspect of the protocol because the solution is proprietary to each network.

In the next sections, I explore each of aforementioned aspects of the network layer in detail.

7.1 Data Packets

ISO and IP data packet formats are remarkably similar, partly because the information to be carried in a data packet is fairly simple (source, destination, fragmentation info, special requests, and data) and partly because ISO basically started out with the IP data packet, expanded the addresses, and made minor changes.

The IP packet format is usually written as a sequence of 32-bit chunks. The ISO packet format is written as a sequence of octets.

The IP data packet format is specified as follows:

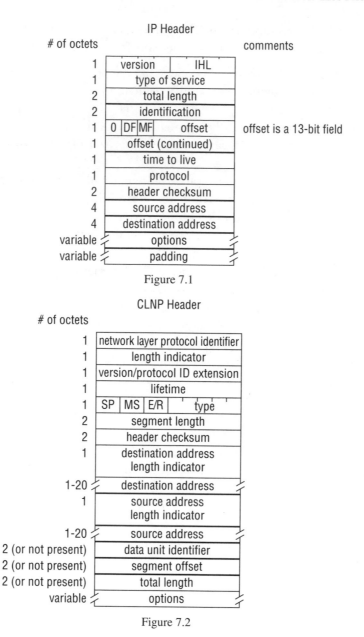

Figure 7.1

Figure 7.2

In the following subsections, I go through the two different formats field by field, showing where each field fits into each format.

7.1.1 Destination Address

Both protocols have a field indicating the address of the destination. The structure of addresses is quite different in the two protocols, though, as discussed in Chapter 6. In IP, an address is 4 octets long. In CLNP, an address is variable-length, with a maximum of 20 octets. Because of the variable-length addresses, CLNP requires a **destination address length indicator**, a 1-octet field that specifies the number of octets in the destination address.

7.1.2 Source Address

Both protocols have a field indicating the source address. Again, in IP, this field is 4 octets long. In CLNP, it is variable-length, with a 1-octet **source address length indicator** field.

7.1.3 Header Length

This field is called **IHL** (Internet Header Length) in IP and **length indicator** in CLNP. In IP, the unit is in 32-bit words; in CLNP, the unit is in octets. In IP, the field is 4 bits long; in CLNP, the field is 1 octet long. Thus, the maximum header length in CLNP is 254 octets (the value 255 is reserved), whereas in IP, the maximum header length is 60 octets (15 × 4). In IP, the header must be constructed so as to be a multiple of 4 octets, since the header length unit in IP is in 4-octet chunks. That is why the IP header requires the **padding** field—to allow the header to be a multiple of 4 octets.

Forcing the header to be a multiple of 4 octets is not unreasonable, since some implementations might be more efficient if the data always started on a 4-octet boundary.

The fact that the IP header cannot be larger than 60 octets can be viewed either as a disadvantage (long source routes and other options might be impossible to specify) or an advantage (we really don't want people spending all the bandwidth on the header).

7.1.4 Datagram Length

Both protocols have a field that indicates the total length, in octets, of the datagram, which consists of the header and a fragment of the original packet (if the packet needed to be fragmented somewhere along its path). In ISO, this field is called **segment length**. In IP, it is called **total length**, which is extremely confusing because this field indicates only the fragment's length, not the length of the original packet before fragmentation. The field was called "total length" because it includes the length of the header in addition to the length of the data in the fragment.

7.1.5 Header Checksum

Both protocols have a 16-bit **header checksum** field. They even both call it "header checksum," but they use different algorithms.

In IP, the header checksum is computed by doing a 1's complement add of all the 16-bit words and then taking the 1's complement of the result. A 1's complement addition of two numbers consists of a normal add, followed by an increment of the total if the add resulted in a carry. This is more robust than an unsigned add, because with a normal add, two bit errors in the most significant bit would cancel out, whereas with 1's complement, the carry from the most significant bit carries over into the least significant bit. Thus, all bit positions are equally protected by the checksum.

In CLNP, the checksum is different. It can be thought of as two 8-bit checksums. The least significant octet is similar to the IP checksum but is performed by doing 1's complement sums based on octets rather than on 16-bit words. The second octet is also calculated using 1's complement arithmetic on octets and is the sum of the value of each octet multiplied by that octet's offset from the end of the header. This might seem very expensive to compute, but it can be computed and verified with adds or table lookups and is not more expensive to compute than the IP checksum.

Note that routers modify fields in the header—most obviously, the **time to live** field, but many other fields as well if the packet must be fragmented. Thus, in addition to verifying the checksum, a router needs to recompute the checksum before forwarding a packet.

If a router recomputes the checksum from scratch after modifying the header, then the checksum really doesn't give very much protection. The main purpose of a network layer checksum is to guard against corruption by a flaky router. The checksum provided by almost all data link layer protocols guards against transmission errors. A flaky router might mangle the packet and then recompute a good checksum for the mangled packet. To reduce the likelihood of a flaky router's introducing undetected errors, CLNP requires routers to incrementally modify, rather than recompute, the checksum. (Though I wonder how that can ever be checked in a conformance test.) IP does not require incremental modification of the checksum.

Dealing with the checksum makes forwarding packets considerably more difficult, especially if the router is required to incrementally modify a packet and several fields have been changed (as in the case of fragmentation). IP always requires routers to verify and modify the checksum. CLNP allows the source to specify in a packet that the checksum is not being used, which allows the routers to spend their cycles on tasks other than verifying and incrementally modifying checksums. In CLNP, if the 2 octets of checksum are 0000000000000000, it means that the checksum is not being used and should not be checked or modified. Reserving the value 0000000000000000 for this purpose is possible because in 1's complement arithmetic, 0000000000000000 and 1111111111111111 are equivalent. Thus, if the checksum computation results in the value 0000000000000000, the value 1111111111111111 is used instead.

7.1.6   Fragmentation Allowed

Both protocols have a 1-bit flag indicating whether or not fragmentation is allowed. In IP, the flag is the middle bit of the 3 bits set aside for **flags** and is called **DF**, for "don't fragment." If this bit is 0, fragmentation is permitted. In CLNP, the flag is called **SP**, for "segmentation permitted." Thus, it is the opposite of IP. In CLNP, if the flag is 0, fragmentation is not permitted.

In CLNP, if the SP flag is 0, the fields **data unit identifier**, **segment offset**, and **total length**, which are useful only for reassembly, are omitted. Although this saves bits by decreasing the size of the header, it introduces yet another case in which the header fields are in different places, which makes building high-performance CLNP routers more of a challenge.

7.1.7   Packet Identifier

Both protocols have a field that consists of a number assigned by the source to the original unfragmented packet. Its purpose is to enable the destination to perform reassembly. Successful reassembly requires the destination to know which fragments belong together. The rule is that two fragments belong to the same original packet if the packet identifier field and the source address, destination address, and protocol fields ("protocol" is relevant only for IP) match.

In IP, the field is called **identification**; in CLNP, it is called **data unit identifier**. In CLNP, the packet identifier field is present only if the **SP** flag is set. In IP, the field is always present.

The packet identifier field should be long enough so that it will not wrap around within a packet lifetime. Both protocols have a 16-bit packet identifier field. Now that technology allows gigabit speeds, this field is definitely too small.

The consequence of an insufficiently large packet identifier field is that multiple distinct packets with the same packet identifier can exist in the network simultaneously (with the same source-destination pair). If they have been fragmented, then the destination can be fooled into combining fragments from different packets. If the transport layer has a checksum, the checksum will probably not match and the incorrectly reassembled fragments will be discarded. There is a small possibility that the checksum would not detect the error—in which case, garbled data would be delivered to the application. There is also the possibility that the transport layer may not have a checksum (which means either that it can tolerate some garbage data or that it deserves what it gets).

The problems associated with a too-small packet identifier field may not be as frightening as they sound, since they only occur when packets are fragmented. If the transport layer uses a packet size that does not require network layer fragmentation, then the packet identifier field is irrelevant (and can even be excluded, in the case of CLNP).

7.1.8   Fragment Offset

Both IP and CLNP have a field indicating the offset at which this fragment belongs in the reassembled packet. This field is 0 in a packet that has not (yet) been fragmented.

Both protocols require fragmentation to occur on 8-octet boundaries, in order to allow efficient reassembly algorithms. In IP, this field is called **fragment offset** and is 13 bits long, with the unit being in 8-octet chunks. In CLNP, this field is called **segment offset** and is 16 bits long, with the unit being in single octets. Since CLNP requires fragmentation on 8-octet chunks, the bottom 3 bits of the segment offset field in CLNP will always be 0. Thus, the fields are equivalent. They are both essentially a 13-bit field indicating the offset in 8-octet chunks. CLNP puts in the extra 3 bits "daring" you to commit the protocol crime of setting them to anything but 0.

In CLNP, the **segment offset** field is present only if the **SP** flag is set.

7.1.9   Prefragmentation Length

Only CLNP indicates the prefragmentation length, with a 2-octet field called **total length** (so as to allow confusion with the badly named IP **total length** field). The pre-fragmentation length shows the length of the original packet, including both header and data, before any fragmentation occurred. The existence of this field allows the destination to know, upon receiving any fragment of a packet, how big a buffer to set aside for reassembly. If the segmentation permitted flag is 0, this field is not in the header, since it is not needed (it is equal to CLNP's **segment length** field when a packet has not been fragmented).

IP has no equivalent field. Thus, the destination must guess at a buffer size and either copy the packet into a bigger buffer if it guessed too small, or use chains of buffer fragments.

7.1.10   More Fragments Follow

Both IP and CLNP have a 1-bit flag to distinguish the final fragment of a packet from the other fragments. In IP, this bit is called **MF**, for "more fragments"; it is set on all fragments except the last and is 0 on the last fragment. In CLNP, it is called **MS**, for "more segments," and is otherwise identical to the IP flag.

In CLNP, the **MS** flag serves no useful function, since the state of that flag can be determined from CLNP's **total length** field. If the offset plus the length of the fragment equals the total length, then it is the last fragment. It exists in CLNP because CLNP's designers started out with the IP packet format and did not notice that the flag was no longer necessary when the **total length** field was added. The **MS** flag in CLNP does no harm, except that it will confuse implementers wondering what it is supposed to be useful for, and it raises the question of what a router or the destination should do if the flag is incorrectly set (indicating that a fragment is the last when it is not or that it is not the last when it is).

7.1.11   Lifetime

Both IP and CLNP have a 1-octet lifetime field. In IP, it is called **time to live**; in CLNP, it is called **lifetime**. In both protocols, the field is initially set to some value by the source and decremented by routers until it reaches 0—at which point, the packet must be discarded.

The time unit in IP is seconds. In CLNP, it is half seconds. Both protocols specify that every router must decrement the field by at least 1. CLNP specifies that routers must overestimate rather than underestimate the amount by which the field should be decremented. I feel the field should simply be a hop count—i.e., each router should modify it by 1.

There are three reasons for having this field:

1. While routing information is propagating, routing decisions can be inconsistent among routers, and packets can loop. The lifetime field enables looping packets to be deleted. A simple hop count field (one in which every router decrements the field by 1) would suffice for the elimination of looping packets.

2. Assuming that the network layer provides the equivalent of network layer multicast addresses or simply that many servers of a certain type might all advertise a well-known network layer address, a source might want to do an expanding search in order to find the closest station that answers a particular address. For this use, again, a simple hop count field would suffice. The source might first issue the packet with a very small count, and then if no reply was received, the source might reissue the packet with a larger count, and continue the process until it either found something or decided that the search was too expensive.

3. Certain transport protocols need assurances from the network layer that packets will not live in the network longer than a certain amount of time, so that they can reuse connection identifiers and similar fields. A hop count would not solve this problem, since a packet might be delayed a very long time at one router.

   However, the granularity of the lifetime field in both protocols and the difficulty of estimation make this field not very useful for this purpose. One example of a situation in which it is impossible to estimate this field is when a router transmits a packet onto a bridged extended LAN. Once the router has successfully transmitted the packet onto its local LAN, the packet can be delayed for up to 2 sec per bridge. With the stipulation in CLNP that every router overestimate rather than underestimate, this would imply that a router would need to decrement the CLNP lifetime field by 30 (half seconds) each time the packet was forwarded onto a LAN. Another example of a situation in which it is not feasible to estimate an absolute upper limit on the delay is when transmitting onto "FDDI" ("fiber distributed data interface"). Usually, there is a very small delay before a station gets permission to transmit on FDDI, but in the worst case, the delay can be as long as 150 sec. Thus, theoretically, in order to comply with the CLNP overestimate constraint, a router would need to decrement the lifetime field by 300 (half seconds), which is larger than the maximum value of the field (255).

   I believe the only reasonable solution to the problem of guaranteeing the transport layer a maximum packet lifetime is to have the transport layer use large enough fields so that given the natural characteristics of the network, there is an acceptable probability that they will not be reused. Pretending that the lifetime field is accurate enough, or that it gives sufficient granularity to be useful and safe, is not realistic. In fact, most router implementations treat the field as a simple hop count. However, this point is controversial. There are people who feel that treating the field as a time value is practical and important to implement.

7.1.12   Version

Both protocols have a field that can be incremented if the protocol is ever modified by the standards bodies in such a way as to change the format. In IP, this field is 4 bits long; in CLNP, it is 8 bits long. In IP, the value is 4; in CLNP, the value is 1.

If **version** is not the constant value 4 in IP, or the constant value 1 in CLNP, the packet is supposed to be discarded without an error being generated (since theoretically, the packet cannot necessarily be parsed to find the source address, to which an error report would be transmitted).

There is no clear distinction between a new version of a protocol and a new protocol. Instead of changing the version field, the standards body could achieve the same effect by assigning a new data link layer SAP or protocol type to the new protocol.

7.1.13   Padding

Both IP and CLNP make provision for **padding** in the header. In IP, the header must be a multiple of 32 bits, since the header length is specified as the number of 32-bit chunks. If the IP header does not end on a 32-bit boundary, the remainder of the 32-bit chunk is filled with 0's. The IP header is variable-length because of the **options** field.

In CLNP, padding is encoded as one of the options. Unlike in IP, padding is never necessary in CLNP, but if it is convenient for the implementation to have the header end on a 16-bit or 32-bit boundary, the padding option can be used.

7.1.14   Protocol

Only IP has the **protocol** field. This 1-octet field allows the network layer at the destination endnode to know which protocol running within the endnode should receive the packet. The "assigned numbers" RFC (RFC 1060) documents which numbers are to be used for which protocols. The most obvious user of IP is TCP (the transport layer in the Internet protocol suite), but the routing protocols and other essential parts of the network layer (like ICMP) are specified as if they were separate protocols running on top of IP, and as such, they also have protocol numbers, and their data is carried inside an IP datagram.

CLNP does not officially have a comparable field. One reason is that a lot of the types of packets that IP assumes are separate protocols running on top of IP (like ICMP) are considered an integral part of CLNP (and are differentiated from data packets by the **type** field, discussed in the following subsection). Another reason is that CLNP assumes that the network layer address actually specifies the process within the destination machine, and not simply the destination machine. Thus, if there are *n* protocols running within an endnode, all using CLNP, the endnode will have *n* network layer addresses.

With the 10589 address convention, the *n* network layer addresses in a machine running *n* protocols on top of CLNP are all identical except for the final octet. Therefore, the final octet of the CLNP destination address serves the same function as the protocol field in IP.

7.1.15   Type

CLNP has a 5-bit field called **type**, which distinguishes the type of network layer packet. An ordinary CLNP data packet is type 28 (binary 11100). An error report packet is type 1. The ES-IS protocol uses types 2, 4, and 6. The IS-IS protocol uses more. Why the CLNP committee chose the number *28* for the first packet format it invented, and the number *1* for the second, is one of life's mysteries. (I asked most of the members of the committee, and their answers ranged from "Why do you care?" to "Oh, yes, I remember there was a big discussion about that, but I don't remember what was said.")

IP has no need for such a field, because it is assumed that all packets will be IP data packets, and any other types of packets would be carried as data inside IP packets, with the protocol field to differentiate them.

7.1.16   E/R

This is a 1-bit flag, in CLNP only, that if set, indicates that the source would like notification, if possible, if the packet cannot be delivered.

Typically, a transport layer will set this bit on the connection-setup packet. Once a transport connection is successfully established, the source might no longer set the E/R bit, so as not to use the network resources that would be required in order to keep it informed about lost packets.

IP has no such field. It assumes that the source would always like to know if there is a problem with delivery of its packets. The router requirements document allows, but does not require, routers to limit the number of notification messages sent. For instance, a router might generate a report only after each *n*th packet.

7.1.17   Type of Service

Both IP and CLNP have a "type of service" field, which is theoretically supposed to indicate something special about the packet that is desired by the source and can intelligently be supplied by the routers.

In IP, the field is 1 octet:

Figure 7.3

1. *Precedence:* A number from 0 ("normal" priority) to 7 ("highest" priority)

2. *D:* A flag indicating whether the source would like low delay (0 is defined as "normal" delay; 1 is defined as "low" delay)

3. *T:* A flag indicating whether the source would like "normal" throughput (0) or "high" throughput (1)

4. *R:* A flag indicating whether the source would like "normal" reliability (0) or "high" reliability (1)

Note the interesting use of the word *normal*—high delay, low throughput, low priority, and low reliability. Would you buy a network from someone who defined *normal* that way? (Don't take that comment seriously, by the way. It's just that I'm desperately trying to keep an entire chapter devoted to packet formats from being deadly dull.)

In CLNP, two options—**quality of service maintenance** (also known as **QOS**, for "quality of service") and **priority**—provide the equivalent function. As is described in the following subsection, any particular option may or may not appear in a packet. In ISO, the "globally defined" quality of service option (option code 201; binary 1100011) is 1 octet long and has the following definition:

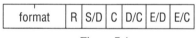

Figure 7.4

*   **Format:** 2 bits. Set to "11" to indicate that this is the "globally defined" type of service.

*   **R:** 1 bit—reserved (i.e., it is an unused bit).

*   **S/D:** 1 bit—"sequencing versus delay." If this flag is set, it indicates that the source is requesting that insofar as possible, its packets should be delivered to the destination in the order in which they were transmitted. This is implemented by having the routers transmit all packets for a particular destination with this bit set along the same path, rather than doing load splitting, when there are multiple equivalent paths to that destination. Not doing load splitting can impact throughput; hence, the "sequencing versus delay" terminology.

*   **C:** 1 bit—"congestion experienced." This flag is transmitted as 0 by the source and is set by a router along a packet's path if the packet needs to be transmitted on a congested link. The intention is for the destination to discover that the path is congested and, through some means, notify the source transport layer that it should decrease its window, so as to place less demand on the network.

This bit is an alternative to the IP scheme of having a router send an explicit "source quench" ICMP message back to the source.

There are interesting trade-offs between the two schemes (the C bit versus source quench messages). The C bit approach avoids adding traffic to an already congested network. However, the information in the source quench message is likely to reach the source more quickly than the information that the C bit was set, since the C bit must first be transmitted all the way to the destination, after which, information from the destination must be transmitted back to the source.

Usually, a source quench message is triggered by a data packet's needing to be discarded due to congestion. The C bit will be set before the network becomes so congested that it must drop packets. And of course, if the network is forced to drop the packet, the C bit will not reach the destination.

Currently, researchers are investigating these issues, including the trade-offs between the C bit and source quench messages, algorithms for setting the bit or generating a source quench message, and algorithms for reacting to the information.

- **D/C:** 1 bit—"transit delay versus cost." This flag, if set, indicates that the source regards low delay as more important than the expense of the path.

- **E/D:** 1 bit—"residual error probability versus delay." This flag, if set, indicates that the source would really prefer that none of its data be corrupted and is willing to have the routers send the packet on a slower path if that path is more reliable.

- **E/C:** 1 bit—"residual error probability versus cost." This flag, if set, indicates that the source is willing to have the routers send the packet on a more expensive path if that path is more reliable.

The last 3 bits in the preceding list have always mystified me. They were standardized without any hint as to how they should be used. There are lots of possibilities that are circular. For instance, setting **E/C** and leaving the other 2 bits clear indicates that cost is more important than delay, delay is more important than error rate, and error rate is more important than cost. This is discussed further in Chapter 9, "Routing Algorithm Issues," section 9.11.2, "Multiple Metrics."

> **Edible, adj. Good to eat, and wholesome to digest, as a worm to a toad, a toad to a snake, a snake to a pig, a pig to a man, and a man to a worm.[1]**
>
> **— Ambrose Bierce**

In CLNP, the **priority** option is the equivalent of the IP **precedence** field. **Priority** is option 205 (binary 11001101) and has a length of 1 octet, with a value between 0 (lowest priority, which CLNP also euphemistically refers to as *normal*) and 15.

Although the congestion-experienced bit really has nothing to do with type of service, this field was a convenient place to stick the bit.

[1] **Ambrose Bierce, *The Devil's Dictionary* (Mattituck, N.Y.: River City Press, 1911).**

7.1.18   Options

Both IP and CLNP have a provision for "options." Each has several options defined, and any subset of them (including none) may appear in any packet.

The general format of options is different in the two protocols. In CLNP, each option is defined by:

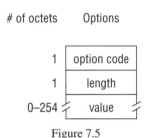

Figure 7.5

In CLNP, options can appear in any order, but no option is allowed to appear more than once.

For the CLNP options **security** and **quality of service**, the most significant 2 bits of the first octet of value have the following meaning:

1. 00 = reserved (i.e., this combination is not used).

2. 01 = *source-address-specific*. (Brace yourself for a mind-boggling definition!) This means that the interpretation of the option is not given in the spec but rather is defined by the authority from which the source got its address.

3. 10 = *destination-address-specific*. (Why not?) This means that the interpretation of the option is defined by the authority from which the destination got its address.

4. 11 = *globally unique*. This means that the interpretation of the option is given in the spec.

I am not aware of any implementations making use of anything other than the globally unique options. The source- and destination-address-specific options are not useful unless the routers are coded to understand and implement them.

The source- and destination-address-specific options might be of use in a private network, with personalized routers (i.e., routers specially coded to handle options as specified by the customers). ISO, being a standards body, was reluctant to specify how to define options—thus, it provided this level of "flexibility." However, just to show that it does have the clout to make rules, it decreed that no option should appear twice. This restriction places a burden on routers (are they supposed to check that no option appears twice every time they forward a packet?) and reduces flexibility. For instance, it precludes using padding in multiple places or using both the globally unique form of an option and the source-specified version in the same packet.

In IP, options are also coded as **code**, **length**, and **value**, but with the following differences:

1. In the **code** octet, 1 bit specifies whether a router, upon fragmenting the packet, should copy the option into every fragment (if the **copy** flag is set) or just leave the option in the first fragment.

2. Instead of defining the bottom 7 bits as the code, the IP designers chose to subdivide these bits into two fields, giving the first octet of an option the following format:

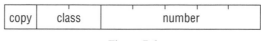

Figure 7.6

For convenience, I will refer to the **copy/class/number** octet as the "option code," even though it also contains the **copy** flag.

There is no particular reason why **class** and **number** could not be considered a single 7-bit field identifying the option. But IP decided to mark options as being either *control* (class 0) or *debugging and measurement* (class 2). Classes 1 and 3 are reserved. Class 2 is only used for a single option—**Internet timestamp**. All the other defined options have the class field equal to 0.

3. There are two options in IP that are only a single octet long—i.e., the only octet is the option code. Rather than waste an octet specifying that the option has 0 length, IP defines those options as not having the length octet, since a length of 0 is implied by the option code.

The options that are just 1 octet long are:

1. **End of option list:** IP option 0. (CLNP does not have, nor does it need, an equivalent option.) This indicates that the option list is ended. If the header length were in units of octets, this option would not be required; however, since the header length is in units of 32-bit chunks, this option indicates where the header ends. Note that since the padding is required to be transmitted as 0, the transmitter will automatically add this option when the header length is a nonintegral number of 32-bit chunks. This option may be introduced by a router after a packet is fragmented (i.e., the router may fragment the packet, and the header length may change due to an option's not being copied, which might result in the header's being a nonintegral number of 32-bit chunks). Also, if after fragmentation, the header becomes an integral number of 32-bit chunks, this option can be omitted.

2. **No Operation:** IP option 1. The equivalent option in CLNP is "padding," option 204 (binary 11001100). In CLNP, the length octet must be present even if the length equals 0, which indicates that only the option type and option length octets are present, so that with CLNP, it requires at least 2 octets to include the padding option.

The no operation option can appear any number of times in IP and might be used, for instance, to align the beginning of a subsequent option on a 32-bit boundary. In either IP or CLNP, this option can be deleted or introduced by a router anxious to modify a packet in a nondestructive manner.

Other IP options require data in addition to the option number. The format for the other options in IP is that an option length octet follows the option code, indicating the number of octets in the option. The option code octet is counted, as well as the option length octet, so the smallest value possible for the option length octet is 2. Some options are variable-length. Others are fixed-length but still require the option length octet.

Both IP and CLNP have about the same options defined. These are:

1. **Security:** Intended to specify how sensitive the information in the packet is, so perhaps the routers would choose routes that stay within the country or routes upon which link encryption can be done. Of course, neither spec says what should be done about the security option, and as long as the routers don't have special code enabling them to do something intelligent with it, the security option will have no effect (other than possibly saving a spy some time by identifying the packets in which he or she might be interested). The CLNP spec does say that if the security option is specified in a packet but a router doesn't implement that option, the router should drop the packet. The only problem is that it doesn't specify what "implementing" the option means.

2. **Source routing:** There are actually two different source routing options. In the first, "strict source routing," the entire list of routers is specified. In the other, "loose source routing," the source specifies several intermediate addresses along the route that the packet must not miss visiting, in the order specified, during its journey.

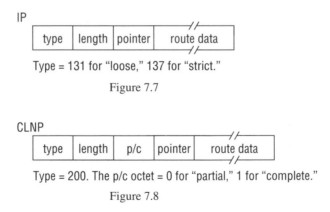

Type = 131 for "loose," 137 for "strict."

Figure 7.7

Type = 200. The p/c octet = 0 for "partial," 1 for "complete."

Figure 7.8

In both IP and CLNP, an octet in the option value field is a pointer into the route, indicating the next destination to which the packet should be routed. (In IP, it is the first octet. In CLNP it is the second octet, since the first octet is used to distinguish partial source routing from complete source routing.) The remainder of the option value field consists of the sequence of addresses that the packet must visit. In IP, since addresses are fixed-length, the sequence of addresses is just that. In CLNP, since addresses are variable-length, each address consists of a length field (giving the length of the address) followed by the address.

Strict source routing is useful when the source does not trust the routers to route properly (as when the network is broken) or when, for security reasons, the source wishes to make sure that the packet does not stray from the specified path—for instance, because the source suspects some router of having been compromised by the enemy.

Loose source routing is useful when not all of a network recognizes all addresses. For instance, a packet may originate in a portion of the network in which the routers would not recognize the destination address. If the packet is first directed to an intermediate address, with a "smarter" router that does recognize the destination address and whose address is recognized in the first portion of the network, the packet can proceed. Several intermediate destinations may be required in order for the packet to reach the final destination.

Another use of loose source routing is to allow the source to control some aspects of the route, similar to our ability to select a long-distance carrier when making a phone call.

In IP, a node has a different address for each link upon which it resides. Thus, a router (which presumably resides on multiple links, since otherwise, it wouldn't be particularly useful as a router) has several addresses. In IP, the source routing options specify that when an intermediate destination is reached, the router overwrites the hop in the route that specified its address with its address on the outgoing link. For example, if the source route consisted of A–B–C, when router B is reached, B makes a decision as to which link it should forward the packet on, in order to route to C. If B's address on the outgoing link is not "B," then it modifies the route with its alias on the outgoing link, which might be "D." Then the route will be A–D–C.

In IP, loose source routing is option 3; strict source routing is option 9. In CLNP, both are option 200 (binary 11001000), and loose and strict are distinguished by the first octet of the option value, which is 0 for "partial" source routing (ISO's word for "loose," since "loose" probably offended someone) and 1 for "complete" source routing ("strict" was probably also deemed objectionable).

An interesting mechanistic difference between the handling of source routing in IP and CLNP is that in IP, the next hop in the source route is overwritten onto the destination address field in the header. This would have been awkward in CLNP, since addresses are variable-length. Thus, in CLNP, the destination address field remains constant throughout the packet's journey, whereas in IP, it always points to the next place, as specified by the source, that the packet must visit. In both IP and CLNP, routers were not required to implement loose source routing, and they were supposed to process the packet normally (as if the option were not specified) if the option was specified in a packet. This can cause packet looping in CLNP (see Homework problem 6), and as a result, CLNP was modified to make implementation of partial source routing mandatory, which fixed the problem.

IP does not have the problem because, as just indicated, it requires the next destination to be written into the destination address field. This allows source routing to work even when intermediate routers other than those specified in the source routing header ignore the source routing option.

3. **Route recording:** This option is used to trace the path that a packet has taken. Each router that handles the packet adds its address to the route.

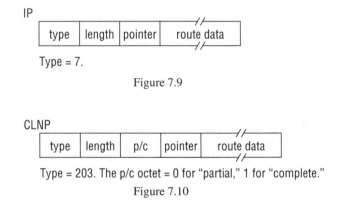

Figure 7.9

Type = 203. The p/c octet = 0 for "partial," 1 for "complete."

Figure 7.10

In CLNP, there are two types of route recording, "partial" and "complete," just as with the source routing option. If complete route recording is specified, then every router must add its address to the route. If a router receives a packet with complete route recording specified, and it does not implement route recording, it must drop the packet. If partial route recording is specified, then a packet is allowed to arrive at the destination with only some of the route recorded, since routers that do not implement partial route recording merely ignore the option if it is present. The missing hops will be routers that do not implement this option.

IP only specifies one type of route recording, which is equivalent to ISO's partial route recording, because in IP, it is not mandatory for routers to implement route recording and routers are not instructed to drop packets with this option if they do not implement route recording.

In both IP and CLNP, route recording has the same format as source routing. As in source routing, IP specifies that the router should write its address on the outgoing link into the route. CLNP does not need to specify which address a router should write into the route, because in CLNP, routers are assumed to have only a single address.

In both IP and CLNP, the source makes the record route option **value** field as long as it thinks is necessary. Routers do not increase the length of the header as a result of adding their address to the route.

Both IP and CLNP specify that when the route is full, the packet is forwarded on without modification to the route field, even if (in CLNP) complete route recording is specified. There is a subtlety in CLNP. Suppose that a packet is traveling the following path:

Figure 7.11

Since CLNP addresses are variable-length, it could be that complete route recording is being done, and router R4 discovers that there is insufficient room in the route data to put its address. If it merely forwarded the packet on, it could be that R5, with a shorter address, might write its address into the route data, which would confuse someone trying to make sense out of the supposedly complete, but in fact truncated, route. Thus, when R4 discovers that it cannot fit its address into the route, it sets the "pointer" octet to all 1's, indicating that no more route recording is to be done.

In IP, route recording is option 7; in CLNP, it is option 203 (binary 1100 1011). Complete route recording is distinguished from partial route recording by the first octet of option value, which is 0 for partial route recording and 1 for complete route recording.

4. **Internet timestamp:** This option, offered by IP, is option 4, class 2. CLNP has no equivalent.

The format is:

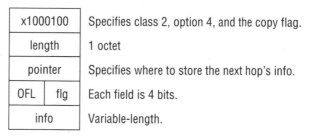

Figure 7.12

The **info** field is either a sequence of 32-bit timestamps, marking the local time at each router at which the packet was received, or it is a sequence of (address, timestamp) pairs, with each router recording its address as well as the timestamp.

If **flg** is 0, the routers just record the timestamp. If it is 1, they record their address plus the timestamp. If it is 3, it indicates that the source specified the addresses of the routers that should store their timestamps, with space in between for the timestamps to be stored.

As with route recording, the source allots whatever size it wishes for the timestamp recording, and when it fills up, routers increment the **OFL** ("overflow") field, indicating how many timestamps—or (address, timestamp) pairs—were not stored due to lack of space.

The timestamp is a right-justified, 32-bit timestamp in milliseconds since midnight universal time.

7.2   Error Reports and Other Network Feedback to the Endnode

Although IP and CLNP provide datagram service, they are thoughtful enough to provide notification of trouble and other information to an attached endnode, if possible.

In CLNP, an error report has the same format as a data packet, except that the **type** field (the bottom 5 bits of the fifth octet) is equal to 1, indicating that it is an error report, rather than 28 (binary 11100), which is a data packet.

When a router R cannot forward a packet from source S, R will send S an error report if S has set the **E/R** ("error report requested") flag in that packet's header. The source address will be R; the destination address will be S. The reason for discard is put into the error report's header, coded to look like the other options. It has code 1100 0001, its length is 2 octets. The value of the first octet is the type of error that is listed below. The value of the second octet is a pointer into the header where the error occurred. There are lots of error types, and it is in no way obvious what they all mean. The error types were defined prior to the definition of any sort of routing protocol that would have provided a sensible context for them. Luckily, most of the defined error types do make sense, and they include most errors that one would want reported. The error types are as follows:

error code	meaning
0	Reason not specified
1	Protocol procedure error
2	Incorrect checksum
3	Congestion
4	Header syntax incorrect, header can't be parsed
5	Segmentation required, but SP set to 0 (segmentation not permitted)
6	Packet incomplete (header or total length doesn't match unfragmented packet size)
7	An option appeared twice
128	Destination address unreachable

129	Destination address unknown
144	Unspecified source routing error
145	Syntax error in source routing field
146	Unknown address in source routing field
147	Specified source routing path not acceptable
160	Lifetime expired while packet in transit
161	Lifetime expired at destination during reassembly
176	Unsupported option not specified (That's the wording in 8473, and it is supposedly self-explanatory. What it is intended to mean is that the packet contains an option that this router never heard of, and that option is such that it should be dropped by a router that doesn't support it. Unfortunately, 8473 says that if there's an option the router never heard of, the router should assume it is safe to ignore the option and forward the packet, so this error should never occur.)
177	Unsupported protocol version
178	Unsupported security option
179	Unsupported source routing option
180	Unsupported recording of route option
192	Reassembly interference

The data portion of the error report packet contains at least all of the doomed datagram's network layer header but may contain more. It is friendly of a router to provide at least enough more than the network layer header so that the entire transport header is included. This enables the source to match the returned datagram with the user process.

An error report packet has the "segmentation permitted" flag off. If an error report packet needs to be forwarded but is too long, a router will truncate the packet.

In IP, the functionality provided by CLNP error reports is provided by the ICMP protocol. The ICMP packet is carried in the data portion of an ordinary IP packet. The "protocol" field in the IP header will indicate ICMP. The basic format of ICMP messages is:

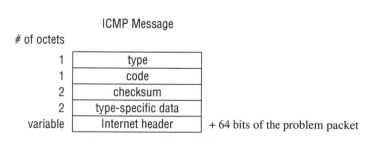

Figure 7.13

The ICMP message types are:

> 0 = echo reply
>
> 3 = destination unreachable
>
> 4 = source quench
>
> 5 = redirect
>
> 8 = echo request
>
> 11 = time exceeded
>
> 12 = parameter problem
>
> 13 = timestamp request
>
> 14 = timestamp reply
>
> 15 = information request
>
> 16 = information reply
>
> 17 = address mask request
>
> 18 = address mask reply

The message types "destination unreachable," "time exceeded," and "parameter problem" together provide the functionality in CLNP error report packets.

The general format of these ICMP error report messages is:

1. **Type:** 1 octet.

   > 12 = parameter problem.
   >
   > 11 = time exceeded.
   >
   > 3 = destination unreachable.

2. **Code:** 1 octet.

   a. In *time exceeded*:

   > 0 = died in transit
   >
   > 1 = died while being reassembled by destination.

   b. In *destination unreachable:*

   > 0 = net unreachable.
   >
   > 1 = host unreachable.
   >
   > 2 = protocol unreachable.
   >
   > 3 = port unreachable.

        4 = fragmentation required but not allowed by DF.

        5 = source route failed.

    c. In *parameter problem*: Code unused, set to 0.

3. **Pointer:** 1 octet. Used only in *parameter problem*. It is a pointer into the header indicating where a problem was found.

4. **Unused:** 3 octets.

5. **Internet header** + 64 bits of doomed datagram.

The other ICMP messages are:

1. *Echo:* An echo request can be used to decide whether some destination is reachable. Any IP machine receiving an echo request is supposed to respond with an echo reply.

    An echo request is known as a "ping." *Ping* can also be used as a verb. To *ping* node X means to send X an echo request. This is a method of testing whether X is alive, well, and reachable.

    a. **Type:** 1 octet.

        8 = echo request message.

        0 = echo reply message.

    b. **Code:** 1 octet = 0.

    c. **Checksum:** 2 octets. 16-bit 1's complement checksum of the ICMP message.

    d. **Identifier:** 2 octets. A number that helps the echo requester match the reply to the request.

    e. **Sequence number:** 2 octets. Another number that helps the echo requester match the reply to the request.

    f. **Data:** Variable. Anything echo requester wants to put in. (It will be copied into echo reply.)

    The **identifier** and **sequence number** fields can be thought of as a single 4-octet field that allows the echo requester to match the reply with the request. It was written as two fields because the suggested use was for the identifier to correspond to the TCP (transmission control protocol) or UDP (user datagram protocol) port number and for the sequence number to be incremented on each request.

2. *Timestamp request* or *timestamp reply:*

    a. **Type:** 1 octet.

        13 = timestamp request message.

        0 = timestamp reply message.

   b. **Code:** 1 octet = 0.

   c. **Checksum:** 2 octets. 16-bit 1's complement checksum of the ICMP message.

   d. **Identifier:** 2 octets. A number that helps the requester match the reply to the request.

   e. **Sequence number:** 2 octets. Another number that helps the requester match the reply to the request.

   f. **Originate timestamp:** 4 octets. Timestamp put in by the requester to indicate the most recent known time before transmission of the timestamp request.

   g. **Receive timestamp:** 4 octets. Timestamp put in by the replier to indicate the time that the request was received.

   h. **Transmit timestamp:** 4 octets. Timestamp put in by the replier to indicate the time that the reply was transmitted.

3. *Information request* or *information reply:*

   a. **Type:** 1 octet.

      15 = information request message.

      0 = information reply message.

   b. **Code:** 1 octet. = 0.

   c. **Checksum:** 2 octets. 16-bit 1's complement checksum of the ICMP message.

   d. **Identifier:** 2 octets. A number that helps the requester match the reply to the request.

   e. **Sequence number:** 2 octets. A number that helps the requester match the reply to the request.

The *information request message* is used by a host that does not know the "network" number of the LAN on which it resides. The information request message is sent with the network portion of the source and destination addresses in the IP header equal to 0, and the reply has the addresses in the IP header fully specified.

    The *information request* ICMP message is largely obsolete. A much more practical scheme for finding out the missing information is with the BOOTP protocol.

4. *Address mask request* or *address mask reply:*

   a. **Type:** 1 octet.

      17 = address mask request message.

      18 = address mask reply message.

   b. **Code:** 1 octet. = 0.

   c. **Checksum:** 2 octets. 16-bit 1's complement checksum of the ICMP message.

   d. **Identifier:** 2 octets. A number that helps the requester match the reply to the request.

   e. **Sequence number:** 2 octets. Another number that helps the requester match the reply to the request.

   f. **Address mask:** 4 octets.

   The address mask request message is used by a host that does not know its address mask. The reply contains the correct address mask. This message is described in RFC 950. It was added to ICMP after RFC 792 was published.

5. *Source quench:*

   a. **Type:** 1 octet. = 4.

   b. **Code:** 1 octet. = 0.

   c. **Checksum**.

   d. **Unused:** 4 octets.

   e. **IP header** + 64 bits of the dead datagram.

   The source quench message informs the source that the network is congested and that the source should attempt to lower its demand on the network. This message serves the same purpose as the "congestion-experienced" bit in the CLNP header. The IP method (sending a source quench message) has an advantage over the CLNP method, in that a source quench is delivered to the source, which is where the information may be used, but it has the disadvantage of causing an extra message to be generated in a congested network.

6. *Redirect:* This message is discussed in Chapter 8.

Homework

1. Suppose you are a router that needs to forward a fragment of size n onto a link that can only handle packets of size m. Give the values of all the appropriate header fields, as a function of what they were in the received packet, as they should be transmitted for each outgoing fragment. Do this for both CLNP and IP.

2. Why is the "packet identifier" field not needed for X.25?

3. Both IP and CLNP specify that besides the packet identifier field, the **source address** and **destination address** fields (and in IP, the **protocol** field as well) should also be checked to determine whether two fragments belong to the same original packet. What does this imply about the algorithm for assigning packet identifiers?

    Suppose that the two protocols instead specified that only the **source address** and **packet identifier** fields were to be checked to determine whether two fragments belong to the same original packet. What advantages and disadvantages would this modification have? Take into account the probability of wraparound of the packet identifier field as well as CPU and memory in the source and destination stations.

    Suppose that this modification were made to the two protocols. Would stations implemented according to the old specification interwork properly with stations implemented according to the new specification?

    Suppose that the two protocols instead specified that only the **packet identifier** field was to be checked to determine whether two fragments belonged to the same original packet. Would this work?

4. IP does not have a "prefragmentation length" field. How can a destination reassemble packets without this field?

5. In the source routing options in IP, a router R that is one of the intermediate destinations overwrites the hop in the route that specifies R with its address on the outgoing link. Under what conditions will the router's overwriting of its specified address with its address on the outgoing link not cause the option value to be modified? Draw a picture of a network, specifying the routers' addresses on each link, and give a source route that would not be modified upon reaching the destination.

    If IP did not specify that routers must overwrite their address on the outgoing link, what would happen if the destination attempted to use the specified route (but in reverse order) when reaching the source?

6. How can a loop be created in CLNP as a result of a router's ignoring the partial source routing option? Why does mandating the implementation of partial source routing in CLNP fix the problem?

    Why doesn't IP have the same problem?

7. In IP route recording, would it be easier, harder, or neither easier nor harder to reconstruct a route if the routers recorded their address on the link from which the packet arrived rather than their address on the link on which they will forward the packet?

8. Suppose that a router implemented the **S/D** bit by choosing the path to a particular destination based on the source address in the packet. In other words, if

there are two equivalent paths to destination DEST, the router might send all packets with the S/D bit set on the first path if the source address was numerically even, and send all packets with the S/D bit set on the second path if the source address was numerically odd. Would this be a good or bad idea? If some routers did it this way and others did it the "standard" way (sending all packets to DEST on the same path if the S/D bit was set), would there be any problems with the schemes interworking?

Chapter 8
Network Layer Neighbor Greeting

Neighbor greeting is one of three more or less orthogonal aspects of a network layer protocol, as described in Chapter 7, "Connectionless Data Exchange." Neighbor greeting is the process by which endnodes find adjacent routers, distinguish adjacent nodes from those only reachable through a router, and find the data link layer address of adjacent nodes. It is also the process by which routers find the network layer address and data link layer address of adjacent endnodes.

In ISO, this portion of the protocol is defined in document 9542, commonly known as the "ES-IS" protocol. In TCP/IP, most of this is defined in either ICMP or ARP.

8.1. The Problem

Handshaking between neighbors is different when the neighbors are attached with a point-to-point link or a LAN. First I'll explore the specific problems in each situation, and then I'll discuss the ISO and IP solutions.

8.1.1   Endnodes Attached via Point-to-Point Links

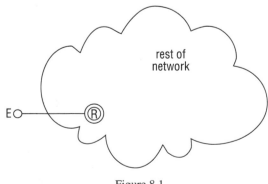

Figure 8.1

When an endnode E is attached to the network with a point-to-point link, the only necessary part of the neighbor discovery protocol is for the router R to discover E's network layer address. This enables R to route packets to E and to announce E's network layer address to other routers, so that they can direct packets destined to E toward R.

In ISO, this is accomplished by having the endnode periodically transmit a packet known as an *end-system hello*, or *ESH*, that announces its network layer address. This periodic announcement of the endnode's network layer address is really sufficient to allow the network layer to operate. There is no reason for the endnode on a point-to-point link to know the identity of the adjacent router. When the endnode has a packet to transmit, all it needs to do is transmit the packet with the destination's network layer address. Since there are only two nodes on a point-to-point link, there is no need for a data link layer address. ("Hey, you! Yes, of course, I mean you. Who else would I be talking to? The cable?")

In IP, there's an even more trivial protocol for handling endnodes attached to point-to-point links—the router must be configured with the IP address and mask for each of its links. No protocol between the endnode and router is required. Although the protocol is indeed simple (the simplest protocol is no protocol at all), the IP strategy requires significantly more configuration than the ISO method.

8.1.2   Endnodes Attached via LANs

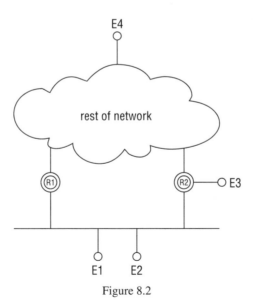

Figure 8.2

As I discuss the mechanisms in the IP and ISO schemes, I will refer to the following problems and show how each mechanism solves one of these problems:

1. As in the point-to-point case, the routers on the LAN (R1 and R2) need to know the network layer addresses of their neighbor endnodes so that they can announce to the rest of the network that they can reach E1 and E2.

2. The routers on the LAN need to know the data link layer addresses of their neighbor endnodes so that they can fill in the appropriate destination address in the data link layer header when forwarding a packet the final hop to the destination endnode.

3. The endnodes on the LAN (E1 and E2) need to know the data link layer address of at least one router so that they can forward packets through the router when necessary.

4. When E1 needs to communicate with E2, it should be possible for E1 to send packets directly to E2 rather than having to transmit each packet initially to a router and then having the router forward the packet to E2. If this were not possible, forwarding packets via the router would still work, but it would result in a doubling of intra-LAN traffic.

5. When E1 needs to communicate with E3, it should be possible for E1 to find out that R2 is a better router to use than R1. If this were not possible, things would still work, but when E1 talks to E3, the LAN traffic will be doubled if E1 chooses R1 rather than R2 because each packet from E1 to E3 would result in two packets transmitted on the LAN: one from E1 to R1 and another from R1 to R2.

6. If R1 and R2 were broken, it should still be possible for E1 and E2 to communicate. In order for that to happen, E1 and E2 need to find out each other's data link layer address.

8.2 The ISO Solution

In the ISO solution, there are three types of messages:

1. *End-system hello, or ESH:* As with a point-to-point endnode, a LAN endnode periodically transmits an ESH, announcing its presence. On a LAN, the data link layer destination address is a special group address listened to by the routers ("intermediate systems," in ISO terminology).

2. *Intermediate-system hello, or ISH:* This message is similar to the ESH, except that it is periodically transmitted by a router and is transmitted to a special data link layer group address listened to by the endnodes.

3. *Redirect message:* This message is transmitted by router R to endnode E, after E sends R a packet to forward, with network layer destination address D, and R notices that it forwards the packet back onto the same link from which it arrived, either directly to D or to a more optimal router. The contents of the redirect inform E that for destination address D, it really ought to send to the data link layer address that R used when forwarding the packet back onto the LAN.

The periodic transmission of ESHs by the endnodes on the LAN enables the routers to learn the network layer addresses of the endnodes, so that they can announce these destinations to the other routers in the network (thus solving problem 1), as well as find out the data link layer address corresponding to the network layer address for each endnode (solving problem 2).

The periodic transmission of ISHs by the routers on the LAN enables the endnodes to learn the data link layer addresses of the routers (solving problem 3) and their network layer addresses.

A slightly simplified version of the endnode algorithm (I'll explain in a minute the additional protocol needed) is:

1. Listen for ISHs. Store each data link layer address from which an ISH is received in a cache (the "router cache") and time it out if a new ISH is not heard within a specified period.

2. Keep a cache (the "destination cache") of <destination network layer address, data link layer address> correspondence.

3. When transmitting to destination D:

    a. If D is in the destination cache, with data link layer address X, transmit the packet with data link layer destination address X.

    b. If D is not in the destination cache and there is at least one router in the router cache, transmit the packet to a data link layer address (any of them) in the router cache.

       The final case, in which D is not in the destination cache and the router cache is empty, will be deferred for a moment so the simple case can be explained.

4. Upon receiving a *redirect* message with the information that data link layer address X should be used when forwarding to network layer address D, put <D, X> in the destination cache.

The way things work is that initially, E1 and E2 build up their router cache. When E1 wishes to transmit a packet to E4, it chooses the data link layer address of one of the routers. When E4 is the destination, either router will forward the packet through the network. One might be slightly more optimal than the other, but unless the chosen router actually forwards the packet back onto the same link from which it was received, no redirect will be generated.

When E1 wishes to transmit a packet to E3, E1 will, as before, choose the data link layer address of one of the routers. If it chooses R2, everything is fine. If it chooses R1, everything is still fine, but R1 forwards the packet over the LAN to R2 and sends E1 a redirect, telling E1 that in order to talk to E3, it should use R2's data link layer address (solving problem 5).

When E1 wishes to transmit a packet to E2, it will again choose the data link layer address of one of the routers. The data packet will get forwarded by the chosen router, but that router will also send a redirect to E1 informing it to use E2's data link layer address when communicating with E2 (solving problem 4).

So far, problem 6 hasn't been solved. What happens when there is no router on the LAN? Maybe there never was, because the entire network consists of one LAN. Maybe there were routers, but they are all out to lunch. The topology then is:

Figure 8.3

The additional endnode protocol rules for handling this case are:

1. When transmitting to destination D, if D is not in the destination cache and the router cache is empty (the case I postponed discussing earlier), transmit the data packet to the group address ALL ESs.

2. If you are an end system and receive a data packet from the data link layer address ALL ESs, and the network layer address matches yours, accept the packet (otherwise, discard it) and transmit your ESH to the data link layer source address in the received data packet.

3. If you are an end system and receive an ESH informing you that network layer address D corresponds to data link layer address X, put <D, X> in the destination cache.

These additional rules solve problem 6. If there is no router, E1 multicasts the data packet to E2, unfortunately bothering all the other endnodes on the wire with a "wrong-number" packet, but E2 responds with its ESH, so that E1 will address future packets for E2 with E2's data link layer address. As the protocol is specified, when E2 responds with a data packet to E1, it will go through the same procedure, initially multicasting to ALL ESs, receiving E1's ESH, and putting E1 in its destination cache.

When E1 wishes to communicate with E3 (an endnode not on the LAN), E1 will also multicast the packet to ALL ESs, since it does not know that E3 is not on the LAN. E3 will not receive the packet, since no vendors to date have implemented an interface to the "ESP medium." Hopefully, the upper-layer protocol at E1, upon not receiving a reply, will stop transmitting packets to E3 or will at least not retry frequently.

The cache timeouts are specified in the ISO protocol. All three protocol messages (ESH, ISH, and redirect) contain a "holding timer" indicating how long the corresponding cache entry should be kept in the cache. Each node on the LAN can have its own configured time for how long it thinks neighbors should remember it. If a node specifies a particular holding timer value, its period at which it transmits hellos should be about three times smaller than that holding timer value, so that a modest percentage of lost or delayed hello messages will not cause neighbors to assume that the node is down.

There is one additional subtle detail of the ISO scheme. When a redirect message points toward a router, the network layer address of the router is included in the redirect. This information allows an endnode, when it notices (through lack of received ISHs from router R) that R has gone down, to delete entries in the destination cache that are pointing toward R. Therefore, the destination cache contains an indication of whether the redirect is toward a router, and if so, it also contains the router's network layer address.

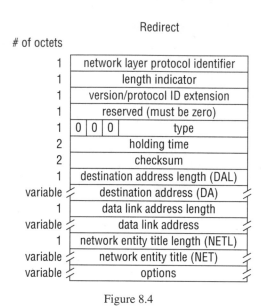

Figure 8.4

8.3   The TCP/IP Solution

In IP, the link number is a part of the network layer address, recognizable by all the nodes attached to the link. As explained in Chapter 6, "Network Layer Addresses," an IP node knows its 32-bit IP address as well as a 32-bit mask. The mask has 1's in the bits corresponding to the "link" portion of the address. If your IP address is X and your mask is Y, to determine whether a node with IP address Z is on the same link, you AND the mask Y with X and AND the mask Y with Z, and if the result is the same, Z is on the same link.

Also, IP routing does not route to the destination endnode. Instead, it routes to the destination link. This is really the same as saying that there is no level 1 routing (the LAN provides the level 1 routing).

Again referring to the set of problems that I said needed to be solved by the neighbor discovery mechanism, problem 1 is solved in IP by manual configuration of the routers attached on the LAN. Routers know the set of network layer addresses reachable on one of their links because they have been manually configured with the link number and mask of each of their links.

There are three protocol messages in IP to solve the remaining problems:

1. *Address resolution protocol (ARP) query:* This is a message sent to the data link layer broadcast address indicating a network layer address for which the transmitter seeks a corresponding data link layer address.

2. *Address resolution protocol response:* This is a message transmitted in response to an ARP query by the node whose network layer address was queried. It contains the desired data link layer address.

3. *Redirect:* This message, which is specified in the ICMP protocol, contains the network layer address of another router.

When a node N on link L wishes to transmit a packet to a network layer address D that is also on link L, N first transmits an ARP query to the data link layer broadcast address, with data indicating that N seeks D's data link layer address. All nodes on L are bothered with the packet (even non-IP nodes, since the ARP query is transmitted to the broadcast address), and all but D throw it away after examining the data and discovering it is not their network layer address that is being queried. If D receives the ARP query and sees "D" inside, D replies with an ARP response, transmitted to the data link layer source address in the received ARP query.

When N receives the ARP response, it makes an entry <D, DL address> in a cache known as the "ARP cache."

With the aforementioned procedures, plus some configuration or the use of an initialization protocol such as RARP or BOOTP so that endnodes know L's address and mask, problems 2, 4, and 6 are solved.

Problem 3 involves having endnodes find the routers. There is no standardized method for solving this in IP. To date, the best solution has been to manually configure each endnode with the network layer address of at least one router. If the endnode has been manually configured with the address of only a single router, and that router happens to be down, then that endnode will not be able to communicate with nodes off the LAN.

Various implementations have used a number of ad hoc methods to less inelegantly solve the problem of having endnodes find routers. An example involves making an assumption that the routers will be running RIP (a routing protocol) and listening to the data link layer addresses from which RIP messages are broadcast. It would be possible to merely copy the relevant portion of ES-IS (have the routers periodically advertise), but a decision to do this has not yet been made. A working group is studying the problem. As of the writing of this book, the working group's proposal consists of having the routers issue the equivalent of ISHs, but very infrequently (say, every 10 min)—sufficiently infrequently that a new endnode coming up would not want to wait for a periodic ISH, thus necessitating an additional mechanism for the endnode to query the routers to get them to generate hellos.

I prefer a more adequately frequent hello interval from the routers. Not only does it avoid the extra query mechanism, but it also gives useful information regarding when a router has crashed. If a router only transmits hellos every 10 min, then it would take a long time for an endnode to notice that the router has gone down (since an endnode probably shouldn't assume that a router is down if it misses only a single hello). Either traffic will be sent into a black hole for 20 to 30 min until the endnode realizes that the router has gone down, or endnodes will need to "ping" the routers whenever they fail to reach a destination. This will result in far more traffic on the wire than just having the routers issue hellos more frequently (such as every 10 sec), as in the ISO scheme.

Problem 5 is solved by redirect messages, as in ISO. There is one difference, however. The only useful piece of information in a redirect message is the data link layer address that should have been used when communicating with the destination. In IP, that information is not included in the redirect. Instead, the network layer address of the router to which the packet should be forwarded is provided. When E1 wishes to communicate with E3 and sends the packet to R1 rather than R2 for forwarding, R1 will send a redirect to E1 indicating R2's network layer address. At this point (unless R2 is already in E1's ARP cache), E1 must do an ARP query to R2 to obtain the relevant data link layer address. Although this is rather ugly, it does not have any significant performance implications. I asked why it was done that way and received two answers:

1. ICMP (which describes the redirect message) was invented before LANs, so the concept of needing a data link layer address did not exist.

2. "It would be a gross layer violation to provide a data link layer address in a network layer protocol message." I don't believe this argument at all, but it was spoken in a tone of voice that indicated I would be ill-advised to attempt to pursue the matter further at that time with the individual in question.

8.4   Review

To review the two approaches, and still using the figure presented at the start of subsection 8.1.2:

1. Routers R1 and R2 need to find out which network layer addresses are reachable on the LAN. In ISO, this is accomplished by having the endnodes periodically broadcast ESHs. In IP, this is accomplished by manual configuration of the routers, together with the convention that the link number is included in the IP address.

2. E1 wishes to communicate with E2. In ISO, this is solved by having E1 initially transmit to one of the routers—say, R1—and having R1 forward the packet to E2 and send a redirect to E1. E1 then makes a destination cache entry for E2 and sends future packets directly to E2. In IP, E1 knows that E2 is on the LAN because E1 has been configured with (or has acquired) the LAN number and mask. E1 initially sends an ARP query to E2; after receiving an ARP response, E1 stores E2 in its ARP cache and thereafter sends packets directly to E2.

3. E1 wishes to communicate with E3. In both protocols, if E1 chooses the "wrong" router, R1, that router forwards the packet anyway and sends a redirect. The only difference is that in IP, an additional ARP query might be needed to find R2's data link layer address.

4. E1 wishes to communicate with E4. In both protocols, E1 chooses either router, and the packet is forwarded without complaint.

5. R1 and R2 are down, and E1 wishes to communicate with E3. Neither protocol will succeed in getting E1 to converse with E3 because there is no connectivity between them. In ISO, E1 will send the packet to the group address ALL ESs, which bothers all the ESs and gets no response. In IP, E1 will send the packet to one of the routers and get no response.

   If at some point some mechanism (similar in functionality to ES-IS) is added to IP to inform the endnodes that the routers are down, then E1 will know it cannot reach E3. In the IP mechanism, even in the absence of a means for E1 to know that the routers are down, E1's "useless" packet to the router is less costly than ISO's "useless" packet multicast to ALL ESs because the IP message does not cause software interrupts at all the endnodes on the LAN. (However, this situation only occurs when all the LAN routers are down.)

6. R1 and R2 are down, and E1 wishes to communicate with E2. In ISO, E1 sends the packet to the group address ALL ESs, which bothers all the ESs but does get a response from E2, which transmits its ESH to E1. E1 thereupon puts E2 into its destination cache, and future transmissions work as desired. In IP, E1 knows that E2 is on the LAN and does an ARP query to get the data link layer address. In this case, the ISO and IP schemes are functionally almost identical. The only difference is that in ISO the multicast packet actually carries the data. In IP the ARP query and response must be transmitted before the first data packet between E1 and E2 can be transmitted.

7. R2 has gone down, but E2's information indicates that traffic for E3 should be redirected toward R2. In ISO, lack of receipt of ISHs from R2 will alert E2 that R2 has gone down. When E2 notices this, it scans its destination cache for entries using R2's network layer address and deletes them. In IP, there is no mechanism for E2 to discover that R2 is down.

8.5   Comparison

Both the ISO and TCP/IP schemes require a certain amount of control traffic on a LAN. In ISO, the overhead is primarily due to ESHs (there are so few routers that the overhead due to ISHs is insignificant). In TCP/IP, the overhead is due to ARP queries and responses. Evaluating the significance of the bandwidth usage in either scheme is an interesting research problem.

In IP, endnodes are forced to waste CPU cycles receiving and discarding ARP queries for other nodes. In ISO, endnodes are forced to waste CPU cycles when a node wishes to communicate with another node, but only when there are no routers on the LAN. In ISO, even if the entire topology is a single LAN, so no routers are needed, if the CPU cycles spent receiving and discarding data traffic destined for other nodes get to be a nuisance, a router can be added to the LAN. Despite the fact that it never attaches to another link, the router can eliminate the need for multicasting data messages. If the router is known to be required only to stop the nuisance of multicast data messages, a very simple box (which I'll call a "pseudorouter") will suffice. It need not implement any routing protocol (since the entire network consists of just one link). Homework problem 1 asks what functions a pseudorouter must perform.

The ARP versus ES-IS debate is highly charged. ES-IS was designed the way it was because:

1. It was assumed that CPU cycles in endnodes were precious. If this assumption is true, then the fact that ES-IS does not force endnodes to get software interrupts when two unrelated nodes start communicating (as ARP does) is an important advantage.

2. ES-IS was designed before the structure of ISO network layer addresses was standardized. Thus, there was no way to include a link number in an ISO address.

3. Even if it had been possible to define the structure of ISO addresses so as to include the link number, it was felt that establishing the restriction that every link must have its own link number placed too great a burden on the level 2 routing. Rather, it seemed preferable to lump as many little LANs and point-to-point links into a single area as was possible without overloading the level 1 routing in the area.

The people who hate ES-IS think that:

1. The bandwidth consumed by ESHs is too high and is much higher than ARP traffic.

    No careful analysis has been done to truly compare the two schemes with respect to their relative use of bandwidth. Theoretically, once ARP caches are built up, no further bandwidth use is required. However, if ARP cache timers are too long, then invalidating incorrect entries becomes a problem.

    Furthermore, if a node wishes to communicate with a node that is down, it will need to do an ARP query, since there is no way to distinguish an incorrect ARP entry from a dead destination. It could be argued that ES-IS uses *less* bandwidth, if assumptions are made about the frequency with which endnodes seek conversations with other endnodes and about reasonably small ARP caches in the endnodes.

    My intuition says that the bandwidth used by the two schemes does not differ significantly, and that neither scheme uses enough bandwidth to degrade network performance significantly, so bandwidth should not be the criterion for choosing one scheme or the other.

2. Too much bandwidth and too much memory in the routers are consumed by forcing routers to keep track of every endnode instead of just keeping track of the links. I'd answer this by saying that ISO *allows* you to assign a different area number to each LAN—in which case, knowledge of the individual endnodes on the LAN would not be propagated off the LAN. ISO just doesn't *force* an area to be a single LAN. Thus, if several LANs and point-to-point links can be aggregated into an area, and level 1 routing can handle the area appropriately, then keeping track of endnodes should not be an issue.

Homework

1. What functions must be performed by a pseudorouter, as defined in section 8.5?

2. Give arguments for why the background traffic caused by ARP queries and responses would be more than, less than, or (relatively) equal to the background traffic caused by ESHs.

3. If the link number on which a node resides were standardized to be a recognizable portion of the ISO address, what changes might be made to the ISO protocol? (Assume that ISO would not implement ARP because of the desire to avoid forcing endnodes to consume CPU cycles receiving and discarding ARP messages.)

4. A *broadcast storm* is an event causing a flurry of messages. Some storms only last a few seconds; others persist indefinitely or for such a long time they might as well be never-ending. Broadcast storms have chiefly been observed with the IP protocols. One of the main implementation decisions that cause storms is the decision (in the Berkeley Unix endnode IP implementation) that an endnode should attempt to forward a packet that it mysteriously receives with a network layer address of a different endnode. This is what you, as a good citizen, would do if you found a neighbor's letter wrongly placed in your mailbox. However, it is not a good thing for an endnode to do.

   Suppose an IP endnode is incorrectly configured and it thinks that its data link address is all 1's, i.e., the data link layer "broadcast" address. What happens when someone attempts to transmit a data packet to that node? Give the sequence of events.

Chapter 9
Routing Algorithm Issues

> **More than any time in history mankind faces a crossroads. One path leads to despair and utter hopelessness, the other to total extinction. Let us pray that we have the wisdom to choose correctly.**
>
> **— Woody Allen[1]**

In this chapter, I discuss the third piece in the network layer protocol, the routing algorithms and protocols. There are basically two types of distributed routing algorithms:

1. Distance vector

2. Link state

All the popular network layer routing protocols are based on one or the other. In this chapter, I consider these distributed routing protocols generically. In later chapters, I examine specific routing protocols derived from them.

I also discuss, generically, other problems that arise in routing, such as supporting multiple types of service, modifying routes to account for current traffic distribution, supporting a connection-oriented interface, and providing WAN multicast.

9.1 Distance Vector Routing

Distance vector routing is sometimes known in the literature by other names. Probably the least sensible name for it is "old ARPANET routing." It is also sometimes referred to as "Bellman-Ford," after the people who invented the algorithm from which distance vector routing is derived.

Distance vector routing requires that each node maintain the distance from itself to each possible destination. The distances are computed using the information in neighbors' distance vectors.

Imagine that you are sitting at the intersection of several roads.

[1] **Robert Byrne, *1911 Best Things Anybody Ever Said* (New York: Ballantine Books, 1988), 82.**

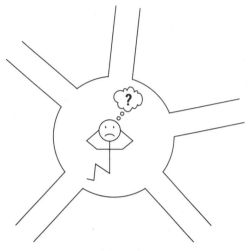

Figure 9.1

Your job is to post signs of the following form:

Figure 9.2

You have been told that you must post a complete set of signs (one for each town), but you haven't even been told the names of all the towns. The only thing you have been told is the name of the town in which your intersection is located (for instance, "Hereville"). You can start by constructing a sign like this:

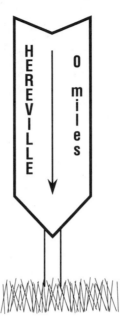

Figure 9.3

How can you proceed further? Luckily, you know that at every intersection, someone has been hired to do the same work you're doing. You can fulfill your obligation as follows:

1. Measure the distance to the nearest intersection down each of the roads radiating from your location.

2. Keep track of the set of signs posted at each of the neighboring intersections.

Now calculate the distance to each town independently by figuring out which direction will yield the smallest total distance. For instance, in Fig. 9.4, there are five possible ways to get to Littleton.

If you go down Highway A, it will be 31 miles to the intersection, from which (according to the sign there), Littleton is an additional 159 miles, yielding a total distance of 190 miles. If you go down Highway B, the total distance will be 22 + 206, or 228 miles. Highway C yields a distance of 4 + 319, or 323. Highway D yields 112 + 74, or 186. And Highway E yields 81 + 180, or 261. Thus, the best way to get to Littleton is down Highway D. The sign you post should read "Littleton 186" and point down Highway D.

The trouble with our age is all signposts and no destination.

— Louis Kronenberger [2]

Now the question is, "How did your fellow sign painters get *their* information?" Amazingly enough, they can be doing the same thing you are—i.e., scouting down each

[2] **James B. Simpson, *Simpson Contemporary Quotations* (New York: Thomas Y. Crowell Company, 1964), 314.**

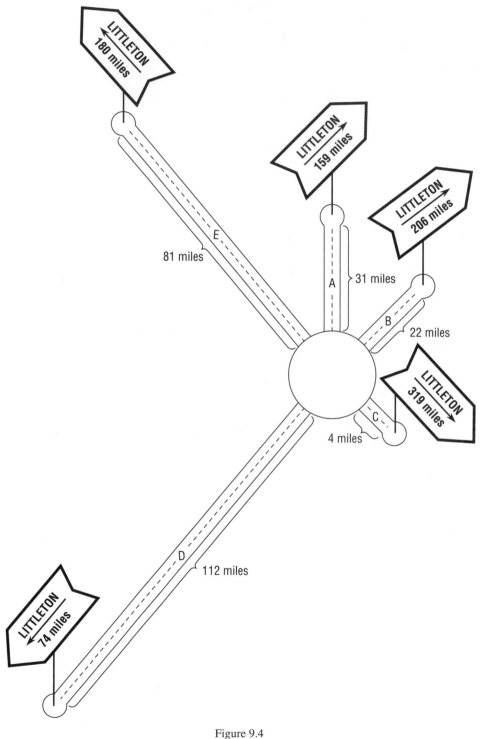

Figure 9.4

of their roads to look at the signs at neighboring intersections and basing their information on those signs. The process will work. You have to keep checking to make sure your neighbors have not changed anything on their set of signs, and you have to keep modifying your signs if any of your neighbors change their signs, but this process will eventually converge to correct information.

In a computer network, the protocol is stated as follows:

1. Each router is configured with its own ID.

2. Each router is also configured with a number to use as the cost of each link. (Or a fixed value like 1 is used as the cost of each link, or some sort of measurement is done to calculate a number to use as the cost).

3. Each router starts out with a distance vector consisting of the value "0" for itself and the value "infinity" for every other destination.

4. Each router transmits its distance vector to each of its neighbors whenever the information changes (as well as when a link to a neighbor first comes up and probably also periodically).

5. Each router saves the most recently received distance vector from each of its neighbors.

6. Each router calculates its own distance vector, based on minimizing the cost to each destination, by examining the cost to that destination reported by each neighbor in turn and then adding the configured cost of the link to that neighbor.

7. The following events cause recalculation of the distance vector:

   a. Receipt from a neighbor of a distance vector containing different information than before.

   b. Discovery that a link to a neighbor has gone down—in which case, the distance vector from that neighbor is discarded before the distance vector is recalculated.

This algorithm seems somewhat magical, and it is. The intuition behind why it works is that for a particular destination D, D knows the proper distance to D—i.e., 0. When D sends its distance vector to its neighbors, they now have a good route to D. When they send their distance vectors to their neighbors, those nodes will have good routes to D. If the optimal route from D to A is D–C–B–A, then A will discover its best route to D after D sends a distance vector to C, followed by C's sending a distance vector to B, followed by B's sending a distance vector to A. Every destination is being calculated independently.

> **We are here and it is now. Further than that all human knowledge is moonshine.**
>
> **— H. L. Mencken[3]**

[3] Byrne, *1911 Best Things*, 109.

It might be hard to understand why distance vector routing works, because my information depends on your information, which depends on my information ... However, this algorithm is sufficiently robust that it works properly even if the implementers or network users do not understand or believe in it. It is easy to code and is therefore attractive.

9.1.1   Why Not Distance Vector?

If distance vector works, why is it the "old" ARPANET routing algorithm? The chief problem with distance vector routing is its slow convergence. While routing information has only partially propagated through a computer network, routing can be seriously disrupted. Since a single link change may affect many routes, it is important for routing to recover as quickly as possible after a topological change.

Distance vector routing can take a very long time to converge after a topological change. The reason for this can be seen from the following simple topology.

Figure 9.5

Let us think only about everyone's distances to destination C. C calculates its distance to C as 0. To keep things simple, assume that the cost function is hops, so that the cost of each link is 1. B calculates its distance to C as 1. A calculates its distance to C as 2.

Now let us assume that C dies or that the link between B and C breaks. Noticing that a link has broken, B must discard the distance vector it received from that link and recalculate its distance vector. Unfortunately, B will not conclude at this point that C is unreachable. Instead, B will decide that it is 3 from C, based on having a neighbor (A) at a distance of 1 from B that has reported a distance of 2 to C. Since B's distance vector has now changed, it will transmit the changed vector to each of its remaining neighbors (in this case, only A). A, as a result of having received a modified distance vector from neighbor B, will recalculate its own distance vector and conclude that C is now 4 away. A and B will continue this process until they count to infinity. Furthermore, during this process, both A and B will conclude that the best path to C is through the other node. Packets for C will get bounced between A and B until they die of old age.

Counting by ones to infinity might seem as if it would take a very long time (try it sometime). It will, but not as long as you might imagine. First of all, computers keep getting faster. But more relevantly, "infinity" in distance vector routing is a network-management-settable parameter, which is usually set to some value on the order of 20 (if the cost function is hops) or 20 times the largest link cost in the net (if the cost function is something other than hops).

At just about every computer networks conference, someone presents a paper proposing a "fix" for the slow-convergence problem in distance vector routing. Some of the fixes are extremely expensive (like reporting the entire path to each destination, in addition to the cost to the destination, in the distance vector). Others (like what is referred to as "holddown") are kludges based on timers, which tend to further slow down convergence in many cases. Others involve complex protocol in an attempt to coordinate all the routers. Some are too complex to understand, and one tends not to get around to reading them before another paper appears explaining why the previous approach didn't work and giving in its stead an even more complex protocol. Although certain fixes improve things somewhat, even if the counting-to-infinity problem could be solved, distance vector routing will always converge less quickly than link state routing, because information cannot propagate through a node until that node recalculates its routing information.

One popular technique used to speed up convergence of distance vectors is known as "split horizon." It does no harm and speeds up convergence in many cases. However, split horizon does not solve the "count-to-infinity" problem in all cases. The rule in split horizon is that if router R forwards traffic for destination D through neighbor N, then R reports to N that R's distance to D is infinity. Because R is routing traffic for D through N, R's real distance to N cannot possibly matter to N. N's distance to D cannot depend on R's distance to D. In the simple case of the three-node network in Fig. 9.5, split horizon will prevent counting to infinity. A will have reported to B that A's distance to C is infinity. When B's link to C breaks, B has no alternate path to C and immediately concludes C is unreachable. When B informs A that C is now unreachable, A now knows C is unreachable.

Split horizon does not work in arbitrary cases, however. Consider the following picture:

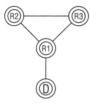

Figure 9.6

When the link to D breaks, R1 concludes that D is unreachable because R2 and R3 both have reported to R1 that D is unreachable because of the split horizon rule. R1 reports D's unreachability to R2 and R3. Now the scenario might differ slightly depending on the timing of events, but the results will be similar. When R2 receives R1's report that D is unreachable, R2 concludes that the best path to D is now through R3. R2 will conclude that R2 is now 3 from D, report D as being unreachable to R3 because of split horizon, and report D as being reachable to R1 at cost 3. R1 now thinks that D is reachable through R2 at a cost of 4. The counting-to-infinity problem still exists.

In the following section, I will examine link state routing and explain why it converges more quickly as well as the other advantages it offers.

9.2 Link State Routing

The basic idea behind link state routing is very simple:

1. Each router is responsible for meeting its neighbors and learning their names.

2. Each router constructs a packet known as a "link state packet," or "LSP," which contains a list of the names of and cost to each of its neighbors.

3. The LSP is somehow transmitted to all the other routers, and each router stores the most recently generated LSP from each other router.

4. Each router, armed now with a complete map of the topology (the information in the LSPs yields complete knowledge of the graph), computes routes to each destination.

The following subsections examine each of these steps, some of which are nontrivial.

9.2.1   Meeting Neighbors

On a point-to-point link, neighbors can meet each other simply by transmitting a special packet over the link, identifying themselves. On a LAN, neighbor greeting is usually done by periodically transmitting the same sort of special packet to a predefined group address. Sometimes (as in IP, where a link is considered a neighbor), the identity of the addresses reachable over a particular interface is manually configured.

9.2.2   Constructing an LSP

Once the identity of neighbors is known, constructing an LSP is not at all difficult. It is a simple matter of formatting.

A router R generates an LSP periodically as well as when R discovers that:

* It has a new neighbor.

* The cost of the link to an existing neighbor has changed.

* A link to a neighbor has gone down.

9.2.3   Disseminating the LSP to All Routers

Once router R generates a new LSP, the new LSP must get transmitted to all the other routers. This is the most complex and critical piece of a link state routing algorithm. If it isn't done correctly, various bad things can happen, including:

1. Routers will have different sets of LSPs. This means that they will be calculating routes based on different information. Many routes can become nonfunctional as a result of a disagreement among routers about a single link.

After a link changes state, any routing algorithm will require some short amount of time for updated knowledge of the link's state to propagate throughout the net. However, a faulty LSP distribution algorithm can cause knowledge of a link's state to propagate to only some of the routers, resulting in disruption of the routing for many orders of magnitude longer than necessary.

2. LSP distribution can become "cancerous," a condition in which the number of LSPs rapidly multiplies until all network resources are spent processing LSPs. Later in this section, I examine an LSP distribution scheme used in the ARPANET that can get into this state.

I'll start by designing an LSP distribution scheme. Ordinarily, it would be possible in a network to distribute information using the information in the routing database. For instance, when router S generates a new LSP, it could transmit a copy, as data, to each other router. However, LSPs cannot be transmitted based on the assumption that the routing database makes sense, because this creates a chicken-or-the-egg problem (known more impressively as a *recursion* problem)—LSP distribution relies on the routing database, but the routing database relies on the LSPs. So the distribution scheme cannot make any assumptions about the information in the routing databases. It has to work no matter what kind of information is in those databases.

A simple scheme for routing that does not depend on having any routing information is *flooding*, in which each packet received is transmitted to each neighbor except the one from which the packet was received. Then, to prevent a single packet's spawning an infinite number of offspring, a packet could have a hop count (or a diary of the route—sound familiar?), and when the hop count reaches some threshold, the packet can be dropped. This will create an exponential number of copies of each packet, which can be an annoyance but is guaranteed to deliver a copy of the packet to every node, provided that packets are not lost (which they undoubtedly will be in the congestion caused by exponential growth).

Luckily, when it is LSPs rather than data packets that are being distributed, we can do far better. Because each router R retains the most recently generated LSP from each router S, R can recognize when it is receiving a duplicate of S's most recently generated LSP, and R can refrain from flooding the packet more than once. If each router floods S's most recently generated LSP only once, then the flooding will not create an exponential number of copies. Instead, the LSP will travel over each link in the network only once.

A simple LSP distribution scheme is as follows: If an LSP is received from neighbor N with source S and the LSP is identical to the one from S that is stored, then ignore the received LSP (it is a duplicate). If the received LSP is not identical to the one from S currently stored, or if no LSP from S is stored, store the received LSP and transmit it to all neighbors except N.

The problem with this scheme is that R cannot assume that the LSP most recently received from S is the one most recently generated by S. Two LSPs from S could travel along different paths to R and might not be received in the order in which S generated them.

9.2.3.1 Timestamps

How can R know which of S's LSPs was generated most recently? One attractive possibility is a timestamp in the LSP, which would enable R to look at two LSPs and know that the one with the later timestamp was more recently generated. One problem that might occur with timestamps is that if S accidentally generated an LSP with a timestamp 15 years in the future, or if the timestamp on one of S's LSPs got corrupted so it appeared to be from that far in the future, then none of S's LSPs for the next 15 years would be believed, since all the nodes would assume that they had a more recent LSP from S.

If the timestamp has global meaning—i.e., the routers' clocks are synchronized to within a few minutes—then R can do a "sanity check" on the timestamp in S's LSP. If R receives an LSP with a timestamp that appears to be too far in the future, R rejects the LSP. Similarly, if R receives an LSP with a timestamp too far in the past, R can delete the LSP to save memory, since a node that hasn't issued a new LSP within some amount of time can be considered unreachable or dead.

However, if the timestamp does not have global meaning, R cannot do any sort of sanity check on the timestamp in S's LSP. If a timestamp got corrupted, or if S, through temporary flakiness, issued an LSP with a bad timestamp (one in the future), S's real LSPs would be rejected by other nodes.

A globally synchronized timestamp would make LSP distribution a little simpler, but synchronizing clocks requires special hardware and is a more difficult problem than distributing LSPs. Thus, it is preferable to devise a solution to LSP distribution that does not depend on globally synchronized clocks. Currently deployed routing protocols do not rely on clocks and instead use a scheme involving a combination of a "sequence number" (a simple counter) and an "estimated age" field in each LSP.

9.2.3.2   Sequence Number/Age Schemes

A sequence number is a counter. Each router S keeps track of the sequence number it used the last time it generated an LSP, and when S needs to generate a new LSP, it uses the next sequence number. When it receives an LSP from S, router R compares the sequence number of the received LSP with the one from S stored in memory (if one is stored there) and assumes that the one with the higher sequence number is the more recently generated.

The sequence number approach has various problems that must be solved:

1. The sequence number field is of finite size. What happens if it reaches the maximum value?

   It is tempting to make the field large (say, 64 bits) and then assume that no node will ever issue enough LSPs to cause the field to reach the maximum value. The problem is that the sequence number on an LSP can become corrupted to a value near the maximum, or a router could mistakenly generate an LSP with a very large sequence number. So the protocol must provide for some way to continue operating even if the sequence number for some router's LSP reaches the maximum value. If the sequence number reaches the maximum value, it must either "wrap around," or be reset. Early LSP distribution schemes assumed that the sequence number field would wrap around. Let us start by making that assumption.

"Wrapping around" means that the sequence number starts at some value (say, 0), increases to some maximum value (say, n), and then goes back to 0. It is important to be able to compare two sequence numbers. Given two sequence numbers a and b, a is considered to be less than b if $|a-b| < n/2$ and $a < b$, or $|a-b| > n/2$ and $a > b$. Pictorially, the sequence number space can be considered a circle, and given any point a on the circle, the numbers in the semicircle on one side of a are greater than a, and the numbers in the other semicircle are less than a.

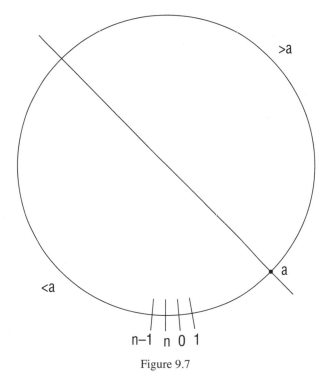

Figure 9.7

2. What happens if router S goes down and forgets the sequence number it was using? If it starts again at 0, will its LSPs be believed by the network, or will they look older than the LSPs that S had issued before it crashed?

3. Suppose that the network partitions into two halves—say, East and West—with router S in the East. Suppose that the sequence number S used before the network partitioned was x and that the partition lasts for long enough that S's sequence number used in the East partition wraps around and starts looking smaller than the last sequence number seen for S in the West partition. Some mechanism must exist so that when the network partition is repaired, and East and West merge, the nodes in the West will believe S's current LSPs.

To solve the preceding problems, a second field, known as the "age" of the LSP, is added to each LSP. It starts at some value and gets decremented by routers as it is held in memory. When an LSP's age reaches 0, the LSP can be considered too old, and an LSP with a non-0 age is accepted as newer regardless of its sequence number.

This is the general idea behind sequence number/age schemes for LSP distribution. Let us study the first such scheme, designed and deployed in the ARPANET. On the surface, it seems logical enough, but as we shall see, it has a spectacular failure mode.

9.2.3.3   The ARPANET LSP Distribution Scheme

An LSP contains:

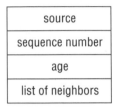

Figure 9.8

When router R generates an LSP, it sets the "source" to "R," the sequence number to be 1 greater (mod n, the size of the circular sequence number space) than the sequence number of R's previously generated LSP, and the "age" to be the maximum value.

When a router other than R receives R's LSP, the router accepts it and overwrites any stored LSP from R provided that the sequence number of the received LSP is greater than the sequence number of the stored LSP (according to arithmetic in the circular sequence number space). If the age on the stored LSP is 0, the received LSP is accepted regardless of sequence number. (The received LSP will have a non-0 age, because LSPs with 0 age are not propagated.) When a router accepts an LSP, it propagates the LSP to each neighbor except the one from which the LSP was received.

When a router holds onto an LSP for some specified time, it decrements the age field. When the age of an LSP reaches 0, the LSP is not propagated further, but it is kept in the database and used for routing calculations.

To get a feel for the actual parameter values used in the ARPANET, age was a 3-bit field, with units being 8 sec. The age started out as 56 sec (7×8) and was decremented every 8 sec.

Each router was required to generate a new LSP within 60 sec. Also, a router was required to wait for 90 sec before issuing its initial LSP upon startup, which gave its old LSP a chance to age to 0 and gave the newly started router an opportunity to acquire a fresh LSP database, since all the other routers would have issued new LSPs in that 90-sec interval.

On the surface, this scheme seems logical enough. But distributed algorithms can be very tricky.

One night, the ARPANET stopped working. Diagnosis was difficult, because ordinarily, network management was done by sending and receiving messages over the network—which, at this point, was nonfunctional. In this case, a core dump indicated that the local router (at BBN, the site from which the ARPANET was maintained) had its queues filled with LSPs. Furthermore, the LSPs were all from some source router S, and S's LSPs had three different sequence numbers: a, b, and c, where $a < b < c < a$.

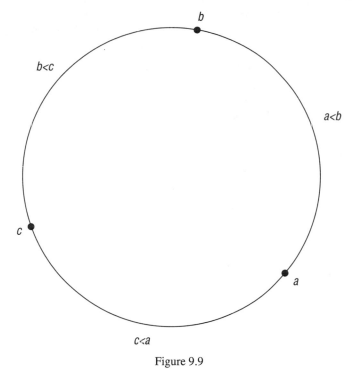

Figure 9.9

The world is round and the place which may seem like the end may also be only the beginning.

— Ivy Baker Priest [4]

Once the network gets into such a state, there is no way for it to recover. If any router has a stored LSP from S with sequence number b, then if it sees an LSP from S with sequence number c, it will overwrite the one in memory and make copies of the LSP for each of its neighbors. Furthermore, a router will flood the LSPs in precisely the order that will cause its neighbors to accept every one (first a will be flooded, then b, then c, then a . . .).

Why didn't these LSPs age out? The reason is that a router only decrements the age field on an LSP after it sits in memory for 8 sec. These LSPs were not getting stored in memory long enough for the age field to be decremented but instead were being received and immediately propagated further. This is an excellent example of a network layer "virus."

Once the problem was diagnosed, it was nontrivial to figure out how to fix the network. One possibility was to find a human at every router site to halt the router, and only after every router was manually halted could the routers be brought back up. This is not very practical. It requires knowing the telephone number of someone at every site who would be able to manually halt the router, making a lot of phone calls, and hoping that someone responds at every site. Furthermore, if some sites were overlooked, then when the network was restarted, S's LSPs might still be lurking in some routers' memories,

---

[4] *Parade* magazine (Feb. 16, 1958), quoted in Simpson, *Simpson Contemporary Quotations*, 324.

ready to reinfect the entire network. Also keep in mind that we are assuming the telephone network would operate properly. Imagine if the telephone network were the one with the network layer virus, so that people could not even be contacted by phone!

The particular approach chosen at the time was to devise a patched version of the router code that specifically ignored LSPs from S. The local router was halted and rebooted with the patched version. Then its neighbors were halted and rebooted with the patched version. Then their neighbors, and so forth, until the entire network was running the patched version of the code. Only after every router was running the patched version of the code was it possible to reboot the routers, one by one, with the real code.

In this case, it was particularly lucky that the people who designed the algorithm were also the implementers and the field service people. All routers were implemented on identical hardware and were running the same software. Is this true of the networks on which you depend today? The ARPANET "incident" (to borrow terminology from the nuclear power industry) occurred because of a single malfunctioning router. That router, instead of failing by stopping outright, failed by first emitting a few well-formed LSPs with random sequence numbers with its dying gasp and then stopping. The ARPANET was completely nonfunctional and would have remained nonfunctional forever (had there not been manual intervention), although all the remaining routers were functioning properly. It seems very unlikely that a router would fail in exactly that way, but it did happen. And furthermore, the same packets could as easily have been injected by a malicious node attached to the network. We should learn from this incident that distributed algorithms must be designed with care.

In the next subsection, I describe the LSP distribution scheme accepted as the best known today. It is used in most of today's link state routing protocols, including DNA Phase V (where it was originally developed and documented), the ISO's IS-IS, and OSPF. It has been proved self-stabilizing by Professor Nancy Lynch from MIT.

The basic improvements introduced are:

1. *Self-stabilization:* No matter what sequence of events occurs, no matter how corrupted the databases become, no matter what messages get introduced into the system, once all defective or malicious equipment is disconnected from the network, the network will return to normal operation within a tolerable period of time (less than an hour, say).

2. *Efficiency:* The ARPANET scheme required every router to generate a new LSP every minute, since the LSP lifetime was only on the order of a minute. The ARPANET parameters could not simply be increased, because that would have required an even longer delay upon start-up (90 sec is already too long—they certainly couldn't have cranked that up to 90 min). The improved scheme still requires periodic regeneration of LSPs, but it can be done on the order of once an hour.

3. *Responsiveness:* The ARPANET scheme required a router to wait 90 sec before participating in the network. The improved scheme has no such requirement, except in the very rare case in which the sequence number space for some router

becomes exhausted. And when that happens, only that single router must wait for its LSP to age out and be purged before it can participate in the network.

9.2.3.4 New, Improved LSP Distribution

As before, an LSP contains:

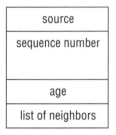

Figure 9.10

The sequence number is a linear space. It starts at 0, and when it reaches its maximum value, no other LSP from that source will be accepted (until the LSP times out). The sequence number field should be large enough (say, 32 bits) that it will never reach the maximum value, except as a result of malfunctioning nodes' generating bad sequence numbers.

The age field is set to some value (say, max age) by the router that generates the LSP. Max age should be on the order of an hour. Every router that handles an LSP must decrement the age field by at least 1 and should further decrement it as it sits in memory.

When a router receives a new LSP and determines that it should be transmitted on some of its links, it should not immediately queue the LSP. Rather, it should flag the LSP in memory as needing to be queued, with a separate flag for each link. In this way, fairness can be enforced for use of the bandwidth, since the memory will be scanned round-robin for LSPs that need to be transmitted. Queues will not be permitted to be filled with multiple LSPs from the same source. If an LSP with a higher sequence number arrives before the previous LSP is transmitted, the LSP with the higher sequence number will overwrite the LSP with the smaller sequence number, and the first LSP will never be transmitted (which is exactly the behavior desired). In addition, we will require that LSPs be acknowledged, and also insist that an acknowledgment not be generated immediately but rather that a flag be set to indicate that an acknowledgment for that LSP should be sent to that link. Thus, each LSP in router R's memory has $2 \times k$ flags associated with it, where k is the number of links connected to R. Half the flags are known as "send flags," where the j'th flag's being set indicates that the LSP should be transmitted to the j'th link. The other k flags are "ack flags," where the j'th flag's being set indicates that an acknowledgment for that LSP should be transmitted to the j'th link.

When bandwidth on a link becomes available, the LSP database is scanned round-robin for an LSP that has a send flag or an ack flag set for that link. If the flag found is a send flag, the LSP itself is transmitted on that link. If the flag found is an ack flag, an acknowledgment for that LSP is transmitted on the link, and the ack flag is cleared. (If the ack is lost, the neighbor will retransmit the LSP.)

LSPs	Flags	Neighbor 1	Neighbor 2	Neighbor 3	. . .	Neighbor k
R1 #27	send flag	✓	✓			✓
links	ack flag			✓		
R2 #15	send flag					
links	ack flag					
R3 #152	send flag		✓	✓		✓
links	ack flag	✓				
R4 #6	send flag	✓		✓		
links	ack flag		✓			✓
R5 #33	send flag	✓				
links	ack flag					
R6 #47	send flag					
links	ack flag			✓		

Figure 9.11

When an LSP is initially accepted from the j'th link, the LSP is written into the LSP database, and all send flags except the j'th are set and all ack flags except the j'th are cleared. The j'th send flag is cleared, and the j'th ack flag is set. If a duplicate LSP is received from link j, the j'th send flag is cleared and the j'th ack flag is set. If an ack is received from link j corresponding to an LSP in memory, the j'th send flag as well as the j'th ack flag are cleared for that stored LSP.

This improved scheme also tries to ensure that all routers will time out an LSP at about the same time. This is important because if one router had a much faster clock, it might time out an LSP much more quickly than other routers, and routing could be severely disrupted while the routers are making decisions based on different LSP databases. Thus, this scheme requires that an LSP be reflooded when its age becomes 0 and that a router receiving an LSP with 0 age that has the same source and sequence number as an LSP in memory overwrite the stored LSP with the newly received LSP.

Once an LSP's age becomes 0, router R deletes the data associated with the LSP (the list of links), but R must hold the LSP header for long enough to successfully transmit it to each of R's neighbors. The improved scheme allows R to delete an LSP with 0 age after all R's neighbors have acknowledged the LSP with 0 age or after some time (on the order of a minute) has elapsed since the LSP's age became 0.

This scheme further stipulates that R must not accept an LSP with 0 age if no LSP from the same source is already in R's memory. The reason for this is as follows:

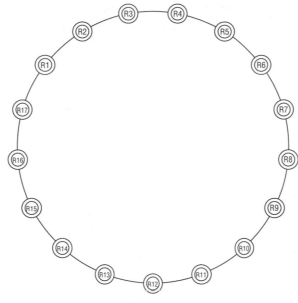

Figure 9.12

Never mistake motion for action.

— Ernest Hemingway [5]

Suppose that R1 has an LSP with 0 age and none of the other routers has that LSP. Perhaps R1 has just received the LSP from R17, which deletes it when R1 acknowledges it. Then R1 will transmit it to R2 and delete it when R2 acknowledges it, and so forth. The LSP will constantly be transmitted around the circle and never go away. The rule that a router merely acknowledges and does not store or propagate an LSP with 0 age when no corresponding LSP appears in the database prevents this. This example would not present a terrible problem, since the protocol specifies that an LSP with 0 age not be used in the routing calculation. It is just a bit untidy to allow random LSPs to wander aimlessly about the net.

This new, improved protocol assumes that all links in the network are point-to-point links. When some routers are connected via LANs, the LSP distribution scheme needs to be modified to take that into account. This portion of the scheme is done differently in IS-IS and in OSPF, so it is explored in Chapter 10, when I discuss specific routing algorithms.

9.2.4 Computing Routes

Once a router has a complete set of LSPs, it has complete knowledge of the network. There are straightforward algorithms to calculate routes, given a complete knowledge of the network. The algorithm that routers always seem to use is based on Dijkstra. The basic algorithm can be stated as follows.

---

[5] **Quote 531 from Byrne,** *1911 Best Things*, **378.**

First, there are several databases:

1. The link state database, which consists of the latest LSP from each other router.

2. PATH, which consists of (ID, path cost, forwarding direction) triples. This is the set of nodes for which the best path from the computing router has been found. The best path's cost and the direction in which the router should send packets to optimally reach the destination are listed in the triple.

3. TENT, which has the same data structure as PATH—namely, triples of the form (ID, path cost, forwarding direction). The name *TENT* comes from *tentative*, which signifies that the paths indicated in TENT are only possibly the best paths. Once it is determined that a path is in fact the best possible, the node is moved from TENT to PATH.

4. The forwarding database, which consists of (ID, forwarding direction). This allows a router, when making a forwarding decision, to look up the ID of the destination and forward the packet along the specified direction. It is simply PATH minus the path cost element of the triples.

The Dijkstra algorithm is as follows:

1. Start with "self" as the root of a tree. This is done by putting (my ID, 0, 0) in PATH.

2. For the node N just placed in PATH, examine N's LSP. For each neighbor M of N, add the cost of the path from the root to N (the second item in N's triple in the PATH data structure) to the cost of the link from N to M (as listed in N's LSP). If M is not already in PATH or TENT with a better path cost, add (M, computed path cost, direction to get to N) to TENT.

    (If N is self, with the special direction "0," then just indicate that the packet should go directly to M.)

3. If TENT is empty, terminate the algorithm. Otherwise, find the triple (ID, cost, direction) in TENT with minimal cost. Move that triple to PATH and go to step 2.

Let us work through an example.

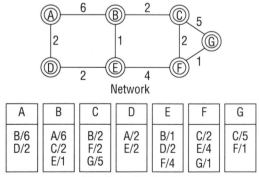

Network

A	B	C	D	E	F	G
B/6	A/6	B/2	A/2	B/1	C/2	C/5
D/2	C/2	F/2	E/2	D/2	E/4	F/1
	E/1	G/5		F/4	G/1	

Link State Database

Figure 9.13

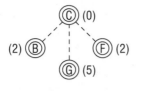

1. Place C in path.
   Examine C's LSP.

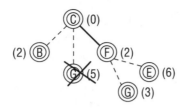

2. Place F in path.
   Examine F's LSP.
   Better path to G found.

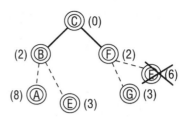

3. Place B in path.
   Examine B's LSP.
   Better path to E found.

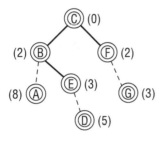

4. Place E in path.
   Examine E's LSP.

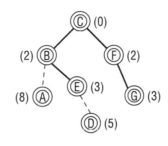

5. Place G in path.
   Examine G's LSP.

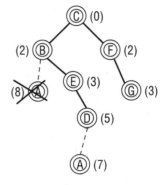

6. Place D in path.
   Examine D's LSP.
   Better path to A found.

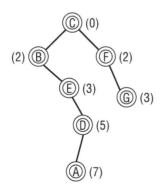

7. Place A in path.
   Examine A's LSP.
   No nodes left.
   Terminate.

Note: The number following the node name represents the cost of the
best path known from C to that node.

Figure 9.14   The Dijkstra computation as done by C

9.3   Comparison of Link State and Distance Vector Routing

In this section I compare link state routing and distance vector routing according to criteria such as resource utilization, robustness, speed of convergence, and other functionality.

9.3.1   Memory

Assume that every router in the net has k neighbors and that there are n nodes in the network. In order to run distance vector routing, a router needs to keep a distance vector from each of its k neighbors. Each distance vector is $O(n)$, since it contains information about all the n destinations. This yields a total memory requirement of $O(k \times n)$.

In link state routing, each router must keep n LSPs, one from each node in the network. Each LSP contains information about each neighbor of the node that generated the LSP, so each LSP is proportional to k. This yields a total memory requirement of $O(k \times n)$.

There are some situations in which distance vector routing does give a significant memory savings, though. In the higher levels of hierarchical routing, it is not necessary to compute routes to each router. If there are significantly more level n routers than level $n - 1$ subnetworks—for instance, s level $n - 1$ subnetworks, n level n routers, and each level n router having k neighbor level n routers—then the memory requirement for distance vector routing would be $O(k \times s)$, whereas for link state routing, it would be $O(k \times n)$. This is because in distance vector routing, the distance vectors would only apply to the s level n destinations. In link state routing, an LSP from each level n router must still be kept, even if routes to the routers need not be computed.

9.3.2   Bandwidth Consumed

It is difficult to compare the bandwidth consumed by the two algorithms. Proponents of either type of protocol can demonstrate a topology in which their favorite uses far less bandwidth than the other.

For instance, distance vector routing fans point out that a link change only propagates control messages as far as the link change's routing effect. In the case of two parallel links, knowledge of the failure and recovery of one of the links while the other remains up will not generate any routing control traffic beyond the link, whereas in link state routing, the link change would trigger an LSP, which would be propagated to all the routers.

Link state routing fans point out that a single link change can cause multiple control packet transmissions over a single link in distance vector routing because of the counting-to-infinity problem, in which the distance vectors must be tossed back and forth a few times. In link state routing, of course, each LSP only needs to travel on each link once. Also, in link state routing, a single link change will cause a single LSP to be transmitted through the network, where the LSP is a fixed size independent of the network. With distance vector routing, a single link change can effect the cost of paths to a significant fraction of the nodes. This can cause many routers to have to transmit a large distance vector because the distance to all effected destinations will need to be updated.

Although this issue deserves to be studied with more care than it has been, again I feel that the bandwidth used in either algorithm is modest and should therefore not be the criterion by which one algorithm or the other is chosen.

9.3.3   Computation

Running Dijkstra's algorithm requires CPU proportional to the number of links in the net ($n \times k$) times the log of the number of nodes in the net, so it is $O(n \times k \log n)$. An optimization to Dijkstra proposed by Anthony Lauck from Digital eliminates the factor of log n, which arises because of the step in the Dijkstra calculation where the element in TENT with the smallest path cost must be chosen. In order to eliminate the need to do a linear search through all the elements in TENT to find the one with the smallest path cost, TENT should be kept sorted. The factor of log n comes about because of the CPU involved in inserting a new entry into TENT with binary search.

The optimization requires keeping the elements in TENT hashed according to path cost. This can be accomplished provided there are not too many possible values of path cost. Then the bins can be searched in numerical order to find all the elements in a particular bin, move them to PATH, and then move to the next bin when that bin has been emptied.

Thus, we can consider the computation necessary to compute the Dijkstra tree as $O(n \times k)$. To run distance vector routing, the entire matrix of k distance vectors must be scanned, yielding an algorithm requiring the same CPU—namely, $O(n \times k)$. However, distance vector computation may require many passes before it is completed, so one pass through the computation may not suffice.

Often, the routing computation does not need to completely calculate routes from scratch. For instance, if a distance vector from a neighbor is received that is identical to the last distance vector from that neighbor, except for a change in cost to a single destination, then the entire distance vector need not be recalculated. Instead, only the cost to that destination must be recalculated. Note, though, that a single link change can cause the cost of paths to many destinations to change simultaneously.

Likewise in link state routing, if the only topology change that has occurred is that an endnode has come up or gone down, a minimal amount of calculation can adjust the forwarding database accordingly. Less obviously, in link state routing, if a single link changes cost, even if it is a link between routers, there is a way of adjusting the calculated shortest-path tree rather than recomputing from scratch. This algorithm,[6] known as "incremental computation of the shortest-path tree," was developed and deployed in the ARPANET, but its performance was never formally studied, especially when additional

[6] McQuillan, Richer, and Rosen, "The New Routing Algorithm for the ARPANET," *IEEE Transactions on Communications*, May 1980, 711–19.

questions are considered, such as the expected computation required when more than one link changes cost.

The true computational costs of link state versus distance vector routing have never been adequately studied and are a good area for research. In my opinion, the CPU costs of the two algorithms are comparable, and both are reasonably modest. Router boxes should be engineered with sufficient CPU to handle the routing computation, which need not be done at forwarding rates but rather can take a second or so in background. An underpowered router is not as serious a problem as an underpowered bridge; however, since the cost of routers is a very small portion of the entire cost of a network, it is an unwise economy to use inadequate packet switches, which can cause unnecessarily lost packets, degrading throughput. They can also disrupt routing, because they might be too slow to recompute routes after topology changes. And they can constrain the growth of the network, because the routers' inability to handle the extra memory might preclude the addition of more nodes.

9.3.4 Robustness

Both algorithms can be completely disabled by a single router that is not following the rules. This can be caused by incorrect software, incorrect configuration, hardware faults, or even a malicious attempt to sabotage the network. In link state routing, a malfunctioning router might:

- Claim to have a link that does not exist

- Claim not to have a link that does exist

- Use a strange pattern of sequence numbers for its own LSPs

- Fail to forward packets

- Fail to forward or acknowledge LSPs

- Corrupt the data in other routers' LSPs

- Corrupt the sequence number in other routers' LSPs

- Corrupt the age in other routers' LSPs

- Calculate incorrect routes

As a safeguard against nonmalicious corruption of LSPs, most link state routing algorithms include a checksum in the LSP that is inserted by the source and not modified by any other routers. Since the age field must be modified by other routers, it is not generally covered by the checksum, or if it is, routers are required to incrementally modify the checksum as a result of modification to the age field (although this is a difficult requirement to enforce through conformance tests).

The remaining failures tend to cause problems with routes that have the misfortune of passing through the faulty router, but they do not cause global misrouting.

In contrast, in the ARPANET experience with distance vector routing, there were multiple times in which a faulty router transmitted a distance vector consisting of all 0's. This created a black hole with an enormous "gravitational field," which caused routers to route packets to the single router in the network that was malfunctioning.

> **One hundred thousand lemmings can't be wrong.**
>
> — Graffito [7]

To truly compare the robustness of the two schemes, one would have to take into account how likely various error scenarios are and how profound a disruption each might cause.

I believe that the difference in robustness between the two schemes is not great, but I feel that link state routing (properly designed—i.e., without the ARPANET bug) is more resilient to nonmalicious malfunctions and that malfunctions are more likely to be detectable. This is another area in which careful study would be valuable.

9.3.5 Functionality

Link state routing does provide more functionality:

1. It is easier to discover the topology of the network, since full knowledge of the topology can be acquired by querying a single router. In contrast, with distance vector routing, mapping the network would be a difficult task, involving querying most, if not all, of the routers.

2. Troubleshooting a network will be easier in link state routing—again, since a single router can be queried, and from its LSP database, all the broken links can be discovered (assuming that the original topology was known).

3. Source routing is more powerful with link state routing. I am not referring to the bridge style of source routing but rather to the network layer's feature of allowing the source to place a route in the packet header. Since the source can easily acquire the topology of the network, it can calculate routes based on such considerations as avoiding a particular router that it finds suspicious.

4. Implementation of really general types of service routing is more practical with link state routing.

9.3.6 Speed of Convergence

Between the time a topology change occurs and the time all the routers have recomputed routes based on the new topology, routing in the network is disrupted, from minimally to severely, depending on the topological change. It is thus vital to keep the network in the "converged" state as high a percentage of the time as possible.

---

[7] **Quote 558 from Byrne, *1911 Best Things*, 249.**

Link state routing will converge more quickly than distance vector routing. For one thing, distance vector routing has the looping problem discussed earlier in the chapter, and even if that were solved, distance vector routing would still converge more slowly, since a router cannot pass routing information on until it has recomputed its distance vector. In contrast, a router can recognize a new LSP and forward it before recalculating routes.

I think that the route convergence issue is the truly critical point of comparison between link state and distance vector routing. The chief argument in favor of distance vector routing is that it might require less memory, but since the cost of routers, and the cost of memory in routers, is such an insignificant portion of the cost of a network, it seems ill-advised to save a bit of money on routers at the expense of having the network broken a larger amount of the time.

9.4   Load Splitting

> **Two roads diverged in a wood, and I—**
> **I took the one less traveled by,**
> **And that has made all the difference.**
>
> **— Robert Frost [8]**

If the traffic load is spread among several paths, network capacity will be increased. Both algorithms under discussion can easily be enhanced to allow keeping several paths to a destination.

With distance vector routing, if the paths through more than one neighbor are equally minimal, then all such optimal paths can be saved. The forwarding database will consist of a set of neighbors (instead of a single neighbor) to which traffic for a particular destination can appropriately be sent.

With link state routing, it is also easy. As noted earlier, the data structures TENT and PATH are triples of the form (ID, path cost, forwarding direction). In order to keep track of multiple optimal paths, "forwarding direction" should be a set of forwarding directions. Thus, TENT and PATH will be triples of the form (ID, path cost, {set of forwarding directions}).

When a new path to destination DEST is found, or when a path better than any discovered so far is found, the entry in TENT will be as before. When a new path to DEST is found with the same cost as the one already in TENT, then a set union is performed with the set of forwarding directions already stored with DEST and the set of forwarding directions stored with the node through which the new path to TENT was found.

For example, suppose that node A is being added to PATH, and its triple is (A, 35, {neighbor 5, neighbor 7}). One of A's neighbors is B, at a cost of 7. Thus, the path to B through A has a cost of 42. Suppose that B is already in TENT, with the triple (B, 42, {neighbor 1, neighbor 3, neighbor 7}). Then the set union of {neighbor 1, neighbor 3,

---

[8] *New Enlarged Pocket Anthology of Robert Frost's Poems* (New York: Washington Square Press/Pocket Books, 1977), 223.

neighbor 7} and {neighbor 5, neighbor 7} is performed, yielding {neighbor 1, neighbor 3, neighbor 5, neighbor 7}, and B's triple is modified in the data structure TENT to be (B, 42, {neighbor 1, neighbor 3, neighbor 5, neighbor 7}).

Now that the forwarding database contains a choice of neighbors for each destination, an algorithm must be devised for selecting among the choices when forwarding a data packet. One possibility is to always take the first-listed choice, but then we needn't have gone to the trouble of storing multiple choices in the forwarding database. Other possibilities are:

1. Note the last choice made and move through the list of neighbors in the forwarding database round-robin as packets are forwarded to that destination.

2. Choose a neighbor at random from among those listed in the forwarding database.

3. Do either of the above, but enhance the process to make forwarding to neighbor N less likely if the link to N is more congested than the links to other neighbors listed in the forwarding database.

No definitive study has been done to guide us in making the choice. Round-robin is simple and only requires a modest addition to the database, to store the last-chosen neighbor for each destination. Random choice is attractive, provided that the cost of choosing a random number is not high. Enhancing the schemes by taking congestion into account is also attractive, but without additional protocol, this approach will not adjust to traffic that is more than one hop downstream—it will only adjust to the queues at the local router.

In some respects, it can be argued that load splitting is undesirable. The transport layer would prefer getting uniform service so that it can perform such calculations as round-trip delay and maximum packet size along the path. Load splitting will also increase the number of out-of-order packets. If the network layer is analyzed all by itself, it is clear that load splitting is a good idea, in that it will increase network capacity. However, if the annoyance to the transport layer is somehow taken into account, it is no longer obvious that load splitting is desirable.

Future applications might be designed so that service variance and packet shuffling would not be an issue. For instance, a file transfer could be designed so that every packet will have sufficient information to enable the data to be stored on disk when the packet arrives at the destination. Lost information could then be requested at leisure. Round-trip delay would not have to be calculated because there would be no need for the source to estimate when to retransmit an unack'ed packet. Instead, the destination would explicitly request any information that did not arrive. Out-of-order packets would also not be an issue.

If applications evolve similarly to what I've just described, then the argument for load splitting would be obvious, since there would be no disadvantages to doing it.

9.5   Link Costs

Should the cost of a link be a fixed number, or should it be a quantity that varies with the utilization of the link?

If the cost is a fixed number, should it be automatically determined at link start-up, by some sort of algorithm in which the bandwidth and delay are measured and a number is calculated that is a function of the measured characteristics? Or should it be left solely to the discretion of the network manager to assign the number, based either on the characteristics of the link or on knowledge of the expected traffic matrix, so that traffic can be discouraged from using links that are likely to become congested with that matrix?

The alternative to establishing a fixed quantity is to have the routers measure the delay on each link and increase the link's cost as its utilization increases, thereby encouraging traffic to seek an alternate, and perhaps less congested, route.

These are important and interesting questions, and they have not been adequately studied.

The proponents of having link costs vary with traffic offer two major arguments:

1. Traffic will be routed more optimally if the current traffic conditions are factored into the link costs and thus into the route calculations.

2. Having link costs assigned by network management requires additional configuration, which is undesirable both because it involves unnecessary work and because it introduces yet another place where human error can create problems.

The proponents of fixed link costs argue that:

1. If the cost of a link is a fixed quantity, routing information about the link only needs to be generated if the link goes down or recovers. This is a far less frequent event than changes in the traffic pattern on the link. Thus, with fixed link costs, there will be a lot less control traffic, which might more than offset the gain in network capacity that could be realized by using more optimal routes.

2. Between the time when a link changes cost and the time when knowledge of that revised link cost has successfully reached all the routers and they have all completed their routing computations, routing is disrupted in the network, since routers are making routing decisions based on different data. If link costs are frequently changing, the network will more often be in an "unconverged" state, in which routing will be disrupted to some degree, ranging from not at all to globally and severely. When the network is in an unconverged state, looping data packets will consume a significant portion of the network capacity that was perhaps gained by more optimal routing. The proportion of time that the network is in an unconverged state is also an annoyance, since packets might be dropped and even transport layer connections might not survive the disruption. Although "network quality" is an intangible and hard-to-measure factor, it must be taken into account when comparing the schemes.

If fixed costs are used, there is still the question of whether to have the costs assigned by humans or calculated by the routers upon link start-up. And if the costs are human-assigned, another question is whether the costs should be a simple function of the characteristics of the link, such as its bandwidth and delay, or whether the costs should take into account the expected traffic matrix in the network.

The proponents of traffic-matrix-dependent costs argue that network capacity will be increased if costs depend on the traffic matrix and are set so as to optimize flow. The opponents argue that attempting to optimize to that degree is a complex task, and it is likely to be done incorrectly, since the operating topology will differ from the topology on which link costs were optimized if new nodes are added to the network or if links or routers are down, and furthermore, the actual traffic matrix might differ from the expected one. Simple link costs in which all equivalent links (all links of the same delay and bandwidth) are assigned the same value are safer.

An additional approach for optimizing traffic flow in a network that has not been implemented anywhere is to have congestion information transmitted around the network in a manner that does not change the link costs but is only used by routers as advice for choosing among equivalent paths. This has the disadvantage of introducing more control traffic (the congestion information) but may enhance network capacity.

I would like to see more study done on these questions.

My opinion on all this is that attempting to increase network capacity a very small amount through complex and costly algorithms is a bad idea. I believe that the difference in network capacity between the simplest form of link cost assignment (fixed values depending on the delay and total bandwidth of the link) and "perfect routing" (in which a deity routes every packet optimally, taking into account traffic currently in the network as well as traffic that will enter the network in the near future) is not very great. And the difference between simple routing and the more optimal routing that can be gained by constantly monitoring delays on each link and adding control traffic to keep all the other routers informed is probably negligible, especially when the added bandwidth consumed by the routing information is taken into account.

If fixed costs are used, I do not feel that fancy "traffic matrix" algorithms that are run on the assumed topology in order to optimize traffic flow are a good idea, since I believe that the assumptions under which the numbers are generated are almost guaranteed to be incorrect (topology will evolve as nodes and links are added; topology will change as nodes and links fail; traffic patterns are not necessarily predictable). And I don't believe that the percentage of network capacity that could theoretically be gained is large enough to warrant the complexity and risk.

Having routers measure the characteristics of links and set the costs at link start-up seems like a good idea. It eliminates the possibility of human error, makes the network more "plug and play," and does not add any control traffic or increase the time during which the network is unconverged. Nobody has implemented such a scheme, however.

My position on these issues is only an opinion, and there are certainly people in the field who strongly disagree. Careful evaluation of this area would be very helpful.

9.6   Migrating Routing Algorithms

An interesting problem is how to change the routing algorithm in an operational network. It is undesirable to require that the entire network be brought down while all the routers are simultaneously reloaded with code for the new algorithm. It is preferable to modify each router, one at a time, and somehow keep the network functioning.

If a network is hierarchical, the entire network need not be switched at once. Rather, each level 1 subnetwork can be switched at different times, as can the level 2 subnetwork that connects the level 1 subnetworks. It is possible for a level 2 router to be running one algorithm at level 2 and a different algorithm at level 1.

In the following subsections, I describe two strategies for migrating from one algorithm to another.

9.6.1   Running Both Algorithms

The strategy of running both algorithms was implemented in the ARPANET when the system was switched from distance vector to link state routing. The original ARPANET code ran only distance vector routing. An intermediate version of the code ran both distance vector and link state routing. It transmitted and processed distance vectors as well as LSPs. The two algorithms did not interact, in the sense that the link state algorithm computed routes based solely on the information received from LSPs. If only a single router, R, was running the intermediate version of the code while all the other routers were running the original code, the link state algorithm in R would conclude that the entire network consisted of R and its attached endnodes. Likewise, the distance vector computation was based solely on received distance vectors. The intermediate version of the code also contained a network-management-settable switch that specified whether the routes chosen should be based on the forwarding database computed by the distance vector routing or by the link state routing. A third version of the code ran only link state routing.

At first, the network consisted solely of routers running the original code. Then, one by one, routers were modified to run the intermediate version of the code, all of them with the network-management-settable switch specifying that they should route based on distance vector routing. Only after every router was running the intermediate version of the code (so that the LSP database would compute correct routes) was it possible to modify the routers, one by one, by changing the setting of the network-management-settable switch, to start using the link-state-computed forwarding database.

During the time when all routers were running the intermediate version of the code but forwarding based on distance vector routing, the sanity of the link state algorithm could be checked by comparing the forwarding databases computed by both algorithms.

Once all the routers were running the intermediate version of the code but using the link-state-computed database, it was no longer necessary to run distance vector routing, and the third version of the code could be loaded into the routers, one by one.

The disadvantage of this approach is that during the time when the intermediate version of the code was running, the memory, bandwidth, and CPU requirements were doubled, since both routing algorithms were running.

9.6.2 Manual Node-by-Node Switch

The strategy of doing a manual node-by-node switch is more disruptive of a network when the changeover from one algorithm to the other occurs, but the theory is that the changeover can hopefully be accomplished in an hour or so, and it is the simplest and lowest-cost strategy to implement.

The basic idea is that the code for the new algorithm should be designed so that nodes running the new algorithm look to nodes running the old algorithm like endnodes in the portion of the network running the new algorithm, and nodes running the old algorithm look like endnodes to the portion of the network running the new algorithm. In this way, it is possible to migrate in both directions. If a level 1 subnetwork is running the old algorithm, then from one location, that router can be rebooted with the new algorithm. It will allow communication with its old-algorithm neighbors. Once they are rebooted with the new algorithm, communication is possible with their neighbors, and so forth. If a portion of the network has been reloaded with the new algorithm and it is determined that the new algorithm is not behaving satisfactorily, then a single site can be rebooted with the old algorithm, and then the neighbors of that site (which are accessible as endnodes), etc.

This method is conceptually simple. It has the disadvantage of severely disrupting the network while the migration occurs, but it does not involve any intermediate code requiring twice the resources (enough memory, CPU, and bandwidth to run two algorithms). Also, implementing two routing algorithms to run simultaneously is more difficult than the sum of implementing each of the two algorithms individually, since when they are running simultaneously, care must be taken to ensure that resources are shared fairly between the two processes.

This strategy is the one adopted for migrating DECnet from distance vector (used in phase IV) to link state (used in phase V).

9.7 Address Matching

There is more to life than increasing its speed.

— Mahatma Gandhi [9]

Address matching is the most critical part of making a high-performance router, since a router's performance is based on how quickly it can forward a packet. To forward a packet, a router must extract the destination address from the packet and find the matching forwarding database entry.

[9] **Quote 29 from Byrne,** *1911 Best Things*, **11.**

In level 1 routing, a portion of the network layer address corresponds to an entry in the forwarding database. For instance, in ISO, the "ID" field is the field on which level 1 routers make their routing decisions. A level 1 router must have an entry in the forwarding database exactly matching the ID portion of the destination address in the packet. In IP, there really isn't any level 1 routing, but finding the proper entry in the ARP cache involves essentially the same problem.

In contrast, in level 2 routing in both ISO and TCP/IP, there might be several forwarding database entries that match a particular destination address, and it is the most specific or longest address that must be found.

For instance, in TCP/IP, each entry in the forwarding database will correspond to a 32-bit address and a 32-bit mask. The destination address field in a packet contains a 32-bit value. The router must find the forwarding database entry with the mask with the most 1's that matches that destination address. The following examples all match destination address 11001111 01011100 00000000 10000111:

1. Value: 11001111 01011100 00000000 10000111

    Mask: 11111111 11111111 11111111 11111111

2. Value: 11001111 01011100 00000000 00000000

    Mask: 11111111 11111111 00000000 00000000

3. Value: 11001111 01011100 00000000 00000000

    Mask: 11111111 11111111 11100000 00000000

In the preceding examples, it is the first item that should match the destination address, because the mask is the most specific. However, as IP is specified, there can be ambiguities if noncontiguous subnet masks are used. For instance, suppose the following two entries were in the forwarding database:

1. Value: 11001111 01011100 00000000 00000000

    Mask: 11111111 11111111 11111110 00000000

2. Value: 11001111 01011100 00000000 00000111

    Mask: 11111111 11111111 00000000 01111111

Both masks have the same number of 1's, and both match the destination address. The IP standards do not specify which entry, in this case, should be considered a match. If one router chose the first entry and another chose the second, then a routing loop could result.

As discussed in Chapter 6, "Network Layer Addresses," noncontiguous subnet masks are not particularly useful, they are extremely confusing, and they make it difficult to build efficient routers. If subnet masks are contiguous (i.e., if they have the property that no 1 bit appears to the right of any 0 bit), then the longest-matching-address-prefix algorithms (to be described in subsections 9.7.1 and 9.7.2) can be used to efficiently find the forwarding database entry for a particular destination.

In ISO, level 2 routing is based on address prefixes, and finding a match in the forwarding database involves finding the longest matching address prefix.

In the following subsections, I describe two algorithms for efficiently finding the longest matching address prefix in the forwarding database for a particular destination address. These algorithms apply to both ISO and IP (provided that noncontiguous subnet masks are outlawed). If noncontiguous subnet masks are allowed in IP, then it is possible in the general case that no efficient algorithm exists. Trying every mask in the forwarding database might be the best algorithm.

As I describe the address-prefix-matching algorithms, I'll assume for clarity that addresses are alphabetic strings of variable length and that address prefixes are just initial substrings. The forwarding database consists of a "dictionary" of address prefixes. The destination address consists of a string, and the problem is to find the longest initial substring of the destination address that is included in the forwarding database.

9.7.1   Trie

The trie algorithm is described by Knuth.[10] The addresses in the forwarding database are put into a tree data structure. Each vertex represents a string. The root consists of the null string. There are 26 pointers from each vertex, where the first pointer consists of the string at the vertex plus the letter *A*, the next pointer consists of the string plus the letter *B*, and so forth. If no string in the dictionary contains the vertex's string plus some letter, that pointer either is missing or points to a vertex indicating failure.

Each vertex also has a flag associated with it, which indicates whether that string, terminated there, is in the dictionary. In Fig. 9.15 the flag is indicated with an asterisk.

Assume, for instance, that the dictionary consists of the following strings:

A

AB

ABCD

ABCDEQG

ABF

ABRACADABRA

ZMJ

ZZZZ

The data structure would then look like this:

[10] **Donald E. Knuth**, *Sorting and Searching*, **vol. 3 of** *The Art of Computer Programming* **(Reading, Mass.: Addison-Wesley, 1973), 481–500.**

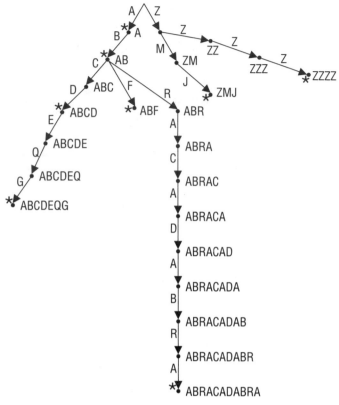

Figure 9.15

To search for the string "ABCDEFGH," the "A" pointer would be followed from the root, and it would be noted that "A" is a legal initial substring in the dictionary. Now the job is to try to find a longer one. Then the "B" pointer is followed, and it is noted that "AB" is the longest initial substring found thus far. Next, the "C" pointer is followed, which leads to a vertex that isn't marked as being the end of a string in the dictionary. So "AB" is still the longest initial substring found so far. Next, the "D" pointer is followed, which leads to vertex "ABCD," which is marked as being in the dictionary, so "ABCD" is remembered as the longest match found thus far. Next, the "E" pointer is followed, but "ABCDE" is not in the dictionary, so "ABCD" is retained as the longest match found thus far. Next, it is noted that no "Q" pointer exists, so the longest match found thus far—i.e., "ABCD"—is the longest match.

To search for the string "ZABC," first the "Z" pointer would be followed from the root. The string "Z" is not in the dictionary, so no longest match has been found thus far. Next, the "A" pointer is followed, but there is no "A" pointer, so since no longest match has been found thus far, it indicates that no suitable initial substring of "ZABC" is in the dictionary—i.e., the destination is unknown or unreachable, and the packet cannot be forwarded.

Maintaining the data structure is not difficult. To add an entry, follow the pointers to where it would be in the tree. If no pointers exist for that string, they should be added. If the vertex for the string already exists, then the vertex merely needs to be marked as being in the dictionary. To delete an entry that has children, the vertex associated with the string is simply unmarked as a legal termination point. To delete an entry that has no children, the vertex and the pointer pointing to it are deleted, and the parent vertex is examined. If it has other children or is marked as a legal termination point, it is left alone. Otherwise (it is not a legal termination point and there are no remaining children), that vertex, too, is deleted, and so on up the tree until a vertex that has other children or is marked as a termination point is found.

This algorithm requires lookup time proportional to the average length of the strings in the dictionary, regardless of how many entries the dictionary contains.

9.7.2 Binary Search

Ordinary binary search will not quite work, because it is not an exact match that is being sought but rather a longest initial substring. However, with a few enhancements, a binary search scheme can work.

First, a string length L must be found that is longer than any of the strings in the dictionary. Then each entry in the dictionary is made into two entries—one padded out to length L with 0's and another padded out to length L with 1's. Again, for human readability in this explanation, I will use a to represent 0, the smallest number, and z to represent the highest numerical quantity. I'll use lower-case for the padding—again, just for readability. In a real implementation, some mechanism must exist so that the data can be differentiated from the padding. (For instance, the length of the unpadded string can be kept with the entry.)

These items are sorted and stored in order. The dictionary presented in the preceding subsection will now consist of the following items:

```
Aaaaaaaaaaaa
ABaaaaaaaaaa
ABCDaaaaaaaa
ABCDEQGaaaaa
ABCDEQGzzzzz
ABCDzzzzzzzz
ABFaaaaaaaaa
ABFzzzzzzzzz
ABRACADABRAa
ABRACADABRAz
ABzzzzzzzzzz
Azzzzzzzzzzz
ZMJaaaaaaaaa
ZMJzzzzzzzzz
ZZZZaaaaaaaa
ZZZZzzzzzzzz
```

Additionally, each entry consisting of string "FOO" padded with z must point back to the entry representing the longest prefix of "FOO" that is in the dictionary. For instance:

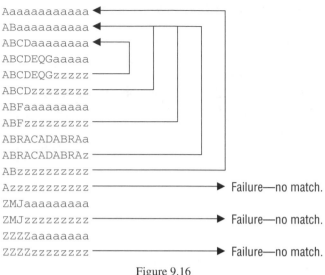

Figure 9.16

The way the search is done is that the location where the destination address would appear in the sorted table is found. If the next smaller entry is padded with *a*, then that is the initial substring. If the next smaller entry is padded with *z*, then the longest initial substring is the one to which the pointer points.

For example, let us search for destination address "ABCDEFGH." In this case, it would fit between "ABCDaaaaaaaa" and "ABCDEQGaaaaa." Since "ABCDaaaaaaaa" is padded with *a*, the unpadded part of that entry—i.e., "ABCD"—is the longest matching substring.

Now let us search for destination address "ABCDEYBVNG." In this case, it would fit between "ABCDEQGzzzzz" and "ABCDzzzzzzzz." Since "ABCDEQGzzzzz" is padded with *z*, the pointer from that entry must be followed. It points to "ABCDaaaaaaaa," so "ABCD" is the longest matching substring.

The efficiency of lookups with this algorithm depends on the log of the number of entries in the dictionary. Maintaining the data structure is more painful than with trie. To add an entry, a lookup must first be done to find the longest matching initial substring of the string to be added that is already in the dictionary. The two entries for the string to be added (padded with *a* and padded with *z*) must be added to the table, with a pointer from the string padded with *z* to the initial substring found (or an indication that none exists). Next, any entries pointing to a smaller initial substring for which the added entry would be a valid substring must have their pointers modified. This can be done by performing a scan of all entries between the two new entries (the string to be added padded with *a* and with *z*). The pointers for all examined entries should be modified to point to the newly added entry if appropriate (i.e., if the newly added string is a valid substring).

In deleting an entry, care must be taken to account for any entries that might point to it. One possibility is not to delete an entry immediately but rather indicate that it isn't really a legal substring anymore and store the pointer for the longest substring that *is* in the dictionary there. Thus, entries that pointed to the deleted entry will have to follow two pointers. When enough entries have been deleted so that table space needs to be recovered, or lookups are being slowed by having to sequentially follow too many pointers, then the table can be rebuilt.

Another possibility is to scan all items in the database between the two entries to be deleted (from the string padded with *a* to the string padded with *z*), modifying pointers along the way as necessary.

Another implementation issue is that the database would probably not be kept as a linear list but would instead be organized as a binary tree. Then, issues such as tree-balancing algorithms must also be considered, but there are well-known algorithms for tree balancing and traversal.

9.8   Implementing a Connectionless Service

In this section, I'll describe the most common method of implementing a connectionless service. There is only a single type of packet to route, and that is a data packet. Each data packet has a destination address. No state is kept in routers about conversations in which endnodes are currently participating.

A router receives a data packet and makes a decision as to which link to forward the packet upon, based on the destination address (and possibly also the type of service—to be discussed later in the chapter).

The routing computation has computed a forwarding database, which matches a destination with a routing decision at the local router. The forwarding database will be different in each router. (One router will route a packet for destination DEST to neighbor FOO, and another router will route a packet for DEST to neighbor BAR. The second router might not even *have* a neighbor FOO.) A router receives a data packet, looks at the network layer destination address, finds the entry in the forwarding database corresponding to that destination, and routes the packet on the link specified in the forwarding database.

The characteristics of the network can vary a great deal during the course of a conversation. Routes can change, either very frequently (such as with every packet) if load splitting is being performed by the network, moderately frequently if routes change in an attempt to adapt to current traffic patterns (traffic-sensitive link costs), or less frequently if routes change only as a result of changing topology. The endnode will experience varying quality of service in terms of delay, maximum packet size before fragmentation becomes necessary, and higher probability of packet reordering as routes change.

Even if routes do not change, service characteristics can vary a great deal during the course of a conversation as a result of competition with other traffic.

9.9   Implementing a Connection-Oriented Service (X.25)

In this section, I'll discuss two methods of implementing a service interface with the X.25 guarantees—i.e., that all packets be transmitted in order with no duplication or loss, or else the call will be disconnected. Some X.25 providers use the first strategy, and some use the second.

9.9.1   Circuit Method

In the circuit method, routers keep the same sort of forwarding database as in connectionless networking, which maps network layer destination addresses to output ports (neighbors to which packets should be forwarded). The choice of routing algorithm, and whether multiple paths to a given destination are computed, is proprietary to the network provider.

There is another database, which I'll refer to as the "call-mapping database," that maps (call number, port) pairs to (call number, port) pairs. When a call request packet is received on port x, with call number C1 and destination address DEST, the router consults its forwarding database to determine a reasonable output port, y, for forwarding traffic for DEST. It also chooses a call number that is not currently used on port y—say, C2. The router will forward the call request packet, substituting C2 for C1, and make the call-mapping database entry (C1, x)/(C2, y). Data packets do not carry a destination address, only a call number. Thus, if a data packet with call number C2 is received on port y, the call-mapping database will be consulted and find (C1, x) as the associated call number and port. In the data packet, C2 is overwritten with C1, and the packet is forwarded onto port x. Likewise in the other direction. If a data packet with call number C1 is received on port x, the call number is overwritten with C2, and the packet is forwarded onto port y.

Often, with networks built this way, a certain number of buffers are reserved for each item in the call-mapping database. If a call request comes in and the call-mapping database is full or all the buffers are reserved, the call is refused by the network (like a "fast busy signal" in the U.S. telephone network).

Since the number of calls is limited, if the network completes a call, a certain level of performance is guaranteed. When the network gets to a particular level of utilization, further calls are refused but service is not degraded for those calls already in progress. This is in contrast to a connectionless service, in which service for all users would be degraded democratically.

Usually, in a network built this way, a router holds onto a data packet only until the downstream router acknowledges it. Consequently, if any router along the path fails, there is no way for the network to recover lost packets, and the network will disconnect the call under these circumstances.

9.9.2   End-to-end Reliable Connections over Datagrams Method

Another way to provide an X.25 interface is to build a connectionless network but have additional code in routers that might have endnode neighbors. The additional code is a protocol similar to a full-service transport layer. When a router, R1, receives a call request packet from an attached endnode, E1, with destination address E2 and call number x, R1 consults its routing databases to find out the router, R2, to which endnode E2 is attached. R1 then sets up a connection to R2—i.e., an end-to-end service between the two routers that ensures that every packet transmitted by R1 gets received by R2 in order, with no loss, duplication, or misordering. Besides R1 and R2, no other routers keep state regarding the conversation between endnodes E1 and E2. Load splitting might be implemented within the network, and different packets of the conversation might travel different routes. R2 will hold onto data packets until all earlier ones have been received. R1 will hold onto packets until R2 has acknowledged them.

9.9.3 Comparison

With the second method for building an X.25 interface, no service guarantees are made. As long as the end routers have sufficient space to hold the state regarding the end-to-end connection, the call will be accepted by the network. Buffers in intermediate routers will not be reserved, and packets might be dropped en route (but the source router will be able to retransmit them).

A network built according to the second method will be able to handle more calls, since buffers and bandwidth can be shared. With the first method, if traffic is at all bursty, the resources reserved for a particular call will be wasted when no data is being sent.

The first method enables routers to forward data packets more quickly and easily, since the routing decision is based on a small call number rather than a larger network layer address.

With the second method, an alternate route can be found if an intermediate router or link fails. The routing algorithm will adapt to the changed topology, and routes will be recalculated. Although packets in transit will most likely be dropped while the routing algorithm is adapting, the source router will fail to receive acknowledgments for those packets and will retransmit them.

9.10 LANs

In describing the routing algorithms, I assumed that all links in the network were point-to-point links. There are extra issues to be considered when some of the links are LANs.

9.10.1 Making the LAN a Node

A LAN is equivalent to full connectivity between every pair of nodes on the LAN. However, routing algorithms tend to have overhead proportional to the number of links in the network, so it is not advisable to expand a LAN with n nodes into n^2 links (see Fig. 9.17).

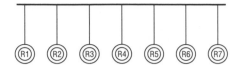

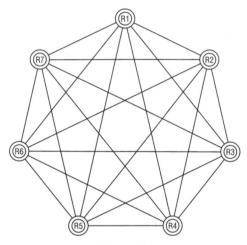

Figure 9.17

In link state routing, it is advisable to consider the LAN itself as a node in the network (see Fig. 9.18). This is done by having the routers on the LAN elect one router to be the "designated router," through a simple process such as choosing the router with the highest or lowest ID. The designated router names the LAN and constructs an LSP on behalf of the LAN. The name of the LAN is the concatenation of the designated router's ID with an additional field to differentiate among multiple LANs for which that router might be designated.

Each router on the LAN reports only a single link in its LSP for the LAN—i.e., a link to the LAN itself (in this case, neighbor R1.5).

R1 issues an LSP for itself claiming a link to R1.5. R1 issues an additional LSP on behalf of the LAN, which lists all the nodes on the LAN, including the endnodes, in the case of ISO (in IP, information about endnodes is not propagated). Thus, all the endnodes on the LAN will appear in only a single LSP rather than being listed in the LSPs of all the routers on the LAN.

9.10.2   Disseminating Routing Information

It is more efficient to disseminate routing information taking advantage of the capabilities of the LAN. However, the LAN service is datagram (especially if the LAN's multicast capability is exploited).

The most obvious thing routers should do is to multicast routing information (like LSPs or distance vectors) to a multicast address listened to by all the routers rather than transmitting individual copies to all the neighbor routers. But routing information must be delivered reliably. There are various methods for ensuring reliable delivery:

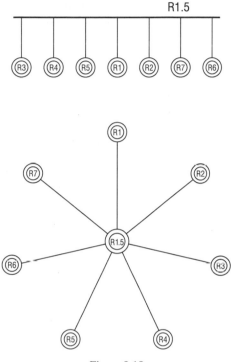

Figure 9.18

1. Have each router transmit an acknowledgment to the router that multicasted a routing message.

    If multicast were not exploited, the source router, R, would have sent an individual message to each of the other routers. Assume that there are n routers on the LAN. Then R would transmit $n-1$ messages and receive $n-1$ acks, resulting in $2n-2$ messages for each routing message. If R instead multicasts the message but still collects acknowledgments, then there are n messages—the single multicast by R and the $n-1$ acks.

    This scheme is similar to the one chosen by OSPF, which is a link state routing protocol for IP. (OSPF is discussed in more detail in Chapter 10.)

2. Have each router retransmit each routing message fairly frequently. The period between retransmissions should be about equal to the amount of time that a router would have waited, in the absence of having received an ack, before retransmitting.

    This is a reasonable scheme for distance vector routing, in which each router has only a single piece of routing information to transmit. It would not work at all well with link state routing, in which each router has an LSP from each other router in the network.

The reasoning behind this approach is that it is very simple. If the amount of routing traffic is modest (in distance vector routing, with ten routers on the LAN, each retransmitting a distance vector every 10 sec, the overhead is really quite tolerable), then this scheme cannot be faulted for generating too much overhead. It also does not necessarily consume more bandwidth than a scheme involving explicit acks. If there are n routers on the LAN, and the information changes more frequently than n times the periodic retransmission time, then this scheme actually takes *less* bandwidth than an explicit-ack scheme. Most likely, the information changes less frequently than that, but we must keep in mind that elimination of the acks does offset things somewhat.

Also, periodic transmissions in the absence of anything useful to say do less harm than a scheme that requires a lot of packets while topology is changing. So again, the periodic-transmission scheme is attractive because its "nonessential" use of bandwidth takes place during times when there would have been no control traffic anyway.

Furthermore, this approach cannot be faulted for being less reliable than a scheme involving acknowledgments, provided the retransmission timer is the same as the periodic timer. In other words, in an explicit-acknowledgment scheme, if a message is missed, some time will elapse before the transmitter notices the lack of an ack and retransmits. If that time is, say, 10 sec, then a scheme requiring periodic transmissions every 10 sec will recover from lost messages just as quickly.

This scheme was used in phase IV DECnet, which was a distance vector routing protocol.

3. Provide periodic database summaries.

In a link state scheme, an alternative to explicit acknowledgments of individual LSPs is the scheme devised for phase V DECnet (and adopted by ISO in IS-IS). A special packet, known as a *sequence numbers packet*, or *SNP*, is periodically transmitted by the designated router. It contains the latest sequence numbers of all the LSPs. If, based on receiving an SNP, a router R detects that it has missed an LSP, it can explicitly request the LSP from the designated router. If R detects that the designated router has missed an LSP (because the LSP is not mentioned in the SNP or one with a smaller number from that source is mentioned), then R knows that it should retransmit the LSP.

As with the frequent-retransmissions scheme, if the period with which SNPs are broadcast is the same as the retransmission time that would be used with an explicit-acknowledgment scheme, the SNP approach is as robust and responsive as an explicit-acknowledgment scheme.

Again, similarly to the frequent-retransmissions scheme, the extra bandwidth consumed by the periodic transmission of SNPs is offset by the elimination of the explicit acknowledgments and is bandwidth better spent because it involves having a constant low level of traffic instead of having all the control traffic bunched around the time topology changes occur.

A disadvantage of the SNP scheme is the processing required of the routers that receive an SNP. Each time an SNP is received, the link state database must be checked against the information in the SNP. When no LSPs have been recently transmitted, the check will merely verify that the databases remain synchronized. This may not be too much of a disadvantage because if no LSPs have been recently transmitted, the router should have CPU cycles to spare. Also, it might be an advantage to periodically compare databases, in the event that somehow the databases have become corrupted.

9.11   Types of Service

The term *types of service* has been defined in various ways. This section discusses some of the things that people mean when they use this term.

9.11.1   Handling Directives

A handling directive is a special way that the user would like a packet handled, but it does not involve a specially chosen route. An example of a handling directive is *priority*, in which the user requests preferential treatment in terms of placement in queues and perhaps selection of the priority field in the data link header when the packet is forwarded. Other examples are *don't fragment* and *error report requested*.

Any number of handling directives can be implemented, but they must be predefined before the router is implemented, there must be a way of specifying each one in the packet header, and the algorithms for dealing with each one must be implemented. If two or more handling directives are selected on a particular packet, the algorithms for each one must be executed.

9.11.2   Multiple Metrics

If one set of metrics cannot satisfy all users, links could be assigned a set of costs—for instance, one for bandwidth and one for delay. An example of a metric that is very different from delay or bandwidth is money. Some links cost money per packet. Others are "free." Now, as we all should realize, there's no such thing as a free link—it's just a matter of who pays. But some users might want to minimize the money spent, and they might be willing to use an otherwise undesirable path if it costs less money. Routing would be calculated independently for each type of cost, and the forwarding decision would be based on destination address and chosen metric.

What happens if someone wants to consider more than one of the orthogonal characteristics of the link? For instance, suppose that someone wants to optimize delay and bandwidth but is not concerned about other types of costs. What is the cost of a link when two or more independent metrics are supposed to be simultaneously optimized?

Should the costs of the chosen metrics be combined? What sort of combination should be chosen? It could be the sum, the product, or some weighted quantity assigning more weight to one characteristic than another. It could be that the user considers one characteristic much more important, and a second chosen characteristic is to be used only as a tiebreaker among paths whose cost is equal according to the first chosen characteristic.

Another possibility is to consider each combination of characteristics as a separate metric. This gives the maximum flexibility in choosing the most sensible method of combining the values but will be more costly if characteristics are often combined, since n characteristics become 2^n possible combinations of characteristics, yielding 2^n different metrics, which must be manually assigned per link and for which routing must be computed and forwarding databases kept.

The way multiple metrics are specified in IS-IS, there is one metric known as the *default metric*. Every router must implement the default metric, and every link must carry a cost according to the default metric.

Implementation of other metrics is optional. Each router specifies a set of (metric number, cost) pairs for each link. It is possible for a router to report a different set of metrics on different links, but every link must report a value for the default metric. A router that does not report a particular metric on any of its links does not need to compute routes according to that metric. If a router only reports a value for the default metric on each of its links, it will only compute a single set of routes.

When a user requests routing according to some metric other than the default metric, a route with that metric (one that traverses only routers and links that support that metric) is chosen if such a route is available. Otherwise, the route calculated according to the default metric is chosen. With this strategy, routers that have not implemented different metrics will interwork with routers that have.

The implications of multiple metrics should be considered carefully. A route computed according to a metric other than the default metric is constrained, somewhat arbitrarily perhaps, to use certain links (those supporting the requested metric). The computed route may be wildly nonoptimal, since it is restricted to some arbitrary subset of the links and routers.

An amusing scenario, suggested by Ross Callon, involves use of the "money" metric. Suppose that most of the links do not support the money metric, but some of the links do cost significant amounts of money to use, and therefore, the managers of the routers attached to those links regard it as important to warn users that the links are expensive, by reporting the money metric for those links. The links that are "free" do not bother reporting a money metric cost. Then someone wants to save money and selects the money metric. The route computed will be a circuitous one that visits enough of the expensive links to reach the destination. In this case, the money spent will be maximized.

The type of service that can be specified in an IP header consists of a 3-bit "TOS" field, where "delay," "throughput," and "reliability" each have 1 bit. According to the IP router requirements, this specifies eight different metrics. If a user specifies both delay and reliability by setting both bits, and if there is at least one route where every link in the path reports a cost according to the metric of delay plus reliability, but not throughput, then the packet is routed according to the best of those routes. If no such route exists, then the packet is routed according to the default metric—i.e., the one where none of the 3 bits is set in the TOS field.

The TOS field in ISO is an option and, as such, might not appear in a packet header. If it does not, the packet is routed according to the default metric. If it does, it might specify "source-specific" or "destination specific"—in which case, the standard does not specify the meaning, and the default metric is used. If the packet does contain the globally specified quality of service, there are 3 relevant bits:

1. *E/C:* "Residual error probability versus cost"

2. *E/D:* "Residual error probability versus delay"

3. *D/C:* "Transit delay versus cost"

Four metrics are defined:

1. Default (intended to be bandwidth)

2. Delay

3. Expense

4. Error

The metric chosen for each setting of the bits is specified in IS-IS as follows:

E/C	E/D	D/C	Selected Metric
0	0	0	expense
0	0	1	default
1	1	0	default
0	1	0	expense
1	0	0	delay
0	1	1	error
1	0	1	delay
1	1	1	error

Personally, I dislike the added complexity of multiple metrics, especially as implemented (where not all metrics are reported for each link). I think that any potential gains in terms of better routes will be more than offset by the overhead and by the likelihood of extreme sub-optimality due to misconfiguration or misunderstanding of the way multiple metrics work.

9.11.3   Policy-Based Routing/Constraints

When people use the terms *policy-based routing* or *policy-based constraints*, they mean routing where the use of certain links and routers is outlawed. This is different from optimizing a metric, where no paths are outlawed but some are preferred to others. Constraints are motivated by:

1. Assumptions that there is not really a giant network to which you attach and then become part of it, but rather that there are a bunch of autonomous routing domains, and the administrators agree to connect to a few other routing domains.

   For example, if nets A and B decide to connect together, and B and C decide to connect together, this does not give A permission to route traffic to C. Traffic will flow from A to C only if networks A and B explicitly agree to connect to each other, and B and C agree to connect to each other, and A and C agree to send traffic to each other through B, and B agrees to carry transit traffic between A and C.

2. Laws in various countries, or policies corresponding to the applications running, which might constrain the legal routes. For instance, Canadian law requires traffic originating and terminating in Canada to be routed solely within Canada, so a route that entered the United States and then returned to Canada would be illegal.

   These laws are sufficiently complex, and sufficiently likely to change, that a particular law should not be built into the routing algorithm. Rather, routing should somehow be parameterized such that any policy could be entered manually.

3. Policies of certain networks, which might restrict the types of traffic they will carry. For instance, the ARPANET is only supposed to be used for government business.

Providing different routes for different types of traffic makes routing close to intractable.

People would like to have the route to destination DEST depend on any combination of the following:

1. Source routing domain

2. Source node

3. Application

4. Content of the message (for instance, a mail message regarding government business is allowed to traverse the ARPANET, but not a message recommending science-fiction books)

5. The route the packet has traversed so far

I'm sure there are other factors that people will think should be considered in a routing decision. Obviously, the more such criteria, the more difficult routing becomes, especially if it is deemed important for routers to forward packets quickly.

There are several general methods for attempting to deal with these issues, none of them completely satisfactory. Most of the work going on in this area involves interdomain routing, since the assumption is that within a domain, any route should be legal. There are two efforts. One is known as "BGP" ("border gateway protocol") within the TCP/IP community, with an ISO version of BGP that is called "IDRP" ("interdomain routing protocol"). Another is called "IDPR" ("interdomain policy routing").

BGP/IDRP is a distance vector protocol that I describe in the section of Chapter 10 dealing with interdomain routing. IDPR is much more ambitious and is not yet well defined. BGP/IDRP is likely to become a standard in both arenas.

Now I'll discuss the generic approaches to providing policy-based routing without concentrating on a specific protocol.

9.11.4   Static Routes

Static routing is the conceptually simplest solution. Humans can consider whatever they want in determining the desired routes. The main problem with static routes (other than the hassle of manual configuration, together with the fact that this approach will not work unless all routers are configured properly and compatibly) is that static routes cannot adapt to topological changes.

9.11.5   Filters

A filter is an additional algorithm executed in a packet switch that decides which packets it will forward and which it will refuse to forward. For instance, a filter could reject packets from a particular source address or source routing domain.

Filters can be useful, and indeed essential, to enforce restrictions on access to resources, but they do not solve the general problem because a packet that is not allowed to use one route to a particular destination might have another, perfectly legal route to that destination. There must be a way to ensure that the packet will traverse a legal route when one is available rather than penalizing the user because the network happened to decide to route the packet on a restricted route.

9.11.6   Source Routing

The theory behind source routing is that the source can have any policy it wishes and merely specify the route in the packet header. The main problems with source routing as the solution to providing policy-based routing are that the source must have access to a current topological map in order to be able to select a route that is not only desirable but works, and that there has to be some way for the source to know the characteristics of other routing domains, links, and switches (whatever criteria it is using for selecting a route). Assuming that it is not a human calculating a path, the computer must be given enough information so that if a new routing domain, switch, or link is attached to the network, the algorithm will know the relevant characteristics.

9.11.7   Routing-Domain-Specific Policy

Routing-domain-specific policy is the approach taken by BGP/IDRP. The assumption is that routing constraints apply equally to all links and routers within a routing domain.

Thus, any policy restrictions can be expressed in terms of the routing domains in the path. Each "border gateway" (a router connecting two routing domains) has a set of policies that it uses to choose a route to a particular destination. Here are some examples of such policies:

- Never use routing domain X for any destination.

- Never use both routing domains X and Y in any particular route.

- Don't use routing domain X to get to a destination in routing domain Y.

- Don't use routing domain X unless you are also using routing domain Y.

- Don't use routing domain X unless no alternative path exists.

- Don't use routing domain X unless the next best alternative path is at least cost C worse.

BGP is a distance vector routing protocol in which each entry in the distance vector gives the sequence of routing domains in the path to the destination. Distributing the sequence of routing domains has two purposes:

1. It solves the counting-to-infinity problem.

2. It allows policy decisions to be made based on the routing domains in the path.

When a border gateway makes a decision regarding the path to a destination, it considers all the routing domain sequence routes it has learned from its neighbor border gateways. It first discards all the routes that are precluded by policy and then uses some algorithm to calculate the "preference" of the remaining routes. The route with the highest preference is advertised in its distance vector.

This approach allows routes to be computed for some policies but certainly not all. Once a border gateway makes a route choice, the other routes are not available to border gateways farther from the destination. For instance, assume the following topology:

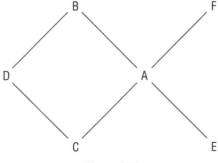

Figure 9.19

Suppose that F and B are routing domains that only U.S. citizens are allowed to use; C and E are routing domains that only French citizens are allowed to use; and A and D are open to everyone. With these rules, when E wants to transmit to D, it must travel route

E–A–C–D. When F wants to transmit to D, it must travel F–A–B–D. However, A will make a choice as to its route to D. If it chooses A–C–D, it will make F unhappy, since D will become unreachable to users within F. If it chooses A–B–D, it will make E unhappy, since D will become unreachable to users within E. Source routing will allow things to work, but it is unfortunate to require users within E or F to know that source routing is needed and to know a set of source routes that might work (there could be multiple legal paths, but not all of them may be functional at any moment due to links' or routers' being down).

9.11.8 Service-Class-Specific Policy

Suppose that a link had a small number of independent characteristics—for instance, whether the link crossed national boundaries, whether it was commercial or military. If that were the case, then each router could advertise the characteristics of each of its links as a set of flags, one for each characteristic.

A packet would contain a list of characteristics that all the links in the path must meet. If link state routing is used, then a route can be computed when a new set of characteristics is seen. A route meeting characteristics i, j, and k can be computed by rejecting all the links that don't have the i, j, and k flags set. If a router had sufficient CPU, it could compute a route every time it forwards a packet. More realistically, it is improbable that a very large number of different combinations of characteristics would be requested during any particular time interval, so a router could compute for a few combinations known to be popular and then compute and cache for others as seen. The overhead to support this sort of service class is not too odious, since it only involves a bit vector of perhaps 30 flags, for each link in the net, and cached routes for the combinations that are actually requested.

This type of service class is clean and general, but it assumes that the characteristics can be reasonably well defined. This is not the approach being taken in any of the emerging routing standards.

9.12 Congestion

Congestion control is a very difficult problem in a network. If congestion conditions start and resolve more quickly than information can propagate around the network, then the problem is completely intractable.

I've always felt that a network that is reasonably underutilized does not need any congestion control mechanisms; a network that is seriously overutilized will not work well no matter what type of congestion control mechanisms are invoked. And the difference between the tolerable utilization levels in a network with no congestion control mechanisms and one with the best congestion control mechanisms that can be devised is probably a few percent.

An analogy is the highway system. When traffic is light, everything works fine. But at 5:00 P.M. in Boston, nothing helps—traffic lights, radio reports of congestion areas ("all of metropolitan Boston"), police directing traffic, etc.

That said, I'll explain the work going on in congestion. The belief is that congestion can be alleviated in a connectionless network by informing users that they should lower their use of the network. This can be done by advising the transport layers in the data sources that the network is becoming congested—at least, in the direction of a particular destination. In IP, this information is provided through the source quench messages in ICMP. In ISO, the information is piggybacked in the data packet headers. The ISO mechanism doesn't add traffic to an already congested network but has the disadvantage of informing the destination rather than the source. However, since most transport layers provide end-to-end flow control, the destination can cause the source to lower its demand on the network by shrinking the source's window.

These mechanisms are promising if traffic is caused by a few high-volume sources. If traffic is caused instead by the existence of an enormous number of sources, each with a transport window of 1, then these mechanisms will not help.

9.13   WAN Multicast

In this section I discuss the ability to do multicast within a LAN, i.e., why people want it, workarounds when it is not provided, dangers of providing it, and methods of providing it.

9.13.1   History

LAN technology made the ability to multicast convenient and (deceptively) inexpensive. It is convenient and inexpensive for the transmitter, which can transmit a single copy of a packet and reach multiple recipients. It is convenient for the medium, since a single copy of the packet reaches all recipients anyway. However, multicast is not so inexpensive for the receivers. Since it is difficult for the hardware to do perfect filtering of many addresses, a receiver that wishes to receive any multicast addresses winds up processing software interrupts for "wrong numbers"—i.e., destination addresses it is not interested in receiving.

Multicast is used on LANs chiefly for autoconfiguration—helping clients and servers find each other. The two models, as described in Chapter 2, are *solicit* and *advertise*. Soliciting is when a client queries for a server; advertising is when a server announces its presence to clients.

With the emergence of bridges, multicast was no longer so obviously inexpensive. In bridged LANs, multicast packets are transmitted along the spanning tree to all LANs. In a single LAN, if there were one recipient, it would require no more bandwidth to transmit a multicast packet than a unicast packet. However, in a bridged extended LAN, if there were indeed only a small number of recipients of a multicast packet, or if all the recipients were in one location (residing on one LAN), it could take a significant amount of extra bandwidth to transmit a multicast packet (which will be delivered and broadcast onto every LAN) rather than multiple unicast packets, one to each recipient.

9.13.2 Reasons for WAN Multicast

Once people got used to the capability of multicasting, it was natural to ask why it could not be provided in a wide area network. There were several potential applications for WAN multicast, as indicated in the following list, and it was argued that others might emerge, given the opportunity to experiment with the technique.

1. Advertisement by servers.

2. Solicitation of servers by clients.

3. Conference calls, where a conversation is taking place among a group of individuals. Rather than requiring the source of each packet to make individual copies for each recipient, the network could provide a multicast address for the conversation, all the packets of the conversation could be addressed to the multicast address, and the network would deliver the multicast packets to all recipients.

4. Dissemination of datagram information (e.g., weather reports or stock market prices) of potential interest to many recipients, who might "tune in" temporarily to hear the information.

5. Dissemination of mail to large numbers of recipients. Rather than keeping track of all the recipients, the source can transmit a single multicast message and any interested recipient can listen for it.

6. Dissemination of information that must be reliably delivered to many recipients—for instance, downline load.

It is important to keep in mind the potential applications of WAN multicast in order to be able to evaluate the best method of providing it.

9.13.3 WAN Multicast in TCP/IP

Steve Deering designed a form of WAN multicast for his Ph.D. thesis at Stanford, and it is likely to become a standard within the TCP/IP protocol suite. The basics of the design are as follows:

1. A convention is defined for recognizing a particular network layer address as being a multicast address.

2. A convention is defined for mapping a network layer multicast address to a LAN data link layer address—at least, for 802 LANs.

3. A protocol is defined ("internet group management protocol," or "IGMP") that consists of endnodes' informing their adjacent routers about the network layer multicast addresses they wish to receive. A group of hosts that might wish to communicate with each other using the mechanisms of wide area multicast is known as a *host group*. The network layer multicast address used by the host group is known as a *host group address*.

4. The routing algorithm (whatever one is used) is modified so that each router R can inform all the other routers about which network layer multicast addresses are being listened to by R's neighbors.

5. The routing algorithm is modified so that each router calculates a separate spanning tree for each source (see Fig. 9.20).

6. When a data packet is transmitted with a network layer multicast address as its destination, the packet is propagated through the spanning tree selected based on the source address of the packet, but with the spanning tree's branches pruned to eliminate those branches that do not lead to any listeners of that network layer multicast address (see Fig. 9.22).

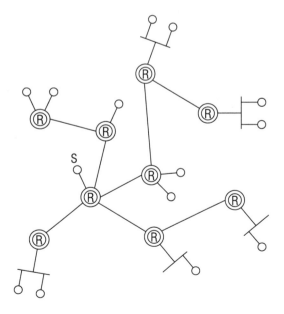

Figure 9.20   Spanning tree for S

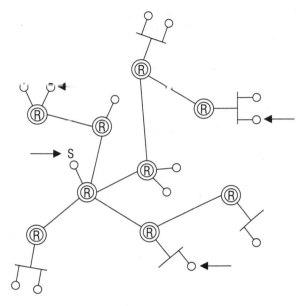

Figure 9.21   Listeners for multicast address M

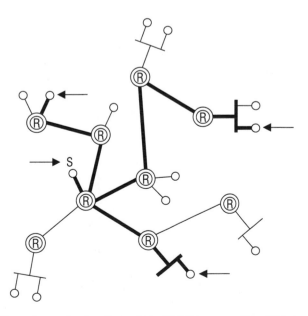

Figure 9.22   Pruned spanning tree for packet with NL source = S and NL destination = M

9.13.4   Recognizing an NL Multicast Address

The IP convention for recognizing a network layer address as being a multicast address is that in a multicast address, the top 4 bits of the address are "1110." That yields 28 bits to be assigned for IP multicast addresses.

9.13.5   Mapping NL Multicast to DL Multicast

When the network layer destination address is a multicast address, and the packet is transmitted onto a LAN, what should the data link layer destination address be? Before answering that, it is important to realize that applications are being considered for NL multicast that would be high-traffic. Previous use of data link layer broadcast attempted to minimize the amount of traffic. But the NL multicast is being designed assuming high-bandwidth applications like video teleconferencing.

One possibility for choosing a data link layer address for transmitting IP multicast messages is to always transmit such messages to the data link layer broadcast address. This would not be very "socially responsible," though, because there are protocols that require conforming nodes to listen to packets addressed to the data link layer broadcast address. Increasing the number of protocols that use the broadcast address would increase the number of software interrupts. This problem could be alleviated if hardware were extended to filter packets based on the protocol type.

Another possibility is to choose the data link layer multicast address for "all IP hosts." Although this at least does not bother non-IP hosts, it does require IP hosts to deal with a potentially lethal dose of software interrupts.

Ideally, every IP multicast address would map to a distinct data link layer address. Since there are 28 bits of IP multicast address (as noted in the preceding subsection, the top 4 bits of the address are the constant "1110"), this would require 20 bits of high-order constant. An ordinary block of addresses that one might obtain for an 802 LAN gives 24 bits of high-order constant. If 16 consecutive address blocks could be obtained, then the IP community would have its 28 bits.

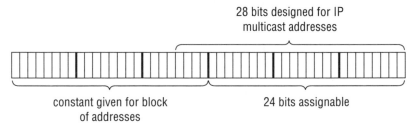

Figure 9.23

It was considered impractical economically and politically to obtain 16 consecutive address blocks for IP multicast. Economically, it would have cost $1,000 per block. Politically, it was impossible because the IEEE does not want people asking for lots of blocks and has a policy against granting consecutive blocks to one organization in order to discourage schemes such as this. So instead, the IP community decided to reserve half the multicast addresses in its single address block. That yielded only 23 bits for IP multicast. But that was workable. It simply meant that the mapping is done by looking only at the bottom 23 bits of the IP multicast address. Thus, 32 different IP multicast addresses will map to the same data link layer multicast address if the bottom 23 bits are the same in all 32 addresses. It is just an example of imperfect multicast filtering, which is already the case with the standard chips.

9.13.6   IGMP Protocol

The IGMP protocol contains two types of messages, "host membership query" and "host membership report." The query is transmitted by a router. When it is transmitted on a LAN, the data link layer multicast address "all IP endnodes" is used. The response is transmitted to the multicast address derived from the group address being advertised.

Note that because a router must be able to receive all the responses, the IGMP protocol requires a router to be able to receive all the 2^{23} possible data link layer multicast addresses derived from IP host group addresses. This requires routers to listen promiscuously to all LAN multicast traffic.

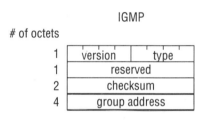

Figure 9.24

The **version** is set to 1. The **type** is either 1 (for a host membership query), or 2 (for a host membership report). The **checksum** is the usual IP checksum calculated on the 8 octets defined in the accompanying illustration. When transmitted in a query, the **group address** is 0, and when transmitted in a host membership report, it is the 4-octet address of the host group being reported.

9.13.7   Propagating Host Group Information to All Routers

In link state routing, propagating host group information to all routers involves having each router include in its LSP the host group addresses that adjacent endnodes wish to receive.

9.13.8   Calculating a Spanning Tree per Source

In link state routing, it is not conceptually difficult to calculate a spanning tree per source. The link state database contains all the information required to calculate a spanning tree using any node as the root. It is just expensive in terms of memory and CPU, since the Dijkstra algorithm must be run from the point of view of every location in the network, and information about the spanning tree for each source address must be kept.

9.13.9 Pruning a Spanning Tree for a Multicast Address

It is desirable to confine a multicast so that it does not propagate into portions of the network in which no endnodes are listening for a particular multicast address. This is done by examining a given spanning tree and discarding branches in which no listeners exist.

When a router receives an IP packet with a multicast address as the network layer destination, it is supposed to do the following two things:

1. Select a spanning tree based on the network layer source address

2. Prune that spanning tree based on the network layer destination address

9.13.10 My Opinion on IP-Style Network Layer Multicast

The mechanisms described in the preceding subsections for providing the functionality of network layer multicast are very expensive in terms of bandwidth and CPU and memory in the routers. Moreover, I feel that the functionality itself is potentially dangerous. The IP community has had many problems with "broadcast storms" on LANs. The storms were always the result of misconfiguration or implementation bugs. Given the collective wisdom of the IP community, each of the categories of broadcast storms could be analyzed and fixes could be found.

However, if network layer multicast is provided, then lots of user applications will be utilizing it. Any one of these applications that has been improperly designed, implemented, or configured could cause a network layer broadcast storm. Network layer broadcast storms are more serious than LAN broadcast storms because the latter could only disable a single LAN (or a set of bridged LANs), whereas the former could disrupt an entire network. Also, the LAN broadcast storms were basically the result of a single protocol—IP and ARP. Network layer broadcast storms could result from many applications designed by all sorts of groups.

Since providing NL multicast is not harmless, the benefits should be weighed carefully against the disadvantages before this functionality is deployed. The sorts of applications for which NL multicast is considered potentially useful are:

1. Finding the nearest server of some type—say, a "FOO server."
    This can be supported without WAN multicast in one of two ways:

    a. Have a yellow-pages-type naming service, where all the FOO servers register their addresses and someone wanting a FOO server chooses one. This mechanism may not easily give the very closest FOO server, but people could certainly choose based on area address (get one in their area). Or if people really want to be able to optimize the choice, it might work to have a simple mechanism for asking the advice of a neighbor router regarding which of a set of addresses is closest. I'd guess that it doesn't matter whether the optimal server is chosen.

b. Have all FOO servers advertise that they are a particular well-known NSAP. Then, ordinary level 1 routing will route to the nearest FOO server. (This works with ISO addressing but not with IP addressing, since IP addresses must be different for each link.)

2. Carrying on a "conference call" among a group of people.

My feeling is that if there are not very many participants, sending individual copies of each packet to each participant will suffice. I can't believe that a significant amount of network traffic will be based on conference calls, and if only a minute proportion of the traffic on the network is due to conference calls, then there is no reason to optimize it.

3. Sending material that needs to get reliably delivered to multiple participants.

My feeling is that the solution to this requirement is not a datagram WAN multicast but rather a fancy mail facility containing several distribution sites to which the mail gets reliably delivered, with each distribution site, in turn, reliably delivering the mail to the users for which it is responsible.

4. Providing datagram information—like weather reports, news, or stock prices—to which many people might sometimes want to listen but that doesn't have to get delivered reliably.

This seems to me like a good application of WAN multicast, but I'd think it could be supported by an extremely simple WAN mechanism. The solution I'd propose is to support broadcast only on a single LAN or in a single area. A single spanning tree would be calculated for the area, and any network layer multicast addresses would be disseminated to all the nodes in the area. Perhaps it might be worthwhile to have an optimization for point-to-point links, where the endnode tells the router which network layer multicast addresses it wants to see, thus enabling the router to filter the "junk mail."

This limited form of WAN multicast would be considerably simpler and would require lower overhead to maintain than an IGMP-type solution, in which hosts on LANs tell their routers which multicasts they are listening to, and those routers tell all the other routers in the area (as well as in other areas?). This approach isn't "optimal" in the sense of data distribution, since it involves sending a multicast through an entire area, including those portions of the area where nobody is interested in the multicast. But the kinds of applications that would use WAN multicast for this purpose might indeed interest enough of the area to warrant sending the multicasts everywhere.

And in special cases where only two LANs in the area are known to contain interested listeners, two copies of the packet could be sent—one copy to be multicast on the first LAN, the other to be multicast on the second LAN.

Thus, my opinion is that we should either do without network layer multicast or provide just a very simple mechanism.

The mechanisms proposed for IP can be simplified, although the multicast data will not be routed as optimally. The simplifications suggested in the following list will save bandwidth due to control traffic, which might more than offset the loss in optimization of multicast data traffic.

1. I would not calculate more than a single spanning tree. With a spanning tree per source, it is assured that data will travel an optimal route from the source to each listener. However, a single spanning tree would suffice for all multicast traffic—it just means the route to each listener might not be optimal.

2. I would not propagate host group listener information throughout the network. This would lower the amount of bandwidth used to provide the functionality. Every multicast would travel to all the routers within the distance specified by the source (or within the level 1 subnetwork specified by the source).

3. I would not attempt to have routers calculate the set of NL multicast addresses being listened to on a LAN. Instead, I'd have each NL multicast transmitted onto the LAN, as with the mechanism provided by data link layer multicast—the multicast travels through the entire LAN, and the endnodes decide whether or not to read the message.

   It might be worthwhile to enhance ES-IS so that on a point-to-point link, an endnode can inform the neighbor router of the set of network layer multicast addresses it wishes to receive.

This is another area where it would be useful to conduct an unbiased, careful evaluation of the trade-offs—to determine whether the expense and potential hazards of the mechanisms will be offset by the proposed optimizations and the functionality that could be provided.

9.14   Partition Repair—Level 1 Subnetwork Partition

Suppose that some links break in a level 1 subnetwork, thereby partitioning the subnetwork into two or more pieces. If one of the pieces has no other connections, then it becomes a separate network. Nodes within that piece will be able to talk only to nodes within that piece. There is nothing, short of repairing the links connecting that piece with the rest of the network, that will restore communication between that piece and the rest of the network.

However, if each partition contains a level 2 router, and the level 2 router has level 2 links to the rest of the network, there can be a path from one partition to the other partition, through the level 2 network.

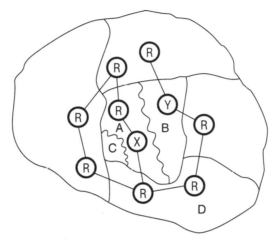

Figure 9.25

A subnetwork partition presents several problems (see Fig. 9.25):

1. A cannot talk to B, even though there is a physical path, since A's address and B's address look to level 1 routers as if they reside in the level 1 subnetwork, so the level 1 routers will attempt to deliver the packet via level 1 routing, fail, and declare the destination unreachable.

2. C cannot talk to anyone. This is not really a problem, since there is no physical path out of C's partition.

3. D may or may not be able to communicate with B. Packets for B from D might get routed by the level 2 network toward B's partition, or they might get routed toward A's partition.

This partition problem is a real annoyance, because it can create strange symptoms, in which some nodes can communicate and others cannot. Also, depending on the topology of a given level 1 subnetwork, a single failure can partition the subnetwork, and partitions can happen frequently.

The best solution known for dealing with subnetwork partitions is documented in IS-IS and is as follows:

1. Level 2 routers residing in level 1 subnetwork FOO identify the partition of FOO in which they are located (this may be all of FOO if FOO is not partitioned). They accomplish this by finding the level 2 router, X, with the lowest ID within the partition. This will distinguish one partition from another because X cannot reside in multiple partitions of FOO or else FOO would not be partitioned. X is known as the "partition-designated level 2 router." The level 2

router that is elected partition-designated level 2 router is responsible for noticing and repairing partitions.

2. Level 2 routers report the name of the partition in which they reside in their level 2 link state packets. For instance, a level 2 router in FOO will report in its level 2 LSP that it resides in FOO, partition X.

3. Level 2 router X checks to make sure that all level 2 routers reporting that they reside in FOO also report X as the partition name.

4. If some level 2 router reports attachment to FOO, partition Y, then X concludes that FOO is partitioned.

5. Level 2 router X and level 2 router Y have the task of repairing the partition. This is accomplished by having X and Y establish communication over the level 2 path connecting them (there must be a level 2 path connecting them because the level 2 LSPs listing X reach the routers that know about Y and vice versa). X and Y treat the level 2 path as a virtual level 1 link.

6. X and Y report, in their level 1 LSPs, that they have a level 1 link to each other. They report this as a virtual link, but it is treated by level 1 routing as an ordinary link. LSPs are exchanged over the link, and data traffic is forwarded over the link.

7. X and Y use the level 2 path as a level 1 link. This is accomplished by encapsulating every packet that must be sent over the link in an extra network layer header, with the source and destination network layer addresses being X and Y (or vice versa).

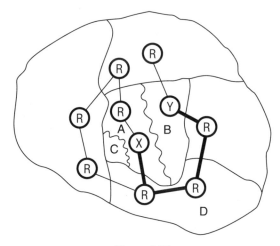

Figure 9.26

At this point, FOO is no longer partitioned. When A transmits a packet for B, the packet travels, via ordinary level 1 routing, to B. The only unusual thing is that one of the links used in the path is the virtual link between X and Y.

When choosing the partition-designated level 2 router, it is important that level 2 routers within FOO consider only level 2 routers reachable via nonvirtual links. Otherwise, as soon as X and Y establish communication, either X or Y would be elected partition-designated level 2 router, and they would both conclude that FOO was no longer partitioned, whereupon they would bring down the virtual link (thereby reestablishing the partition).

Homework

1. With standard LSP distribution, each LSP gets transmitted over each link at most twice. An alternative is to have routers run the bridge spanning tree algorithm and transmit LSPs over the resulting spanning tree. What are the pros and cons of such an LSP distribution scheme? Consider such factors as how quickly an LSP reaches all routers and how many packet transmissions it takes for the LSP to reach all routers.

   Would using the bridge spanning tree violate the principle that the protocol for distributing routing information must not rely on the routing information?

2. Under what circumstances is it possible for router A to forward packets for router B through router C, even though routers A and B are neighbors?

3. What is the worst-case number of distance vector messages that might be generated as a result of a single node's coming up in a network? Remember, you can postulate any topology, any assignment of link costs, and any timing of message generation and delivery.

4. Suppose that A and B are neighbors, but A thinks the cost of the link to B is x, whereas B thinks the cost of the link to A is y. Will this cause any problems with distance vector routing? How about with link state routing?

5. Under which method of implementing a connection-oriented network layer is there a higher probability of a call's being disconnected by the network? Why?

6. Give a topology in which, as a result of disagreement between the routers about a single link, many routes are disrupted. Give a topology in which, as a result of disagreement between the routers about a single link, no routes are disrupted.

7. Consider the following variant of split horizon. In traditional split horizon distance vector routing, R tells neighbor N that R considers D unreachable (or R does not report anything about D to N) if N is the neighbor R uses when forwarding packets to D. Modify the rule to be that R informs all neighbors N for which N's distance to D is less than R's that D is unreachable. Will this modification work? How does this compare with traditional split horizon.

   How about if the rule is modified to be that R informs all neighbors N for which N's distance to D is less than *or equal to* R's that D is unreachable. Will this modification work? How does this compare with traditional split horizon and the modification in the first half of this problem?

8. In link state routing, the designated router names the LAN using its ID as part of the name. Why do you think the DR's ID is part of the LAN ID?

9. Assume an X.25 network is implemented using the circuit method. Assume that buffers are reserved in all the intermediate routers when a call is set up. Will delays on the path then be constant?

10. Assume an X.25 network is implemented using the circuit method. Assume that router R1, processing a call setup between S1 and D1, chooses call number 47 on its port-to-neighbor router R2. Suppose R2 is processing a call setup between S2 and D2 in the meantime and decides that call should be forwarded to R1, and R2 chooses call number 47 on its port-to-neighbor router R2 for the S2/D2 call. Is this a problem? If it is, what can be done to fix it?

11. Rewrite the algorithm in section 9.2.3.4 to combine the two flags "ackflag" and "sendflag" into a single flag.

Chapter 10
Specific Routing Protocols

The shortest distance between two points is usually under repair.

— Anonymous

This chapter covers the specifics of several routing protocols. I start the discussion of each protocol by describing some of the concepts required in order to understand the protocol, then show the specific packet formats.

The discussion begins with intradomain protocols:

1. RIP, which is used for routing IP

2. IS-IS, which is used for routing CLNP

3. OSPF, which is used for routing IP

4. "Ships in the night," which is a method of routing multiple protocols

5. "Integrated routing," which is another method of routing multiple protocols—in particular, CLNP and IP

Next, the interdomain protocols are discussed:

1. Static routing

2. EGP, which was deployed in the IP Internet many years ago

3. BGP, a proposed replacement for EGP for interdomain IP routing

4. IDRP, which is basically BGP rewritten for ISO

10.1 Intradomain Routing Protocols (RIP, IS-IS, OSPF, S.I.N, Integrated Routing)

10.1.1 RIP

RIP ("routing information protocol") is a very simple distance-vector-based routing protocol. The only specification of it (RFC 1058) was written after the protocol was widely deployed in various implementations. Although the implementations differ in subtle details, distance vector routing is so simple and robust that interworking between RIP implementations is not a significant problem.

A distance vector protocol has each router transmit (destination address, cost) pairs to that router's neighbors. In RIP, there are two types of packets:

1. Request

2. Response

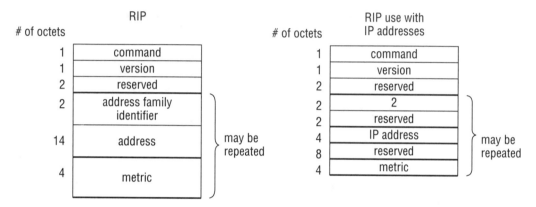

Figure 10.1

The portion of the packet starting from **address family identifier** and ending with **metric** can appear up to 25 times in one packet, which means that up to 25 destinations can be reported in a single packet.

Command distinguishes *requests* (which equal 1) from *responses* (which equal 2). A request might be transmitted by a router that has just recently come up or by a router that has timed out information about a particular destination. A request asks for information about either all destinations or only some specific destinations. If the request does not specify any destinations, it implies that the requester is asking for information about all destinations. Responses are the messages that actually contain (destination address, cost) pairs. They are sent for one of three reasons:

1. They are sent periodically. If a distance for a particular destination has not been reported by a particular neighbor for some time, the information is discarded. Thus each destination must be reported to each neighbor periodically. The period given in the RIP spec is once every 30 sec.

2. They are sent in response to a query.

3. They may be sent when information changes. If the cost to destination FOO as reported to neighbor X has become different from the last cost to FOO reported to X, then it is a good idea to transmit the updated information to X immediately. Not all RIP implementations do so, however.

Version equals 1. **Address family identifier** equals 2 for IP. An implementation that does not support the address family identifier for a particular destination ignores that destination and processes the remainder of the RIP message. If the address family identifier equals anything other than 2, then the 14 octets following the address family identifier are used as defined for that address family. In fact, RIP has only been used for IP.

An ISO address requires 21 octets (up to 20 for the address, plus the length octet). Fortunately, since 21 octets will not fit into a 14-octet field, nobody will be tempted to use RIP for routing CLNP.

In RIP, **IP address** is the 4-octet IP address. There is no provision for passing around a mask. The mask must be inferred based on whether the address is class A, class B, or class C. There are some special cases in which the inferred mask differs from a class A, B, or C standard mask:

1. RIP can be used with subnets, but the routers have to be aware of the subnet mask for a particular network number. For example, if class B network number 168.29.*.* is known by router R to be subnetted, with mask 255.255.252.0, then a destination address with the top 2 octets equal to 168.29 will be assumed to refer to a subnetwork specified by the value of the top 22 bits of the destination address.

2. If bits are set in what the router regards as the "host" portion of the address, then the address is assumed to refer to a host, and to have a mask of 255.255.255.255.

   The host portion of the address is the part other than the "network" number, which is inferred based on whether the address is class A, B, or C. In the case of preconfigured knowledge of subnets, the host portion of the address is the part in which the preconfigured subnet mask has 0's.

3. If the address reported in a RIP update is 0.0.0.0, it is considered a *default* destination, with a mask equal to 0.0.0.0. All destination addresses match. If a destination address was not known to be reachable based on all the other reported destinations in RIP, then the packet would be routed toward the destination 0.0.0.0.

   Terminology note: The IP community refers to a destination reported in a routing message as a *route*. It refers to 0.0.0.0 as the *default route*. And a destination with a mask of 255.255.255.255 is known as a *host route*. I wish the IP community wouldn't do that. People already find names, addresses, and routes sufficiently confusing. Then again, terminology doesn't impact performance, robustness, or anything that really matters.

Notice that 32 bits are allocated for the **metric** field, which has a maximum value of 16 in RIP! The number *16* was chosen because of the "counting-to-infinity" behavior of distance vector protocols. Given such a small value of maximum path cost, most implementations use a simple hop count as the cost metric, because anything else would quickly add up to more than 15. The reason 32 bits are allocated for the field is so that important fields in the message are conveniently aligned on 4-octet boundaries.

As a result of RIP's not having been documented until after several implementations were deployed, there are subtle differences between implementations. For instance, some implementations keep the most recently received distance vector from each neighbor. Others discard the distance vectors after computing their own. When the link to a neighbor is known to have gone down, a distance vector protocol should at that point discard the distance vector received from that neighbor and compute a new distance vector. However, some RIP implementations retain forwarding information that points to a neighbor that is down. (The neighbor was selected as the next hop to certain destinations before connectivity to the neighbor was lost.) Only after the computed route to destination D times out does a router discard the information regarding that destination. Then the router may (depending on the implementation) wait for new information to arrive, or it may query its neighbors. This timer-based distance vector implementation converges even more slowly than necessary and requires more bandwidth than necessary.

The extra-slow convergence is due to RIP's not requiring that a router R1 immediately discard the information previously received from a neighbor R2 upon discovering that the link to R2 has gone down. When a router loses contact with a neighbor, it should throw away any information previously received from that neighbor and recompute a new distance vector based on stored information from other neighbors. RIP implementations also converge slowly because RIP does not require a router to keep distance vectors from all neighbors. When information about a destination times out, some implementations must query all their neighbors to reobtain information for that destination before another route can be computed.

The excess bandwidth required by RIP is caused by the need for frequent periodic retransmission of routing updates.

With any luck, one of these days, a different acronym will apply to RIP.

Every one to his taste, as the woman said when she kissed her cow.

— Rabelais, *Pantagruel* [1]

10.1.2   IS-IS

ISO's standard for routing CLNP is known as IS-IS because all the other names (e.g., 10589: "Intermediate system to Intermediate system Intra-Domain routeing information exchange protocol for use in Conjunction . . .") are worse. IS-IS is a link state routing algorithm, which was designed at Digital for phase V DECnet.

10.1.2.1   Choosing a Level 2 Router

As explained in Chapter 6, "Network Layer Addresses," an ISO (connectionless) network layer address looks like this:

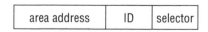

Figure 10.2

[1] *The Pocket Book of Quotations*, (New York, Pocket Books, 1952) 390.

When a level 1 router receives a data packet, it examines the **area address** portion of the destination address in the packet's CLNP header. If it matches the router's area address, then the router routes based on the **ID** portion of the address. Otherwise, the router forwards the packet toward a level 2 router. Since in IS-IS, a level 1 router R does not know which level 2 router is closest to the destination area, it simply forwards the packet to the nearest level 2 router.

A level 1 router knows which routers in the area are level 2 routers because there is a field in the level 1 LSP that indicates whether the router is level 1 or level 2. All routers (level 1 and level 2) within an area generate level 1 LSPs in that area. Level 2 routers also generate level 2 LSPs, which are propagated through the level 2 network.

10.1.2.2 Area Addresses

As discussed in Chapter 6, "Network Layer Addresses," an *area* is a level 1 subnetwork. Level 2 destinations consist of *address prefixes*, and routing is to the longest matching address prefix.

An area can have multiple area addresses, which serves the purpose of allowing migration of an area from one address to another, merging of two areas, or splitting an area into pieces.

If an area has three area addresses—say, A1, A2, and A3—then a packet is routed via level 1 routing if the area field in the destination address matches any of these three addresses.

A router is configured with a set of area addresses, known as its *manual area addresses*. A level 1 router R will refuse to consider an adjacent node S to be a neighbor if R and S's manual area addresses do not overlap. The hello messages that R and S send each other include their manual area addresses. If at least one of the area addresses reported by S matches at least one of the area addresses reported by R, they will be neighbors.

In addition to including its manual area addresses in its hello messages to its neighbors, a router includes its manual area addresses in its LSP. All level 1 routers take the set union of all the area addresses reported in the area's LSPs to find the complete set of area addresses for the area. If the area portion of the destination address of a packet to be forwarded matches any of the area addresses reported in LSPs within the area, then the packet is routed by level 1 routing.

There is a limit to the number of area addresses for an area. Originally the limit was fixed at three. One of the last ISO modifications to the spec allows the limit to be a parameter, *maximum area addresses.*

Unfortunately, routing would be disrupted if different routers in an area had different values for that parameter. To ensure that all routers in an area agree on the value of maximum area addresses, the parameter value is inserted into the header of IS-IS control packets. For backward compatibility with implementations that were built to the previous version where the value of three was fixed, a value of zero for maximum area addresses means three. The header field where maximum area addresses are written was a reserved field in the earlier version of the IS-IS spec. Therefore, implementations built before the change will have set the value to zero and will ignore it upon receipt.

If the number of different area addresses in the union of all the sets of area addresses reported in level 1 LSPs exceeds x, where x is the value of maximum area addresses, then the x that is numerically lowest is considered to be the area addresses of the area.

To merge area A into area B, the following procedure is employed:

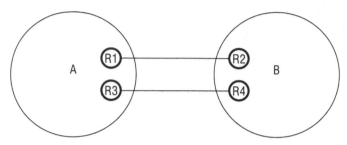

Figure 10.3

Area address B is added to R1's configured set of area addresses (which is now the set {A, B}). As soon as R1 is configured, R1 and R2 will become neighbors and exchange LSP databases. R1 will pass all of area B's LSPs into area A. All routers in area A will accept both "A" and "B" as the name of the area, and the two smaller areas will be merged into one big area with two area addresses, A and B.

One-by-one, all the routers in A are configured to accept B as an additional address for their area. After all the routers in the original area A are so configured, they can be reconfigured one-by-one to have only address B configured. Even when there remains just a single router with {A, B} as the set of area addresses, the entire area still has two addresses. When that router is reconfigured to have only address B configured, then the area reverts back to having a single area address—namely, B.

10.1.2.3 Multiple Metrics

Each router must be configured with a *cost* for each link to which it is attached. This cost is included in its LSPs when reporting that link. If the network administrator feels that a single metric won't please all the users, links can be configured with up to three additional costs. The original cost is known as the *default* metric and must be configured for every link.

When a router receives a data packet for forwarding, it must know what metric the user would like employed for computing the route to the destination. The router determines this based on the "quality of service" (QOS) option in the data packet header. In IS-IS, there is a mapping defined between the setting of the bits in the quality of service option and the four metrics.

The four metrics are:

1. *Default:* Intended to correlate (inversely) with bandwidth

2. *Delay:* Intended to correlate with the amount of delay on the link

3. *Expense:* Intended to correlate with the amount of money it costs to use the link

4. *Error:* Intended to correlate with the flakiness of the link

When, according to the setting of the QOS bits in a data packet, IS-IS infers that the user really wants a route computed according to a metric other than default, the routers attempt to find a route that consists solely of links that have a reported cost according to the desired metric. If no such path exists, then the packet is routed according to the default metric.

E/C	E/D	D/C	Chosen Routing Metric
0	0	0	Expense metric
0	0	1	Delay metric
0	1	0	Expense metric
0	1	1	Default metric
1	0	0	Default metric
1	0	1	Delay metric
1	1	0	Error metric
1	1	1	Error metric

Since the default metric is supposed to correspond to bandwidth, and none of the QOS bits mentions bandwidth, it is amusing that the only way one can specify the default metric is to either leave the QOS option out entirely or specify a nonsensical setting of the bits that should be illegal since it is circular. There are only two settings that have been assigned the default metric. If a bit such as E/C is set to 1, it means that error rate is more important than monetary cost. If the bit is set to 0, it means that cost is more important than error rate. There's no third setting of the bit by which the user can state his or her real feelings, which might be that both characteristics are equally uninteresting. The first setting of the bits that IS-IS maps onto the default metric is E/C = 0, E/D = 1, D/C = 1, which means that error rate is more important than delay, which is more important than cost, which is more important than error rate. The other is E/C = 1, E/D = 0, D/C = 0, which means that cost is more important than delay, which is more important than error rate, which is more important than cost.

None of the members of the 8473 committee with whom I've talked admits to actually liking the QOS encoding.

As I've stated before, I am extremely unenthusiastic about multiple metrics. Using any metric other than default constrains the route to go through a somewhat arbitrary subset of the links (those for which the router's manager has configured a cost for the metric in question), which can yield wildly nonoptimal routes. If users decide to include the QOS option, perhaps to ask for sequenced delivery of packets (the **S/D** bit) or to find out about congestion (the "congestion-experienced" bit), I find it hard to believe that they'll have read 10589 closely enough to know that they have to set the E/C, E/D, and D/C bits to total nonsense in order to get the safe, "normal" default metric. However, the situation really isn't all that bad. If nobody configures links with anything other than the default metric, everything will work fine. Better even, because routers won't have to compute and store four sets of routes.

10.1.2.4 LAN Designated Router

IS-IS does not treat a LAN with n routers as n^2 point-to-point links, which, as discussed in Chapter 9, "Routing Algorithm Issues," would be quite inefficient. Instead, it pretends that the LAN itself is a router in the network. One router on each LAN gets elected *designated router*, or *DR*, on the LAN. The DR gives a name to the LAN, which consists of the ID portion of the DR's address plus an additional octet, in case that DR is designated on multiple LANs. The DR informs all the routers on the LAN of the LAN's name. In their LSPs, all the routers (including the DR) announce just a single link for the LAN, which is a link to the LAN itself. Then the DR issues an additional LSP, this one on behalf of the LAN, which lists all the routers and endnodes on the LAN.

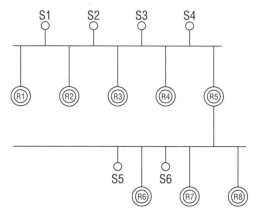

Figure 10.4

Suppose that R5 is DR on both LANs shown in Fig. 10.4. It might name the top LAN R5.1 and the bottom LAN R5.21. R1, R2, R3, R4, and R5 will all claim a link to neighbor "R5.1" in their LSPs. R5.1 claims links to neighbors R1, R2, R3, R4, and R5 in its LSP, which is generated by R5. Likewise, R5, R6, R7, and R8 will all claim a link to neighbor "R5.21." R5.21, in an LSP generated on its behalf by R5, will claim links to neighbors R5, R6, R7, and R8 (see Fig. 10.5).

10.1.2.5 Reliable Propagation of LSPs on LANs

As stated in Chapter 9, "Routing Algorithm Issues," the most straightforward method of reliably distributing LSPs on LANs would consist of having each router transmit an explicit acknowledgment for each LSP. Every router would have to ensure that every other router on the LAN received every LSP.

The scheme chosen by IS-IS requires no explicit acknowledgments on a LAN. Instead, a router that transmits an LSP on the LAN transmits it once, to a multicast address to which all the routers listen, and assumes the transmission was successful.

Periodically, the DR summarizes the state of its LSP database by multicasting to all the routers on the LAN a packet consisting of the IDs and sequence numbers of all the LSPs in the database. This packet is known as a *complete sequence numbers packet*

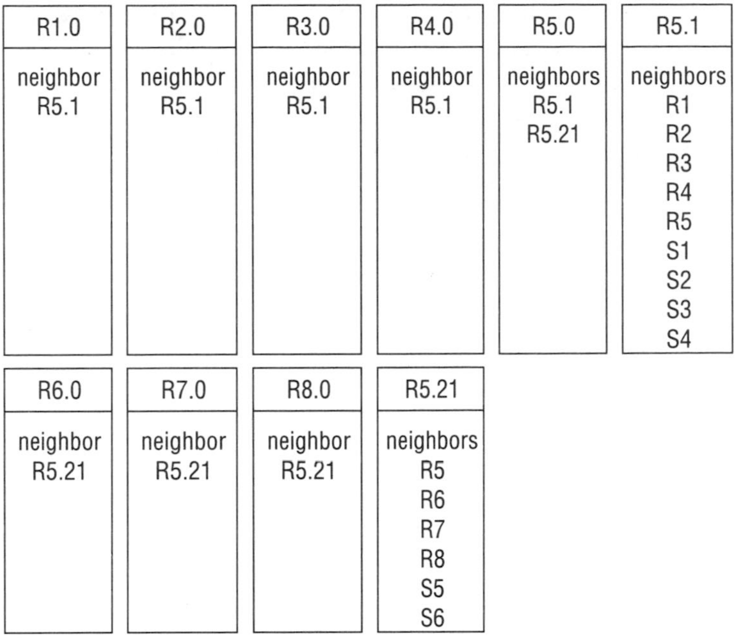

R1.0	R2.0	R3.0	R4.0	R5.0	R5.1
neighbor R5.1	neighbor R5.1	neighbor R5.1	neighbor R5.1	neighbors R5.1 R5.21	neighbors R1 R2 R3 R4 R5 S1 S2 S3 S4

R6.0	R7.0	R8.0	R5.21
neighbor R5.21	neighbor R5.21	neighbor R5.21	neighbors R5 R6 R7 R8 S5 S6

Figure 10.5

(CSNP). If a router R detects, based on the received CSNP, that the DR has missed an LSP that R has, R transmits that LSP on the LAN. R detects that the DR has missed an LSP because the LSP either was not listed in the CSNP or was listed with a lower sequence number. If R detects that the DR has a more recent LSP than R, R explicitly requests the missing LSP. R does so by using a *partial sequence numbers packet* (PSNP), which is similar to a CSNP except that the PSNP does not claim to include all LSPs in the database. A PSNP can be used either to explicitly request transmission of a specified set of LSPs or to acknowledge a set of LSPs.

10.1.2.6   Big Packets

It is possible for LSPs and CSNPs to be so large that they cannot fit into a single packet as transmitted on a link. The same sort of fragmentation and reassembly could be performed on LSPs and CSNPs as would be performed on data packets. Instead, IS-IS has two different mechanisms, one for CSNPs and one for LSPs, that avoid fragmentation and reassembly.

There are two problems with using standard fragmentation and reassembly:

1. *Wasted bandwidth:* If a single fragment is lost, all the fragments must be retransmitted.

2. *Slower-than-necessary propagation of LSP information:* A fragment of an LSP cannot be propagated until all the fragments have been received and reassembled.

IS-IS avoids these problems by using the following mechanism for keeping control packets small enough so they don't need hop-by-hop fragmentation: The LSP's **source** field consists of 8 octets. The first 6 octets are the ID of the router that issued the LSP.

The seventh octet is zero when the router issued the LSP on its own behalf. The seventh octet is nonzero when the router is the DR on a LAN and the router issued the LSP on behalf of the LAN. The eighth octet can be considered the "fragment number."

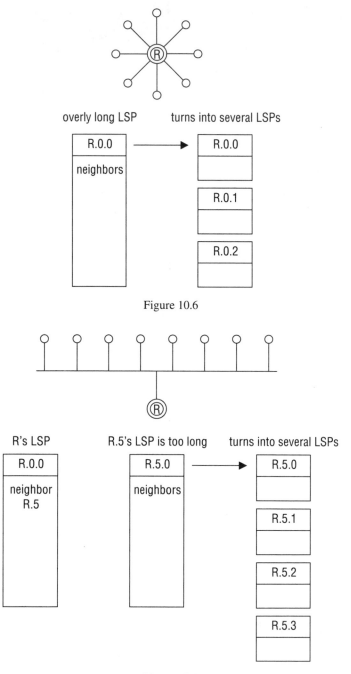

Figure 10.6

Figure 10.7

Suppose that router R's LSP is so large that it needs to be divided into three packets (see Fig. 10.6). R will generate three LSPs, one from source R.0.0, one from source R.0.1, and one from source R.0.2. If R is generating an LSP on behalf of a LAN for which R is DR, and R has named the LAN R.5, then the LAN's LSP will come from "source" R.5.0. If the LAN's LSP is large enough to require four packets, then there will be four LSPs—from R.5.0, R.5.1, R.5.2, and R.5.3 (see Fig. 10.7).

For the purposes of propagating the LSPs, R.x.i and R.x.j are totally different sources, with totally independent sequence numbers. If a single fragment is lost, only that fragment need be retransmitted. And any fragment can be forwarded as soon as it is received. It is only when routes are computed that a router combines all of R.x's LSP fragments into one logical LSP. The IS-IS scheme has the additional advantage that if only a single link changes, only the LSP fragment that has changed as a result of that link change must be reissued by the source router.

The scheme for avoiding fragmentation and reassembly of CSNPs is that a CSNP includes an address range for the LSPs reported within the CSNP (see Fig. 10.8). If an LSP's ID fits within the address range and it is not reported in the CSNP, it is assumed to be missing from the CSNP transmitter's database. The receiver of a CSNP makes no assumption about LSPs that do not fall within the address range. The transmitter of an overly large CSNP can transmit CSNP pieces in any order, and even with overlapping address ranges. The only requirement is that for any possible address, the DR must eventually (in a timely fashion) transmit a CSNP that includes that address in the address range.

CSNP

address range 27.3.0 to 35.0.5	
27.3.0	sequence number 22
27.3.1	sequence number 5
31.0.0	sequence number 291
31.5.0	sequence number 102
31.5.1	sequence number 92
31.5.2	sequence number 61
31.5.3	sequence number 153
31.7.0	sequence number 22
35.0.0	sequence number 6
35.0.1	sequence number 17
35.0.2	sequence number 17
35.0.3	sequence number 3
35.0.4	sequence number 14
35.0.5	sequence number 22

Figure 10.8

10.1.2.7 Partitioned Areas

Level 2 routers have two LSP databases. One consists of the level 1 LSPs for the area in which the level 2 router resides. The other consists of the level 2 LSPs that have been broadcast through the level 2 subnetwork. A level 2 router R in area FOO generates two LSPs: a level 1 LSP that R generates in area FOO and a level 2 LSP that R generates and broadcasts in the level 2 subnetwork. R's level 1 LSP contains information indicating that R is a level 2 router. Level 1 routers must know which routers in the area are level 2 routers, so that they can forward out-of-area packets to a level 2 router.

If area FOO is partitioned, it means that FOO has broken into two or more pieces, and level 1 routing cannot route between the pieces. Each piece is called a *partition*. If FOO is not partitioned, it will consist of a single partition. Level 2 routers examine the level 1 LSP database to find the set of level 2 routers in the partition. They elect (based on ID) a single level 2 router to be the *partition-designated level 2 IS*. (Sorry—I tried unsuccessfully to come up with a shorter, but still descriptive name for that.)

Assume that X is the partition-designated level 2 IS. Each level 2 router in FOO reports "X" in its level 2 LSP. A partition of FOO can be detected based on an examination of the level 2 LSPs. If some level 2 routers claim to reside in FOO and have X as the partition-designated level 2 IS, and others claim to reside in FOO and have Y as the partition-designated level 2 IS, then FOO is partitioned. It is the responsibility of level 2 routers X and Y to "repair" FOO by using the level 2 path between X and Y as a level 1 *virtual link* in FOO. Once they establish communication over the virtual link, the virtual link is reported by X and Y in their level 1 LSPs within FOO. Level 1 routers treat the virtual link as a normal link and compute routes that might include the link (see Fig. 10.9).

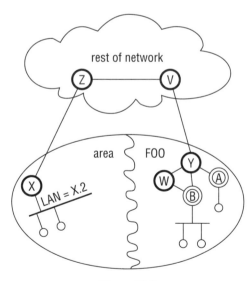

Figure 10.9

The only subtlety is that level 2 routers must be sure that the partition-designated level 2 router is a router that can be reached via "real" level 1 links and not "virtual" links, or else as soon as the partition is repaired, X and Y will conclude that the area is no longer partitioned and turn off the virtual link, thus repartitioning the area. That means that the level 2 routers must first run the routing algorithm to calculate paths without the virtual links in order to determine which of the level 2 routers are reachable within the partition.

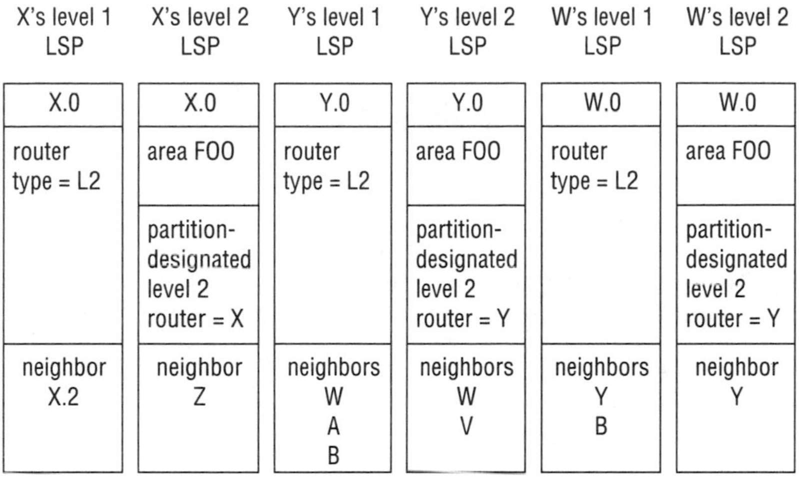

X's level 1 LSP	X's level 2 LSP	Y's level 1 LSP	Y's level 2 LSP	W's level 1 LSP	W's level 2 LSP
X.0	X.0	Y.0	Y.0	W.0	W.0
router type = L2	area FOO	router type = L2	area FOO	router type = L2	area FOO
	partition-designated level 2 router = X		partition-designated level 2 router = Y		partition-designated level 2 router = Y
neighbor X.2	neighbor Z	neighbors W A B	neighbors W V	neighbors Y B	neighbor Y

Figure 10.10   Before partition repair

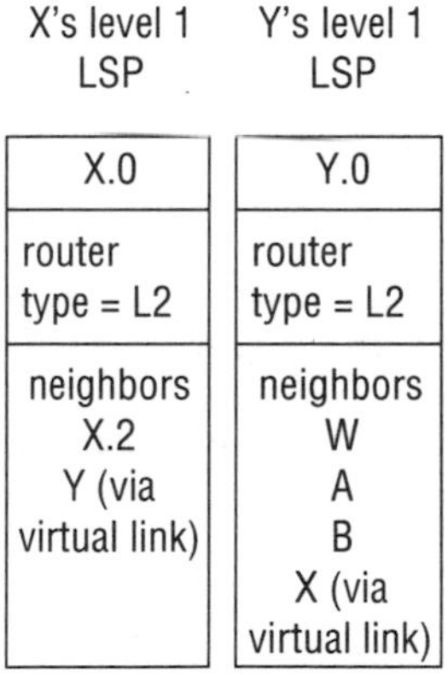

X's level 1 LSP	Y's level 1 LSP
X.0	Y.0
router type = L2	router type = L2
neighbors X.2 Y (via virtual link)	neighbors W A B X (via virtual link)

Figure 10.11   LSPs that change after virtual link between X and Y is established

Partition repair is optional in IS-IS. A level 2 router indicates its support of partition repair in its LSPs. As long as at least one level 2 router in each partition implements the partition-repair capability, the area partition will be repaired.

10.1.2.8   Partitioned Level 2 Network

The network consisting of level 2 routers must be connected. IS-IS does not attempt to repair a partitioned level 2 network by using a level 1 path (see Fig. 10.12).

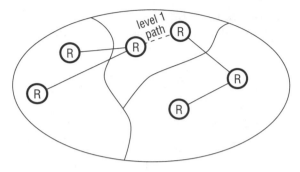

Figure 10.12

10.1.2.9　LSP Database Overload

A router will be configured based on an assumption regarding the size of the network it will need to support. There are two reasons why this assumption might be incorrect:

1. *Static overload:* In this case, either the router has been underconfigured, or the area has grown illegally large. Until nodes are disconnected from the network, the router will not be able to participate as a router.

2. *Temporary overload:* In this case, the router is properly configured for the size of the area, but a temporary situation has caused the LSP database to be larger than expected. An example of such a situation is when the designated router, R1, on a LAN goes down, and another router, R2, takes over. R1 will have issued an LSP on behalf of the LAN, with the LAN having an ID of R1.x. Then R2 will issue an LSP on behalf of the LAN, with an ID of R2.y. Until the R1.x LSPs age out and can be removed, twice as much room will be occupied by the LAN information.

Most routing protocols do not specify what a router should do when memory for the routing database is exceeded. Traditionally, implementations have done one of the following:

1. *Crash:* This is OK but makes it difficult to use network management to reconfigure the router, since the router will not be reachable via the network. Also, if the overload is only temporary, it is inconvenient to have to manually restart the routers.

2. *Work with the random subset of routing information that happens to fit:* This is not OK. A single router routing based on incomplete information can cause global routing disruption.

IS-IS specifies what a router must do when the routing database exceeds its allocated memory. A router that cannot fit a new LSP into its database simply refuses to acknowledge it. The neighbor will continue trying to transmit the LSP. If the overload is a temporary problem, the router will eventually be able to accept it.

A router forced to refuse an LSP sets a flag in its LSP indicating that its LSP database is overloaded. Other routers treat the overloaded router as an endnode. Since a refused LSP will be retransmitted within a few seconds, a router that has not needed to refuse an LSP for a time longer than the LSP retransmission time clears its flag, indicating that it is no longer overloaded.

10.1.2.10 Multiarea Bridged LANs

Note to the reader: This section is quite independent of the rest of IS-IS and can be skipped if for some reason you are not fascinated with the notion of multiarea bridged LANs.

Routers keep track of neighbor routers by periodically sending IS-to-IS hello messages. They are similar in function to the ESH and ISH messages in the ES-IS protocol. Level 1 routers listen to the multicast address ALL LEVEL 1 ISs. There is a separate multicast address for ALL LEVEL 2 ISs. The reason for having different addresses for level 1 versus level 2 ISs is to allow LANs in different areas to be connected via bridges without merging the areas. The connection is made solely as a means of creating connectivity between the level 2 routers.

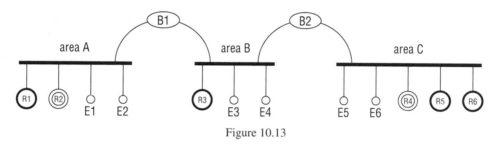

Figure 10.13

Routers transmit IS hellos to the multicast address ALL ESs, according to the ES-IS protocol. Routers also transmit IS-to-IS hellos to the multicast address ALL LEVEL 1 ISs. Level 2 routers additionally transmit level 2 IS-to-IS hellos to the multicast address ALL LEVEL 2 ISs.

The bridges in a multiarea bridged LAN are manually configured to filter traffic with the destination addresses ALL LEVEL 1 ISs and ALL ESs, but to forward traffic with the destination address ALL LEVEL 2 ISs. In this way, the endnodes will autoconfigure the correct area address. If the bridges forwarded the IS-to-ES hellos, then ESs in area A would see the ISHs from areas B and C as well and would not know the correct area address. They also might choose an IS in area B or C for forwarding off the LAN, which would probably be less optimal than choosing a router that is closer.

The level 2 routers will see each other as neighbors and be able to forward traffic between each other, but the level 1 routers will not see the IS-to-IS hellos from other areas.

When E1 wishes to communicate with E6, it will transmit a data packet to one of the routers it knows about—namely, R1 or R2 (see Fig. 10.13). Suppose it chooses R2. R2 will forward the packet to the nearest level 2 router—in this case, R1. Because R2 is forwarding the packet onto the same link from which the packet arrived, R2 will transmit a redirect message to E1, redirecting E1 to R1's data link layer address on the LAN.

R1 will forward the data packet to R5. Although R1 forwards the packet onto the same link from which it arrived, R1 will not send a redirect to R2, because it knows that R2 is a router neighbor and a redirect would be ignored. R5 will then forward the packet to E6.

Again, although R5 is forwarding the packet onto the same link from which it arrived, R5 will not transmit a redirect to R1 because R5 knows that R1 is a router neighbor.

When E1 transmits the next data packet, it will transmit the packet to R1, because of its having received a redirect from R2. R1 will forward the packet to R5. This time, R1 will send a redirect to E1, pointing toward R5's data link layer address. R5 will forward the packet to E6 without issuing a redirect to R1.

When E1 transmits the third data packet, it will transmit the packet to R5. R5 will forward the packet to E6 and issue a redirect to E1 because R5 knows that E1 is not a router neighbor. R5 in this case doesn't know for sure that E1 is an endnode, because the bridge does not forward E1's ESHs. But the rule is that R5 transmits a redirect unless it knows that it shouldn't.

When E1 transmits the fourth data packet, it will use E6's data link layer address, and the packet will not be forwarded by any routers.

10.1.2.11 Packets Used by IS-IS

Now that you understand most of IS-IS's subtle features, I can explain the packet formats. There are three basic types of packets:

1. *IS-to-IS hello:* This packet allows neighbor routers to keep in touch with each other.

2. *LSP:* This packet includes information about a router's neighbors and is broadcast to all the routers.

3. *SNP ("sequence numbers packet"):* This packet is transmitted by router R to inform R's neighbors about the sequence numbers of LSPs R has received. It can serve as an acknowledgment to individual LSPs, as a method of requesting information upon start-up, or as a method of ensuring that neighbor routers have identical LSP databases. It allows LSP distribution on a LAN without individual explicit acknowledgments.

All the IS-IS packets start out with the following fields, each 1 octet long. They are formatted like the data packet in CLNP.

# of octets	Common Fixed Header
1	protocol identifier
1	header length
1	version
1	ID length
1	packet type
1	version
1	reserved
1	maximum area addresses

Figure 10.14

Protocol identifier   A constant, equal to 131 decimal.

Length   Length of the fixed header—a useless field with useless information, but included so that the IS-IS packets wouldn't be self-conscious about looking too different from data packets as defined in 8473.

Version   = 1. (See also the sixth field on this list.)

ID length   The size of the ID portion of an NSAP. If it's between 1 and 8, inclusive, it indicates the size of the ID portion; if it's 0, it means that the ID portion = 6 octets; if it's 255, it means that the ID portion = 0 octets.

Packet type   Tells the type of packet (LSP, etc.).

Version   = 1. (Yes, it's redundant, but the redundancy doesn't hurt anything.)

Reserved   Transmitted as 0; ignored on receipt.

Maximum area addresses   Number of area addresses permitted for this area. If the field is 0, the number is 3. Else, the field is the number of area addresses allowed for the area.

I will refer to the aforementioned fields as the "common fixed header" in the description of the IS-IS packet formats.

Each type of packet has some more of the "fixed" part of the header—fields that are always present—followed by a "variable" part of the header, with multiple fields coded thusly:

Code   1 octet   Tells the type of field

Length   1 octet   Tells how many octets in what follows

Value   Length   Data specific to the type of field

10.1.2.11.1 IS-to-IS Hello

The purpose of the IS-to-IS hello is to enable routers to coordinate with their router neighbors. On point-to-point links, it is very similar to an ES hello or an IS hello. It basically gives the IS's network layer address, together with the "holding time," which is how long the receiver of the IS-to-IS hello should hold the information before assuming the router is down. There is a network-management-settable parameter "hello timer," which is the interval between transmission of hellos. The holding time transmitted in the IS-to-IS hello is equal to three times the value of the hello timer. A small hello timer value allows the routing protocol to recover from failures faster because a router death will be detected quickly, but it involves more overhead since it requires more frequent transmission of hellos.

There are two main types of IS-to-IS hellos, one for transmission on point-to-point links and the other for transmission on LANs. The IS-to-IS hello on a LAN contains additional information, such as the ID of other routers on the LAN, that helps to ensure that connectivity between neighbors is bidirectional. There are actually two types of LAN IS-to-IS hellos. One is for use by level 2 routers, and one is for use by level 1 routers. The level 1 LAN IS-to-IS hello is transmitted to the multicast address all level 1 ISs, and the level 2 LAN IS-to-IS hello is transmitted to the multicast address all level 2 ISs.

The point-to-point IS-to-IS hello is packet type 17. The first 8 octets (the portion of the IS-IS packets that is common to all the IS-IS packet types) were defined in the preceding subsection. The remaining part of the fixed portion of the point-to-point IS-to-IS hello is:

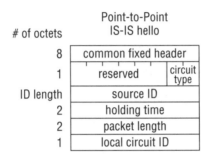

Figure 10.15

Circuit type is one of the following:

• 1 = level 1 only.

• 2 = level 2 only. The transmitter is a level 2 router that has been manually configured to use this circuit only for level 2 traffic. Such a router will not transmit an IS-to-ES hello on a LAN. The purpose of transmitting this parameter in IS-to-IS hellos is to detect misconfiguration.

• 3 = both level 1 and level 2. The transmitter is a level 2 router that is allowed to use the circuit for both level 1 and level 2 traffic.

Source ID is the ID portion of the transmitting router's network layer address.

Holding time is the time at which neighbors can legally declare this router dead if they haven't gotten a hello from it.

Packet length is the length of the entire IS-to-IS hello message, in octets.

Local circuit ID is an identifier for this interface, unique relative to the transmitting router's other interfaces. For network management purposes, it is sometimes useful to have a unique "name" for a link in the network. The unique name of a point-to-point link is the concatenation of the ID of the router whose ID is lower with the local circuit ID that that router assigned to the link. Thus, if a point-to-point link connects routers 492 and 581, and router 492 assigned the link the ID 12 and router 581 assigned the link the ID 3, then the link is known as 492.12.

The variable-length fields in a point-to-point IS-to-IS hello are:

1. **Area addresses:** The code for this field is 1. This is the set of area addresses manually configured into this router. The data consists of maximum area addresses, each preceded by an "address length" octet.

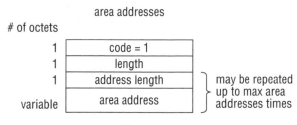

Figure 10.16

2. **Padding:** Code 8. This allows the packet to be padded to any length. The padding can contain any arbitrary values and is ignored by the receiver.

3. **Authentication:** Code 10. The value contains two fields. The first octet is the type of authentication. The only one really defined is type 1, which is *cleartext password*. A router may be configured, for each interface, with a transmit password and a set of receive passwords. If a transmit password is configured for a particular interface, the router will include the authentication option in its IS hello on that link. If a router R receives an IS hello containing a password, and R has been configured with a set of receive passwords on that interface, then R rejects the hello unless the password matches one of the configured receive passwords.

    The other type of authentication "defined" is *routing domain private authentication method*, which is designated as type 255 but is not actually defined in the standard.

    Password authentication might offer a modest amount of security on point-to-point links, but it offers none on a LAN, at least as defined. It certainly creates a lot of configuration complexity and ensures that misconfiguration will cause problems.

The level 1 LAN IS-to-IS hello is packet type 15. The level 2 LAN IS-to-IS hello is type 16. It has the same fields as a level 1 LAN IS-to-IS hello. The fixed part of the header contains:

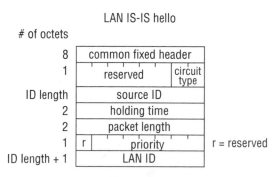

Figure 10.17

Circuit type, **source ID**, **holding time**, and **packet length** are the same as defined for the point-to-point IS-to-IS hello.

Priority is the transmitting router's priority for becoming designated router on the LAN, with higher numbers having a higher priority.

LAN ID is the name of the LAN, as assigned by the designated router. It consists of the DR's ID plus an extra octet to differentiate this LAN from others with the same DR.

The variable-length fields defined for level 1 LAN IS-to-IS hellos are shown in the following list. In the first three cases, the definitions are the same as were given earlier in this subsection for point-to-point IS-to-IS hellos.

1. **Area addresses:** Code 1.

2. **Padding:** Code 8.

3. **Authentication:** Code 10.

4. **IS neighbors:** Code 6. This is a list of the other routers on the LAN from which the transmitting router has recently heard IS-to-IS hellos.

    The data consists of a sequence of 6-octet IDs. In this case, it is OK to assume that the ID is exactly 6 octets, because this really is defined for 802 LANs. For instance, if there were a new kind of LAN with 8-octet IDs, then a new kind of IS-to-IS hello would be defined for use on that new type of LAN.

10.1.2.11.2   LSP

There are two types of LSP—level 1 and level 2.

A level 1 LSP is packet type 18. The remaining fields in the fixed part of the header are:

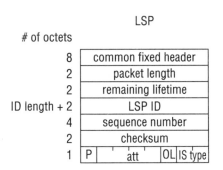

Figure 10.18

Packet length is the length of the entire LSP.

Remaining lifetime is the "age" field, as discussed in Chapter 9, "Routing Algorithm Issues," subsection 9.2.3, "Disseminating the LSP to All Routers."

The first ID length number of octets of **LSP ID** consist of the ID of the router that generated the LSP. The next octet is non-0 if the LSP is generated on behalf of a LAN (the router that generated the LSP is the designated router on the LAN and has transmitted the LSP on behalf of the LAN). The next octet is the fragment number, used when an LSP is so large that it needs to be broken into pieces.

Sequence number is, again, as discussed in subsection 9.2.3.

Checksum is computed as in a data packet. It starts with the LSP ID field and goes to the end. The remaining lifetime field is purposely omitted from the checksum computation so that intermediate routers will never legitimately modify the checksum as computed by the router that originally generated the LSP.

P is a flag that indicates whether the router that generated the LSP supports partition repair. This is only relevant if the LSP was generated by a level 2 router.

Att is a 4-bit field consisting of the four flags shown in the following list. It is only relevant if the level 1 LSP was generated by a level 2 router. Each flag indicates whether this level 2 router can reach at least one other area according to the specified metric.

Bit 4: Default metric

Bit 5: Delay metric

Bit 6: Expense metric

Bit 7: Error metric

OL, bit 3, if set, indicates that the router that generated the LSP has run out of room in its LSP database. A router with this bit set in its LSP is treated as an endnode by other routers (i.e., no routes are computed through that router).

IS type is a 2-bit field for which only two values are defined:

- 1 = level 1 router.

- 3 = level 2 router.

The variable-length fields defined for the level 1 LSP are:

1. **Area addresses:** As defined for previous packets.

2. **Authentication:** As defined for previous packets, except that the acceptable set of passwords is in the network management parameter "area receive passwords," plus the router's own "transmit password."

   I think authentication in LSPs is especially dangerous and useless. Any intruder listening in can discover an acceptable password, so it does not enhance security. But it does create the potential for global disruption of routing if a single router has the wrong set of area receive passwords and therefore decides to reject an LSP that the other routers accept. Such a problem will be extremely difficult to detect and correct (since network management commands can't be delivered unless the network is operational). It's hard enough to get routing to work without creating a giant opportunity for the LSP databases to become unsynchronized. The set of area receive passwords is separately managed at each router. If it is not identical at all routers, it becomes likely that different routers will accept different subsets of the LSPs. Authentication was put in for political reasons. Adding it to the spec is "harmless," in that it need not be used.

3. **IS neighbors:** Code 2. Multiple router neighbors can be listed in one occurrence of this field provided that the links to those neighbors have identical costs and flags. If the links to different router neighbors have different costs, then this field appears multiple times.

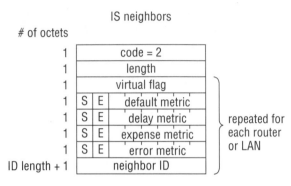

Figure 10.19

Virtual flag indicates whether the link is a true level 1 link or a path through the level 2 network used as a level 1 link in order to repair a partitioned area.

S indicates whether the metric in question is supported. A value of 0 for the flag indicates that the metric is supported. **Default metric** must have this bit clear, since it must always be supported.

E is a flag indicating whether the metric is *internal* (has meaning within the routing domain) or *external* (the destination's reachability was learned through an interdomain routing protocol that had no metrics or whose metrics were impossible to combine with the routing domain's metrics, for some reason).

Note: Ideally, this bit would never be used. It is extremely inconvenient not to be able to compute the metric on an interdomain path. The metrics need not have the same meaning. The only important thing is that the path cost always increase at every hop.

There are two types of protocols that inspired the need for this bit. One is EGP, which does not provide a metric. The other is RIP, which provides a metric but has a maximum value of 15, which is much smaller than allowed by most other protocols. It is extremely dangerous in a routing protocol to permit the cost of a path to decrease along the way. If part of the path is computed with RIP, the accumulated path cost to the destination would almost certainly need to be mapped down into a very small number so that the information could be fed into RIP.

The terms *external* versus *internal* are not exactly correct for this bit. Instead, the terms *comparable* versus *incomparable* should really be used.

Neighbor ID is the ID portion of the network layer address of the neighboring router.

4. **Endnode neighbors:** Code 3. This field is encoded similarly to router neighbors, except that it is assumed that many endnodes might be neighbors on a common link,

and as such, the cost to all the endnodes will be the same. Therefore, this field reports the costs according to all the metrics once and then lists all the endnode neighbor IDs for which those costs apply. If the links to different endnode neighbors have different costs, then the endnode neighbor field appears multiple times.

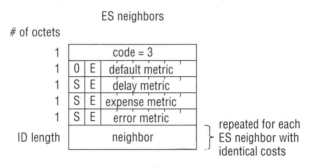

Figure 10.20

The level 2 LSP is packet type 20. The only difference between the encoding of a level 1 LSP and a level 2 LSP is that the level 2 LSP does not contain a field for endnode neighbors. Instead, it contains a field for "prefix neighbors," which are the equivalent of endnodes for level 2 routers.

Prefix neighbors (code 5) is encoded like endnode neighbors in a level 1 LSP, except instead of neighbor ID with a length of ID length, it is a sequence of (**address prefix length**, **address prefix**) pairs. The address prefix length is in units of semioctets. This means that an address prefix need not be an integral number of octets.

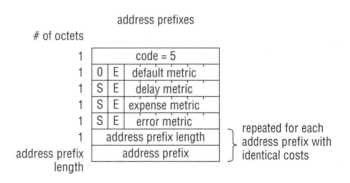

Figure 10.21

10.1.2.11.3 Sequence Numbers Packet

A sequence numbers packet describes the LSPs in the LSP database in a compact format, so that neighbor routers can ensure that their databases stay consistent. A sequence numbers packet is never forwarded. It is only transmitted between neighbors.

There are two main types of sequence numbers packets. A "CSNP" ("complete sequence numbers packet") includes every LSP in the database. Because a CSNP may not fit into a single packet, a CSNP actually contains an "address range," and all LSPs within that range are considered to be included.

A "PSNP" ("partial sequence numbers packet") contains some subset of the LSPs. Nothing can be inferred about LSPs that are not included in a PSNP. A PSNP is primarily used to acknowledge one or more LSPs. It can also be used to request transmission of a specific LSP.

Since there are two LSP databases—level 1 and level 2—there are CSNPs and PSNPs for each of the levels. That makes four explicit types of SNPs:

- Level 1 CSNP

- Level 2 CSNP

- Level 1 PSNP

- Level 2 PSNP

Other than the address range, which consists of the two fields **start LSP ID** and **end LSP ID**, which is included in CSNPs but not in PSNPs, the encoding of all the SNPs is the same.

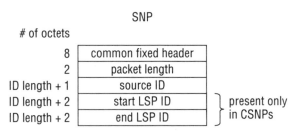

Figure 10.22

The packet types for SNPs are:

- Level 1 CSNP = 24.

- Level 2 CSNP = 25.

- Level 1 PSNP = 26.

- Level 2 PSNP = 27.

The **source ID** field is the ID of the router that generated the SNP. Note: This field could have been only ID length octets long, since it is generated by a router, not on behalf of a LAN. The extra octet is transmitted as 0.

The **start LSP ID** and **end LSP ID** fields are ID length + 2 because an LSP on behalf of a LAN is ID length + 1, and a fragmented LSP requires an extra octet to indicate the fragment number.

The variable-length fields in SNPs are:

1. **LSP entries:**

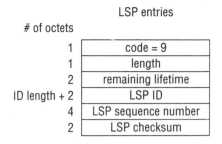

Figure 10.23

The preceding information summarizes the state of a particular LSP. The **checksum** is included in case the same source generates two different LSPs with different data but the same **sequence number**. This can happen due to faulty behavior on the part of the source, corruption of LSP data, or a source's crashing and then restarting with a duplicate sequence number. The checksum is an inexpensive method of checking for this problem with a high probability of catching it.

2. **Authentication:** As described in the earlier discussion of IS-to-IS hellos.

10.1.3   OSPF

IS − IS = 0

— T-shirt distributed at an IETF (Internet Engineering Task Force) meeting.

(Note: I do not agree or approve, but do concede that the T-shirt was clever.)

OSPF stands for "open shortest path first." *Open* implies that the protocol is not proprietary. *SPF* is the phrase some people use to refer to link state routing algorithms. OSPF is very similar to IS-IS, partly because there are only so many ways one can build a link state routing algorithm and partly because a lot of the ideas came from IS-IS.

10.1.3.1   General Packet-Encoding Issues

OSPF does not have variable-length fields in the protocol packets, nor does it have any provision for adding fields that will be ignored by previous-version routers. This permits compact encoding and faster processing of packets but makes extensibility less possible. For instance, addresses in OSPF are exactly 8 octets.

OSPF runs "on top of" IP. That means that an OSPF packet is transmitted with an IP data packet header. The **protocol** field in the IP header (which is set to 89 for OSPF) enables OSPF packets to be distinguished from other types of packets that use the IP header.

10.1.3.2 Terminology

OSPF uses different terminology than IS-IS. The *backbone* in OSPF is what I have been referring to as the level 2 network. A *backbone router* in OSPF is a level 2 router. An *area border router* is a backbone router that attaches to more than one area. An *internal router* is a level 1 router. An *AS boundary router* is a router that attaches to routers from other autonomous systems—i.e., an interdomain router. (The IP community refers to a "domain" as an *autonomous system*. I don't like the term *autonomous system* because I visualize a single computer when I hear the word *system*.) OSPF refers to the packets that advertise link state information as "Link State Advertisements," or LSAs. LSAs are functionally equivalent to the IS-IS LSPs. So that you need not assimilate another acronym, I will refer to the OSPF link state information as an LSP.

10.1.3.3 Area Partitions

In OSPF, level 2 routers are configured to report address summaries that include all the IP addresses reachable within the area. For instance, if one LAN in the area contains addresses having the form 5.7.*.*, and another contains addresses having the form 5.12.*.*, and it is known that no addresses outside the area have the form 5.*.*.*, then the level 2 router can report that "5.*.*.* is reachable in this area."

OSPF has no automatic mechanism for repairing area partitions. A human could reconfigure the address summaries after an area partition, and routing would start working again. Or, the theory goes, if one is worried about area partitions, then the level 2 routers need not be configured with summary addresses, and they can instead report each individual IP address reachable within the area. In that case, a partitioned area would just automatically break into two areas. However, if summary addresses are not used, then there is no routing hierarchy.

10.1.3.4 Level 2 Partitions

Although it is probably preferable for the level 2 network to be connected via "real" backbone links, it is possible for a human to configure two level 2 routers to be end-points of a *virtual level 2 link*. The purpose of configuring such a link is to repair a partition of the level 2 network. OSPF does not have any method for routers to automatically notice either that a virtual level 2 link is required or that such a link is no longer required. All this is managed by humans.

As indicated in subsection 10.1.3.1, OSPF routing messages are carried inside an IP header. When an OSPF routing message is transmitted between level 2 routers X and Y, the destination specified in the IP header is Y and the source in the IP header is X. However, when X forwards a data packet over the virtual link to Y, the data packet already has an IP header, which contains as the source the ultimate source of the data packet (say, A) and the ultimate destination of the data packet (say, B). In order for it to be possible to forward a data packet between X and Y, the level 1 routers along the virtual link must recognize that packets for out-of-area destination B have to be forwarded toward level 2 router Y (see Fig. 10.24).

An alternative strategy (not used by OSPF) uses *encapsulation*. Level 2 router X receives a data packet with IP source A and IP destination B. X determines that the packet should be forwarded through level 2 router Y over the virtual link between X and Y. X puts an additional IP header on the packet, which specifies X as the IP source address and Y as the IP destination address. Since Y resides in the same area as X, the level 1 routers in the area will have no problem forwarding the packet to Y. When Y receives the data packet, it removes the outer IP header added by X and continues forwarding the packet.

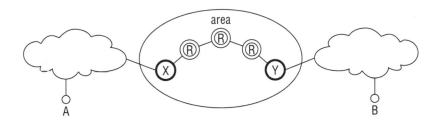

Data Packet between X and Y with OSPF (No Encapsulation)

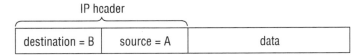

Data Packet between X and Y If Encapsulation Were Used

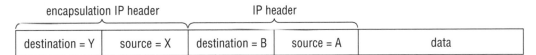

Figure 10.24

The OSPF approach requires level 1 routers to have level 2 information, since they must know how to forward a packet destined for another area. The OSPF designers rejected the encapsulation approach because encapsulation does present some complications. If the encapsulated packet is too large it must be fragmented, and this, in turn, requires that Y be able to perform reassembly.

10.1.3.5 Finding the Right Level 2 Router

OSPF feeds a summary of the level 2 destinations into the area, so that internal routers can choose a more optimal exit point out of the area—i.e., take into account the distance from the level 2 router to the destination.

If feeding the level 2 information into some area turns out to be too expensive, the area can be configured as a *stub area*, which is done by individually configuring each router in the area. In a stub area, the level 2 routers announce "default route" as the summary of all the IP destinations reachable outside the AS. Information about IP destinations that are outside the area but still within the AS continues to be fed into an area, even if it is configured as a stub area. The reasoning given was that the level 2 routing information inside the AS is unlikely to be extensive.

If an area is configured to be a stub area, the routes out of the area to destinations outside the AS become the same as the routes used by IS-IS, and it becomes impossible to configure virtual links through the area.

10.1.3.6   LSP Propagation on a LAN

OSPF has a different means of reliably propagating LSPs on a LAN than IS-IS. In OSPF, the designated router is responsible for collecting explicit acknowledgments for each LSP from the other routers.

Since the DR in OSPF keeps a lot of state regarding which routers have which LSPs, it would require a lot of time and protocol messages for another router to take over in the event that the designated router crashed. Therefore, OSPF elects not only a designated router but a "backup designated router." The backup DR also listens to all the explicit acknowledgments and keeps track of which routers have received which LSPs.

When a router R has an LSP to propagate on the LAN, R does not multicast the LSP to all the other routers. Instead, R transmits it to the DR. But rather than send the LSP to the DR's personal data link address, R transmits it to the multicast address ALLDROUTERS, to which both the DR and the backup DR listen. When the DR receives the LSP, the DR multicasts the LSP to ALLSPFROUTERS. Then the DR collects acks for that LSP, which are transmitted to the multicast address ALLDROUTERS. If the DR does not receive an ack from a subset of the routers, it sends explicit copies of the LSP to each router in that subset.

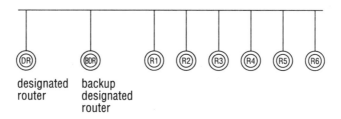

Figure 10.25

The protocol is as follows:

1. R3, say, receives an LSP and needs to forward it onto the LAN.

2. R3 multicasts the LSP to ALLDROUTERS.

3. DR and BDR receive the LSP.

4. DR multicasts the LSP to ALLSPFROUTERS.

5. Assume that all the routers receive the LSP correctly.

6. BDR, R1, R2, R3, R4, R5, and R6 all send an explicit ack to the multicast address ALLDROUTERS.

7. Assume that DR does not receive acks from R2, R5, and BDR within the timeout.

8. DR retransmits the LSP three times, once to R2's data link address, once to R5's data link address, and once to BDR's data link address (and waits for acknowledgments).

10.1.3.7 Designated Router Election

OSPF has the equivalent of IS-to-IS hello messages. They are called simply "hello" packets. Once a DR and backup DR are elected, OSPF makes every effort to keep them, even if another router subsequently comes up with a higher priority or ID.

In contrast, IS-IS simply selects, from the list of routers, the one with the highest priority, with IDs breaking ties.

10.1.3.8 Authentication

As with IS-IS, OSPF has an "authentication" field in all its packets. Indeed, authentication was added to IS-IS to overcome the claim by some in the IP community that IS-IS could not be a contender for an IP IGP (interior gateway protocol) without authentication.

Authentication is done slightly differently in OSPF. As with IS-IS, there is a separate password per link. However, in IS-IS, there is a transmit password and a set of receive passwords for each link. In OSPF, there is only a single password per link. This creates two problems:

1. It makes it difficult to migrate a link from one password to another.

2. It makes things less secure on a point-to-point link, since an intruder need only listen for a message from the other node on the link in order to determine the password. (Imagine two spies. "Tell me the password." "No, you tell me first.")

Authentication in LSPs is handled differently in the two protocols. In IS-IS, the router that originally generated the LSP puts in the authentication field. In OSPF, the LSP itself does not contain an authentication field. Instead, the authentication field is in the header of a link state update packet, inside which, one or more LSPs are packaged. The authentication field in OSPF is added by a router that is propagating the information to a neighbor, not the original router that generated the LSP, as in IS-IS. This may make configuration of passwords easier in OSPF, since a password is a local phenomenon. It also makes it less likely for a misconfigured password in a router to cause global disruption, as it can in IS-IS when an LSP is accepted by some routers and rejected by others.

Another difference is that in IS-IS, the authentication field is variable-length. In OSPF, it is 64 bits. If authentication involves a simple password scheme, a 64-bit field is sufficient for the marginal amount of security that such a scheme can offer. However, if some sort of public key cryptographic scheme were desired (which, in my opinion, is the only sort of scheme that might offer any security), a 64-bit field is too small.

10.1.3.9   Neighbor Initialization

When a link between two neighbor routers comes up, OSPF has a protocol for synchronizing their LSP databases. First, it must be determined which of the neighbors will be the "master" in the initialization protocol and which will be the "slave." This is determined based on ID. The one that is chosen master then sends a description of its LSP database (similar to an IS-IS PSNP) by transmitting "database description" ("DD") packets, each one containing a portion of the database (since it is assumed that the entire database description will not fit into a single packet) and each having a sequence number. The slave acknowledges each database description packet by sending a database description packet with the same sequence number containing information about the slave's LSPs. When the master receives a database description packet from the slave with the same sequence number as the last one the master transmitted, the master sends the next group of information in a DD packet with a sequence number that is 1 higher than the preceding sequence number. The master continues sending DD packets in this manner until it has described all the LSPs in its database, indicating the last packet by clearing the **M** bit in the DD packet.

If the slave requires more DD packets than the master in order to describe the LSPs in the slave's database, the master will know that the slave is not finished because the **M** bit will be set in the slave's DD. At this point, the master must continue sending empty DD packets until it eventually receives one from the slave with the **M** bit clear.

When router R1 discovers, as a result of receiving database description information from neighbor R2, that R1 is missing some information, R1 sends "link state request packets" to obtain the missing information from R2. If R1 discovers that R2 is missing some LSPs, R1 transmits those LSPs to R2.

If OSPF had defined the sequence of DD packets to be the equivalent of IS-IS's CSNP (complete sequence numbers packet) rather than IS-IS's PSNP (partial sequence numbers packet), then only one of the two routers would have had to inform the other of the LSPs in the database.

In contrast, in IS-IS, when a point-to-point link comes up between neighbor routers R1 and R2, each router assumes that the other router has no LSPs and marks all LSPs as needing to be transmitted to that neighbor. Additionally, each neighbor transmits a CSNP. If R2 receives R1's CSNP, then R2 will note that R1 already has the LSPs and will clear the flags reminding R2 to transmit the LSPs to R1. The CSNP in IS-IS is merely an optimization. In IS-IS, when a new neighbor router comes up on a LAN, no special protocol is required. The designated router's periodic CSNP will keep the LSP databases in all the routers on the LAN synchronized.

10.1.3.10   Types of LSPs

There are five types of LSPs in OSPF:

1. *Type 1—router links advertisement:* This is very similar to an IS-IS LSP. It is flooded only within the area and contains information about the router's neighbor routers (via point-to-point links) and the LANs to which the router is

attached. It can also be generated by a "backbone" router and flooded within the backbone—in which case, it is equivalent to an IS-IS level 2 LSP.

2. *Type 2—network links advertisement:* This is similar to an IS-IS LSP generated on behalf of a LAN. The OSPF network links advertisement is generated by the designated router on a LAN, lists all the routers on the LAN, and is flooded only within the area (or within the backbone, if it is level 2).

3. *Type 3—network summary link advertisement:* This is level 2 information that is injected into an area to describe networks reachable from outside the area. It is generated by an area border router (a level 2 router that is connected to more than one area) and is flooded into an area. An area border router attached to both area 1 and area 2 will generate a different network summary link advertisement for distribution within area 1 than for distribution within area 2.

    A type 3 LSP is also used by area border routers to summarize the destinations within the area to the backbone. When the contents of the type 3 LSP contain information about an area, it is flooded to the backbone.

    Note that a type 3 OSPF LSP can report only a single IP destination. Therefore, an area border router will generate many type 3 LSPs. For each area A to which it has a link, it will generate one type 3 LSP for each IP destination outside A within the AS. It will also generate one for each (summary) IP address within A and flood that to the backbone.

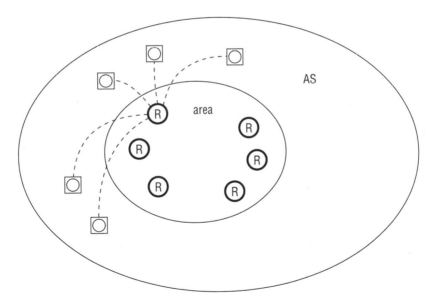

Figure 10.26 Type 3 LSP Information.
(Each level 2 router reports its cost to each IP destination in AS, indicated by ▣.)

4. *Type 4—AS boundary routers summary link advertisement:* This is more level 2 information injected into an area. It describes the cost of the path from the

router that generated the type 4 LSP to an AS boundary router. As with type 3, type 4 LSPs carry only a single destination.

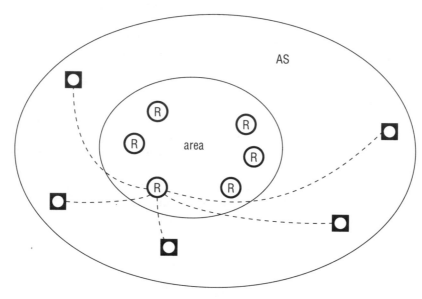

Figure 10.27   Type 4 LSP information.
(Each level 2 router reports its cost to each AS boundary, indicated by ▣.)

5. *Type 5—AS external link advertisement:* This is also level 2 information that is flooded to all the routers throughout the entire AS. It describes the cost from the AS boundary router that generated the type 5 LSP to a destination outside the AS (see Fig. 10.28). As with type 3 and 4 LSPs, because the type 5 LSP carries only a single destination, an AS boundary router will generate many type 5 LSPs.

The combination of type 4 and type 5 LSPs informs level 1 routers about IP destinations reachable outside the AS. Assume that there are k level 2 routers in some area, j AS border routers in the AS, and n IP destinations reachable outside the AS. With the OSPF scheme, each of the k level 2 routers will report the cost of the path from itself to each of the j AS border routers, and level 1 routers will also receive the LSP generated by each of the j AS border routers, each one reporting at least some of the n externally reachable IP destination addresses.

OSPF could have had each level 2 router report the distance from itself to each of the n externally reachable IP destination addresses rather than the chosen scheme, which was to have each level 2 router report its distance to each AS border router and then have the border routers report the distances from themselves to each externally reachable IP destination. OSPF made the decision that it did based on certain topological assumptions, under which the OSPF scheme uses less memory than the variant scheme. (See Homework problem 10.)

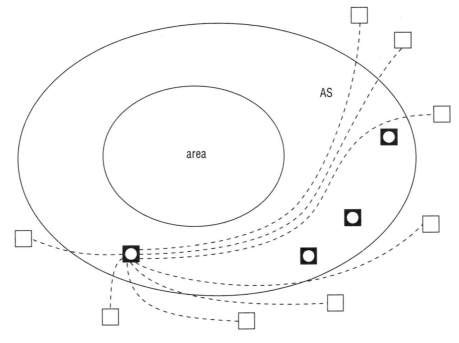

Figure 10.28   Type 5 LSP information.
(Each AS border router reports its distance to each IP destination outside the AS indicated by ☐ .)

10.1.3.11   Packet Encoding

All OSPF packets start with the following 24-octet header:

common header

# of octets	
1	version
1	packet type
2	packet length
4	router ID
4	area ID
2	checksum
2	authentication type
8	authentication data

Figure 10.29

- **Version:**   2.

- **Packet type:**

    1 = hello

    2 = database description

3 = link state request

4 = link state update

5 = link state acknowledgment

- **Packet length:** Number of octets in the OSPF packet.

- **Router ID:** The network layer address (the IP address) of the router that generated the packet.

- **Area ID:** The ID of the area to which the packet belongs (or 0 if it is a level 2 packet).

- **Checksum:** The same checksum algorithm as for an IP data packet.

- **Authentication type:**

    0 = no authentication

    1 = simple password

    2–255 = currently undefined

- **Authentication data:** For authentication type 1 (the only defined type), it consists of a 64-bit quantity.

10.1.3.11.1   Hello Packets

Hello packets are similar to the IS-to-IS hello packets in the IS-IS protocol. They are transmitted between neighbors and never forwarded.

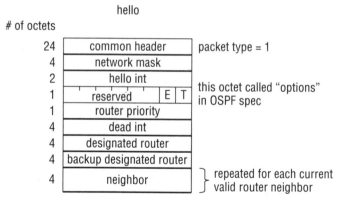

Figure 10.30

- **Network mask:** The mask for the link configured in the router generating the hello. If this field does not match the receiving router's mask configured for the link, the receiving router rejects the hello and does not accept the transmitting router as a neighbor.

- **Hello int:** The number of seconds between this router's hello packets. Interestingly enough, a receiving router will reject the hello and refuse a transmitting router as a neighbor if the receiving router's configured **hello int** on that link is not identical to the transmitting router's **hello int.** In contrast, IS-IS makes no restriction that neighbors must have identical hello intervals.

• **Options:** Only the bottom 2 bits are defined. The bottom bit is **T**, which indicates whether the router supports multiple routing metrics. This seems to imply that a router must either support exactly one metric (default) or support all of them (eight metrics, which is all possible settings of the 3 types of service bits in a data packet header).

   The next bit is **E**, which indicates whether or not the router considers the area to be a stub area. If the receiving router has not been configured identically with the transmitting router, the hello will be rejected.

• **Router priority:** Used in the election of designated and backup designated routers. A router with a higher number is more likely to become designated router. A priority of 0 means that the router will never become designated router or backup designated router, even if no other routers are up.

• **Dead int:** The number of seconds before a router declares a neighbor router dead if no hellos have been received. As with hello int, if this time doesn't exactly match the configured time in the receiving router, the receiving router will reject the hello.

• **Designated router:** The ID of the router that the transmitting router thinks is the designated router (or 0 if the transmitting router thinks there is no DR).

• **Backup designated router:** The ID of the router that the transmitting router thinks is the backup designated router (or 0 if the transmitting router thinks there is no backup DR).

• **Neighbors:** The list of 4-octet IDs of routers from which hellos were received on the link within dead int seconds.

10.1.3.11.2 Database Description Packets

When a link first comes up between two routers, R1 and R2, one of the routers (the one with the higher ID) becomes *master* and the other becomes *slave*. Once the identity of the master is known, the master transmits a sequence of database description packets (as many as necessary to include all LSPs in the database). Each fragment of the database description packet contains a sequence number. The slave acknowledges each fragment, and only after fragment number n is acknowledged does the master transmit fragment number $n + 1$.

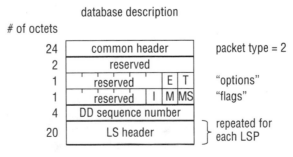

Figure 10.31

- **Options:** The **E** and **T** bits, as described in the preceding subsection.

- **Flags:** Bit 8 (least significant)—**M/S** ("master/slave"). If set, this bit indicates that the transmitting router is the master. If not set, it indicates that the transmitting router is the slave.

  Bit 7—**M** ("more"). If set, this bit indicates that this is not the final database description packet.

  Bit 6—**I** ("init"). If set, this bit indicates that this is the first in the sequence of database description packets.

- **Database description packet sequence number:** The sequence number of the database description packet. The beginning value should be chosen to be "unique," to minimize confusion with previously transmitted database description packets.

- **LS headers list:** For each LSP advertised, the following:

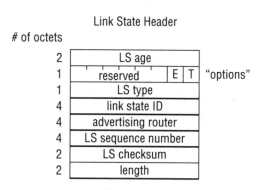

Figure 10.32

These are described in subsection 10.1.3.11.6, in which link state packets are discussed in detail.

10.1.3.11.3   Link State Request

A link state request packet (OSPF packet type 3) contains a description of one or more LSPs that a router is requesting from its neighbor. A router discovers that it needs LSPs after exchanging database description packets with the neighbor.

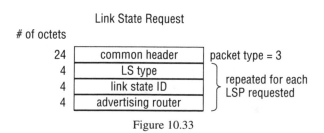

Figure 10.33

The fields **LS type**, **link state ID**, and **advertising router** are defined in subsection 10.1.3.11.6, "Link State Advertisement."

10.1.3.11.4   Link State Update

Link state update packets are OSPF packet type 4. They contain one or more link state advertisements.

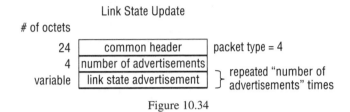

Figure 10.34

10.1.3.11.5   Link State Acknowledgment

Link state acknowledgments are OSPF packet type 5. They contain one or more link state advertisement headers, each of which is 20 octets long.

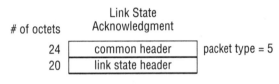

Figure 10.35

10.1.3.11.6   Link State Advertisement

A link state advertisement is basically what is called an LSP in IS-IS. As described in subsection 10.1.3.10, there are five types of LSP in OSPF. All of them start out with the following 20-octet header:

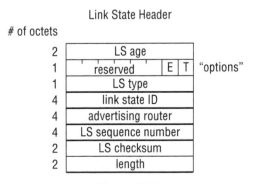

Figure 10.36

LS age is an estimate of the number of seconds since the LSP was generated.

Options, as defined in subsection 10.1.3.11.1, carries the **E** bit (meaning that the router believes the area is a "stub" area) and the **T** bit (meaning that the router can handle multiple types of service).

LS type is one of the following:

- 1 = router links

- 2 = network links

- 3 = summary link (reachable IP "subnetwork numbers")

- 4 = summary link (reachable AS boundary routers)

- 5 = AS externally reachable IP "subnetwork numbers"

Link state ID is defined differently, depending on the type of LSP:

- *Type 1:* The ID of the router that generated the LSP

- *Type 2:* The IP address of the DR on the LAN

- *Type 3:* The IP address of the link being reported as an IP destination

- *Type 4:* The router ID of the AS boundary router to which the distance is being reported

- *Type 5:* The IP address of the link being reported as an IP destination

Advertising router is the ID of the router that generated the LSP.

LS sequence number is the sequence number of the LSP.

LS checksum is the Fletcher checksum of the complete contents of the LSP. (For details on computation of a Fletcher checksum, see Annex C of ISO 8473, the CLNP specification.)

Length is the number of octets in the LSP.

10.1.3.11.7   Router Links Advertisement

A router links advertisement is a type 1 LSP.

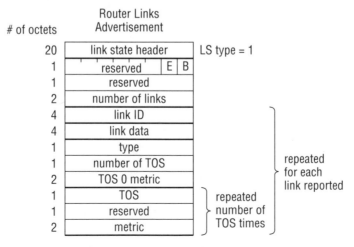

Figure 10.37

When set, bit **E** (which stands for "external") indicates that the router that generated the LSP is an AS boundary router.

When set, bit **B** indicates that the router is an area border router.

Number of links is the total number of links that the router that generated the LSP has in the area. (In IP, a link is considered to reside in exactly one area, whereas a router can reside in multiple areas. In contrast, in ISO, a router is considered to reside in exactly one area, whereas a link can connect two areas. Thus, in IP, some of the router's links may be in one area, and some may be in another.)

Link ID identifies what is connected to the router via the link being reported. For each type of link, the link ID consists of the following:

* *Link type 1:* ID of neighbor router
* *Link type 2:* IP address of the designated router on the LAN
* *Link type 3:* IP "subnetwork" number
* *Link type 4:* ID of neighbor router

Link data consists of the subnetwork mask when the link is type 3 (stub LAN). Otherwise it is the IP address of the router that generated the LSP on the advertised link.

Type is the type of link, which is one of the following:

1 = point-to-point link to another router

2 = connection to a "transit" LAN

3 = connection to a "stub" LAN

4 = virtual link

Number of TOS specifies the number of costs reported for the link, not counting TOS 0, which is required.

The OSPF spec claims that **TOS** is represented exactly as it is in the IP header's TOS field, which consists of:

IP header TOS field

Figure 10.38

Thus, there are theoretically 64 potential types of service, since the 3 **precedence** bits and the **D**, **T**, and **R** bits can all take any value. However, the intention is that the precedence bits be ignored, and TOS only applies to the **D**, **T**, and **R** bits. That means there are potentially 8 different TOSs. But even that is likely to change. The IP community is considering adding another metric, for "monetary expense," since ISO has it and some people consider it useful. The IP community is also considering banning the setting of multiple bits in the TOS field. If the monetary expense bit is added, there would be potentially 16 different TOSs. If the setting of multiple bits is disallowed and the monetary expense bit is added, there would be only 4 different TOSs, which would make the metrics in OSPF equivalent to the metrics in IS-IS.

10.1.3.11.8 Network Links Advertisement

A network links advertisement is a type 2 LSP.

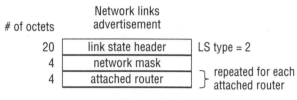

Figure 10.39

Network mask is the mask for the LAN's IP address.

Attached router is the ID of a router on the LAN that is a neighbor of the DR.

10.1.3.11.9 Summary Link Advertisement

A summary link advertisement is generated by an area border router and flooded into the area. LSP types 3 and 4 are both considered summary link advertisements. Type 3 reports the cost to a "subnetwork" number outside the area. (Note that the backbone is considered an area. An area border router also generates a type 3 LSP for the IP addresses inside the area and floods them into the backbone.) Type 4 reports the cost to an AS border router. A summary link advertisement reports only a single destination. Therefore, each destination reported requires its own LSP header. For instance, if *n* subnetwork numbers are reachable outside the area, then each area border router will generate *n* type 3 LSPs, each with its own 20-octet LSP header, 4-octet mask, and 4-octets for each metric reported.

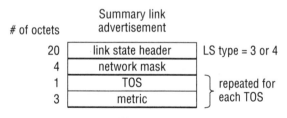

Figure 10.40

The **network mask** is only relevant for type 3 LSPs. For type 4 LSPs, it is set to 0.

10.1.3.11.10 AS External Link Advertisement

An AS external link advertisement is a type 5 LSP. These LSPs are generated by AS boundary routers and flooded to the entire AS, except for stub areas. Like type 3 and 4 LSPs, each type 5 LSP can report only a single destination. Thus, if *n* subnetwork numbers are reachable outside an AS, each AS boundary router will generate *n* LSPs.

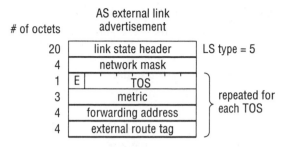

Figure 10.41

Network mask is the mask for the advertised destination.

E is a flag indicating whether the metric reported can be considered comparable with the metric for that TOS used within the AS. If it is comparable (E = 0), then the total cost to the advertised destination can be calculated by summing the cost to the AS boundary router with the cost that the AS boundary router reports to the advertised destination. If it isn't comparable (E = 1), then there is no way to compare the internal cost with the external cost, and therefore, the AS boundary router advertising the smallest distance to the destination is chosen, and the cost to the AS boundary router is ignored.

TOS is the same as the TOS field in an IP data packet header, but without the **precedence** bits.

Metric is the advertised cost to the destination.

Forwarding address is used to optimize the final hop. If the advertising AS is advertising a destination that can more optimally be reached by a different router on the same LAN, then the advertising AS puts that router's address into the forwarding address field. Otherwise, it leaves the field 0. Without this field, in certain topologies, a route might traverse an extra LAN hop.

External route tag is 4 octets of information that the OSPF designers thought might be useful to an interdomain routing protocol, but the OSPF spec does not specify what that field would contain. One idea for information that could be carried in the external route tag field was to include the "autonomous system number" of the next AS hop on the path to the advertised destination. An AS number is defined as a 16-bit quantity that is globally administered by the same authority that administers IP addresses. The AS number is not part of an IP address. It was invented for the EGP protocol. Other interdomain routing protocols may use the AS number as well, for whatever purpose might be found for it.

Although the purpose of the OSPF external route tag field is not clearly defined, the following reasons were given for providing this field:

1. The tag might contain the IP address of the interdomain router that advertised the destination.

    The theory is that this information would enable an interdomain router R1 that wishes to forward a packet through the domain to interdomain router R2 to determine whether the intradomain routing protocol (OSPF) has stabilized and will route the packet toward R2.

In my opinion, since routing algorithms always take some time to converge, there is no reason for performing a special check in this situation.

2. The tag might contain the number of the autonomous system from which the information about that destination address was learned.

This information might be of use to the obsolescent EGP protocol, since EGP requires that information learned from AS 1 not be transmitted back to another EGP router from AS 1. When EGP is replaced by BGP, however, this field will no longer be useful for that purpose.

3. It might allow the interdomain routing protocol (for instance, EGP) to pass information to other interdomain routers in the same domain without requiring them to communicate directly.

Although this might be more efficient than n^2 pairwise links between the n interdomain routers in a domain, it requires all the intradomain routers to store information they will ignore, and it is only useful if the amount of information that the interdomain routers wish to transmit to each other is no larger than 4 octets per destination address. This amount of information might be sufficient for EGP, but it is not sufficient for BGP.

10.1.4   Ships in the Night

"Ships in the night," abbreviated "S.I.N.," is the method of implementing multiprotocol routing that existed before the concept of integrated routing. It consists of running all the routing protocols in parallel. Logically, it is the same as buying a separate router for each routing protocol supported. The only difference is that they are all implemented in the same box.

When a multiprotocol router receives a packet, it must determine which logical router should receive the packet. Although it is possible that no packet (data or control) in network layer protocol X is a legal packet in network layer protocol Y, this is unlikely, especially if X and Y are independently developed standards. Therefore, there must be a mechanism in the data link layer for distinguishing between packets of the different protocols.

On LANs, the **SAP** field (or the **protocol type field**, if the SNAP SAP is used) distinguishes the network layer protocol that must receive the packet. On point-to-point links, either some proprietary mechanism must exist, or the data link protocol must be enhanced to include a field to distinguish among multiple network layer protocols. The PPP ("point-to-point") protocol developed by the IP community [2] is an example of a protocol for a point-to-point link (in this case, a protocol that gives datagram service) that includes a field in the data link layer header specifying the network layer protocol that should receive the packet.

[2] **D. Perkins, "The Point-to-Point Protocol for the Transmission of Multiprotocol Diagrams Over Point-to-Point Links," RFC 1171, July 1990.**

10.1.5 Integrated Routing

The idea behind integrated routing is that the routers run a single routing algorithm—in this case, IS-IS. The single routing algorithm allows the routers to compute paths between themselves and all other routers. Then, additionally, each router R informs other routers, in R's LSPs, of the set of destinations that R can reach. The destinations need not be restricted to ISO addresses just because the routing algorithm was originally developed for ISO. Reachable destinations can be IP addresses or addresses from other protocol suites.

IS-IS packets have been encoded in such a way that it is possible to enhance them with additional fields and still remain compatible with routers that do not implement the new features.

The fact that only a single routing algorithm is required does not eliminate the other protocols necessary to support a protocol suite. To support ISO, routers need to implement ES-IS and be able to parse the data packet format. To support IP, routers need to support ARP, ICMP, and the IP data packet format. Endnodes are completely unaffected by the type of router. For instance, an IP endnode will work with an OSPF router, a S.I.N. router running OSPF and IS-IS in parallel, or an integrated router that supports both IP and ISO using IS-IS.

The fields added to IS-IS:

1. Inform routers about the reachability of addresses in other protocol suites—in this case, TCP/IP destinations

2. Inform routers about which protocols are supported by which routers

3. Include any other information specifically needed by a particular protocol suite

Integrated routing was originally called "dual routing," because it was capable of routing both IP and CLNP. However, there is hope that additional network layer protocols will be added, in which case, the name *dual* will no longer be appropriate, since it implies exactly two.

10.1.5.1 Types of Routers

A router is defined as "supporting protocol X" if it can parse protocol X's data packets and implements the neighbor-handshaking protocols required by protocol X (e.g., ARP, ICMP, ES-IS).

All routers implementing "integrated routing," as defined here, use the same format of routing control packets (LSP, SNP, IS-IS hello). Not all will necessarily support all protocols.

For now, let us assume that the only two protocols in question are ISO and IP. There are three possible types of "integrated routers":

1. Those that support both ISO and IP

2. Those that support only IP

3. Those that support only ISO

A router that supports only IP ignores the portion of LSPs that discusses reachability of ISO endnodes (in level 1 LSPs) and ISO address prefixes (in level 2 LSPs). A router that supports only ISO ignores the portion of LSPs that discusses reachability of IP destinations. A router R1 will refuse to be neighbors with a router R2 unless R1 and R2 support at least one protocol in common. Thus, an IP-only router will not become neighbors with an ISO-only router. A dual router will be neighbors with any of the three types of router.

It is simpler to constrain an area to carry only IP data traffic if any IP-only routers reside in the area. And likewise, it is simpler to constrain the area to carry only ISO data traffic if any ISO-only routers reside in the area. If this constraint is considered too odious, encapsulation can be used. A dual router, noticing that it needs to forward a protocol X packet to a neighbor router that supports only protocol Y, encapsulates the packet in a protocol Y header and routes it to a router farther along the path that supports both protocols and can remove the encapsulated header. However, encapsulation is messy, and it can be avoided by ensuring that all routers support both protocols.

If all the level 2 routers support both protocols, then some areas can be IP-only, others ISO-only, and still others dual.

10.1.5.2   IP Hierarchy

When dual routing reports an IP destination, it includes the 32-bit address and the 32-bit mask. A level 2 router is configured with addresses that it advertises to the level 2

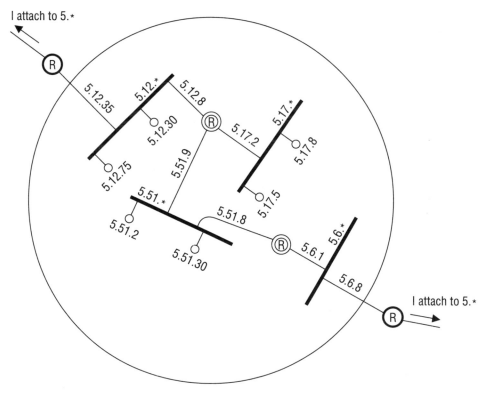

Figure 10.42

network as being reachable within the area. With the use of a shorter mask, this enables the contents of the area to be summarized compactly.

The protocol would work correctly if a level 2 router simply gathered together all the IP addresses reachable within the area and reported them in its level 2 LSP. However, if IP addresses are assigned wisely, it is possible to summarize many reachable addresses by reporting a single address with a shorter mask. For instance, in the accompanying illustration, assuming that no link with an address starting with "5" resides in any other area, the address summary "5.*" will cover all the addresses reachable within the area. It would be too difficult for the level 2 router to try to infer 5.* as the most efficient encoding of the area, and it would be impossible if not all addresses of the form 5.* were reachable within the area. Instead, a level 2 router must be manually configured to report 5.*.

If a level 2 router is configured to report "X.*" as reachable within the area, it reports X.* as reachable provided that at least one address within the area matches X.*. It also reports in its level 2 LSP any IP addresses within the area that are not subsumed by the configured address summaries.

10.1.5.3   Type of Service Routing

The IP data packet header gives three criteria for routing metrics:

> *D:* Delay

> *T:* Throughput

> *R:* Reliability

Since these criteria can be selected in any combination, this gives eight possible settings of the TOS field in an IP header. OSPF supports provision of a different assignment of metric for each combination. IS-IS only provides four metrics, however, and one of the IS-IS metrics is "monetary cost," which has no representation in the IP header.

The mapping from the TOS field in the IP packet header to the IS-IS chosen metric is as follows:

D	T	R	Chosen Metric
1	0	0	Delay
0	0	1	Reliability
All others			Default (throughput)

Despite my lack of enthusiasm for multiple routing metrics, I will nevertheless explain the trade-offs between the OSPF method of supporting multiple routing metrics and the integrated routing method.

OSPF gives greater flexibility, because it allows eight possible metrics to be used. On the other hand, using all combinations multiplies the CPU overhead and memory required for the forwarding database by 8. There is no way to lump multiple settings of the metrics together into one entry. For instance, it might be sensible to say that any setting in which the D bit is set should use the delay metric, regardless of the setting of the other 2 bits. However, in OSPF, the default metric will be used unless there exists a path from source to destination consisting of links that have been assigned costs according to exactly the combination of metrics specified in a data packet's TOS field.

In my opinion, the bits in the IP header were never intended to be used in combination. I think the intent was that the user select either delay, throughput, or reliability as the criterion for optimizing the route. If that is indeed the case, then OSPF and IS-IS are equivalent. Both allow selection of one of the three metrics.

10.1.5.4   IP Information

It is obvious that IP addresses (including masks) that are reachable have to be included in level 1 and level 2 LSPs. The format of the information is as (IP address, subnet mask, metrics) triples. Reachable IP addresses can be reported as either *internally reachable*, meaning that the reported destinations are reachable within the AS, or *externally reachable*, meaning that the reported destinations are reachable outside the AS.

Additional information (i.e., besides reachable IP destinations) is required for multiprotocol operation, however. Assuming that not all routers will support every protocol suite that could be supported with integrated routing, it is necessary for routers to announce which protocol suites they support, to prevent data packets in a foreign format from being transmitted to a router that does not handle that protocol. The protocols supported must be announced in hello messages, so that routers know the capabilities of their neighbors. The protocols supported are also announced in LSPs, for two reasons. One is to detect misconfiguration, if mixing of X-only and Y-only routers in the same area is prohibited. The other is to give sufficient information so that a router that supports both X and Y can encapsulate an X protocol packet in a Y header when forced to forward the packet through a Y-only neighbor, in those cases in which router mixing is considered sufficiently desirable to warrant solving the problem through encapsulation.

The next piece of additional information for IP is the router's IP interface. This is required in hello messages because, in IP, it is necessary to know the IP address of a neighbor router in order to send an ICMP redirect. An IP address of a router is also included in the router's LSP, which is only required if encapsulation is used either for mixing of X-only and Y-only routers or on virtual links.

The final piece of additional information is known as "interdomain routing protocol information" (which I'll abbreviate as "IRPI"). It is included in level 2 LSPs and serves any function that might be served by the tag field in OSPF but is more flexible, since it is a variable-length field. The IRPI field is intended to be useful to the interdomain routing protocol and is ignored by the intradomain routers. Possible uses of the IRPI field (beyond the uses of the OSPF tag field, which could also be supported if anyone thought they were desirable) include the following:

1. The IRPI field could allow interdomain routers to find each other. In other words, certain level 2 routers would also be interdomain routers. The interdomain routers within a routing domain would be able to discover which of the level 2 routers within the domain were also interdomain routers because of the inclusion of the IRPI field in the level 2 LSPs.

2. If there were many interdomain routers within a domain, and they wished to share information with all the other interdomain routers within the domain, they could include the information in the IRPI field in the level 2 LSPs, which automatically get flooded to all the level 2 routers in the domain. The alternative is for each interdomain router to individually transmit the information to each other interdomain router. The latter mechanism is more efficient if there are only a small number of interdomain routers, since it does not require carrying an extra field in the level 2 LSPs that must be stored (although ignored) by all the level 2 intradomain routers.

10.1.5.5 Packet Formats

The packet formats are IS-IS, enhanced with the fields described in the following two subsections. These fields are all in the variable portion of the IS-IS packets, in which fields are encoded with a **code**, **length**, and **value**.

10.1.5.5.1 Added to Hellos

The **protocols supported** field is code 129. The **length** is equal to the number of protocols supported. The **value** is a list of octets, each one representing a protocol supported. There is a registry of network layer protocols, with a code for each, in ISO/TF 9577. The "network layer protocol ID" is known as the "NLPID." The NLPID is the first octet of all the ISO network layer packets.

Also in the hello packet is the **IP interface address** field (code 132), which includes one or more IP addresses for the interface over which the hello is transmitted. The **length** is 4 octets per interface address reported, and the **value** is a sequence of IP addresses.

10.1.5.5.2 Added to LSPs

The **protocols supported** and **IP interface address** fields are included, exactly as defined for hellos in the previous section, 10.1.5.5.1.

Furthermore, IP reachability information is included. **Internal reachability information** is code 128 and is included in both level 1 and level 2 LSPs. **External reachability information** is code 130 and can only be included in level 2 LSPs generated by routers (not by DRs on behalf of a LAN). This field, whose length is a multiple of 12 octets, is a sequence of the following information:

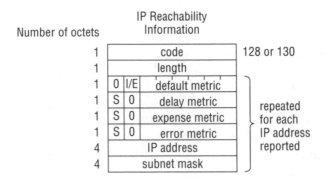

Figure 10.43

The bits marked as "0" are reserved, which means they are transmitted as 0 and ignored on receipt. Since the metrics to a destination inside the AS must be reported with the internal metrics, the **I/E** flag can only be set when reporting IP external reachability information. When set, the I/E flag indicates that the metrics are not comparable with internal metrics. When clear, it indicates that the metrics can sensibly be combined with the internal metrics (the destination is outside the AS, but the metrics for reaching it are comparable with the internal metrics).

You are allowed to be slightly confused about why the protocol reports a cost according to the "expense" metric when there is no way to specify in an IP data packet that the user wants the packet routed according to that metric. This cost is reported in case the IP data packet format is ever modified in the future to include a bit for specifying the expense metric.

Interdomain routing protocol information is code 131.

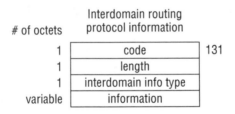

Figure 10.44

The **interdomain info type** field indicates the interdomain routing protocol for which the field contains information. For instance, it might be BGP information or information for some other interdomain routing protocol.

The **information** field itself is ignored by intradomain routing and is used only by the specified EGP.

10.2 Interdomain Routing Protocols (Static Routing, EGP, BGP, IDRP)

Interdomain routing is really analogous to a level 3 routing protocol. Level 1 routing works within an area, and level 2 routing connects areas. Similarly, intradomain routing (which is the combination of level 1 and level 2 routers) works within a routing domain, and the interdomain routing protocol connects the routing domains.

The reason interdomain routing protocols are different from intradomain routing protocols is because it is assumed that routing domains don't really want to be combined into one big happy melting pot of a network. Routing domains are independently funded. When a domain routes transit traffic, resources are being consumed. Therefore, some domains might be willing to route some sorts of traffic and not others. Some domains might have different charging policies, and users might wish to control the route so as to optimize monetary cost. Routing domains don't trust one another. They don't trust the routing algorithms running in other domains to be implemented properly, and they don't want bugs in other domains or in the interdomain routing protocol to affect the routing within the routing domain. And it is assumed that all sorts of administrative rules will restrict the legal routes. Within a routing domain, if you can physically travel a particular path, it is legal. Between routing domains, it might be that the only legal paths are ones for which bilateral agreements have been made between the owners of the domains. Or laws within a country might restrict the legal routes (for instance, Canadian traffic must not exit and then reenter Canada). Or network X might agree to be a transit network only for military business.

Interdomain routing is not well developed. Nobody is very happy about any of the current protocols, but they will have to do until something better comes along.

In this section, I describe four interdomain routing protocols. The first is not really a protocol at all. It is simply static routing. The second is EGP, the IP community's first interdomain routing protocol, which was documented in RFC 827. The IP community refers to an interdomain routing protocol as an "EGP" (for "exterior gateway protocol"). Since I find it very confusing to discuss EGP as an example of an EGP, I will use the term *interdomain routing protocol*, and only use the term *EGP* when discussing the specific protocol documented in RFC 827. The third protocol is BGP (for "border gateway protocol"). The fourth protocol is IDRP (for "interdomain routing protocol").

10.2.1 Static Routing

Static routing means that information is manually configured into routers that directly connect to other routing domains. Ordinarily, manual configuration is to be avoided whenever possible, but in the case of interdomain routing, static routing has some attractive features:

1. Often, links between routing domains are expensive to use, and there are long periods of time during which no data traffic needs to flow on the links. Thus, it is attractive not to require any routing control traffic on such links.

2. Very complex policies can be accommodated.

3. Since no interdomain routing protocol is operating, there is no possibility of global disruption caused by faulty interdomain routers in another domain.

The chief disadvantages of static routing are:

1. It does not adapt to changing topologies. For instance, if link L3 goes down, R1 would not know that it must change the route for destination DEST from link L1 to L2 (see Fig. 10.45).

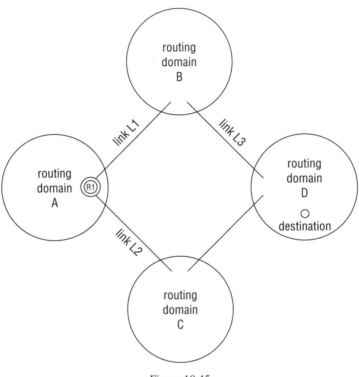

Figure 10.45

2. Inconsistent manually configured databases can cause looping of interdomain traffic.

3. Manual configuration is a lot of trouble.

In certain very simple topologies, assuming ISO addresses are used, static routing requires minimal configuration.

In Fig. 10.46, assume that each routing domain uses the DTE ("data terminal equipment") address of the point of attachment to the public network as the most significant portion of the area addresses within the domain. In that case, the only interdomain routing information required is to configure the routers attached to the public network with the address prefix of the public net and an algorithm to extract the DTE address from an area address. No unnecessary traffic needs to flow between the domains. Only when data traffic must flow between two domains is a link initiated.

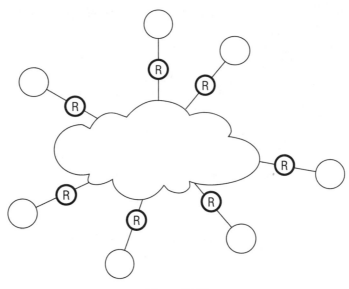

Figure 10.46

Fig. 10.47 shows a routing domain that has multiple points of attachment to various public networks.

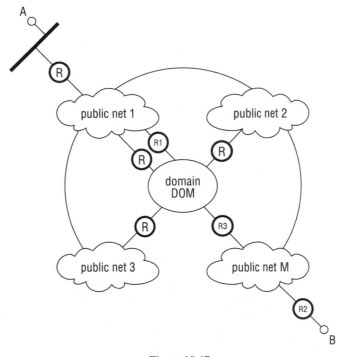

Figure 10.47

What should the routing domain DOM show in its area address? And what should appear in the static configurations of routers in other domains regarding addresses within DOM? Here are three possibilities:

1.   DOM uses one of the points of attachment in its addresses. Routers in other domains make no special entries for addresses in DOM. Instead, they know how to reach prefixes specifying each of the public networks.

     This will work, but it constrains the route by which DOM is reached. For instance, if DOM chooses R1's point of attachment and R1 is down, then A will not be able to reach addresses in DOM. If R1 is up, B will have a nonoptimal route for reaching DOM, since the packet will first be routed toward public net 1.

2.   DOM uses all the points of attachment and has multiple legal addresses. Remote routers have no special configuration regarding DOM.

     One problem with this approach is that there is a limit to the number of area addresses for an area. Another problem is that the address chosen by a source constrains the route. If it chooses an address corresponding to a dead router's point of attachment, DOM will be unreachable. If it chooses an address corresponding to an inconveniently located point of attachment, the route will be nonoptimal. Smart software in the source node that attempts the addresses in order of geographic preference could alleviate these problems.

     Another problem with multiple area addresses is that this approach multiplies the storage required in the server that maps names to addresses. Name-to-address resolution is handled in a higher layer, but it is interesting how choices made in the network layer affect higher layers.

3.   DOM chooses one address. It might not even correspond to any of the points of attachment. At least one interdomain router in each routing domain would have a static entry regarding how to reach addresses in DOM. For instance, router R2 would have an entry in its database corresponding to the link onto public net N indicating that the address prefix that defines addresses in DOM is reachable on that link by dialing the DTE address corresponding to R3.

The ISO addressing and configuration give network managers a great deal of flexibility. Engineering trade-offs can be made with clever decisions.

Despite static routing's disadvantages, I would like to see it tried for interdomain routing, because it eliminates any need for cooperation between routers in separate domains, and because it does not require a routing protocol to be operating continuously on potentially expensive interdomain links. If after a trial period, ISO networks grow so large that static routing is unworkable, then an interdomain routing protocol could be added.

This will not happen, however. Static routing will not work for IP because the address space is not large enough. Since an interdomain routing protocol must be developed for IP, it will be adapted for ISO. Indeed, this is happening. BGP is being developed for IP, and the ISO-ized version (with changes to accommodate ISO addresses instead of IP addresses) known as "IDRP" ("interdomain routing protocol") is likely to become an ISO standard.

10.2.2 EGP

EGP was the first interdomain routing protocol. Nobody likes it, but something was needed. And despite EGP's problems, the Internet has been limping along with it for many years and has managed to survive.

The EGP protocol has three aspects:

1.   Neighbor acquisition

2.   Neighbor reachability

3.   Routing information

10.2.2.1 Neighbor Acquisition

The EGP spec says nothing about how routers decide to become EGP neighbors. An *interior EGP neighbor* is a router within a particular AS with which EGP information is exchanged. An *exterior EGP neighbor* is a router in another AS with which EGP information is exchanged. Theoretically (according to the EGP spec), an EGP neighbor must be a single IP hop away. However, the single IP hop can be over a WAN. If the WAN is an ISO network, for instance, then the EGP protocol messages would be transmitted inside an ISO network layer header, as if they were ordinary ISO data packets. There is no reason why the WAN cannot be running IP as the network layer, and then the EGP packet would be contained inside an IP header.

Anyone who isn't confused about when routers become EGP neighbors and what the rules are for configuring routers to initiate being EGP neighbors does not understand EGP.

Now, for those of you still following, if router A has been configured to initiate a neighbor relationship with router B, then A transmits a "neighbor acquisition" message to B. If B has been configured to accept a neighbor relationship with A, it will transmit a "neighbor acquisition reply." If not, it will transmit a "neighbor acquisition refusal." If one of the routers wishes a "divorce," it transmits a "neighbor cease" message, to which the other router replies with a "neighbor cease acknowledgment."

Neighbor Acquisition

# of octets	
1	version number = 1
1	type = 3
1	code
1	info
2	checksum
2	AS number
2	identification number

Figure 10.48

Version number is 1.

Type is 3, designating this as a neighbor acquisition message of some sort.

Code is one of the following:

> 0 = neighbor acquisition request
>
> 1 = neighbor acquisition reply
>
> 2 = neighbor acquisition refusal
>
> 3 = neighbor cease
>
> 4 = neighbor cease acknowledgment

"Info" depends on the message type:

1. For a refusal message, 1 indicates that the transmitter is out of table space, and 2 indicates that there is an administrative prohibition against becoming neighbors.

2. For a cease message, 1 indicates that the transmitter is planning on going down soon, and 2 indicates that the neighbor relationship is no longer needed.

Checksum is the 16-bit 1's complement of the 1's complement sum of the EGP message starting with the EGP version number field.

AS number is the AS number of the router that generated the message.

The **identification number** aids in matching requests and replies.

10.2.2.2   Neighbor Reachability

The neighbor reachability aspect of EGP consists of two routers that are neighbors with each other sending messages back and forth to ensure that they are still alive and able to communicate. Each router periodically sends a "hello," and the other responds with an "I heard you" message.

Hello/I heard you

# of octets

1	version number = 1
1	type = 5
1	code
1	status
2	checksum
2	AS number
2	sequence number
1	minimum polling interval
1	reserved
2	last poll ID number

Figure 10.49

Type is 5.
Code is 0 for "hello," 1 for "I heard you."
Status is one of the following:

> 0 = No status given.

1 = "You appear reachable to me."

2 = "You appear unreachable to me due to neighbor reachability information."

3 = "You appear unreachable to me due to network reachability information."

4 = "You appear unreachable to me due to problems with my network interface."

The **sequence number** aids in matching requests and replies.

Minimum polling interval is the minimum number of minutes that the transmitting router would like the receiving router to wait between hello messages.

Last poll ID number gives the identification number of the most recent routing update message received from the router to which this *hello* or *I heard you* is being transmitted.

10.2.2.3   Routing Information

Basically, EGP is similar to a distance vector routing protocol. But there is one astounding difference. Instead of specifying the cost to a destination, a router merely reports whether or not the destination is reachable. EGP was designed for a very specific topology—namely, the assumption was that there was a "core" system to the Internet, which was the ARPANET, and that various routing domains attached to the core, usually with a single router.

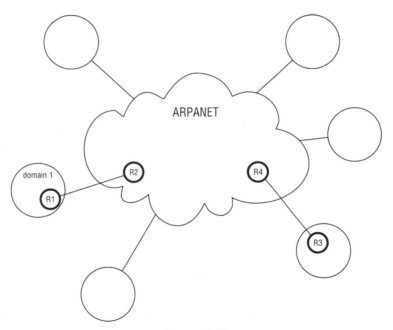

Figure 10.50

R1 discovers, through the intradomain routing protocol operating in domain 1, which IP "network numbers" are reachable inside domain 1. R1 informs R2 of that list of network numbers. R2 informs the other routers in the core domain, so that they will route traffic for any of the network numbers in domain 1 toward R2. R2 also informs R1 of all the network numbers reachable outside domain 1.

Note that this protocol does not work if there are any loops in the topology. For instance:

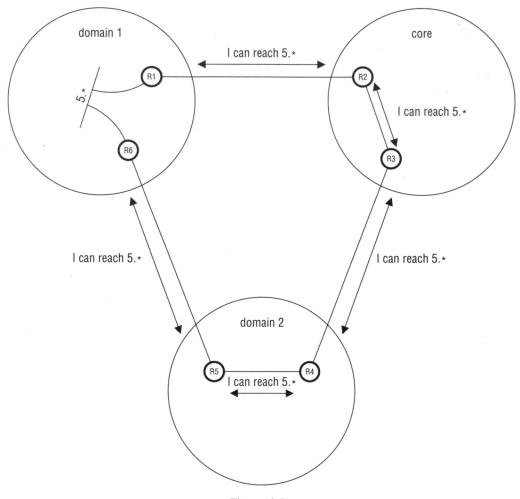

Figure 10.51

Assume that IP network number 5 is reachable in domain 1. R1 will inform R2 that 5 is reachable via R1. R2 will inform R3 that 5 is reachable via R2. R3 will inform R4 that 5 is reachable via R3. R4 will inform R5 that 5 is reachable via R4, and R5 will inform R6 that 5 is reachable via R5. Meanwhile, in the other direction, R6 will inform R5 that 5 is reachable via R6, etc.

When the core has a packet for network number 5, it has a choice. It will send the packet via either R2 or R3. If it sends the packet to R2, R2 has a choice. It knows it can send the packet to either R3 or R1. If it sends the packet to R1, and R1 is sensible, then R1 would deliver the packet to domain 1, since it ought to prefer reaching a destination it knows is reachable in the domain via intradomain routing. If, however, R2 sends the packet to R3, then R3 has no reason to prefer the "clockwise" direction in which the packet has been traveling and is equally likely to send the packet back to R2. The packet does not keep a diary of its travels. It will eventually be dropped when the "lifetime" field becomes 0, but until then, the Internet will have no idea which way to send the packet, and it is as likely to loop as to get delivered.

Surprisingly, the EGP routing update message does include a metric when reporting the reachability of a destination, but the EGP designers explicitly preclude making routing decisions based on the metric, on the theory that metrics in different domains might be incomparable. For instance, RIP only allows a metric as large as 15. Other routing protocols would probably allow much larger metrics. If a router wishes to report the reachability of a destination with cost 59 with one metric, and has to translate it into the RIP metric in order to pass the information across an IP routing domain routed with RIP, the metric would somehow have to be compressed into a much smaller number. The decision was to deal with incomparable metrics by mandating a loop-free topology and ignoring the metrics.

Another subtlety of the EGP protocol is that a routing message includes the IP addresses of other routers, and for each router listed, there is a list of destinations. The purpose of this is to allow a single router on a LAN to speak on behalf of other routers on the LAN. If a router were not allowed to speak on behalf of other routers on the LAN, then each pair of routers on the LAN would need to be exchanging EGP information. It is more efficient to funnel routing information through one router, which gathers information from all the other routers and keeps all the other routers informed.

If the router with which all the other routers communicate simply advertised the set of all destinations it has learned about through the other routers on the LAN, then all traffic for the advertised network numbers would be sent to the transmitting router, and an extra hop might be required on the LAN (see Fig. 10.52).

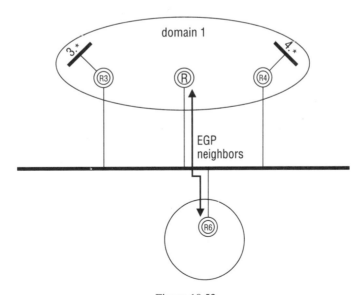

Figure 10.52

Suppose that R is an EGP neighbor of all the other routers, and no other routers are neighbors with each other (which is a legal configuration). This might be desired instead of having all the routers communicate in a pairwise fashion. If R simply advertised reachability of all the network numbers to R6, then R6 would send traffic for network 4 to R, which would forward it to R4. To eliminate the extra hop, R does not simply advertise reachability of network 4 but rather advertises that network 4 is reachable via router 4.

EGP network reachability messages can be transmitted in response to a poll or on the initiative of the transmitter. What would initiate transmission of an unsolicited network reachability message is not defined, but presumably, such a message is sent either periodically or when the information changes.

A network reachability poll looks like this:

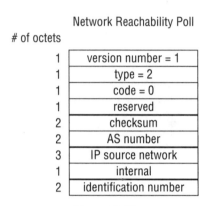

Figure 10.53

The EGP network reachability packet looks like this:

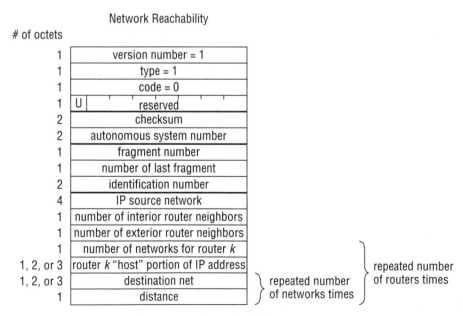

Figure 10.54

The **U** bit indicates whether the routing message is being sent in response to a poll (0) or is being sent unsolicited (1).

The **autonomous system number** is a globally unique 16-bit number identifying the autonomous system (the routing domain). It is globally unique because each IP routing domain is supposed to acquire an AS number from the IP addressing authority.

The **fragment number** is used in case a routing message does not fit into a single packet. If the routing message does fit, the field is set to 0.

The **number of last fragment** is the number of the final fragment, or 0 if the message did not require fragmentation.

The **identification number** is copied from the poll, so that responses can be matched to polls.

The **IP source network** gives the network portion of the address of the LAN on which all the routers mentioned in the message reside. The field is 4 octets long, but only the network portion of the address is nonzero. For example, if it is a class A network number, the second, third, and fourth octets of the IP source network field will be 0.

The sum of the next two fields (**number of interior router neighbors** and **number of exterior router neighbors**) indicates the number of routers on behalf of which the transmitter of this routing message is including reachability information. Interior routers (i.e., routers in the same AS as the EGP transmitter) are listed first.

The **number of networks** indicates the number of IP destination addresses reported on behalf of the router—say, R—listed in the next field.

The **router IP address** is the IP address of R, which can reach the network numbers advertised next. It only includes the "host" portion of the IP address. Therefore, it is 1, 2, or 3 octets, depending on whether the IP source network field at the beginning of the packet is class A (in which case, the bottom 3 octets of R's IP address are listed), class B, or class C.

The **destination network address** is the IP address of a destination network. The field is 1, 2, or 3 octets, depending on whether the address is class A, B, or C.

The **distance** is claimed in the EGP spec to be the number of hops from R to the advertised destination, but it is really assumed to be a metric that has meaning only within R's AS.

10.2.3 BGP

BGP is intended as a replacement for EGP. Neighbor BGP routers communicate over a reliable transport layer connection. The purpose of running on top of the transport layer is so that the BGP protocol can assume that communication with neighbors is reliable.

BGP is a distance vector routing protocol. But instead of transmitting the cost to a destination, a BGP router transmits the sequence of autonomous system numbers in the path to the destination IP address. Each BGP router R is configured with algorithms to rank routes. R calculates its preferred route to a particular IP address and announces that route in its routing message to its BGP neighbors.

Because BGP enumerates the route to each destination, it does not suffer from the counting-to-infinity problem that most distance vector routing protocols have.

10.2.3.1 BGP Attributes

A BGP update message describes the route from the BGP router R that generated the update message to a particular destination D. As part of the description of the route to D, R includes some number of fields, each of which is called an *attribute*. BGP has defined some terms that apply to attributes. Note that the definitions of the words in the following list apply only to BGP. I personally find the BGP terminology very confusing and hope that the way in which these words are used by BGP does not propagate beyond BGP.

1. *"Well-known" versus "optional"*: A well-known attribute is one that all BGP implementations must recognize—i.e., be able to understand when received. The term BGP uses to describe the opposite of *well-known* is *optional*. An optional attribute is one that need not be recognized by all BGP implementations.

2. *"Mandatory" versus "discretionary"*: A mandatory attribute is one that must appear in the description of a route. A discretionary attribute need not appear.

3. *"Partial"*: An attribute marked as "partial" has been passed along, unmodified, by a BGP router that has not implemented the attribute. BGP has not invented a word for the opposite of partial.

4. *"Transitive" versus "nontransitive"*: A transitive attribute is one that can be passed along unmodified by a BGP router that has not implemented the attribute. After this occurs, the attribute is marked as partial. A nontransitive attribute is one that must be deleted by a BGP router that has not implemented the attribute.

Most combinations of these attributes make no sense. For instance, if an attribute is mandatory, then it has to be well-known, since a BGP router must include a mandatory attribute in every route it describes. If an attribute is well-known, then the transitive/nontransitive distinction makes no sense, since all BGP routers along the path will have implemented the attribute—in which case, there is no reason to specify what a BGP router that has not implemented the attribute should do with it. The combinations that "make sense" are "well-known mandatory," "well-known discretionary," "optional transitive," and "optional nontransitive."

The attributes currently defined by BGP are as follows:

1. *Origin:* This has one of three values:

    a. "IGP" means that the information was originally learned from the routing protocol operating within the AS in which the destination resides and is therefore assumed as trustworthy.

    b. "EGP" means that the information was learned from the EGP protocol. As stated earlier, EGP does not work in the presence of topological loops. Therefore, if the origin field on a route is equal to EGP, the route would probably be less preferred than a route whose origin is equal to IGP.

c. The third value of origin is named "incomplete." It seems to have two uses. One is to indicate that the path was learned through some means other than EGP or IGP. For example, it might have been learned through static configuration. The other use is to mark an AS path that has been truncated because it is associated with a destination that is now unreachable. Since the AS path is classified as a mandatory attribute, it must appear, even though the destination is being reported as unreachable.

The origin attribute is classified as well-known and mandatory.

2. *AS path:* This is an enumeration of the autonomous systems along the path to the destination. An AS is identified by a 2-octet number.

    This attribute is classified as well-known and mandatory.

3. *Next hop:* This is the IP address of a router R2 on the same subnet as the BGP speaker R1 that is announcing the route to destination D. The purpose of including this attribute is that it is sometimes better to have R1 announce routes on behalf of R2. If the next hop attribute were not present, then the packet would actually be forwarded through R1. The presence of the attribute indicates that although R1 is announcing the route, it is actually R2 toward which packets should be forwarded.

    Next hop is classified as well-known and mandatory. (Note: It really ought to be well-known and discretionary, but when I pointed that out to one of the BGP designers he agreed and said, "Oh, well." No real harm done; it just means the attribute must always be reported even though it is often not useful for anything.)

4. *Unreachable:* This attribute, if present, indicates that a formerly advertised route is no longer correct.

    Unreachable is classified as well-known and discretionary.

5. *Inter-AS metric:* This attribute allows a BGP speaker in AS 1 to announce its intra-AS cost to a destination within AS 1. This information is allowed to be used by BGP routers within an AS bordering AS 1 to select a more optimal entry point into AS 1 to reach the destination. However, this metric is not allowed to be propagated by BGP speakers in an AS bordering AS 1 to ASs farther away.

    Note: I think the name *Intra-AS metric* would be more appropriate for this attribute.

    Inter-AS metric is classified as optional and nontransitive.

There is no defined attribute that is optional and transitive.

10.2.3.2 BGP Policies

A policy in BGP is manually configured information that can enable a BGP router to rank routes according to preference. Most routing protocols associate an integer with a path to a destination, which is known as the "cost" to the destination. With an integer, it is easy to rank routes. The route with the smallest cost is the preferred route.

Because BGP does not advertise a cost to a destination, some other means must exist for a router to determine which of several routes it should choose. BGP allows very complex policies. It assumes there is some local method of managing a BGP router to construct a function that will take as input all the information advertised in a BGP update message about a particular destination and output a number. Once different possible routes are mapped to numbers, the routes can be compared. The preferred route would be the one that maps to the smallest number.

10.2.3.3 Message Types

BGP has four types of messages:

1. Open

2. Update

3. Notification

4. Keepalive

The "open" message is the first message transmitted when a link to a BGP neighbor comes up. The "update" message contains routing information. The "notification" message is the final message transmitted on a link to a BGP neighbor, just before the link is disconnected. The "keepalive" message is used to reassure a neighbor, in the absence of routing news, that the transmitter is still alive.

10.2.3.4 Message Formats

All messages start with the following fields:

Common header

```
# of octets
        16  | marker  |
         2  | length  |
         1  | type    |
```

Figure 10.55

The **marker** field is used for authentication. As with authentication in the other routing protocols, it is only a placeholder, created on the assumption that someone will someday invent a reasonable authentication scheme. As of the writing of this book, the only authentication scheme defined in the BGP spec is the null authentication scheme, which requires that the marker field be set to all 1's.

The **length** field is the number of octets in the BGP message, including the header.

The **type** field is one of the following:

1 = open

2 = update

3 = notification

4 = keepalive

10.2.3.4.1 Open Message Format

The "open" message contains the following fields:

Open

# of octets	
19	common header
1	version
2	my autonomous system
2	hold time
4	BGP identifier
1	authentication code
12	authentication data

Figure 10.56

Version is 3.

My autonomous system gives the AS number of the transmitter.

Hold time indicates how long the receiver should wait before assuming that the transmitter is dead. The transmitter agrees to transmit a keepalive and/or an update and/or a notification message before hold time seconds elapse.

BGP identifier is an IP address of the transmitter. A BGP router picks an IP address as its identifier and uses that in all its messages.

Authentication code defines the authentication mechanism. The only authentication mechanism defined is code 0, which is the null mechanism.

Authentication data is a field whose length and contents are defined according to the type of authentication being used. For type 0, the only type defined in the BGP spec, the authentication data field has a length of 0.

10.2.3.4.2 Update Message Format

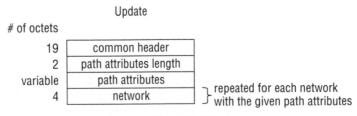

Update

# of octets	
19	common header
2	path attributes length
variable	path attributes
4	network

⎫ repeated for each network
⎬ with the given path attributes

Figure 10.57

The **path attributes** is a sequence of fields, each describing one attribute, and is encoded as follows:

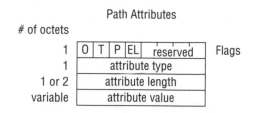

Figure 10.58

Flags

O, if set, indicates "optional."

T, if set, indicates "transitive."

P, if set, indicates "partial."

EL ("extended length"), if set, indicates that the length field is 2 octets; if clear, it indicates that the length field is 1 octet.

Attribute type is one of:

1 = "origin"; length: 1 octet

2 = "AS path"; variable-length

3 = "next hop"; length: 4 octets

4 = "unreachable"; length: 0 octets

5 = "Inter-AS metric"; length: 2 octets

10.2.3.4.3 Notification Message Format

A "notification" message is an error message sent by router R1 to explain to BGP neighbor router R2 why R1 is closing the connection to R2. The notification message contains the following fields:

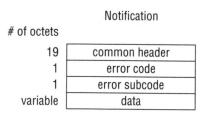

Figure 10.59

Basically, every field in every message that could contain a value that the receiver might reject is covered in the various codes. The **data** field contains the offending field.

The **error codes** are as follows:

1 = *message header error*, for which the subcodes are:

1 = unacceptable marker field value.

2 = unacceptable message length.

3 = unacceptable message type.

2 = *problem with "open" message*, for which the subcodes are:

1 = unsupported version number.

2 = unacceptable AS number.

3 = unacceptable IP address.

4 = unsupported authentication code.

5 = authentication failure (authentication type supported, but marker field is the wrong value).

3 = *problem with "update" message*, for which the subcodes are:

1 = malformed attribute list (for instance, an attribute appears twice).

2 = unrecognized "well-known" attribute.

3 = missing "mandatory" attribute. (Actually, the BGP spec calls this "missing well-known attribute," but that's not what it meant.)

4 = attribute flags error, meaning that there was a conflict between the receiver's notion of what kind of attribute a particular attribute was and what was flagged by the transmitter of the update message (for instance, the receiver thought that attribute number X was optional, but the transmitter set the flag claiming that it wasn't).

5 = attribute length error.

6 = invalid "origin" attribute.

7 = the specified AS path has a loop in it.

8 = invalid "next hop" attribute.

9 = optional attribute error, meaning that the receiver understood the attribute and was able to check the value and discover that it was incorrect.

10 = invalid "network" field. BGP does not pass along a mask when it refers to a destination. Instead, it expects that the reported destination will be a "network number" rather than a "subnetwork number." If any unexpected bits are set in the destination address in an update message, then this error is reported. For instance, this error would be reported if the destination address is a class B network number and any bits are set in the final 2 octets.

4 = *hold time expired*, during which no BGP messages were received from the BGP neighbor.

10.2.3.4.4 Keepalive Message Format

There is no information in a "keepalive" message other than the standard BGP header. A keepalive message is sent when it has been so long since the preceding BGP message had to be sent that the hold timer might expire unless something were transmitted.

10.2.4   IDRP

IDRP started out just being a version of BGP with the fields modified to be suitable for ISO addresses rather than IP addresses. And of course, the document needed to be translated into ISO terminology to make it more fun to read.

However, many modifications to IDRP were suggested once it was introduced into ISO. Most of the modifications improve the protocol a great deal. Some people would like to see these improvements fed back into BGP. Others feel that BGP should cease to exist and, instead, IDRP should be modified to support both ISO and IP addresses, as IS-IS was. Then, rather than having two protocols shadowing each other's modifications, the world would merely have to cope with a single interdomain routing protocol. Sounds good to me.

As of the writing of this book, IDRP is not stable enough for its packet formats to be taken seriously. But the basic concepts are unlikely to change a great deal. This subsection discusses the aspects of IDRP that are different from BGP.

Also as of the writing of this book, there are some extremely complex things in IDRP that I am hoping will be removed from the protocol and that do in fact have a good chance of being removed. Although I describe some of them in this subsection, I do not describe others, since they may be removed, they are not particularly interesting, and reading about them would definitely give you a headache.

Some IDRP terms to remember while reading this subsection: *RD* is a "routing domain." *RDI* is a "routing domain identifier." And *BIS* stands for "border intermediate system," which is merely an IDRP router.

10.2.4.1   Metrics

IDRP actually provides attributes of a path that consist of the cost to the destination according to each of the four possible metrics. The metrics are optional.

In my opinion, the addition of metrics is a vast improvement to the protocol. It means there can be a simple basis for choosing a path rather than relying on configured "policy." IDRP routers should have a default "policy" that consists of choosing the path with the smallest reported metric. The enumerated route would still be an attribute of a path, but the only use for the enumerated route would be to detect routing loops. People who wanted to configure complex policies would be free to do so, but people who just wanted things to work could rely on choosing the route with the smallest metric.

Without the metrics, it is still possible to have a single simple default policy, which is to use the path with the smallest number of listed RDs. But the metric is likely to be a more useful measure of the quality of the path than simply counting the RDs.

10.2.4.2   Confederations

A *confederation* is a group of routing domains. The chief reason for inventing the concept of confederations is to accommodate larger networks by aggregating information. Without confederations, the complete list of RDs along the path to a destination must be reported in the routing update message. With confederations, if several RDs in the path are all in the same confederation, only the confederation need be listed. It is also claimed that confederations simplify configuring policies, since it is easier to configure a policy such as "don't use routes that go through confederation X" than to list a separate "don't use routes that go through RD Y" policy for each of the RDs in confederation X. The belief is that people will not aggregate RDs into a confederation unless there is no need for policies to treat the aggregated RDs differently.

As is always the case when hierarchy is added, confederations trade off storage and other protocol overhead against optimal routing. Once information is aggregated, routes become less optimal.

IDRP requires each routing domain to have an unambiguous identifier, known as an RDI. The RDIs will be assigned the same way NSAPs are assigned. (For those of you who care, the method of assigning them is described in ISO documents 7498 and 8348/AD2.) In fact, an RDI will be an address prefix. The most natural RDI for a routing domain is the IDP of one of the areas in the RD. The address prefix need not describe every system within the RD. It merely needs to be unique—i.e., no other RD can have the same RDI.

A confederation has an identifier as well. A confederation identifier is assigned exactly the same way an RDI is assigned, and indeed, based on the identifier, there is no way of knowing whether the identifier applies to a confederation or an RD. Systems outside a confederation see the confederation as being a normal, single RD. Only IDRP routers within the confederation are aware of the fact that the confederation contains multiple RDs.

Clumping RDs into a confederation restricts the number of possible routes, because IDRP enumerates the RDs along a path. If a path were to exit and then reenter the same confederation, it would appear to have a loop. A confederation cannot be listed in a route twice. For example:

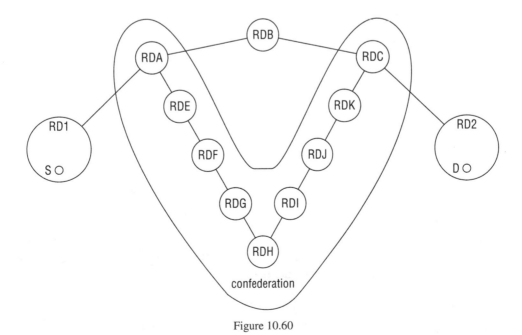

Figure 10.60

In Fig. 10.60, the path RD1–RDA–RDB–RDC–RD2, which is clearly preferable, cannot be used, since a route cannot exit and then reenter a confederation. The only route IDRP will be able to find is RD1, RDA, RDE, RDF, RDG, RDH, RDI, RDJ, RDK, RDC, RD2.

Confederations can be disjoint, overlapping, or nested.

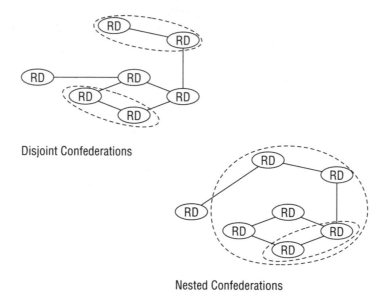

Disjoint Confederations

Nested Confederations

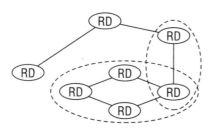

Overlapping Confederations

Figure 10.61

A route is a sequence of RDIs. A confederation identifier looks just like an RDI. Therefore, any of the RDIs in a route can actually be a confederation. Just as with BGP, IDRP routers report the RDs along the path to the destination. Once a group of RDs has been assigned to be in a confederation, the RDIs of RDs within that confederation will no longer be visible outside the confederation. BISs within the confederation will report the RDIs of RDs within that confederation to other BISs within the confederation. But once the route is reported to a BIS outside the confederation, all RDIs of RDs internal to the confederation must disappear in the route, and be replaced with the confederation identifier.

The protocol for accomplishing this involves the following:

1. Each BIS is configured with the RDI of the RD to which it belongs as well as the identifiers of any confederations to which it belongs.

2. Each BIS is further configured with the nesting rules for the confederations to which its RD belongs. If the RD belongs to confederations X and Y, and X is nested within Y, the BIS will be configured to know that X is nested within Y. If X and Y are disjoint or overlapping, the BIS will not be configured with any nesting rules with respect to X and Y.

3. Each BIS exchanges information about RDs and confederation membership with each neighbor. In this way, each BIS knows when it is on the boundary of an RD or a confederation.

4. Routes to a particular destination accumulate outward from the destination (this is just ordinary distance vector routing). When BIS A receives a route from BIS B, and A knows that A is in confederation X and B is not, A makes a note in the route that the route is now entering confederation X. Within X, the route accumulates RDIs for the RDs in X. Finally, the route may get reported to some BIS on the other side of X. The BIS on the boundary must get rid of all RDIs within X before reporting the route to the BIS outside X. The boundary BIS accomplishes this by searching the route backward until it encounters the marker noting that the route entered X. The BIS then deletes that entire section of route and replaces it with the single RDI "X."

5. The method of marking a route as entering a confederation is to first append a 0-length RDI to the route and then append the RDI of the confederation being entered. I'll refer to that marker (the 0-length RDI) as "enter."

6. When a BIS on the boundary of confederations X and Y receives a route from a BIS that is not in X and Y, it adds "enter X enter Y" to the route. If the BIS has been configured to believe that X is nested within Y, then it will append "enter X" after "enter Y." Otherwise, the order is arbitrary.

For example:

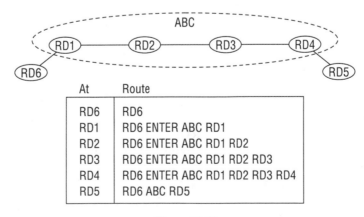

At	Route
RD6	RD6
RD1	RD6 ENTER ABC RD1
RD2	RD6 ENTER ABC RD1 RD2
RD3	RD6 ENTER ABC RD1 RD2 RD3
RD4	RD6 ENTER ABC RD1 RD2 RD3 RD4
RD5	RD6 ABC RD5

Figure 10.62

Now let's consider an example with a confederation BAR, nested within confederation ABC:

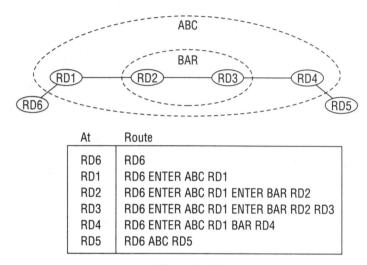

At	Route
RD6	RD6
RD1	RD6 ENTER ABC RD1
RD2	RD6 ENTER ABC RD1 ENTER BAR RD2
RD3	RD6 ENTER ABC RD1 ENTER BAR RD2 RD3
RD4	RD6 ENTER ABC RD1 BAR RD4
RD5	RD6 ABC RD5

Figure 10.63

When a confederation BAR is truly nested inside confederation ABC, network managers would expect BAR to be invisible outside ABC. Policies at BISs external to ABC would not mention BAR. Routes as seen by BISs external to ABC should not mention BAR.

On the other hand, if ABC and BAR overlap and a route travels through both ABC and BAR, it is possible for the route to record that only one of the confederations was visited or that both were visited.

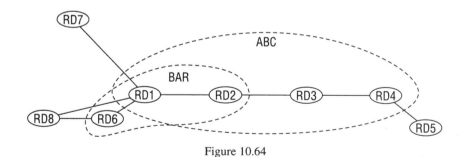

Figure 10.64

In the path RD5–RD4–RD3–RD2–RD1–RD6–RD8, ABC is entered first, then BAR is entered, then ABC is exited, then BAR is exited. By the time it reaches RD8, the route looks like RD5–ABC–BAR–RD8.

In the path RD5–RD4–RD3–RD2–RD1–RD7, ABC is entered, then BAR is entered, then both are exited simultaneously. In that case, when it reaches RD7, the route will look like RD5–ABC–RD7.

In the path RD7–RD1–RD8, BAR and ABC are entered simultaneously and exited simultaneously. If the BIS in RD1 that receives the route from the BIS in RD7 writes "enter ABC enter BAR," then it depends on the order in which the BIS exiting RD1 "cleans up" ABC and BAR. If it processes exiting BAR first, then the resulting route will be RD7–ABC. If it processes exiting ABC first, then the resulting route will be RD7–ABC–BAR. If ABC and BAR are really overlapping rather than one being nested within the other, then it doesn't matter which is chosen. If one is nested within the other, though, it is important that the inner confederation not be visible outside. For this reason, BISs are configured with the nesting rules for the confederations of which they are members.

For instance, in Fig. 10.65, the following nesting rules would be configured.

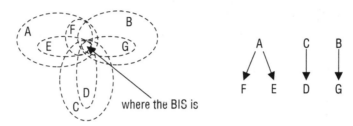

Figure 10.65

10.2.4.2.1   Detecting Confederation Boundaries

Two BISs, A and B, go through an initial handshake to become neighbors. In the handshake, each informs the other of the RD in which it resides, along with the confederations to which it believes it belongs. Assume that A is in RDX and in confederations {L, M, N, P}; B is in RDY and in confederations {M, P, R, V}. A knows that the link to B exits L and N but is internal to M and P. A and B can detect some error conditions with the original handshake:

1. If A and B are in the same RD, they should usually be configured with the same confederations. If they aren't, this may not actually be an error. Instead, it might be due to the fact that a new confederation is being formed and A has been told about it but B has not yet been advised. Therefore, A and B should not refuse to be neighbors because of this anomaly, but they should log an event so that the network manager can eventually fix the situation.

2. If A has been told that M is nested inside L, but neighbor B is in M and not in L, then clearly, M is not nested in L. This is an error, and A should report it.

10.2.4.2.2   Entering Confederations

When a BIS reports a route to a destination in its own RD, or receives a route from a BIS that is not in some of the confederations, it must report that all the appropriate confederations are being entered, and it must do so in an order such that any confederation

F nested within confederation A is reported entered after confederation A is reported entered. For instance, given a BIS located in confederations A, B, C, D, and E with nesting rules "B contained in A," "C contained in A," and "E contained in D," then an order such as "enter A enter B enter C enter D enter E" is legal. Any order is legal as long as A comes before B, A comes before C, and D comes before E.

10.2.4.2.3   Updates Out of a Confederation

When BIS B1 has a neighbor BIS B2 in the same set of confederations, but B2 is in a different RD, B1 simply passes the route to B2. B2 will add its RDI to the route.

When BIS B1 has a neighbor BIS B2, and B1 is in some confederations to which B2 does not belong, then B1 must collapse the portion of the route dealing with any confederations being exited before passing the route to B2.

Assume that confederations A, B, C, D, and E are being exited. Assume, again, that B and C are nested within A and E is nested within D. B1 must start with the inner confederations and proceed to the outer confederations. This is the opposite of the order in which a BIS would report entrances.

For each confederation X, B1 scans backward in the route to find an "enter X" marker.

1. If "enter X" is not found, the route is in error.

2. If "enter X" is found and there are no intervening "enter" markers, then the route from the "enter X" marker to the end is replaced by "X."

3. If "enter Y" is found and B1 thinks that X is nested within Y, then:

    a. Case 1: If there are no RDIs between the "enter X" and "enter Y" markers, then reorder the "enter X" and "enter Y" markers and continue processing as if the "enter X" had appeared after the "enter Y."

    b. Case 2: If there are RDIs between the "enter X" and "enter Y" marker, then X is not nested within Y, and either B1 has been misconfigured or the route is in error.

4. If "enter Z" is found and B1 is not in confederation Z, then B1 declares the route in error.

5. If "enter Z" is found and X is not nested within Z, then the portion of the route between the "enter X" and "enter Z" markers is replaced by "X enter Z."

10.2.4.2.4   Forming a Confederation

It is important to be able to form a confederation in a working network by configuring BISs one at a time.

To form a confederation that has no confederations nested within it:

1. First, the managers of all BISs to which this confederation will be visible must be warned that a new confederation will be formed consisting of a particular set

of RDs. Note that if the new confederation is actually to be nested within another confederation, the existence of the new confederation will not be noticeable to any BISs outside the nesting confederation. Thus, the affected BISs are those within the lowest-level confederation in which this new confederation will be nested. If there are multiple overlapping confederations in which the new confederation will be nested, and the new confederation will not be nested within any smaller confederation that is, in turn, nested within one of the overlapping confederations, the BISs in all those confederations will be affected.

2. The manager of a BIS that has policies regarding any of the RDs in the set that will form the new confederation must modify those policies. The RDs in the set can no longer be differentiated, so if the existing policy is that it's OK to route through some of those RDs but not through others, a single policy regarding the RDs in that set must be formulated.

3. The policy regarding the new confederation must be *added* to the existing set of policies (the confederation will not appear immediately).

4. When enough time has elapsed so that managers have been given ample opportunity to modify the policies at their BISs, the managers of the BISs in the new confederation can start informing those BISs about the confederation.

5. One-by-one, each BIS is informed that it is in the confederation. The order in which the BISs are modified is critical. At all times, the set of BISs that have been informed about the confederation must be connected. Thus, the confederation must be built gradually outward until all the BISs have been modified.

6. When all the BISs in the confederation have been modified, the managers of remote BISs can be informed that the confederation has been fully formed, and the policies regarding the RDs in the confederation can now safely be deleted.

Note that the preceding rules apply as well if the new confederation to be formed is one that is nested within another confederation. The only difference involved when the new confederation is to be nested within a confederation X is that the managers of BISs that are not contained within X need not be informed about the formation of the new confederation. Also note that the BISs internal to X still need to retain their policies regarding the RDs and confederations within X.

10.2.4.3 Reliable Delivery

IDRP includes a reliable end-to-end protocol similar to a transport layer protocol. Each IDRP message to a neighbor contains an acknowledgment number and a sequence number. In contrast, BGP runs on top of TCP, so BGP does not need to implement its own transport layer.

Although it is true that distance vector routing protocols require reliable delivery, they don't require reliable delivery of *every* protocol message. For instance, if router R1 reports that the distance to destination D is 50 and later reports that the distance to D is

41, the earlier message about D need not be delivered. Only the most recent information about D must be delivered. But it was decided that adding a reliable end-to-end protocol that delivered every IDRP message would be simple and that IDRP routing information was unlikely to change so quickly that significant amounts of information would be overwritten by new information before being acknowledged.

10.2.4.4 IDRP Packets

IDRP has the following types of packets:

1. Open

2. Update

3. Error notification

4. Keepalive

5. Checksum

6. Cease

7. Refresh

The first four types have equivalents in BGP. The purpose of the "checksum" packet is to summarize the routing database to ensure that IDRP neighbors are correctly synchronized. The "cease" packet is a way of informing a BGP neighbor that the router that transmitted the packet wishes to close the connection between them. The "refresh" packet is a method of requesting retransmission of some of the routing information.

Since IDRP is not particularly stable as of the writing of this book, I will not give exact packet formats. Furthermore, I will just describe the update and open packets, since they are the only ones that contain complicated information.

All IDRP packets start out with the following fixed header:

Fixed Header

# of octets	
1	interdomain routing protocol ID
2	length
1	version
1	type
4	sequence number
4	ack number
16	validation pattern

Figure 10.66

Interdomain routing protocol ID: A constant specified in the spec.

Length: Number of octets in this packet, including both header and data.

Version: A constant specified in the spec.

Type: One of the following:

>   Open
>
>   Update
>
>   Error notification
>
>   Keepalive
>
>   Checksum
>
>   Cease
>
>   Refresh

Sequence number: Number of this message.

Ack number: Indicates that all IDRP messages from this neighbor with a sequence number equal to or smaller than this one were successfully received.

Validation pattern: This is similar to the **marker** field in BGP. The intention is that depending on the value of the **authentication code** in the open message, this field is either a simple checksum to detect data corruption or a cryptographic integrity plus authentication of the transmitter.

10.2.4.4.1   Open

	Open
# of octets	
29	fixed header
2	hold time
2	maximum PDU size
1	outstanding PDU's (window size allowed)
1	RDI length of transmitter's RD
variable	RDI of transmitter
variable	attributes
variable	confederations
1	authentication code
variable	authentication data

Figure 10.67

Hold time is the maximum number of seconds that the transmitter of the "open" packet will ever wait between successive transmissions of IDRP messages to the receiving router.

Maximum PDU size is the maximum-size packet (in octets) that the transmitting router can receive.

Outstanding PDUs is the maximum number of IDRP messages that may be sent to this IDRP router without receiving an acknowledgment.

RDI length and **RDI of transmitter** give the identifier of the RD in which the transmitting IDRP router resides.

Attributes is a list of all the different attributes for which this IDRP will report routes. For instance, for a particular destination, the route according to each of the four metrics might be different, and therefore, each route must be reported separately.

Confederations is the set of confederations in which the transmitting router resides.

Authentication code indicates the type of checksum to be included in the "authentication data" field.

Authentication data is a noncryptographic checksum if the code equals 1. This field is a 16-octet encrypted checksum if the code equals 2.

10.2.4.4.2   Update

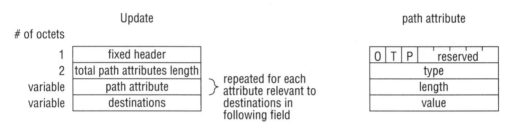

Figure 10.68

Each update packet contains a set of attributes and a set of destinations for which the set of attributes applies.

Flags

> **O**, if set, indicates "optional."
>
> **T**, if set, indicates "transitive."
>
> **P**, if set, indicates "partial."
>
> **Destinations** is a list of address prefixes.

The attribute types are:

1. *EXTINFO:* A 0-length attribute used to flag that at least some of the information in this path attribute has been obtained through some method not specified in IDRP.

2. *RDPATH:* The path to the destination enumerated as a sequence of RDs.

3. *NEXTHOP:* As in BGP, this attribute allows an IDRP router to report routes on behalf of a neighbor IDRP router without incurring an extra hop that would make data packet routing suboptimal.

4. *UNREACHABLE:* A flag indicating that this destination, for which a route has previously been reported, is unreachable.

5. *DISTLISTINCL:* "Distribution list inclusive." Gives a list of RDs to which this route can be passed.

6. *DISTLISTEXCL:* "Distribution list exclusive." Gives a list of RDs to which this route cannot be passed.

7. *MULTIEXITDISC:* This attribute may be used to optimize the entry point into an adjacent RD.

8. *LOCALPREF:* This attribute is intended to inform other IDRP routers in the same RD of the mapping between the route and the numerical preference decided upon, when computing the preference of the route according to configured policy. The idea behind this attribute is that it enables IDRP routers in the same RD to compare in order to determine whether they have been configured with the same policies.

   There is no reason why IDRP routers in the same RD must be configured with identical policies. It is even quite useful in certain cases to configure different policies into different routers. Therefore, I see no justification for having this attribute.

9. *TRANSIT DELAY:* Cost of the route according to the "delay" metric.

10. *RESIDUAL ERROR COST:* Cost of the route according to the "error" metric.

11. *EXPENSE:* Cost of the route according to the "expense" metric.

12. *CAPACITY:* Cost of the route according to the "default" metric, which is intended to represent bandwidth.

13. *SOURCE-SPECIFIC QOS:* Cost of the route according to the source-specific quality of service.

    I can't imagine how this would work or be useful. Nobody on the committee claims to understand this either, but since it is possible to put source-specific QOS into a CLNP packet, at least the draft of IDRP as of the writing of this book contains this attribute.

14. *DESTINATION-SPECIFIC QOS:* Cost of the route according to the destination-specific quality of service. (The opinion I expressed regarding the source-specific QOS attribute applies in this case, too.)

15. *RDHOPCOUNT:* The number of RDs in the route. (Note that due to confederations, this number can be greater than the number of RDIs in the enumerated route.)

Homework

1. Give an algorithm for computing the mask for a particular destination reported in a RIP message.

2. In RIP, assume that a router R does not keep the latest distance vector from each neighbor and throws out the information it has stored that destination D is reachable at cost X via neighbor N after 180 sec have elapsed without receipt of information confirming this.

   What should R do when its information about destination D times out? What should R do if it receives information from neighbor M indicating a shorter path to D through M? What should R do if it receives information from N indicating a longer path to D through N?

3. Suppose that a task force wanted to improve RIP. What suggestions would you make? Now suppose that the task force were operating under the constraint that any improvements in the protocol had to interwork with unmodified current RIP implementations. Indicate whether the benefits of the suggested improvements will be realized if there are still some old RIP implementations around or only if all routers have been modified to implement the new RIP.

4. Give a procedure for IS-IS for changing the area address of an area from A to B, with routers being configured one-by-one so as to cause minimal disruption to the area.

5. Give a procedure for IS-IS for splitting an area with area address A into two areas, one with area address A and one with area address B, with routers being configured one-by-one so as to cause minimal disruption to the area.

6. Design an automatic mechanism for detecting and repairing level 2 network partitions in IS-IS.

7. Suppose that in IS-IS, it were impossible to manually configure more than two area addresses into any single level 1 router. Would it then be possible for the area to have more than two area addresses?

   Now suppose that it were impossible to manually configure more than one area address into any single level 1 router. Would it then be possible for the area to have more than one area address?

8. In IS-IS, once all LSPs have been propagated through an area, is it possible for two level 1 routers in the area to have different opinions regarding the legal addresses for the area? In other words, is it possible for one of the level 1 routers to think that a particular address is outside the area and must be routed to a level 2 router and for another level 1 router to think that that address is inside the area?

9. In IS-IS, why is it necessary for all routers to agree on the value of maximum area addresses? When there are too many area addresses, why is it necessary to specify which subset of the area addresses a router should use?

10. In what topologies would it require less memory to store information about external IP addresses with a scheme in which the level 2 routers report their own distance to each externally reachable IP address instead of the scheme in OSPF, in which the combination of type 4 and type 5 LSPs is used?

11. Compare the LAN LSP distribution mechanisms in IS-IS and OSPF. Under what conditions would OSPF use less bandwidth? Under what conditions would IS-IS use less bandwidth?

12. In OSPF, an AS border router reports each reachable destination in a logically separate LSP. Suppose that an AS border router R crashed after reporting reachability to destination DEST. Suppose that R then restarts but cannot reach DEST and has no a priori knowledge that it used to be able to reach DEST. How will the rest of the network discover that DEST can no longer be reached via R? How long will it take for the rest of the network to discover this?

13. In OSPF, router R has only a single password on a link. In IS-IS, router R has a transmit password and a set of receive passwords. As explained in subsection 10.1.3.8, in OSPF, an intruder can listen for the password and start using it, but in IS-IS on a point-to-point link, the same trick will not work.

    In IS-IS on a LAN, what can an intruder without previous knowledge of the LAN password do in order to participate as a router?

14. Compare the memory requirements for storing link state information about IP destinations in OSPF and integrated IS-IS, both at level 1 and level 2. In particular, assume there are 10 AS boundary routers and that each AS boundary router reports information regarding 10,000 IP destination addresses reachable outside the AS. How much memory will this information require in the level 2 routers in OSPF versus IS-IS? How much memory will this information require in the level 1 routers in OSPF versus IS-IS?

15. Let routers R1 and R2 be neighbors. In OSPF, when the link between R1 and R2 first comes up, R1 needs to send R2 a complete database description, and R2 needs to send R1 a complete database description. As stated in subsection 10.1.3.9, if DD packets were functionally equivalent to IS-IS CSNPs rather than being functionally equivalent to IS-IS PSNPs, then it would only be necessary for R1 to send R2 a complete database description. Why is this true? How would processing of DD packets differ if the sequence of DD packets was treated as a CSNP?

16. Come up with a potential BGP attribute that it would make sense to classify as optional and transitive.

17. In IDRP, come up with an example topology and confederation membership in which there is no legal path between some pair of routing domains. In other words, physical connectivity exists between the two RDs, but because of the way confederations have been assigned, there is no path that IDRP will be able to find. Give an example involving a single confederation. Give an example involving two confederations, with the constraint that the confederations must be physically intact.

18. In IDRP, make rules similar to those given in subsection 10.2.4.2.4 for forming a confederation that has other confederations nested within it.

19. In IDRP, make rules similar to those given in subsection 10.2.4.2.4 for dissolving a confederation that has no confederations nested within it.

20. In IDRP, again, make rules similar to those given in subsection 10.2.4.2.4 for dissolving a confederation, but this time, the confederation to be dissolved has confederations nested within it (which will not be dissolved).

21. Invent a protocol for making distance vector routing reliable when it runs on top of a datagram service. BGP does it by running on top of TCP. IDRP does it by inventing its own reliable end-to-end transportlike protocol. Your protocol should ensure that the latest information gets through, without requiring that earlier, outdated information be transmitted first. Also, you cannot assume that all destinations are reported in each update. Instead, assume that there are many more destinations than can fit in a single update, and that in general, only the destinations for which the path has changed are transmitted in an update. For any particular destination whose path has changed, the update is transmitted and then later retransmitted if an ack has not been received for that destination within some amount of time—say, 10 sec.

Chapter 11
Sabotage-Proof Network Layer Protocols

When people think of a network component's failing, they generally assume that it fails in a *fail-stop* manner—i.e., it reverts instantaneously from working properly to stopping completely. But there can and does occur a different sort of failure, in which a node continues operating but functions incorrectly. This can result from software bugs, hardware faults, or even sabotage.

Chapter 1 mentioned this sort of fault and introduced the term *Byzantine failure*. In this chapter, I'll sketch how a network can be designed to be resilient to Byzantine failures. Such a network will continue operating even if someone has deployed maximally malicious software on some of the routers. It can safely be assumed that the designers of the malicious software thoroughly understand the network layer protocols and have done their best to be disruptive. Despite their best efforts, the resilient network will guarantee that data will continue to be transmitted from a properly functioning source to a properly functioning destination, provided that at least one path of properly functioning routers and links connects the source and destination.

Causing the network to malfunction is known as the *denial of service attack*. In this chapter I describe a method of designing network protocols that will withstand denial of service attacks.[1] The design is practical in the sense that the CPU, memory, bandwidth, and management requirements are not much greater than those for conventional networks. None of today's networks are built this way, which is not surprising because it was only recently demonstrated that sabotage-proof networks were possible. However, networks using the techniques in this chapter may become popular in the near future.

11.1 The Problem

The goal is to design a network that will guarantee that a packet transmitted between two nonfaulty end systems A and B will have a high probability of being delivered, provided that at least one path consisting of nonfaulty components connects the two end

---

[1] **This chapter summarizes the results first presented in R. Perlman, "Network Layer Protocols with Byzantine Robustness" (Ph.D. dissertation, Massachusetts Institute of Technology, 1988).**

systems. No guarantee is made that all messages sent by A for B will arrive at B—just that each packet independently has a high probability of reaching its destination. Node A can compensate for lost packets by using acknowledgments and retransmissions at a higher layer. The network layer makes no attempt to keep conversations private. If privacy is necessary, encryption must be done at a higher layer. Also, the network layer need not certify data that it delivers. For instance, it is possible for some malicious node C to generate data, get it delivered to B, and claim that the data was from A. It is up to the higher layer in B to differentiate between corrupted or counterfeit data and real data, using known cryptographic techniques.

11.2   All You Need to Know about Cryptography

The solution to the problem posed in the preceding section involves some cryptography. In this section, I describe all the fundamentals that are required in order to understand the solution.

There are two basic types of cryptography. In *secret key cryptography,* a magic number known as the *key* is shared by two or more parties. Encryption of message is performed by taking the message and the key and using a mathematical function with those two inputs, generating an *encrypted* message. The reverse operation, *decryption*, also requires use of the key (see Fig. 11.1). The most popular current algorithm for secret key cryptography is known as "DES," for "data encryption standard."

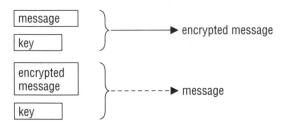

Figure 11.1   Encryption with secret key cryptography

A second type of cryptography is known as *public key cryptography.* In public key cryptography, two magic numbers are actually associated with each user. The first number is known as the *private key,* and the user must keep it secret. The other is known as the *public key,* and the user may advertise it widely. The two numbers are mathematically related, but the mathematical techniques are such that knowledge of one of the numbers does not enable you to calculate the other. Keys are typically hundreds of bits long. If you knew someone's public key and were able to guess the private key, you could verify that the number you guessed was indeed the private key. But since the only known technique for finding the private key, given just the public key, is to guess numbers at random, finding the private key is computationally infeasible.

Encryption of a message for user "Alice" is done with Alice's public key. The decryption operation, which is the inverse of the encryption operation, cannot be done with the public key; it requires use of the private key. Thus, anyone with knowledge of Alice's public key can encrypt a message for Alice, but only Alice will be able to decrypt the message (see Fig. 11.2).

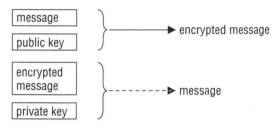

Figure 11.2   Encryption with public key cryptography

Encryption is not needed to design a superrobust network, but a concept known as a *digital signature* is. A digital signature is a number associated with a message, similar to a checksum. In public key cryptography, Alice can generate a signature for a particular message using her private key. Once the signature is generated, the public key is used to verify the signature. Thus, only Alice can generate a signature, but others can recognize Alice's signature. Note that the signature is a function of both the private key and the data. If any of the data is modified, the old signature is no longer valid. This is comparable to the way a checksum operates. If a message is modified, the checksum is no longer valid.

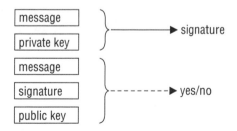

Figure 11.3   Signatures with public key cryptography

Given that anyone with knowledge of the public key can verify a signature, theoretically, someone could forge a signature by trying all possible numbers and then checking to see whether each number satisfies the verification procedure. However, since the numbers are so long, the probability is essentially zero that someone would be able to guess the signature within a reasonable amount of time.

Malicious routers can do anything physically possible, but they cannot do anything supernatural. It is safe to assume that a malicious node cannot guess a legitimate node's private key or forge a signature.

11.3   Overview of the Approach

In this section I'll describe a method of robustly delivering a packet to every possible destination in a network. Although this scheme is not very efficient for delivery of data, which is usually only supposed to be delivered to a single destination, this scheme is efficient for information like LSPs that should be delivered to all the routers. Although this scheme could be used for extremely reliable delivery of data packets, it would likely be used only for delivery of control information that needs to be broadcast. In section 11.3.2 I will describe how to use the control information that is robustly delivered through the techniques described in this section in order to calculate single destination routes for data packets.

11.3.1   Robust Flooding

First, I'll present a design for robust packet delivery based on flooding. With flooding, if a source emits a packet, the packet is theoretically guaranteed to reach the destination if any correctly functioning path to the destination exists. However, the problem is that resources are finite. In order for a packet to successfully travel from one node to the next, link bandwidth has to be available, and the next node must have both sufficient processing available to receive the packet and sufficient buffer space available to store the packet until it can be transmitted on the next link.

The key to accomplishing robust flooding is to structure databases in such a way that every source is guaranteed resources and to utilize digital signatures so that only the source can use its reserved resources.

In a truly resilient network, all the nodes are required to know the public keys of all the other nodes. Theoretically, this could be done by manual configuration, but that would be so inconvenient as to render the entire scheme infeasible. Instead, I will employ a special node known as the *public key distributor,* which distributes a special packet containing the public keys of all the nodes. To guard against Byzantine failure of the public key distributor, I will provide for multiple public key distributors.

Next, I will reserve a buffer for each source at each router. To ensure that only a packet emitted by the source occupies the buffer, the source puts a digital signature into the packet. To ensure that only the latest packet from the source occupies the buffer, the source also puts a sequence number into the packet.

This scheme turns out to be remarkably similar to LSP distribution, as described in Chapter 9. (In fact, after I designed sabotage-proof flooding I noticed that if the cryptography was removed from the design, the resulting protocol was simpler and more robust than previous protocols for flooding LSPs. As a result, I modified the LSP distribution protocol in IS-IS.)

11.3.1.1 Summary of Robust Flooding

The technique outlined in the preceding subsection will guarantee that packets are delivered, provided that at least one nonfaulty path connects source with destination. It is not as efficient as traditional networks because every packet is delivered to all nodes. It is not absurdly inefficient, though, since a packet will only travel over each link once. This makes the algorithm n^2, in the worst case, because there can be at most n^2 links with n nodes. In contrast, transparent bridges will deliver a packet to every destination in O (n), and source routing bridges will deliver an "all paths explorer packet" in O$((b^{13}) \times (p^{13}))$, where $b+1$ is the number of bridges per LAN and $p+1$ is the number of ports per bridge. So robust flooding is less efficient than broadcast using transparent bridges but far more efficient than broadcast using all paths explorer packets with source routing.

11.3.2 Robust Routing

Robust flooding is not very efficient when used for data packet routing, since every packet is delivered to every node. It is useful for broadcasting the public key distributor's information and LSPs, since those packets must be delivered everywhere. But data packets only need to be delivered to one destination.

To make the resilient network nearly as efficient as a conventional network, I'll use robust flooding only for LSPs and public key information. Once every node has a database of LSPs from every other node, I'll have the source node calculate the entire path that it would like to use to the destination.

Traditional network packet forwarding is done by having each router independently make a decision about the next hop. This form of routing only works if all the routers along the path have consistent LSP databases and compatible path-computation algorithms. Allowing the source to compute the route offers the following advantages:

1. All the routers along the path need not have consistent LSP databases. Only the information at the first router must be reasonably accurate, so that that router can find a correct path.

2. The router computing the route can use an arbitrarily complicated algorithm, such as computing routes that avoid certain routers of which the source router has reason to be suspicious because of previous unsuccessful attempts to route through those routers.

Once the source router chooses a route, it sets up the route by launching a special *route-setup* packet, which lists the route. The route-setup packet is cryptographically protected and travels along the route that the data packets will traverse. The routers along the path examine the route-setup packet and record the information that packets from source S to destination D should arrive from a specified neighbor and be forwarded to a specified neighbor. Once a path is set up, data packets travel along it. Data packets are not cryptographically protected. If the path consists of correctly functioning nodes and links, the data packets will get delivered properly. If the path is not correct, it is left to a higher layer to notice the problem and inform the network layer that it would like a different path chosen.

11.4   Detailed Description of the Approach

In this section I describe the details of the design for robustly delivering a packet from a single source to all destinations. I describe the different packet types that are required, the databases, and the amount of information that must be manually configured, as well as the protocols involved.

11.4.1   Robust Flooding

Two types of packets will be flooded through robust flooding. The first type is known as a *public key list* packet. It is generated by one of a few public key list distributor nodes. The second type is generated by any of the nodes in the network. If flooding is used for distribution of data packets, this will be an ordinary data packet. Although flooding can be used for distribution of data packets, I will be using it primarily for distribution of LSPs. For clarity, I will call the type of packet generated by any node and flooded by the network an LSP.

11.4.1.1   A Priori Information

Each node must be configured with the following information:

1.   Its own ID

2.   Its own public and private key

3. N, an upper limit on the total number of network nodes

4.   The identities of, and public keys for, each of the public key distributor nodes

5.   The size of the maximum-size LSP

The public key distributor must also be configured with the IDs and public keys of all the nodes in the network.

11.4.1.2   Dynamic Database

Node R keeps the following: For each public key distributor node for which R has been configured with a key, R sets aside a buffer large enough to hold a packet listing N public keys. Additionally, for each buffer, R keeps a flag for each of its neighbors. The flag can contain three values: "OK," meaning that no action needs to be taken for this public key list packet; "transmit," meaning that this public key list packet needs to be forwarded to this neighbor; or "ack," meaning that an ack for this public key list packet needs to be sent to this neighbor.

For each node reported in a public key list packet, R also reserves a buffer for an LSP and a flag for each neighbor. The flag has the same three possible values: OK, transmit, or ack.

		Neighbor 1	Neighbor 2	. . .	Neighbor k
PKL source = PKD1	OK	✓	✓		
	ack				✓
	transmit				
PKL source = PKD2	OK		✓		
	ack				✓
	transmit	✓			
PKL source = PKD3	OK				✓
	ack		✓		
	transmit	✓			
PKL source = PKD4	OK	✓	✓		✓
	ack				
	transmit				
LSP source = R1	OK	✓	✓		
	ack				
	transmit				✓
LSP source = R2	OK				✓
	ack		✓		
	transmit	✓			
LSP source = Rn	OK	✓			
	ack		✓		✓
	transmit				

Figure 11.4

11.4.1.3 Dealing with Multiple Public Key Distributors

Two strategies can be used for dealing with multiple public key distributors. The first is the "majority rules" strategy, in which a buffer is set aside for a node only if a majority of the public key distributors list that node, with the same public key. The second is the "believe everything" strategy, in which a buffer is set aside for every reported (ID, key) pair. If two public key distributors disagree about node X's public key, with one of them reporting (X, key 1) and another reporting (X, key 2), then two buffers are set aside for X. One buffer is reserved for an X that uses key 1; the other is reserved for an X that uses key 2.

11.4.1.4   Packets

Public Key List

> ID of source
>
> Sequence number
>
> List of (ID, public key) pairs
>
> Signature

LSP Packet

> ID of source
>
> Sequence number
>
> LSP data
>
> Signature

Public Key List Ack

> ID of source (of public key list packet being acknowledged)
>
> Sequence number
>
> Signature copied from public key list packet being acknowledged

LSP Ack

> ID of source (of LSP being acknowledged)
>
> Sequence number
>
> Signature copied from LSP

11.4.1.5   Distribution of Public Key List Packets

Assume that node R receives a public key list packet from neighbor P. First, R verifies the signature in the packet. If the signature is not valid (based on the configured public key for the public key distributor node that is the packet's source), the packet is dropped. If the signature is valid, then the sequence number in the packet is checked against the sequence number of the packet in memory.

1. If the sequence number of the received packet is greater than that of the one in memory, then the packet in memory is overwritten. For that packet, the flag for neighbor P is set to the *ack* value, and the flags for all the other neighbors are set to the *transmit* value.

2. If the sequence number is equal to that of the packet in memory, then for that packet, the flag for neighbor P is set to the *ack* value.

    As a subtle robustness enhancement, the signature in the received packet should be checked against the signature in the stored packet. If the signatures are different, then it means that two different packets have been generated with valid signatures but with the same sequence number. This can happen. For instance, it is possible for the source to crash, restart without knowledge of the sequence number it used before the crash, and issue a new packet with a reused sequence number.

    In this case, R should use the numerical values of the signatures as a tie-breaker and treat the packet with the numerically larger signature as if it had the larger sequence number.

3. If the sequence number is less than that of the packet in memory, then the flag for P is set to the *transmit* value.

Memory is scanned round-robin, and when a link to neighbor P is available, memory is scanned for the next public key list packet with a flag equal to *ack* or *transmit*. If the flag is set to *ack,* then an *ack* for that packet is transmitted and the flag is set to *OK*.

11.4.1.6   Distribution of LSPs

Distribution of LSPs is done the same as with public key list packets. The only difference is that the list of nodes is obtained from the data in the public key list packets instead of being manually configured.

11.4.1.7   Receipt of Acks

If an ack is received from neighbor P, the signature and sequence number are compared with those of the packet in memory. If the signature and sequence number match, then the *transmit* flag is cleared for that neighbor, for that packet.

11.4.1.8   Running Out of Sequence Number

If the sequence number is very large (say, 32 bits or even 64 bits), then it will never reach the maximum value except as the result of a Byzantine failure on the part of the source. In this case, it is reasonable for that node to be disabled until manual intervention occurs. The manual intervention required is to change the public key of the node and reregister it with the public key distributor node(s). At that point, the node becomes, in essence, a brand-new node, starting at the lowest sequence number, and the network will discard all state about the previous incarnation of that node.

11.4.2   Robust Data Routing

Robust flooding is used for distribution of LSPs and public key list packets. Data packets will be routed on a specific route. The source router will generate a route, based on its LSP database. Once a route is chosen, the source generates a special "route-setup" packet, which lists the specified route and travels along that route. Intermediate routers store the source and destination IDs, along with the link from which the packet should arrive and the link onto which the packet should be forwarded.

11.4.2.1   Additional Dynamic Database

For each possible source-destination pair, the following memory is kept:

1. A buffer reserved for a route-setup packet

2. A buffer reserved for the most recently received data packet for that source-destination pair

3. An "RS-ack" flag, which, if set, indicates that an ack should be sent for that route-setup packet

4. An "RS-transmit" flag, which, if set, indicates that the route-setup packet should be forwarded to the next neighbor in the path

5. A "data-transmit" flag, which, if set, indicates that the data packet should be forwarded to the next neighbor in the path

This is a lot of storage (n^2), since room is reserved for every source-destination pair. If each source is limited to a constant number of destinations with which it can be in communication simultaneously, then some storage can be saved. Instead of setting aside a buffer for each source-destination pair, a fixed number of buffers can be set aside for each source. In practice an even smaller number of buffers can be reserved. A router can refuse route requests when no resources are available, as would be done in X.25 networks.

11.4.2.2   Additional Packets

Route-Setup Packet

      Source

      Sequence Number

      IDs of the nodes in the route

      Signature

Route-Setup Ack

      Source (of route-setup packet being acknowledged)

Sequence number (of route-setup packet being acknowledged)

Signature (of route-setup packet being acknowledged)

Data Packet

Source

Destination

Data

11.4.2.3 Receipt of Route-Setup Packets

If the route-setup packet's signature is valid, and if its sequence number is greater than the sequence number of the stored route-setup packet (if any) for that source-destination pair, then the stored route-setup packet is overwritten, and the *RS-ack* and *RS-transmit* flags are set.

11.4.2.4 Receipt of Data Packets

If a data packet is received from neighbor P, with source S and destination D, the route-setup database is scanned for a route for S–D. If such a route exists, and it indicates that packets from S to D should arrive from P, then the data packet is accepted and stored in memory, and the data-transmit flag for that packet is set.

Note that no cryptographic check is made on the packet, and no sequence number is checked. If the route consists of correctly functioning routers, then there is a very high probability that the most recently received packet is the uncorrupted packet most recently generated by the source for that destination. If the route contains a faulty router, then it does not matter what happens, since data cannot be guaranteed to flow along a faulty route. The source must detect that the route has become faulty and select a different route.

I have chosen not to acknowledge each data packet but rather to transmit the data packet once to the next neighbor. Assuming that a simple, reliable data link protocol is used (any standard data link protocol will do), there is a high probability that the data packet will be delivered with one network layer transmission.

The protocol can also include acknowledgments, but then some identification other than source and destination address must be added to the packet so that an ack can be matched with a specific packet. It should not be a strict sequence number, since a corrupted sequence number early in a conversation should not stop the flow of subsequent packets.

11.4.2.5 Nonfunctioning Routes

The robust flooding technique guarantees that if a single functional path exists between S and D, packets will flow along that path. The robust routing technique does not make that guarantee. Although the source is armed with a robustly delivered LSP database, there is no guarantee that a route computed based on that LSP database will consist of correctly functioning routers. For instance, a router could perform all protocols correctly but then drop data packets. It could drop all data packets, or it could discriminate against certain sources or destinations.

Based on complaints from the higher layer, the source can detect that a route is not working. The source can then choose one of several strategies:

1. Select a new route, avoiding as many of the routers in the previous route as possible.

2. Keep track of routers on previously nonworking paths, avoiding them insofar as possible when choosing routes

3. Attempt to find the bad routers by collecting management data

4. Fall back on robust flooding as a routing technique when the chosen route does not work

11.5   Summary

With the design described in the preceding section, forwarding of data packets is as efficient as in a conventional network. Forwarding of route-setup packets, LSPs, and public key list packets is more CPU-intensive than forwarding of data packets because a public key signature must be verified. It is possible with some public key signature schemes—in particular, the RSA(Rivest, Shamir, Adelman) algorithm—to make signature verification much less expensive than signature generation. Signature verification efficiency is much more critical than signature generation efficiency, since signature verification happens so much more frequently.

Byzantine failure of routers in a network should be a very rare event. If that is indeed the case, routes chosen by the source will almost always function properly. If there were to be a Byzantine failure in a router, most probably very few such failures would be occurring simultaneously in the network. In this case, again, most routes will work, and it should be possible to find alternative routes quickly. If it is expected that many Byzantine failures might occur simultaneously, then allowing the fallback strategy of flooding data packets will assure that data packets (like LSPs and public key list packets) will be delivered even if only a single functional path connects the source and destination.

11.6   For Further Reading

For the concepts behind public key cryptography:

> W. Diffie and M. Hellman, "New Directions in Cryptography," *IEEE Transactions on Information Theory* IT-22 (Nov. 1976): 644–654.

For details of the RSA algorithm:

> R. L. Rivest, A. Shamir, and L. Adleman, "On Digital Signatures and Public Key Cryptosystems," *Communications of the ACM* 21 (Feb 1978): 120–126.

For a description of the famous computer science problem known as the "Byzantine generals problem":

> L. Lamport, R. Shostak, and M. Pease, "The Byzantine Generals Problem," *ACM Transactions on Programming Languages and Systems* 4, no. 3 (July 1982): 382–401.

For more details and more variations on robust routing:

> R. Perlman, "Network Layer Protocols with Byzantine Robustness," Ph.D. dissertation, Massachusetts Institute of Technology, Aug. 1988.

Homework

1. What manual configuration is required in order to install a new node in a network? What if the addition of the new node causes the network to grow beyond the configured parameter N? What manual configuration is required to add a new public key distributor to the network?

2. Why is it so much more difficult for a saboteur to cause problems in a network in which the protocols are self-stabilizing?

3. Compare the two strategies for dealing with multiple public key distributors ("majority rule" and "believe everything"). Consider such factors as the amount of memory and bandwidth that might be reserved for nonvalid nodes and the resilience of the network to multiple malicious public key distributor nodes.

4. In robust flooding, suppose that an ack gets lost. What happens as a result?

5. If a public key distributor has a Byzantine failure, what problems can it cause? Can such a failure be detected easily?

   Suppose that a router has a Byzantine failure in its protocol for robust flooding. What problems can it cause? Can this sort of failure be detected easily?

6. Why does a route-setup packet not require a separate flag for each neighbor, as do public key list packets and LSPs?

Chapter 12
To Route or to Bridge: Is That the Question?

In case you aren't completely confused yet about bridges versus routers, I must tell you that very few products are really pure bridges or pure routers. There are brouters, multiprotocol routers, portals, tunnelers, and other strange sorts of mixtures. Furthermore, many of these terms are used in conflicting ways. First, I'll compare bridges and routers, and then I'll explain some of the various mutant forms of bridges and routers that further complicate the issues.

12.1   Bridges versus Routers

What is a bridge? What is a router? Without knowing the answers to those two questions, it is very difficult to do an intelligent comparison. The ISO terminology makes the distinction very clear: A bridge is a data link layer relay; a router is a network layer relay. Very clear, that is, until you wonder, "What is a network layer? What is a data link layer?"

I think that a data link layer should be designed to carry a packet of information across a single hop. If the data link layer assumes multiple hops, then it is hard to imagine what the network layer is supposed to do. With reluctance, I rationalized that transparent bridges operate in the data link layer because the protocol used by the endnodes was designed to work across a single hop. With source routing bridges also defined as operating in the data link layer, I was at quite a loss to devise any definition of a data link layer that would differentiate it from a network layer—until I discovered the true definition of a data link layer, which is: *A data link layer protocol is anything standardized by a committee chartered to standardize data link layer protocols.*

Now that you know what differentiates a bridge from a router, you can ask why bridges and routers should have any functional differences. To be able to discuss this question at all sensibly, I will have to ignore source routing bridges. In my opinion, source routing bridges should really be considered routers. Transparent bridges were designed with the constraint that they fit neatly within the existing data link layer. Source routing bridges were designed by adding protocols more typical of network layer protocols into the end stations. Only because the work was done within a committee dealing with something called a data link layer is source routing (as described in Chapter 4) considered a "bridging function."

The data link layer was designed with the assumption that the nodes communicating via the data link protocol are attached to a common link. The data link header lacks several fields that would be designed into a network layer header—for instance, hop count, fragmentation and reassembly information, congestion feedback, and intermediate destination (next hop), in addition to final destination. There is no handshaking protocol (like ICMP or ES-IS) by which endnodes and routers can become aware of each other.

Another constraint applicable to bridges is that they must work with the 802 addresses. An 802 address cannot be assumed to have any topological significance. Stations were designed so that address assignment would be done at the time of manufacture. Transparent bridges must not require that a station's address depend on its location. They must allow a station to attach to any LAN within a bridged network, using its preconfigured 802 address. In contrast, the network layer address in IP is assigned and configured relative to the LAN to which a node is attached. In ISO, a node can use the 802 address as part of its network layer address, but there is the additional "area" portion of the address to give packet switches a hint about the station's location.

Yet another constraint is that bridges are not allowed to reorder packets from the same source. Protocols designed to work over a network layer expect some packet reordering (or they should; if they don't, they get what they deserve).

Therefore, bridges are operating under constraints that do not apply to routers. Let us examine some of the disadvantages of bridges relative to routers:

1. Bridges can use only a subset of the topology (a spanning tree). Routers can use the best path that physically exists between source and destination.

   This constraint is caused by two factors. The first is that the lack of a handshaking protocol between endnodes and bridges forces bridges to learn the location of stations based on the direction from which traffic is received. The second is that bridges must be transparent—i.e., they do not modify the packet in any way. A packet as transmitted by a bridge cannot be distinguished from a packet as transmitted by the source endnode.

2. Bridge reconfiguration after a topological change is an order of magnitude slower than router reconfiguration after a topological change.

   This is due to the fact that the transparency constraint makes bridge loops much more dangerous than router loops. New bridge connectivity cannot be introduced until it is definitely known to be safe, whereas routers can switch over to new paths as soon as information is received, because temporary loops are not a problem.

3. The total number of stations that can be interconnected through bridges is limited to the tens of thousands. With routers, the total size of the network is for all practical purposes unlimited (at least with ISO).

The reason for this is that network layer addresses contain geographical information. Bridges cannot use hierarchical routing because the addresses have no routing hierarchy.

4. Bridges offer no firewall protection against broadcast storms.

    This is really an unfair complaint against bridges, but it is one of the major reasons that some users have come to dislike them. Bridges are simply doing their job. They are making multiple LANs appear to the upper-layer protocols as if they were a single LAN. A broadcast storm disables a LAN. When LANs are bridged, they become a single LAN from the point of view of the upper-layer protocols, and the broadcast storm therefore disables the entire bridged set of LANs.

5. Bridges must drop packets that are too large to forward.

    The network layer header contains fragmentation and reassembly information. The data link layer header does not. Therefore, bridges must drop a packet that is too large to forward. Also, they cannot send an error message back to the source to let it know why the packet was dropped, because no such packet is defined in the data link header.

6. Bridges cannot give congestion feedback to the endnodes.

    The network layer in IP has "source quench" messages. In ISO, there is the "congestion-experienced" bit in the data packet header. The data link layer has no similar mechanism.

On the other hand, bridges offer some very attractive features relative to routers:

1. Bridges are really *plug and play*. Routers require a lot more configuration.

    This is a significant advantage of bridges. IP routers are more difficult to configure than ISO routers because they require that a distinct address be configured into each port. IP routing requires a significant amount of configuration of endnodes as well (because the endnodes must be configured with an address and a mask, or at least some server must be configured with the address and mask of an endnode that will attach to the LAN). ISO routing requires less configuration than IP routing, but it still requires more configuration than bridging.

    (Again, keep in mind that I am discussing only transparent bridging. Source routing bridges are definitely not plug and play, because each bridge must be configured with a LAN number for each port, and parallel bridge numbers must also be configured.)

2. Bridges have a better price/performance ratio than routers.

    The reason for this is that routers have to parse a network layer header, which is more difficult to parse than a data link header (because of such factors as header checksums that must be modified when hop counts are modified, variable-length fields, and potential options like route recording).

Routers are getting better, however. Once routers are engineered to perform at wire speeds, the fact that they might be more expensive than bridges of the equivalent speed will be irrelevant, because the packet switches constitute such a small percentage of the total cost of a network that the cost differential between bridges and routers will be insignificant.

3. Bridges are multiprotocol.

This issue is becoming less important with the advent of multiprotocol routers. It is often possible to find a multiprotocol router that will handle all the network layer protocols you use.

4. Bridges forward even nonroutable protocols.

Although I wish it were not true, people have designed upper-layer protocols to run directly over the data link layer. Without a network layer, only a bridge will be able to interconnect LANs with respect to such protocols. There is no intrinsic reason why these protocols could not have been designed to run over a network layer. They just weren't. The designers of these protocols really believed that nobody would ever want to use them between LANs. As long as these protocols are in use, bridging will be necessary. Maybe someday they will be replaced by equivalent protocols designed to run over a network layer.

Brouters (described later in the chapter) allow support of such protocols without requiring that other protocols be bridged.

12.2   Extensions to Bridges

In this section, I'll examine various types of features that might be added to bridges to make them more routerlike.

12.2.1   Remote Bridges

The term *remote bridge* simply refers to connecting two bridges with a point-to-point link, instead of having them be neighbors because of their attachment to a common LAN. Since such issues as how to indicate the packet type have not been standardized (see Chapter 3, subsection 3.7.1), remote bridges will have to be bought in pairs, from a single vendor.

12.2.2   Beyond the Spanning Tree

Since a point-to-point link between two bridges has no stations attached, it will remain idle if it is not selected for the spanning tree. Because of the perceived waste of resources, various strategies such as DLS (see Chapter 3, subsection 3.7.2.1) have been developed so that remote bridges can sometimes utilize redundant point-to-point links.

A transparent bridge with DLS becomes slightly more routerlike, because of the fact that it is not restricted to running on the spanning tree. Variations on DLS are also possible, as described in Chapter 3, subsections 3.7.2.2 and 3.7.2.3.

Another strategy for using more than the spanning tree is to employ tunnels, as discussed in Chapter 3, subsection 3.7.2.4. To review, the idea behind tunnels is that a single bridge on each LAN is elected to forward traffic to and from that LAN. The selected bridge on the source LAN encapsulates the packet with some sort of header and routes the packet to the selected bridge on the destination LAN. Bridges on intermediate LANs will not falsely learn the station location because, while the packet is traveling on intermediate LANs, it has a network layer header—i.e., it can clearly be identified as having been transmitted by a packet switch and not by the endnode. The path from source to destination bridge is not constrained to travel on the spanning tree, since the packet is being routed between the bridges rather than being bridged. The proper protocol has taken place among the "bridges" so that they can route packets that have been encapsulated.

Tunnels are not as optimal as one might think, because there is the potential of a hop suboptimality both at the source LAN and at the destination LAN (because the bridges chosen to be the data packet forwarders might be topologically incorrect with respect to that pair of LANs).

It would be an interesting research project to study the various schemes suggested in Chapter 3, section 3.7.2. to see whether they really offer a noticeable performance advantage over simply using the spanning tree. And all these schemes could be compared to routing.

12.2.3   Multimedia Bridges

Some vendors have various capabilities within bridges that require bridges to look at the network layer header. One example is network layer fragmentation. There are some transparent bridges that check the protocol type, and if the protocol type is CLNP or IP and the packet is too large to be forwarded, the bridge will do fragmentation.

The IETF (Internet Engineering Task Force) router requirements working group attempted to define anything that looked at the network layer header as a router. Given that definition, bridges with features such as IP or CLNP fragmentation would be considered routers and would therefore have to conform to the router requirements document and do things like decrement the hop count whenever they forwarded an IP packet and perhaps even support the IP routing protocol. However, the people building multimedia bridges do not consider them to be routers. They view fragmentation as a fairly simple operation that gives their product a lot of functionality and have no interest in providing all the rest of the functionality that would be required in order to turn their product into a full-scale router.

12.3   Extensions to Routers

In this section, I'll describe extensions to routers that give them some of the advantages of bridges.

12.3.1   Multiprotocol Routers

There are two methods of supporting an additional network layer protocol in a router. One method, the "integrated IS-IS" approach, involves integrating support of that network layer protocol into a routing protocol already implemented within the machine. Another method involves adding the extra protocol in a "ships in the night" fashion by implementing a complete routing protocol for that protocol.

These two approaches differ only in terms of how routes are computed. Once forwarding databases are built up for all the supported protocols, data packet forwarding is similar. A data packet arrives at the router; the protocol type is determined from the data link layer information; and the packet is handed to a module designed to parse that network layer header.

It is possible for some of the protocols to be supported with a ships in the night scheme and others with integrated routing. For instance:

Figure 12.1

This multiprotocol router supports seven different network layer protocols, A, B, C, D, E, F, and G. One integrated routing protocol supports A, B, and C; another supports F and G. D and E are each implemented with a separate routing protocol.

Mixing routers that support different subsets of the multiple protocols in a network can be quite complex, especially with integrated routing. If the ships in the night approach is used with each protocol, then a separate route gets calculated for each protocol. Since only the routers that support protocol X participate in X's routing protocol, routes for protocol X are guaranteed to go through only those routers that support X. In contrast, with the integrated approach, routers calculate a single set of routes to all the routers. A protocol X endnode will be declared reachable from some router R, which will support protocol X (otherwise, R could not have declared in its LSP that the protocol X endnode was a neighbor). However, if any of the routers along the path from the source to R do not support protocol X, then there is a problem. The integrated routing approach could calculate a different set of routes for each protocol, but at least the approach chosen by the integrated IS-IS protocol was to calculate only a single set of routes. The proponents of integrated IS-IS believe that all routers will be multiprotocol. If this turns out not to be true, there are two choices:

1. Use encapsulation to "hop over" routers that do not support a particular protocol. When router R1 wishes to forward a protocol X packet to neighbor router R2 that does not support X, then R1 must encapsulate the packet with a network layer header for some protocol that R2 does support, addressing the packet to some router farther along the path toward the destination that understands both protocols and can remove the encapsulating header and let the protocol X packet proceed on its way to the destination.

2. Calculate separate paths for each protocol. The Dijkstra algorithm must be run once for each network layer protocol supported. Each time, the only routers considered are those that have advertised in their LSP that they support the protocol for which routes are being computed.

12.3.2   Single-Protocol Backbone

The multiprotocol routers discussed in the preceding subsection forward packets in "native mode"—i.e., each router along the path of a protocol X packet must be able to parse a protocol X header. If a router supports seven protocols, it must be able to parse seven different network layer headers.

In the single-protocol backbone approach, the assumption is that all routers must be able to parse a single type of network layer data packet—say, protocol X. A router R1 that has a protocol Y neighbor must additionally handle all the endnode/router handshaking protocols required of protocol Y and be able to parse protocol Y data packet headers. When R1 receives a protocol Y packet for forwarding, it figures out which router R2 in the backbone is the appropriate destination router for the protocol Y destination address; constructs a protocol X header with R2 as the network layer destination address; encloses the entire protocol Y packet, including the header, in the newly constructed protocol X header; and forwards the packet toward R2.

R1 has two ways of determining that R2 is the appropriate destination router: It can use either an integrated routing approach or a ships in the night approach. With the integrated approach, the routing protocol used in the backbone would allow each router to advertise all of the destinations it can reach, for each protocol (as integrated IS-IS does). Intermediate routers that do not support protocol Y would ignore the portion of R2's LSP that says, "These are the protocol Y destinations I can reach." These intermediate routers will never see a protocol Y data packet, because router neighbors of protocol Y endnodes will always enclose protocol Y packets inside protocol X network layer headers.

With the ships in the night approach, the backbone is completely unaware of protocol Y. Protocol Y routers R1 and R2 must have some means of finding each other besides the protocol X routing protocol (for instance, manual configuration of each other's protocol X network layer addresses or the use of some sort of multicast capability provided by protocol X). Once R1 knows that R2 also understands protocol Y, R1 communicates with R2 as if R2 were an immediate neighbor with respect to protocol Y by encapsulating protocol Y control messages inside protocol X network layer headers.

Intermediate routers in the backbone would not distinguish R1–R2 control packets for protocol Y from ordinary data packets.

If protocol Y is indeed confined to a few locations within a network, then a single-protocol backbone idea might be attractive, because it requires fewer routers to support protocol Y. If protocol Y endnodes exist on pretty much all the LANs in the network, then there is no reason to encapsulate every protocol Y packet inside a protocol X header, since virtually all the routers would have to support protocol Y anyway. Encapsulation makes the packets longer. It also requires that the decapsulating router support reassembly, which is messy enough when performed at the destination endnode.

The word *portal* is generally used when the box that performs protocol Y encapsulation and decapsulation is not a router in the protocol X backbone but instead is viewed by the backbone as an endnode. This approach is only attractive if there are no boxes capable of routing both protocols. The portal approach requires an extra box on each LAN containing protocol Y nodes and two extra hops for forwarding packets from source to destination.

One problem with single-protocol backbones is perception. If protocol X is the protocol in the backbone and protocol Y is encapsulated within protocol X, then people who really like protocol Y sometimes get insulted. It seems as if their protocol is treated like a second-class citizen. Protocol X packets are transmitted in *native mode* (i.e., with no extra header). Protocol Y packets have to carry the additional protocol X header, which makes them longer. If reassembly is required at an intermediate router because of the encapsulation, throughput for protocol Y can be severely degraded.

The best solution to supporting all the network layer protocols employed in a given network is to use as few network layer protocols as possible. The ideal number is one.

12.3.3   Brouters

A brouter is simply a router that can also perform as a bridge. Assume, for the moment, that the brouter is only a single-protocol router. It supports IP, for instance. When a packet arrives at the brouter, the brouter examines the packet's protocol type. If the protocol type is "IP," then the router code handles processing of the packet as if the box were a simple IP router. If the protocol type is anything other than "IP," then the bridge code handles processing of the packet as if the box were a simple bridge. In essence, a brouter is a bridge and a router implemented in a ships in the night manner.

A brouter can be a multiprotocol router combined with a bridge. For instance, the seven-protocol multiprotocol router presented in subsection 12.3.1 could actually be a brouter.

Figure 12.2

It cooperates in the spanning tree algorithm just as an ordinary bridge would. It cooperates in all the supported routing protocols just as an ordinary router would. When it receives a packet whose protocol type is A, B, C, D, E, F, and G, it processes the packet as a router would. If it receives a packet whose protocol type is anything other than A, B, C, D, E, F, or G, it processes the packet as a bridge would.

12.4   Bridges versus Routers, Revisited

As bridges are becoming more and more like routers, and routers are becoming more and more like bridges, and as almost all products on the market are becoming brouters, what is the real answer to the routers versus bridges question? It might even be possible to configure a multiprotocol brouter so that each protocol can be independently selected for bridging or routing.

Some protocols have to be bridged (e.g., LAT, or Local Area Transport, Digital's proprietary protocol for connecting terminal servers on LANs to hosts located on the same LAN). Any protocol capable of being routed will benefit from the fact that routing offers better paths than bridging. Some protocols derive other benefits from being routed. For instance, IP benefits from being routed because a router offers firewall protection from broadcast storms and also confines ARP traffic to a single LAN. ISO benefits from being routed because ES hellos remain confined to a single LAN, and endnodes wind up choosing a geographically nearby router for forwarding traffic off the LAN.

Although the price/performance advantage that bridges have over routers will become insignificant, bridges will continue to offer some other advantages. Their simplicity (the fact that they need no configuration) and consequent robustness will remain attractive features. The fact that bridges can easily support multicast across many hops might at times be important as well.

12.5   In Closing

Well, I must somewhat regretfully end this book, both because many people would prefer to be able to obtain it before the millennium and because my editor tells me it's getting a bit long. Feel free to contact me with comments, corrections, complaints, and especially compliments. My E-mail is PERLMAN@DSMAIL.ENET.DEC.COM. I can be reached via paper mail at:

> Radia Perlman
> Digital Equipment Corporation LKG1-2/A19
> 550 King St.
> Littleton, Mass. 01460

ARP (address resolution protocol) — A protocol for mapping 32-bit IP addresses to 48-bit data link layer addresses, specified in RFC 826.

AS (autonomous system) — A portion of a network, usually within the control of one organization and usually running a single routing protocol. Routing between autonomous systems is done with a protocol that is defined as being an "interdomain" or "inter-AS" protocol or an "exterior gateway protocol."

The term *autonomous system* within the IP community is synonomous with the term *routing domain* within the ISO community.

bandwidth — The rate of information flow.

BGP (border gateway protocol) — An interdomain routing protocol being standardized by the IETF.

BOOTP (bootstrap protocol) — A protocol defined by RFC 951 to enable a diskless client machine to discover certain information, such as its own IP address.

broadcast address — A group address that by convention, means "everyone." The 802 broadcast address is a bit string of 48 1's.

broadcast storm — A phenomenon of extreme congestion, usually caused by bugs in implementations or ambiguities in protocol specifications.

CLNP (connectionless network protocol) — The ISO protocol, consisting primarily of the data packet format, documented in ISO 8473.

CLNS (connectionless-mode network service) — The ISO term for the datagram network layer service.

confederation — A concept in the IDRP protocol that involves grouping several domains and presenting the group to the outside world as if it were a single domain.

connectionless — A service in which data is presented, complete with a destination address, and the network delivers it on a best-effort basis, independent of other data being exchanged between the same pair of users.

connection-oriented — A service in which a connection-setup procedure must be implemented before data can be exchanged between two users.

CONS (connection-oriented network service) — X.25 is an example of a protocol that provides CONS.

CRC (cyclic redundancy code) — A type of FCS computed by treating bit strings as polynomials with binary coefficients. The CRC is the remainder resulting from division by the CRC polynomial.

CSMA/CD (carrier sense multiple access with collision detection) — A contention scheme for allocating bandwidth on a shared bus. Examples are 802.3 and Ethernet.

datagram — A service in which delivery is on a "best-effort" basis. This term is also sometimes used for a piece of information presented to a network that provides a datagram service.

DCE (data circuit-terminating equipment) — The X.25 term for the device to which an endnode attaches.

DDCMP (Digital data communication message protocol) — A data link protocol developed by Digital Equipment Corporation.

distance vector routing — A type of routing protocol in which each router tells its neighbors its distances to all destinations.

DLS — A Vitalink proprietary enhancement to the transparent bridge standard that in some cases, allows point-to-point links that are not in the spanning tree to be used by bridges for forwarding packets.

DTE (data terminal equipment) — The X.25 term for an endnode.

EGP (exterior gateway protocol) — A term used in the IP community in two different ways: (1) a class of routing protocol for routing between ASs; (2) the specific protocol documented in RFC 827.

encapsulation — Handling protocol A's packets, complete with A's header information, as data carried by protocol B. Encapsulated protocol A packets have a B header, followed by an A header, followed by the information that protocol A is carrying as its own data.

ES-IS (end system to intermediate system protocol) — ISO's protocol, as specified in 9542, for handshaking between routers and endnodes and for mapping network layer addresses to data link layer addresses.

Ethernet — The original CSMA/CD LAN as invented by Xerox and standardized by Digital, Intel, and Xerox.

FCS (frame check sequence) — A quantity transmitted along with a packet to enable the receiver to detect data corruption.

FDDI (fiber distributed data interface) — A 100-Mb token ring being standardized by the American National Standards Institute (ANSI).

filter — To selectively discard packets of a certain type.

functional address — A severely restricted form of multicast addressing implemented by some 802.5 chip sets.

group address — An address to which are sent transmissions intended for receipt by a set of recipients.

HDLC (high-level data link control) — A data link layer protocol.

hop — Forwarding by a packet switch.

IDPR (interdomain policy routing) — A link state interdomain routing protocol being worked on in the IETF community.

IDRP (interdomain routing protocol) — A distance vector interdomain routing protocol derived from BGP and adapted for ISO.

IETF (Internet Engineering Task Force) — An organization, open to anyone who wishes to participate, that helps define the protocols used in the Internet.

IGP (interior gateway protocol) — The IP community's term for the routing protocol used within an AS. The ISO's synonym is *intradomain routing protocol.*

individual address — An address that is intended to correspond to a specific recipient.

IS-IS (intermediate system to intermediate system protocol) — The ISO standard intradomain routing protocol, documented in ISO 10589.

LAN (local area network) — Usually a shared medium with broadcast capability providing logical full connectivity, typically over a limited geographic area the size of a building or perhaps a campus.

link state routing — A type of routing protocol in which each router constructs an LSP listing its neighbors and the LSP is then broadcast to all the routers.

LLC (logical link control) — A sublayer of the data link layer defined by the IEEE 802 committee. Part of LLC defines the multiplexing fields; the other part gives optional types of service that can be run over 802 LANs. LLC type 1 is a datagram service. LLC type 2 is a reliable connection-oriented service. LLC type 3 is semireliable.

LSP (link state packet) — A packet that is generated by a router in a link state routing protocol and lists that router's neighbors.

MAC (medium access control) — A sublayer of the data link layer, defined by the IEEE 802 committee, that deals with issues specific to a particular type of LAN.

MAN (metropolitan area network) — A shared medium bigger than a LAN but smaller than a WAN. An example is 802.6.

MTU (maximum transmission unit) — The largest packet size that can be transmitted between source and destination.

multicast — To transmit information to a group of recipients via a single transmission by the source.

multiplexing — Sharing a communications channel by transmitting messages for multiple destinations with some indication of the intended recipient.

network entity title (NET) — The ISO term for the identifier of the network layer running at a particular node.

NLPID (network layer protocol ID) — The first octet of any of ISO's network layer protocols. This octet enables ISO network layer protocols to be distinguished, even if they are transmitted over a data link that has no "protocol type" or "SAP" field.

NLPIDs can be assigned to non-ISO protocols. The assigned NLPID can sometimes be a convenient method of identifying protocols.

NSAP (network service access point) — The ISO term for the quantity that specifies a client of a network layer running at a particular node.

OSPF (open shortest path first) — A link state routing protocol used for routing IP.

OUI (organizationally unique identifier) — The 3 octets assigned by the IEEE in a block of 48-bit addresses.

PPP (point-to-point protocol) — A data link layer protocol for a point-to-point link with multiplexing capability standardized within the IP community.

promiscuous listen — Having the hardware receive and pass to the upper layers all packets that arrive on a LAN.

protocol type — A multiplexing field that defines the type of packet in which only a single field appears in the packet. In contrast, a SAP type of multiplexing field has a source SAP and a destination SAP, and theoretically, the two SAP values are numerically unrelated.

PVC (permanent virtual circuit) — A concept in X.25 in which a call is administratively set up, with a fixed destination DTE address.

QOS (quality of service) — A field in the CLNP network layer header that is functionally equivalent to the "TOS" field in the IP header.

RARP (reverse ARP) — A protocol defined by RFC 903 to enable a diskless client machine to discover its own IP address. BOOTP accomplishes the same goal and is the preferred protocol.

repeater — A physical layer relay that forwards bits, in contrast to bridges and routers, which forward packets.

RIP (routing information protocol) — A distance vector routing protocol popular for routing IP.

RFC (request for comments) — The document series maintained by the Internet community that records the protocols within the Internet and gives other information.

routeing — The spelling of the word *routing* that vigilant members of the ISO network layer committee pointed out was mandated by the ISO rules, which specify the particular edition of the *Oxford English Dictionary* in which that spelling is used.

routing domain — The ISO equivalent of an AS. *(See* **AS**.*)*

SAP (service access point) — A term that can be employed for the address of a user of a service (as in "NSAP"). In 802.2, it is used to describe a field that further defines an address. For instance, the destination address plus the "DSAP" ("destination service access point") define the recipient of a packet. It differs from a protocol type in that the assumption is that the "SSAP" ("source service access point") and DSAP are numerically unrelated.

SNAP SAP (subnetwork access protocol SAP) — A particular value of SAP reserved by 802.2 for all protocols that do not have a globally assigned SAP value.

spanning tree — A subset of a network in which exactly one path exists between any pair of nodes.

SPF (shortest path first) — The term often used for the Dijkstra algorithm, in which paths to all destinations are computed given complete knowledge of a graph (the LSP database, in the case of a link state routing protocol).

SR bridge — A bridge that only forwards packets with source routing header information.

SR-TB bridge — A bridge that translates between source routing and transparent packets.

SRT bridge — A bridge that forwards both packets with source routing header information and transparent packets.

SVC (switched virtual circuit) — An X.25 connection in which the destination DTE address is specified at connection-setup time, with the connection being set up and hung up by the user as needed.

TCP (transmission control protocol) — The reliable connection-oriented transport layer protocol defined in the Internet suite of protocols.

TCP/IP — A term often used to describe the Internet suite of protocols. Although TCP and IP are only two of the protocols within the suite, for some reason, it has become popular to call the whole suite TCP/IP.

token — Something that is passed between users. In token-oriented LANs, possession of the token gives the possessor permission to transmit.

token bus — A type of LAN standardized within 802.4.

token ring — A type of LAN standardized within 802.5 and FDDI.

TOS — A field in the IP data packet header that specifies the criteria that the source wishes the routers to consider when computing a route for this packet.

WAN (wide area network) — A term usually applied to networks in which there are packet switches called routers.

Ideas for Research

In this section, I will list research problems, and reference sections of the book in which these problems are discussed.

1. Should bridges learn station addresses on a port during the intermediate state between backup and forwarding?

    There are three possibilities. A bridge might not start learning station addresses on a port until that port is in forwarding state. A bridge might start learning station addresses on a port as soon as the port is no longer in backup state. The 802.1 standard calls for two intermediate states between backup and forwarding. In the first state, no learning is done. In the second intermediate state, station addresses are learned.

    What are the performance tradeoffs between these three approaches? (see Section 3.4.2).

2. Bridge Cache Timeout Values

    How short a station learning cache timer can a bridge use before network performance is degraded due to unnecessarily forwarded packets? (see Section 3.4.3).

3. Source Routing Explorer Packet Performance

    Is the potentially exponential behavior of all paths explorer packets a problem in practice? Have people built reasonably large and connected networks with source routing bridges? If they work, why do they?

    In a sample large rich topology, given limited buffering and CPU in the bridges, what can be said about the behavior of the exploration process? If all but the first few explorer packets for a particular station pair get lost, this may not be so bad, since the slower copies are presumably for less optimal routes. However, what does it do to other traffic at the time? Might it cause the best routes to get lost for some other station pair? How long would it take for the congestion burst to die down, given that at most K packets can be queued at each bridge, and each time a bridge reintroduces another copy, it starts the bursts over (see Section 4.5.1).

4. How do ES-IS and ARP compare in terms of total bandwidth use, offloading end systems, responsiveness, and any other measures? This is further discussed in Section 8.5.

5. Dijkstra Incremental Computation

    What is the "point of diminishing returns" on recalculation of the Dijkstra tree from scratch vs doing incremental changes. In the worst case, how does doing an incremental computation based on a single link change compare to recomputing the tree from scratch? In the expected case, how many incremental computations does it take before the expected amount of CPU for recomputing the tree from scratch equals the amount of CPU for doing successive incremental updates?

    This is discussed in Section 9.3.3.

6. Distance Vector Vs Link State Routing

    There are subtle comparisons that can be made about the two routing algorithms. How does the CPU burden compare when factors such as the expected number of link changes, and the expected number of routes disrupted are taken into account. Which is more robust? This is discussed further in Section 9.3.

7. Adjusting routes based on congestion.

    Are the gains of varying link costs according to the amount of congestion on the links worth the cost? Is load splitting a good idea, especially when the effect on the transport layer is considered? If load splitting is used, with a fixed cost metric (one that does not vary according to congestion), how much network capacity is gained if the router considers local queue depths in its forwarding decisions. Is load splitting on "almost equal cost routes" a good idea? Is it a good idea to pass around congestion information in addition to link costs, so that link costs are not affected by congestion, but routers can make decisions on path splitting based on congestion several hops downstream?

    This is further discussed in sections 9.4 and 9.5.

8. Bridge bandwidth use

    Transparent bridges use only a spanning tree. DLS and GDLS allow use of more links. Tunnels allow arbitrary routes, but with the possibility of two extra hops (one at the source LAN, one at the destination LAN). Source routing bridges theoretically allow optimal routes, but the cost of route discovery must be considered. How do all these schemes really compare in terms of performance? See chapters 3, 4, and 12 for more detail on transparent bridges, tunnels, source routing bridges, DLS and GDLS. The summary chapter describes tunnels.

INDEX